S0-AGI-518

FAMILY DEVELOPMENT

EVELYN MILLIS DUVALL, Ph.D.

Family Life Consultant

Family

Development

J. B. LIPPINCOTT COMPANY

Chicago

Philadelphia

New York

Library of Congress Catalog Card Number: 57–9104

3.612.4

PRINTED IN THE UNITED STATES OF AMERICA

Preface

This book attempts to give the mature student a way of looking at family life so that what he or she sees makes sense. It is designed to equip the preprofessional worker with the conceptual tools that will be usable in his or her work with families; and to help the experienced worker get a sharper cutting edge on the tools of his or her profession: teaching, public health work, extension work, social-agency programs, community development, social work, family life education, counseling and research, or whatever involves working with and for families and family members.

The thesis of the book is that families grow through predictable stages of development that can be understood in terms of the development of the individual family members and of the family-as-a-whole. The story of the development of this conceptual framework is told in the Historical Footnote—*Growth of the Family Development Concept* where credit is given those who have had major roles in carving out the concepts up to this writing.

The book is in three parts, and it can be most effectively used in the given sequence. Part I, *Growing Families in Changing Times,* spells out the characteristics of the American family life cycle in midtwentieth century, the influence of social change on family form and functions, the nature of changing patterns of childrearing, and how social class makes for family differences. In addition, Part I describes in detail the developmental task concept and its application to family developmental tasks.

Part II, *Expanding Families,* takes the family from its inception at the marriage of husband and wife through the period of expansion with the coming and rearing of children until they are about to be launched into lives of their own. Part III, *Contracting Families,* starts with the launching of the first young adult "child" from the family and carries the family through its middle and later years, with a final chapter, *The Dynamics of Family Interaction,* discussing and listing services needed for family stability and success.

Each chapter is designed to put into the hands of the readers effective tools for a professional attitude toward families. Consequently, throughout the book, there are outlines and detailed analyses for meeting the problems that arise in the family life cycle such as: child-proofing the home for the rearing of children; checking a child's readiness for school; gathering information on how to prepare a child for a new baby brother or sister; building in safety features in the home during the middle and later years; learning to live with in-laws; adjusting to bereavement.

Readings are more extensive than is usual in a book of this kind so that they may (1) stimulate the student of the family and (2) functionally serve the professional worker who is currently concerned with the problems of families and family members.

Suggested activities are more elaborate and detailed than is traditional in order to serve the teacher, leader, or the situation where a wide variety of dynamically effective methods of study makes the educational experience creatively satisfying. Readers may share the author's gratitude to Dr. Hazel Ingersoll for sharing so generously her original case excerpts and materials for "talkouts" that her students find challenging. The other activities have been gathered through years of family life workshop leadership from scores of competent leaders and teachers, as well as from personal experience.

The photographs used to illustrate the book were selected from a wide variety of cooperative sources, credited picture by picture throughout the text.

More than is usually necessary is the debt of gratitude owed more than a dozen busy professional people who took time out of their full schedules to critically read and in every case add something of their own wisdom and expertness to chapters in their fields of especial competency:

Ruth Albrecht, Ph.D., Research Professor of Family Life, Alabama Polytechnic Institute

Ernest W. Burgess, Ph.D., Family Study Center, University of Chicago

Ruth Shonle Cavan, Ph.D., Associate Professor of Sociology on the Jane Addams Foundation, Rockford College

Allison Davis, Ph.D., Committee on Human Development, University of Chicago

Marion L. Faegre, Arlington, Virginia, formerly with the Children's Bureau

Mary and Lawrence K. Frank, Belmont, Massachusetts, formerly Director of the Caroline Zachry Institute of Human Development

David Fulcomer, Ph.D., Department of Economics and Sociology, Iowa State College

Paul C. Glick, Ph.D., Chief, Social Statistics Branch, Population and Housing Division, Bureau of the Census

Robert J. Havighurst, Ph.D., Committee on Human Development, University of Chicago

Reuben Hill, Ph.D., Research Professor in Family Life, University of North Carolina

Hazel L. Ingersoll, Ph.D., Professor of Family Relations and Child Development, Oklahoma Agricultural and Mechanical College

Leland H. Stott, Ph.D., Leader, Longitudinal Studies Project, Merrill-Palmer School

David B. Treat, Director, The Clara Elizabeth Fund for Maternal Health, Flint, Michigan

Girdie Ware, Department of Family Relations and Child Development, Division of Home Economics, Oklahoma Agricultural and Mechanical College

In crediting these colleagues whose judgment and cooperation are so highly valued, it must be clear that they in no way are responsible for the weaknesses of the finished work; errors of omission and of commission are quite possible without outside assistance!

Authors, publishers, and editors of journals have been generous in granting permission to quote published and unpublished materials, credited in detail where they appear throughout the book.

Without the competent assistance of Joy Duvall Johnson in preparing the final draft of the manuscript for publication, the work might have been indefinitely delayed. That our association in this project occurred through the months in which we awaited the arrival of her firstborn made the work seem doubly creative and certainly made our deadline a living reality.

EVELYN MILLIS DUVALL

Chicago, Illinois
December, 1956

Contents

PART 1

Growing families in changing times

Families run on bursts of emotional energy generated by the interacting personalities of their members. What are the forces that keep a family alive and growing? How do these forces operate in performing family functions? What challenges do American families face as they shift in size and nature, structure and function within our changing society?

To every thing there is a season,
and a time for every purpose under
the heaven:
A time to be born, and a time
to die; a time to plant, and a
time to pluck up that which is
planted; . . .
A time to weep, and a time to
laugh; a time to mourn, and a time
to dance; . . .
A time to get, and a time to lose;
a time to keep, and a time to cast
away; . . .

ECCLESIASTES, III

The family life cycle

F amilies rarely lie idle. They run on bursts of emotional energy generated by the interacting personalities of their members. These dynamic life forces are geared to perform a variety of functions that change
through the years. What the forces are that keep a family alive and growing, how they operate in performing family functions, and how they with-
stand the hazards of conflicting forces, both from within and from without
the family, are important considerations today.

FAMILIES DIFFER IN MANY WAYS

The study of families in America is a study in diversity. It recognizes
that there are many kinds of families developing in a great variety of
ways. Our democratic philosophy establishes the right of each of these
families to find and develop for itself its own fulfillment in a way of life
unique unto itself. Therefore, we cannot speak of *the* American family
any more accurately than we can talk of *the* American child, or *the*
American man, woman, father, or mother, unless at the same time we
recognize the almost infinite variety of forms, functions, statuses, developmental levels, and ways of life inherent in the generalization.

America's forty to fifty million families, or more, are all different. They
are white, black, yellow, red, and many racial mixtures. They have come
from Europe, from Asia, from Africa, from all over the Western hemi-
sphere, and from the islands of the seven seas, bringing with them the
cultural traditions of those lands. They have fared well, and not so well,

in a social system with recognized statuses of lower class, middle class, upper class, and "on the make." They live on farms, in cities and towns, and in the wide suburban areas that circle the metropolitan areas. Some are large families with many children, others are small with few children, and about half have no children at all. There are strict old-fashioned, autocratically controlled families, and flexible democratically oriented families, and many that are a little of both. There are families with a father head, families with a mother head, families with two heads, and some that seem to have no head at all. The list of differences in American family life is long and kaleidoscopic, with few generalizations that hold for all.

There is, however, a predictability about family development that helps us know what to expect of any family at a given stage, regardless of who or where it is. Much as an individual grows, develops, matures, and ages, undergoing the successive changes and readjustments from conception to senescence, no matter who he or she is, so families likewise have a life cycle that is seen in the universal sequence of family development.

THE FAMILY LIFE CYCLE IS COMMON TO ALL FAMILIES

The family life cycle, as a frame of reference, is a way of taking a long look at family life. It is based upon the recognition of the successive patterns within the continuity of family living over the years. It opens the way for study of the particular problems and potentials, rewards and hazards, vulnerabilities and strengths of each phase of family experience from beginning to end. It recognizes the peculiar rhythms and tempos that pulse through family living, now soft and sweet, now loud and tempestuous, now swift, now slow, in movements that every family everywhere knows in its harmonies and dissonances of living together through the years.

Families take form in the marriage and early establishment of the newly married couple. They develop rapidly as husband and wife assume, with the coming of their first child, additional roles as father and mother. As successive children are born, family members enlarge their roles to encompass the additional children as individuals and as members of the growing family group. Each addition to the family brings not only an increase in the number of family members, but a significant reorganization of family living, so that no two children are born in the same family.

As children grow older, their parents are growing older also, changing in their needs and desires, their hopes and expectations, as well as their responses to the demands and pressures of growing children. Concurrently, the children are progressively changing in their relationship to their parents, to their brothers and sisters, and to other relatives.

Families mature as their children grow up, through childhood, into adolescence, and finally into lives and homes of their own. Families that once expanded to accommodate the requirements of growing children, later must contract as they release these same children as young adults. The big bustling years when family life runs at a hectic pace eventually give way to the long slow-moving years of the empty nest, when the middle-aged and aging parents face the later half of their marriage together as a pair. With the prolongation of life these later years present new opportunities and problems.

Each family grows through the years in its own particular way. Just as the individual person is born, grows and develops, matures, and ages, undergoing the successive changes and development from conception through senescence in his own way, so a family lives out its life cycle in its own unique fashion.

STAGES IN THE FAMILY LIFE CYCLE

The family life cycle may be divided into few or many stages, on the basis of several factors. It is possible to think of a two stage family life cycle: (1) *the expanding family stage* taking the family from its inception to the time its children are grown and (2) *the contracting family stage* in which children are being launched by the family into lives of their own and in which the family contracts through the later years with one or both of the original pair still at home. Such a two-stage cycle delineation is usually too gross for definitive study, but the factor of shifting plurality patterns in the family was one of the first used to see stages in the family life cycle.

As early as 1931, Sorokin and others [1] discussed a four stage family life cycle based upon the changing family member constellation within the family: (1) married couples just starting their independent economic existence, (2) couples with one or more children, (3) couples with one or more adult self-supporting children, and (4) couples growing old.

[1] P. Sorokin, C. C. Zimmerman, and C. J. Galpin, *A Systematic Source Book in Rural Sociology* (Minneapolis: University of Minnesota Press, 1931), Vol. II, p. 31.

E. L. Kirkpatrick and others [1] saw the stages of the family life cycle in terms of the place of the children in the educational system in a four-stage cycle: 1) preschool family, 2) grade-school family, 3) high school family, and 4) all adult family.

In plotting the changing income and outgo financial patterns through the family life cycle, Howard Bigelow [2] elaborated on the school placement factor in a cycle he demarked into seven periods: (1) establishment, (2) childbearing and preschool period, (3) elementary school period, (4) high school period, (5) college, (6) period of recovery, and (7) period of retirement. He points out why it is difficult to settle upon any one clear-cut system of delineation of stages of the family life cycle, for all families, when he says,

The length of each of the stages in the typical cycle and the extent to which there is overlapping vary from family to family, depending upon the age of the parents at the time of their marriage, the time of the arrival of their first child, the number and spacing of the children, and the amount and type of education with which they are provided.[3]

The problems of delineating family life cycle stages that will hold for all families are many because families themselves are so varied. Some couples marry early and others not until much later. Some couples have their first baby in the first year of their marriage, others not until years afterwards, and still others never have children. Some babies arrive one after another in quick succession, while others are spaced by as much as a dozen years or more. Some children follow a regular progression through elementary school, high school, and college, while others cease being school children before they are scarcely in their teens. Even more difficult to take into account are the many forms of broken and rebuilt families—with all that is involved in divorce, remarriage, and the establishment of families in which "your children," "my children," and "our children," are all part of the same family. Military service but partially launches many young men from their parental families, for although they leave home, their independence is incomplete when they must return to finish

[1] E. L. Kirkpatrick et al., "The Life Cycle of the Farm Family in Relation to Its Standard of Living," Research Bulletin #121 (Madison, Wisconsin: Agricultural Experiment Station, University of Wisconsin, 1934).

[2] Howard F. Bigelow, "Money and Marriage," Chapter XVII in Marriage and the Family, Becker and Hill, eds. (Boston: D. C. Heath and Company, 1942), pp. 382–386.

[3] Ibid., page 386.

A COMMUNITY FAMILY LIFE PROGRAM

FAMILY FOUNDING

CHILD BEARING

The EMPTY NEST

CHILD REARING

CHILD LAUNCHING

a Elizabeth Fund For Maternal He

Flint, Mich.

The family life cycle is one way of taking a long look at family life. Here we see David Treat (left), Director, Clara Elizabeth Fund for Maternal Health in Flint, Michigan, outlining a community family life program that takes into account the entire family life cycle.

their educational plans and finally get settled in lives of their own. No less indefinite is the status of the girl who may be a wife of an absent serviceman, and yet still a daughter at home with her parents.

Whatever schema for defining family life cycle stages is used, it is merely a convenient division for study of something that in real life flows on from one phase to another without pause or break. The genius of the concept is the explicit awareness that each stage has its beginnings in the phases that are past and its fruition in development yet to come. Being cyclical by definition, the family life cycle and each of the stages within it has no beginning and no end. No matter where you start to study the family life cycle, there are always relevant roots in the near and distant past that must be considered. Wherever you are at the moment, you have grown out of the stage just before and are heading into the stage ahead.

Each family grows through the years in its own particular way. Rich or poor, large or small, in the city or on the farm, every family has a life cycle that is seen in the universal sequence of family development.

This book recognizes and depicts the family life cycle as consisting of eight stages:

Stage I   Beginning Families (married couple without children)
Stage II   Childbearing Families (oldest child, birth to 30 months)
Stage III   Families with Preschool Children (oldest child 2½ to 6 years)
Stage IV   Families with School Children (oldest child 6 to 13 years)
Stage V   Families with Teenagers (oldest child 13 to 20 years)
Stage VI   Families as Launching Centers (first child gone to last child's
             leaving home)
Stage VII   Families in the Middle Years (empty nest to retirement)
Stage VIII   Aging Families (retirement to death of one or both spouses)

The age and school placement of the oldest child are used as criteria of family cycle stage placement from arrival of the first child in the family up to the launching center stage when we shift focus to the situation facing those remaining in the original family. Families as Launching Centers (Stage VI) is the stage that begins with the leaving home of the first child and concludes with the departure of the last child into marriage, military service, work, or whatever pulls him or her as a young adult into a life of his or her own.

This treatment is organized around a modification of the seven stage family life cycle structured by the co-chairmen for the National Conference on Family Life in 1948.[1] It represents a combination of the several factors used in determining family life cycle stages: (a) plurality patterns, (b) age of the oldest child, (c) school placement of the oldest child, and (d) functions and statuses of families before children come and after they leave. This combination of factors seems to be workable for the study of the majority of American families, and to parallel such reliable data as are available to date both from the United States Bureau of the Census, and from less extensive research studies.

OVERLAPPING OF FAMILY LIFE CYCLE STAGES

In defining the stages in terms of the oldest child, the presence of other children in the family is not explicitly recognized. A clean-cut sequence of stages of the family life cycle such as that outlined above seems to occur only in the one-child family. In families with more than one child, there are several years of overlap at various of the stages. The average mother of two or more children is in the period of childbearing for a longer period than Stage II indicates, she has preschool children over a longer span of time than is predicted for Stage III, she has school age children longer than is considered in designating Stage IV, she has teenagers in the home for a longer period than that covered by Stage V, see Chart 1, page 13.

There is no simple solution to the conceptual problem of overlap of stages of the family life cycle in families of more than one child. Since our thesis is that families grow and develop as their children do, our answer to the question of overlapping of stages is that a family grows through a given stage with its oldest child, and in a sense "repeats" as subsequent children come along. We see a family being pushed out into new unknowns in its experience as its oldest child becomes a preschooler, goes to school, gets into the teens, and finally leaves for a life of his own. As younger children come along, they arrive in a family already some-

[1] Evelyn Duvall and Reuben Hill, co-chairmen, *Report of the Committee on the Dynamics of Family Interaction*, prepared at the request of the National Conference on Family Life, (Washington, D. C.: February 1948), mimeographed materials.

what familiar with these normal events and stages of children's growth through the induction given by the eldest. Thus, while a family may be seeing its firstborn into preschool, a younger sibling arrives in a preschool family rather than a childbearing family, because of the family's involvement with the older child also. Actually that family is not solely a childbearing family, because it is already grappling with the problems and pressures of its preschooler, at the same time that it nurtures its newborn. And so it goes through the years that children are in the home. The oldest child is always taking his family with him out into the growing edges of family experience. Younger children necessarily arrive into a different family than that into which the firstborn came, if only in the degree of its experience with children of his age!

THE MARRIED COUPLE AS "FAMILY"

Three stages of the family life cycle, as we define it, deal with the husband and wife as a couple: Stage I as a married couple before children come, and Stages VII and VIII as a married couple after their children have grown and gone.

It might well be argued that a couple without children is not a family, but more accurately a married couple. If we took this position we would name Stage I "Young Married Couple," Stage VII "Middleaged Couple," and Stage VIII "Aging Couple." But, since we are trying to see the whole family in focus through the years, it makes sense to see the newly married couple as "the beginning family" that develops very quickly in the majority of cases into the childbearing family. The norm is for the young married couple to be a family-in-the-making not only in that their children eventually make a family of them, but in that they expect to have children, and think of themselves typically as a pair of potential parents long before children actually arrive. In terms of the time factor alone, many couples spend as much or more of their early married stage as expectant parents as they do as bride and groom.

The middleaged or aging couple who has already been through the childbearing, rearing, and launching stages of the family cycle is still a couple, true. But they are parents of grown children, too. They quite probably have grandchildren. They keep up the home base more often than not. They make a home for varying lengths of time for their married children and grandchildren; perhaps for their own aging parents and other older relatives. They continue to think of themselves as "family"

The middleaged and aging couple is still "family" to their grown children, and to their grandchildren. They keep a home base for the younger members of the family, and more often than not are in the midst of family gatherings, such as we see here.

and to function as family members long after their own children are grown and off in homes of their own. Therefore, we designate them as in the later stages of the family life cycle.

THE LENGTH OF THE STAGES

Americans usually think of a family as one in which there is a father and mother and two or three young children. Advertisements beam on such a picture of family life. Church and school materials often portray this stage of the family life cycle as though it were the only one that mattered. Commercial word pictures commonly assume that the family with young children is *the* family. Holiday sentiments and everyday assumptions put this stage of the family life cycle so much in the foreground that none other seems to exist. Such a stereotype is understandable. Certainly the childrearing and childbearing stages are highly important in family relationships, in the family's contact with school, church, and community, in the development of the personalities of the children, and for the family as a consumer with its bulging appetites for more and ever more goods. Yet this stage of the family life cycle is but a small fraction of the whole. It consists of but a few years, an average of a dozen or so, out of the total of fifty to sixty years in the life of the average family.

In marriage and family life courses, in schools and colleges, it is usual to spend the greater part of the time on the processes that lead to marriage, in the adjustments of the newly married pair, and their functions as expectant and actual parents. This, of course, is justifiable in that it reflects the readiness of the student, as well as the significance of the husband-wife relationship for the stability of the family. Yet at the same time such an emphasis misrepresents the time the married pair have together in the family they have established.

If they are a man and woman of the average ages the U. S. Bureau of the Census reports as typical at first marriage, birth of children, marriage of last child, and death of spouse, then the family cycle they may envisage for themselves is largely ignored in courses that focus solely on the young married couple. As is clearly seen in Chart 1, "The Family Life Cycle by Length of Time in Each of Eight Stages," the husband or wife spends practically one-half of his or her marriage as a middleaged and older person after the children have grown and gone. The Beginning Family Stage is the shortest of them all. The period when there are preadolescent children in the home is roughly the same length of time as that the couple spends in the empty nest between the time the last child has left home and retirement.

The significance of the duration of the various stages not only for education, but for budgeting, housing, health, recreation, home management, and a host of other family resources and services excites the imagination, and will be dealt with in part in the subsequent chapters devoted to each of the stages of the family life cycle.

THE LIFE CYCLE OF THE MIDCENTURY FAMILY MEMBER

With supporting census data for the ages at which men and women typically marry, have their children, and go through the rest of their lives as family members, we can predict in general what may be expected by any individual. Remembering our emphasis on individual difference, we will not expect such a profile to resemble any one person in all particulars. Nor, will we anticipate that any man or woman conform to statistical means and averages. But, in much the same way in which we find reliable the actuarial tables of a life insurance company that tell us of

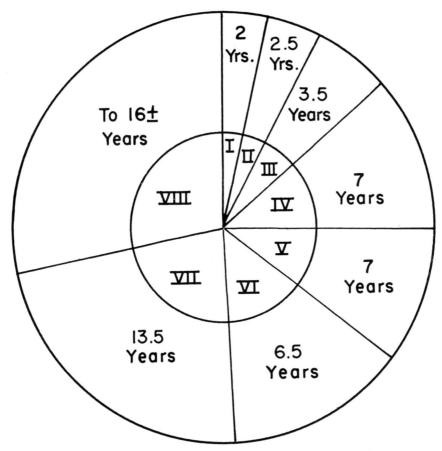

CHART 1. The Family Life Cycle by Length of Time in Each
of Eight Stages [1]

 I   BEGINNING FAMILIES (Married couple without children).
 II CHILDBEARING FAMILIES (Oldest child birth—30 months).
 III FAMILIES WITH PRESCHOOL CHILDREN (Oldest child 30 months—
      6 years).
 IV FAMILIES WITH SCHOOL CHILDREN (Oldest child 6–13 years).
 V   FAMILIES WITH TEENAGERS (Oldest child 13–20 years).
 VI FAMILIES AS LAUNCHING CENTERS (First child gone to last child
      leaving home).
 VII FAMILIES IN THE MIDDLE YEARS (Empty nest to retirement).
 VIII AGING FAMILIES (Retirement to death of both spouses).

[1] Data from U. S. Bureau of the Census for 1950.

our life expectancy, so in a measure, we can plot the generalized family expectancies through which we as family members pass. Just as a man may invalidate his predicted life span by stepping in front of a truck, or coming to a premature death because of some inherited or acquired malady, so too, anyone may personally depart from the generalized profile of family experience at any point in the schema. Such variations do not invalidate the predictions that hold true at a given time for the population as a whole.

Using the norms of our American society, with the United States Census of 1950 data, a woman's life may be outlined as follows. She comes into her family of orientation at birth, she starts school at six, enters her teens at thirteen, and marries at about twenty. At this point she leaves her family of orientation and enters her family of procreation. Her first child is born about two years later, and her last child is born when she is twenty-six years of age. By the time she is twenty-eight, her first child enters school. He becomes a teenager when she is about thirty-five, and marries when she is in her early forties (42–45). Her last child marries before she is fifty (at an average of 47.6, earlier for daughters, later for sons). She shares her middle age in the empty nest with her husband until his death which comes when she is around sixty (61.4) years of age. Then she is faced with nearly sixteen years of widowhood (15.8) until her own demise at age 77.2.

Of course no woman is a cold statistic, but a living person who will pass through several phases distinct from those that have gone before or those that come after in her life. These phases can be seen as a series of long and short pulsations that vary in length and intensity throughout life. She starts with the long pulsation of girlhood that lasts the first thirteen or fourteen years of life. Her career as a young woman is approximately half as long, until she marries in her very early twenties. Then come four short, intensely active phases of about equal length of seven years each: having babies and small children in the home (7 years); having school age children in the home (7 years); having teenagers in the home (7 years); and launching young adult children into lives of their own (6½ years).[1] Now life slows down a bit as she shares the

---

[1] The launching center stage begins with the departure of the first child from the home for marriage, for work, for military service, or in some cases for college or other advanced training that takes him or her away from home as a young adult, and ends with the emptying nest as the last child leaves home for a life of his or her own. The figures used here are taken from the ages at which the first and last child marries, typically in midtwentieth century United States, (See Chart 2 for specific census data).

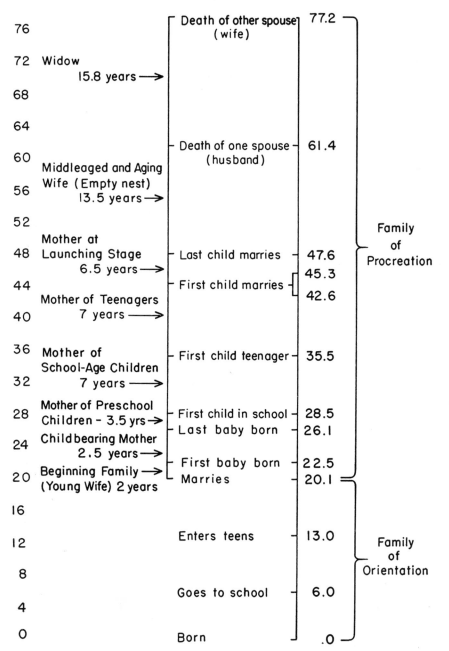

CHART 2. Profile of the Life of the Midcentury Wife and Mother [1]

[1] Data from U. S. Census for 1950 from Paul C. Glick, "The Life Cycle of the Family," *Marriage and Family Living*, Vol. XVII, No. 1, February 1955, pp. 3–9; and from National Office of Vital Statistics, *Births by Age of Mother, Race, and Birth Order United States*, 1953. (Washington, D.C.: U. S. Department of Health, Education and Welfare, Vol. 42, No. 13, December 21, 1955), p. 294.

empty nest with her husband for the long leisurely phase of approximately fourteen years (13.8) until she is widowed by his death when she is in her early sixties (61.4). The last long slow stage of her own aging years is of approximately sixteen years (15.8) duration.

A woman college graduate may expect to marry about three years later than the average American woman. The median age at first marriage for all women who were still in their first marriage in 1950 was 20.6 years. For those women with no high school education, the age at first marriage was 20.1, for those with four years of high school it was 20.8, for those with four or more years of college it was 23.8.[1] The later age at family formation means that the other stages of the family life cycle for the college-educated woman will be likely to come later. The smaller average number of children that college-educated women have offsets the later age at marriage to some extent.[2] The life cycle profile for the college woman and the typical American woman at midcentury therefore tend to parallel each other in the later phases, from the launching center stage onward.

The profile of life as a woman consists of three long periods of about fourteen years each: girlhood, middle years, and aging years. There are five short phases of approximately seven years each: life as a young woman, childbearing years, school-age children's years, teenager's years, and launching-center years. Looking at a woman purely as a reproductive being, we see that she spends the first twenty years of life growing up and getting ready to have children, the next twenty-five years bearing and rearing children, and the last thirty years alone or with her husband after their children have grown and gone.

Seeing oneself as a grown woman focuses attention on the fact that more than half of one's life after marriage remains after children have grown. Such a view of life through the years raises many questions about the kind of education needed not only for the immediate future but for the years ahead. What will a woman need to prepare herself for the long middle years after her parent roles are over? What will be necessary for the period of widowhood that stretches on for fully half of her later years? Does this have implications for life insurance plans? What

[1] 1950 *Census of Population,* Volume IV, *Special Reports,* Part 2, Chapter E, "Duration of Current Marital Status," Table 5.

[2] The average number of children ever born to women 40–44 years old was 2.4 for all American women, and 1.7 for college graduates in 1950, according to Paul C. Glick, personal communication, July 9, 1956.

After a woman marries, there is an intensely active phase of childbearing and rearing that lasts about twenty-five years to be followed by an equally long period that remains after the children are grown and gone. It is easy to see the woman's role in the childrearing stage above. But, can you see her just as clearly twenty-five years from now?

does it say about mate selection that will not unduly prolong the period of widowhood? What is indicated in terms of interests and activities with carry-over possibilities for the later phases of life? One's roles as a woman are played out not just in the quick-moving busy years of young womanhood, but through the ever-changing tempos of the entire family life cycle.

Plotting a profile of the life of the man in the American family using medians and norms projected from 1950 United States Census Data gives us the following outline that differs slightly from that of the American woman. Like her, the male enters his family of orientation at birth, goes to school at six, and becomes a teenager at thirteen. He marries on the average 2.7 years later than the woman, when he is 22.8 years of age. At this point he becomes part of his family of procreation. His first child is born a little more than two years after his marriage when he is not much over twenty-five (25.2). His last child is born when he is 28.8 years of age, and 2½ years later his first child enters school. He becomes

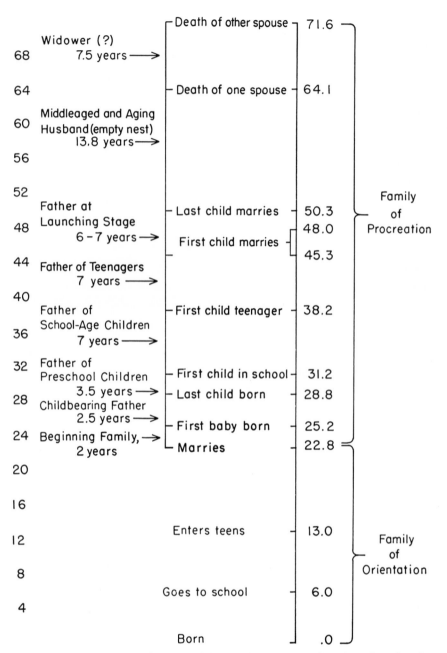

CHART 3. Profile of the Life of the Midcentury Husband and Father [1]

[1] Data from U. S. Census for 1950 from Paul C. Glick, "The Life Cycle of the Family," *Marriage and Family Living*, XVII, No. 1, February 1955, pp. 3–9; and from National Office of Vital Statistics, *Births by Age of Mother, Race, and Birth Order United States, 1953*. (Washington, D. C.: U. S. Department of Health, Education, and Welfare, Vol. 42, No. 13, December 21, 1955), p. 294.

a father of teenagers when he is 38.2 years old. When he reaches his mid-forties (45.3 to 48 years of age) he becomes the father of the bride (or groom) when his first child marries. His last child is married by the time he is barely fifty (50.3). By this time he is probably a grandfather. He and his wife now live in the empty nest, with their parenting roles over, for practically fourteen years. Now, characteristically he is the first spouse to die (64.1). If he survives beyond the average, he enters into retirement soon afterwards, and may or may not be widowed in the years at the latter end of the marriage. The chief differences between the length of the various phases of his life as a man and those of his wife are the slightly longer period before marriage (2.7 years) and the shorter middleaged and aging period due to his shorter life span.

Of course, there is no such thing as the average man. Each man has the particular ages and stages in his life cycle that are peculiar to him. On the average, however, he can anticipate spending most of his adult life as a husband and father. He and his wife will spend the first two years or so as a couple before their first child arrives. Then, after his last child has married and left home he may expect another fourteen years (plus or minus) as a member of a couple again. His second decade of life will be spent in becoming a young man, his third in becoming a father. His forties will be characterized by children and teenagers and young adults being launched into lives of their own. His fifties and sixties, after the peak of childrearing responsibilities are over, will be relatively quiet ones on the family scene, with just himself and his wife and their life as grandparents. The chances are that he will leave his wife a widow, with all the implications of life insurance, retirement plans, housing requirements, and the rest of the factors involved for them both in planning their later years.

ONE GENERATION AFTER ANOTHER

Typically a family develops through a predictable sequence of stages that follow one another in reliable progression. Before one family unit has completed its cycle, its children have been launched to start out on theirs. Most twentieth-century American family members have the privilege of seeing the family life cycle start a second time and sometimes a third as children marry and rear their children who marry and have their children while older members of the family are still living.

| 1900 | 1910 | 1920 | 1930 | 1940 | 1950 | 1960 | 1970 | 1980 | 1990 |

Family of Orientation (Parents' Family)

X is Born

Family of Procreation (Own Family)

X Marries Y

Family of Gerontation'   (Children's Families)

XY's First Child Marries

Family of Gerontation''
(Grandchildren's Families)
XY's First Grandchild Marries

CHART 4. Overlapping of the Life Spans of the Families of Association of the Individual (1950 Census Projections for Average American Women) [1]

Chart 4 is a schematic portrayal of family development from one generation to the next. Using as a base line the length of time married of the original husband and wife, we see their children coming at the usual ages, marrying at the median ages at first marriage, and having their children at ages typical in America today. Thus we see that both original husband and wife survive the marriage of all their children and participate in the induction of sons- and daughters-in-law into the family. Both of the original parents live to see their grandchildren born and raised and most of them married, before their lives are terminated in death. The original woman lives to see the marriage of practically all her grandchildren, and not unusually has the experience of seeing her great-grandchildren well underway before she too passes on. Thus, at midcentury, the American family typically consists of four or more generations in its extended forms. Dr. Ruth Albrecht [2] predicts that, with increased longevity, generations will be added to the family so that five and six generation families seem likely in the future. Chart 5, her "Pattern of an Elongated Family," illustrates how one young person of college age today has eight living antecedents: two parents, four grandparents, and two great-grandparents.

[1] Generations of girls are shorter than generations of boys, since girls marry at earlier ages than do boys.

[2] Ruth Albrecht, "Intergeneration Parent Patterns," *Journal of Home Economics,* Vol. 46, No. 1, January 1954, pp. 29–32.

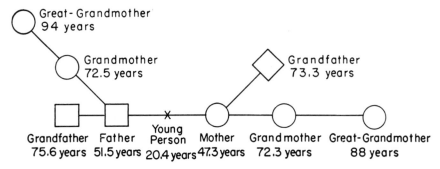

CHART 5.   Pattern of an Elongated Family [1]

The elongated family is not too atypical even now. Albrecht finds that practically half (49 per cent) of the college students she studied had a mean of 7 antecedents still living. She goes on to suggest,

If a girl with two parents, three grandparents, and two great-grandparents marries the boy with two parents and four grandparents, they will have to maintain a social and affectional relationship with 13 parent figures.[2]

Geographical mobility tends to separate members of the extended family, so that face to face contacts between the generations may be few in some modern families. Study of Table 1 shows clearly that in a recent twelve-month period, practically 29 million persons moved to a

TABLE 1. *Mobility of the Civilian Population April 1953 to April 1954* [3]
(Population 1954, age 1 and over, 155,679,000)

Mobility Status			Per cent
Same house (non-movers)			80.7
Different house in the United States (movers)			18.6
Same county		12.2	
Different county		6.4	
Within a state	3.2		
Between states	3.2		
Abroad on April 1, 1953			.6

[1] *Ibid.* p. 31.
[2] *Ibid.* p. 31.
[3] U. S. Bureau of the Census, *Statistical Abstracts of the United States—1955*, Volume 76, pp. 42 and 43. (Based on current population monthly survey published in *Current Population Reports*, Series P–20, Number 57.)

new location. While 80.7 per cent of the civilian population remained
in the same house, nearly one out of five changed residence in a given
year (18.6 per cent).

Even so, current study of 731 families in Detroit, Michigan, finds only
11 per cent of the families with no relatives in the metropolitan area, and
a high frequency of intra-family visiting: 29 per cent daily, 37 per cent
weekly, 20 per cent monthly, and 13 per cent yearly.[1]

TWENTIETH-CENTURY CHANGES IN THE FAMILY LIFE CYCLE

The importance of becoming familiar with the processes of the maturing family has been highlighted in recent years as we have become aware
of the extent to which our population is aging. Today, each of us is
potentially related to an increasing number of older relatives. Even more
pertinent to the individual is the assurance that an increasing number of
us will survive for the middle and later years.

The increase in the life span is a fairly recent phenomenon. There have
been tremendous changes within our century that have given more men
and women added years of life. Today, when more persons of both sexes
survive the early years and when more mothers come through childbearing safely, a larger percentage of our population lives to round out
its life span than formerly did. A brief glance at Table 2 (summarized
United States Census data for 1890, 1940, and 1950), tells us that the

TABLE 2. *Median Age of Husband and Wife at Selected Stages of the Life
Cycle of the Family, for the United States: 1950, 1940, and 1890* [2]

Stage of the life cycle of the family	Median age of husband			Median age of wife		
	1950	1940	1890	1950	1940	1890
A. First marriage	22.8	24.3	26.1	20.1	21.5	22.0
B. Birth of last child	28.8	29.9	36.0	26.1	27.1	31.9
C. Marriage of last child	50.3	52.8	59.4	47.6	50.0	55.3
D. Death of one spouse *	64.1	63.6	57.4	61.4	60.9	53.3
E. Death of other spouse †	71.6	69.7	66.4	77.2	73.5	67.7

° Husband and wife survive jointly from marriage to specified age.
† Husband (wife) survives separately from marriage to specified age.

[1] Robert O. Blood, Jr., report on kinescope program "In-Laws" (No. 11 in the 1956
Marriage Series) University of Michigan Television Center, Ann Arbor, Michigan,
1956.
[2] Paul C. Glick, "The Life Cycle of the Family," *Marriage and Family Living,*
Vol. XVII, No. 1, February 1955, p. 4.

median age of death of husband and wife was from five to ten years later in 1950 than it was in 1890. Since both sexes married at younger ages by from two to four years in 1950 than they did in 1890, both husband and wife can anticipate a total of a decade or more years of marriage and family living now than was typical at the close of the last century.

Summarizing briefly the changes in the family life cycle since 1890, we see the following:

1) Men and women marry at younger ages now than formerly
2) The childbearing period is considerably shorter now than formerly
3) The empty nest, characterized by the marriage of the last child, comes sooner now than formerly
4) More men and women complete their life span as individuals and as a married pair now than formerly
5) There is a longer period together as a couple after children have grown now than formerly. In 1890 the typical family had no such period.

SUMMARY

Families are many and varied. They are similar in that they develop through the years in ways that are in part predictable. Every family develops through a family life cycle in which it becomes established in the marriage of the man and his wife, enters into childbearing and childrearing with the coming of children, becomes an arena of interacting family members as the children grow up, and in time launches the children into lives of their own. The middleaged and aging couple live through their remaining years in an empty nest that is, however, still a home base for their married children, their grandchildren, their other relatives, and so continues to be in fact part of the family life cycle. The eight stages of the family life cycle differ in form and function, in "busyness" and tempo, and in length of time spent in each one before the next stage appears. Each succeeding generation overlaps those that have gone before and those that come after. In recent years there have been significant changes in the family life cycle that tend to elongate the family, increasing the potential number of intergenerational contacts (at the same time that mobility tends to decrease both the number and the influence of actual relationships between members of the extended family), and shifting the length of time spent in each of the various stages of the family life cycle. These changes are part of the matrix of social change that is taken up in the next chapter.

All things journey: sun and moon,
Morning, noon, and afternoon
Night and all her stars;
'Twixt the east and western bars
Round they journey,
Come and go!
We go with them!

GEORGE ELIOT

SUGGESTED ACTIVITIES

1) Read and discuss, *The Fourposter* by Jan de Hartog, a three-act play, Random House, 1951.
2) Review Thornton Wilder's one-act play, *The Long Christmas Dinner.*
3) Plot your own expected life line following the profile for American man or woman in Charts 2 and 3, using your own personal data.
4) Graph the pattern of your extended family of living antecedents according to Albrecht's schema in Chart 5, putting yourself as the young person at point X, and indicating by age and symbol your parents, grandparents, and great-grandparents.
5) Write a paper on woman's education today taking into account the needs that she as a person will have for competency at the various phases in her expected life cycle.
6) Discuss the implications of the family life cycle concept for courses in marriage and family life, in high schools and colleges and in adult education.
7) List the names of ten men and women of various ages, known to you, and opposite each name indicate the stage of the family life cycle in which he or she is. Give supporting data for each designation.
8) List the forms of family life in America today that are *not* explicitly accounted for in the family life cycle stages as outlined in this chapter. Include especially a) couples without children, b) families broken by death, divorce, or separation, c) unmarried parents, d) families with stepchildren, e) others. Describe one such family as you have listed and indicate its possible placement in the family life cycle. Give your reasons for assigning it to the stage you have selected for it.

READINGS

Albrecht, Ruth, "Intergeneration Parent Patterns," *Journal of Home Economics*, Vol. 46, No. 1, January 1954, pp. 29–32.
Bigelow, Howard, "Financing the Marriage," Chapter 13, *Family, Marriage and Parenthood* (Boston: D. C. Heath and Company, Revised Edition, 1955), by Howard Becker and Reuben Hill, eds., pp. 411–414.

Byrd, Oliver E. (ed.), *Family Life Sourcebook* (Stanford, California: Stanford University Press, 1956).

Cavan, Ruth, *The American Family*, (New York: Thomas Y. Crowell Company, 1953), Part Three, "The Cycle of Family Life," pp. 261–612.

Child Study Association of America, "Living and Growing with Our Children: Impact on Parents of Children's Growth Phases," *Child Study*, Vol. XXXII, No. 3, Summer 1955.

Cooley, Donald, "Can You Predict Your Family's Future?" *Better Homes and Gardens*, December 1951, pp. 40 and 140.

Duvall, Evelyn Millis, and Hill, Reuben, *Report of the Committee on Dynamics of Family Ineraction*, National Conference on Family Life, Inc., February 1948. Mimeographed materials.

Duvall, Evelyn Millis, "Changing Roles in the Family Cycle," *Journal of Home Economics*, Vol. 42, No. 6, June 1950, pp. 435–436.

✓Glick, Paul C., "The Family Cycle," *American Sociological Review*, Vol. XII, No. 2, April 1947, pp. 164–174.

Glick, Paul C., "The Life Cycle of the Family," *Marriage and Family Living*, Vol. XVII, No. 1, February 1955, pp. 3–9.

Gutheim, Frederick, *Houses for Family Living* (New York: The Woman's Foundation, 1948).

Hill, Reuben, revision of Willard Waller's *The Family: A Dynamic Interpretation* (New York: The Dryden Press, 1951), Part Five, pp. 375–449.

Hurlock, Elizabeth B., *Developmental Psychology* (New York: McGraw-Hill, 1953).

Kirkpatrick, Clifford, *The Family as Process and Institution* (New York: The Ronald Press Company, 1955), Part III, "Life Cycle of Family Experience," pp. 173–486.

Stott, Leland H., "The Longitudinal Approach to the Study of Family Life," *Journal of Home Economics*, Vol. 46, February 1954, pp. 79–82.

Sussman, Marvin, "Family Continuity: Selective Factors Which Affect Relationships between Families at Generational Levels," *Marriage and Family Living*, Vol. XVI, No. 2, May 1954, pp. 112–120.

*Change doth unknit the tranquil
strength of men.*
                    MATTHEW ARNOLD

*Since you cannot keep life
  Inside a neat fence
You will learn to lean on
  Impermanence.*
                    IRVING FINEMAN

*Remember that there is nothing
  stable in human affairs.*
                    SOCRATES

CHAPTER TWO

Family functions reflect social change

The powerful complex of industrialization, urbanization, and secularization has drastically changed the functions of American families in recent decades. No longer imperative are the once all-absorbing demands of economic productivity, education, medical attention, recreation, protection, religion—all essential functions of the pioneer, rural, old-fashioned large family.

WHAT FAMILIES ARE FOR TODAY

Today's families face subtle functions in terms of the personality development of their members through affectional security, continuity of guidance, and cultural interpretation. Compared with Grandmother's knitting and churning these new functions are bafflingly complex and bewilderingly intangible.

Men and women as fathers and mothers today are engaged in childbearing and childrearing with conscious intent upon socializing and culturizing the child, transforming him or her from an immature human organism into a participating member of society, capable of creative contribution and personal integrity in a complicated, explosive world situation. Parents themselves recognize that they too must continue to develop if they are to find personal happiness and be of some good to others. The garden for human development, both child and adult, continues to be the family in which is found the emotional soil and the spiritual climate for human growth.

The family is therefore the matrix of personality which emerges as the idiomatic patterns of functioning, of habits, ideas, beliefs, values, assumptions, and above all of emotional reactions and persistent feelings, as each child learns to live within his particular family in his or her own individual way.

Families continue to function as primary agents for health, in the selection and preparation of food for adequate nutrition in family meals, in the establishment of attitudes conducive to healthful eating, eliminating, resting, working, and being, as well as in the endless tasks of housecleaning, laundering, dishwashing, and all the other functions that cannot be performed by doctors or outside medical agencies, but must be provided in the home.

Families are the primary agents for basic mental health which cannot be provided by psychiatrists, psychologists, or social workers. Only the family can protect and conserve the mental health of individuals through its quality of interpersonal relationships, the provision of reassurance and comfort, the releases and encouragement that each person needs to keep on striving for fulfillment. Love itself, the prime necessity for mental health, has its genesis in the intimate everyday warmth that husbands and wives, and parents and children generate in interaction with each other.

These things we know today. Present-day American families face a level of family functioning in conscious aspiration unknown in other places and times. The big change in family life in recent decades is in what we, as members, are trying to become. It is no longer enough to make ends meet, or to feed and clothe a child. Today's families in ever increasing numbers are seeking a quality of life for all their members that is truly something new in the history of mankind.

CONTRASTS WITH FAMILIES IN UNDERDEVELOPED AREAS

Millions of people around the world still live a simple agricultural way of life that gives us a vivid impression of our own earlier days. They raise, make, and process most of what they need as families in their own homes and acreages. Whether they be families in the villages of India, the barrios of the Philippines, or the mountain or lake communities of rural Mexico, the pattern is much the same. Each family grows or makes some surplus in the form of small grains, cheeses, vegetables or fruits, ceramic pots, woven reed baskets or hats or mats, handwoven textiles, or whatever the specialty of the area. These "cash crops" are taken periodically to market and sold or bartered for those few commodities that the family does not raise or make for itself. The family builds its own dwelling—a thatched nipa hut of the Philippines, a log cabin in the woods of Northern Canada, or a dark adobe structure characteristic of so many of the people that girdle the globe. What furnishings there are in the home are fashioned by some family member in the ways traditional for the particular group. Small animals feed about the place. Babies play on the floor or are carried about by some older child or mother figure. Old folks doze in the sun nearby. The sick suffer in silence on a corner pallet, and eventually die where they were born—at home.

Water is drawn from the village well, or from some nearby waterhole. What milk there is comes from the family goat or cow or from the open container brought through the streets. Each family protects itself and its belongings from robbers, fire, snakes, and insects as best it can. Each family shares with its neighbors the periodic or chronic invasions of diseases native to the area. Each family is responsible for teaching its members what they are to know with only casual or occasional contacts with formal schooling. The head of the family in this simple folk culture is usually the father, whose authority is backed by the wise old heads of the village and the power of the church or temple whose word is law.

Stepping into such a way of life anywhere around the world is a vivid emotional experience for a twentieth-century American.[1] The tremendous contrast between life in a simple agricultural, nonindustrialized society and in our own complex technological culture is dramatically seen in the ways in which families function, in the things that are important to families, and in the resources available for families.

---

[1] The writer acknowledges the vigor of the education she received in 1954 and 1955, during assignments that took her to work with families and family life leaders in Japan, Hong Kong, the Philippines, the Malay States, Ceylon, through India, Egypt, Jordan, Turkey, Greece, and most recently at the center for fundamental education at Patzcuaro, Michoacan, Mexico. Such personal experiences give meaning to "book learning" and bring home in new ways the similarities and contrasts of people around the world.

Millions of people around the world live in a simple, agricultural way of life such as the family above enjoys here in rural America.

TRADITIONAL LIVING AMONG AMERICAN FAMILIES

Way back in the hills there are still families living as most of us did a few generations ago. In isolated mountain communities families spend their lives making the things they need: food, clothing, shelter, and medicinal herbs, are made, grown, or gathered by their own hands. Many of us remember the smell of fresh-baked bread coming out of the family oven, to be spread with butter just "gathered" from the wooden churn. Only yesterday the hum of the loom and the whirr of the sewing machine turned out the homespun garments that made up the bulk of the family wardrobe. Once the arts of soapmaking, candle dipping, and of preserving meats by smoking, salting, pickling, and drying were everyday realities. The implements and handicrafts of such primitive ways of living are prized as treasures by those of us who live in a far different kind of family life. Yet it was not long ago when through the vast reaches of the United States most families lived just this way. This is our herit-

COURTESY OF THE LIBRARY OF CONGRESS

American families used to draw their water from a well, as is still done in underdeveloped areas around the world.

age. Such ways of life are traditional for us, as they are for most of the peoples of the world.

In sharp contrast, today's American families live largely in cities or suburbs. These families no longer work together to make their living from the land. Now instead of *making* a living, the husband-father goes out to *earn* the living for the family. There are fewer members in today's modern family, and more of them live longer than did their forebears in the traditional American family. Members of today's families live better by working less and enjoy a standard of living unknown to previous generations.

Wherein lie these tremendous differences between the underdeveloped and traditional ways of life and the highly developed modern American families? The simplest answer is to be found in the power of the machine harnessed to do man's will. The genius of mass production is that the more goods we make, the less it costs to make them. The better off people are, the more goods they can buy, thus making lavish economical production infinitely possible. Home industries can no longer compete with the assembly line, so the making of things has moved out of the home and into industry. What happens as families adapt to the shifting social and economic scene that results is an exciting phenomenon that most of us have seen in part with our own eyes in our own and other cultures around the world. Everywhere the picture is basically the same.[1] When modern industrial development comes in, old ways are modified, discarded, and replaced, as the family changes to meet the new needs and take advantage of the new opportunities that arise. In America the shift has involved many interrelated complex changes in family life. Some of those most pertinent to this discussion are treated briefly in subsequent sections.

CHANGES IN AMERICAN FAMILY LIFE IN THE TWENTIETH CENTURY

Families have moved off the farm. In 1850, two-thirds of all American workers were farmers (65 per cent). In the decades that followed there was a steady migration from farms to cities and towns, so that by the middle of the twentieth century, only 14 per cent of America's labor force were agricultural workers.[2] This steady decline of our farming population brought an influx of workers to urban areas that increased within the century from 35 to 86 per cent of the total working population. Two related forces were responsible for this mass migration of families from farms to cities. One was the tremendous increase in jobs available in cities and towns as industrialization opened up and expanded with its good paying positions not only in the factories but also in the many related areas of construction, maintenance, and servicing of larger urban developments. The second factor was the increased efficiency of the farm as it became mechanized. Fewer and fewer workers on larger and larger farms were needed to support the nation. Before modern mechanized farming, a farmer's family did well to support itself on the old place. In 1790, one farmer could produce enough to feed himself and 3.52 others. By 1945, one farm worker could provide for himself and

---

[1] Rajah Manikam and Irma Highbaugh, *The Christian Family in Changing East Asia.* (Report of the East Asia Christian Family Life Seminar—Conference, Manila, November 2–16, 1954). (Manila: The Philippine Federation of Christian Churches, 726 Taft Avenue, Manila, P. I., 1955), 199 pp. Available from the International Missionary Council, 156 Fifth Ave., New York City 10, N. Y. $1.00.

[2] Source: *Statistical Abstract of the United States, 1951,* United States Bureau of the Census, 1951, pp. 11, 174.

COURTESY OF THE LIBRARY OF CONGRESS

You may not remember this type of kitchen range, but your grandmother would. Many there are today who well remember when most of the family's food was grown and processed at home, and then cooked on just such a stove.

13.54 other persons.[1] As people moved off farms and into the cities and towns, families underwent significant changes in form and function, size and nature.

Families have moved from production to consumption. As long as families were mainly agricultural, they raised, made, and processed almost all they needed in the home. Go back far enough and you find the pioneer making an annual journey to the settlement to pick up his salt and coffee, all he needed to supplement what he and his family could provide for themselves. Some of us today can remember when most of the family's foods were grown, prepared, cooked, and preserved at home; when the making of clothing and furnishings were home industries; when educa-

---

[1] See Ruth Cavan, *The American Family*, (New York: Thomas Y. Crowell Company, 1953), pp. 38–40; and M. R. Cooper, G. T. Barton, and A. P. Brodell, *Progress of Farm Mechanization*, October, 1947, United States Department of Agriculture, Miscellaneous Publication No. 630, p. 5.

tional, religious, recreational, and protective services centered in the home.

Today, the main burden of producing things has moved out of the home and into industry. The family is mainly a consuming unit, buying, selecting, and arranging goods made in the factory for use in the home. What used to be "homemade"—bread and butter, bacon, canned goods and clothing, now are mass produced in modern bakeries, dairies, packing houses, food-processing plants, and factories that flood our homes with goods. Not only the essentials of life, but all the pleasant extras in terms of electrical mixers and grinders, stoves and roasters, refrigerators and deepfreezes, washers, driers, and ironers, air conditioners and heaters, radios, record players, and television sets pour out of our factories in tempting challenge to the family pocketbook.

Families have shifted from an economy of scarcity to an economy of abundance. There was a time when goods were so scarce that everything of any possible future use was saved in the home. Some of us remember the string pail, the grease bucket, the paper drawer, and all the rest of the devices by which a family used over and over again the little things that were hard to come by. Today we face the opposite situation in which so much floods our homes that yesterday's philosophy of "make it do" has been replaced with today's "get the new model." Our present-day economy depends upon a steady flow of goods, and an insatiable public. Advertising is designed to make our families discontent with what they have. The trend is to throw out what you have and buy the newer, better, more efficient item. The shift has been from the slow painstaking fashioning of an article that lasted a family for years, to planned obsolescence that calls for selectivity rather than creativity on the part of the family.

Families have become smaller. A large family does not make sense today as it did in Grandfather's day. Then a man was blessed with many sons, and he welcomed every new pair of hands on the place where so much had to be done. Today's city family has neither room nor jobs for the aging and dependent relatives who used to be welcome in the home. Children, once an economic asset, today are a financial liability: ten to twenty thousand dollars are needed to raise a child to maturity[1] in a city home, where space is limited and children's jobs are scarce to nonexistent. Family limitation has become the norm in the American fam-

[1] Louis Dublin and A. J. Lotka, *The Money Value of a Man* (New York: The Ronald Press, Revised Edition, 1946), p. 55. (Details in Table 12, p. 162)

ily. Children today tend to be desired for themselves alone rather than for the work they can do to help support the family as was once the case.

Families work less and live better. It takes fewer people working shorter hours to support a family in a higher standard of living today than yesterday. The working week has dropped in the first half of the twentieth century from approximately 60 to 40 hours a week, according to the Bureau of Labor Statistics. During the same period the real income per family member has more than doubled, from $520 in 1901 to $1,085 in 1948, calculated in 1948 purchasing power dollars. This greater affluence means more luxuries,[1] better diet, increased medical services, longer life, more education and culture, greatly widened horizons through travel, news coverage, magazines, books, radio, television, and expansion of communication generally, now than a few decades ago.

Families are established in larger numbers and at younger ages now. People can afford to get married in larger numbers and at younger ages now than used to be the case. The young wife as well as her husband can find work and jointly support the marriage at least in its first months or years. Neither military service nor continued education deters young people from marrying at earlier ages than ever before. A considerably higher percentage of our population marries today than formerly. In 1890, 63.1 per cent (as compared to 78.6 per cent of the population in 1949) ever married. One of the results of these trends has been for more immature, irresponsible, and inadequate persons getting married now than formerly. For, no longer is it necessary for the man to prove himself capable of supporting a wife before he asks her hand in marriage. He marries at a much younger age (22 rather than 26, comparing 1900 with 1950 median ages for men) while he is still an untried product. The girl today scarcely out of her teens (median age at first marriage for girls in 1950 was barely 20), has had little chance to prove herself as a responsible person before she faces the confusing and complex roles of today's married woman.

Family roles are more complex and flexible today. Men, women, and children worked hard on the old family farm in bygone years. But they knew what was expected of them, and had been prepared rather specifically for the roles they played. A woman had to be a good cook

---

[1] See detailed comparative chart in Evelyn Duvall and Reuben Hill, *When You Marry*, New Revised Edition (Boston: D. C. Heath and Company, 1953), pp. 416 and 417.

since her family would depend upon her food throughout its lifetime. A man had to be a good steady provider, before it was possible for his wife to get a job to supplement his earnings. Both men and women had learned their roles in their own homes before they married. Children had their place in the scheme of things and knew what was expected of them from the beginning. The whole neighborhood agreed on what was man's work, and what was woman's work, and what was to be expected of a child. The family lived according to relatively rigid rules traditionally established and maintained by social and moral pressures of the entire society.

Today both men and women expect a wide variety of roles in each other. These expectations differ from couple to couple and from family to family. In one home, a woman is expected to work outside, in another her place is seen to be in the home. In one family, a man is expected to be a companion to his wife and children, in another his roles are more traditionally defined. In general, the trend is for both husbands and wives to expect more of each other in the intangible roles of understanding companion, stimulating colleague, and loving, sympathetic parent.

The challenge of democratic interaction between family members—husband and wife, parent and child, close and extended family members —imposes new tasks and responsibilities upon all members of the family. Now that the authority of the father-head has been taken over by discussion within the family, decisions are not as quick, nor plans as easily made. Now, when the social pressures of church and neighborhood have declined, every member of every family faces innumerable choices and possibilities. Seeing home as a place good for people to grow up in is life at a much deeper level than seeing it as a "roof over our heads." Its potentialities are tremendous, but its problems, especially for transition generations, are felt in the very warp and woof of family living. It is exciting today to see the family, freed at last from the burden of producing things, facing as its primary function the development of sturdy, wholesome personalities. But such a shift does not come all at once. Each step in the new direction is taken slowly, some with pain, others only after real effort as every member of the family learns its new roles and practices the new innovations that are appropriate in today's family.

It is much harder to learn how to raise a child according to the best child development procedures today than it used to be when anyone with any "common sense" knew what was good for a child. Being a warmly sympathetic and companionable spouse is more difficult than baking a light biscuit or mending the harness. Such arts and skills of human interaction as are expected of family members today open new social and emotional frontiers where few have been adequately prepared by previous experience. Today's family becomes a miniature laboratory at work on the most challenging world-wide problem: how to live together in creative peace, build harmony out of difference, and make democracy work. This is a big order in which many little families fail.

Family instability has increased. Families no longer stay together as they once did. More of them are broken by separation, desertion, and divorce than formerly. There has been a marked rise in the divorce rate decade by decade in the twentieth century.[1] Summary figures are given in Table 3.

TABLE 3. *Divorce Rates per 100 Marriages the Same Year,*
in the United States [2]

Year	Divorces per 100 Marriages
1900	7.9
1910	8.8
1920	13.4
1930	17.4
1940	16.5
1950	23.1

Two facets of the trend in the rise of divorces are notable. One is that the divorce rate has risen most rapidly in the war years. The two most rapid increases in the number of divorces came in the decades between 1910 and 1920 (World War I) and between 1940 and 1950 (World War II). The second is that divorces decline during economic slumps. The only decade in which the divorce rate was lower than that of the previous period is in the 1930's, a period of depression. These tendencies suggest that divorce rates and economic prosperity are closely related. When times are good, a husband and wife who do not get along can divorce and support themselves separately. When jobs are scarce and

---

[1] There was some decline in the divorce rate between 1950 and 1955, which may or may not continue.

[2] *Vital Statistics, Special Reports, Summary of Marriage and Divorce Statistics, United States,* 1949, Vol. 36, No. 2, Federal Security Agency, June 5, 1951, 14, 24, 25; and *News Release,* Federal Security Agency, April 23, 1951, p. 2.

there is little money, the married pair is forced to stay together, for they cannot afford to do otherwise.

Thus far we have seen two reasons for the increased instability of American families. One, family members expect more of each other in terms of personal, intangible qualities that are harder to develop than were the simpler definite roles more easily learned in former times. Two, divorce is more possible as a solution to discord today when neither man nor woman is so completely dependent upon each other for economic support. Insights as to other factors related to divorce are gained in seeing the differential rates among segments of our population outlined below.

The evidence is that divorce is more frequent among some groups than others in America today. In general, the data point in these directions.[1]

Divorces More Frequent	*Divorces Less Frequent*
Among city families	Among farm families
In states with lenient divorce laws	In states with strict divorce laws
In inter-faith marriages	In marriages within same faith
In protestant marriages	In Roman Catholic marriages
Among working class families	Among professional families
Among less educated people	Among better educated persons
Among teenage marriages	Among more mature marriages
In first years of marriage	In later years of marriage
In childless marriages	In marriages with children

The reasons for the increase in family instability are many. The factors involved in understanding who gets divorced and why are complex. There is no question but what the revolutionary social changes of recent decades have blasted relatively stable families out of their old ways that had persisted for many hundreds of years, into new forms and functions with far-reaching repercussions. The eminent historian Arnold Toynbee feels that,

The vital revolution of our time is the emancipation of women, . . . because, in the long run, their emancipation is going to affect everybody's life. Above all, it is going to demand an immense and disturbing psychological adjustment on the part of men, because it implies a revolutionary change in the traditional relations between the sexes.[2]

---

[1] For detailed discussion of differentials in divorce read Ernest Burgess and Harvey Locke, *The Family* (American Book Company, 1953), Part IV, esp. Chap. 20; Evelyn Duvall and Reuben Hill, *When You Marry* (D. C. Heath and Company, 1953), Chap. 14; Clifford Kirkpatrick, *The Family* (Ronald Press, 1955), Chap. 21.

[2] Arnold J. Toynbee, "We Must Pay for Freedom" *Woman's Home Companion*, March 1955, pp. 52, 53.

Freedom of family members to be themselves has increased. Traditionally each family member was subordinate to the group. He had to be. The very survival of the family and its members depended upon family and community solidarity. With the greater resources of our modern way of life has come an increase in individuation. The individual man, woman, and child today expects to be happy. He is encouraged to develop himself and to work out his own problems in his own way. If his marriage is not happy, he can dissolve it. Or, better still, he is encouraged to select early in the courtship the kind of partner whom he can love, who will be good for him to live with, and to prepare with her for their life together. Children now exist not for what they can do to help the family, but rather for themselves as growing persons with rights, privileges, and values recognized as uniquely theirs. Today's child no longer is expected to follow without question in his father's footsteps, but rather more often to find his own interests and talents and choose a vocation that is meaningful to him.

Even the nature of the family is chosen today by its individual members. A couple may or may not have children. They may live much as their parents and grandparents did, or they may establish their own unique family patterns. They may make the old rambling family homestead their home, or more likely, they may choose compact efficiency in a new little suburban dwelling or a city apartment. They may remain rooted close to the place where they grew up, or fare forth through the years over a vast terrain, calling all sorts of places "home" for awhile. They may both work and jointly run the household, or he may be the sole breadwinner, or she may support them both at least for intervals of his military training or further education. They may join forces with other couples in a joint household. They may live at least for a while with his folks, with her parents. They may share their home with relatives. Or, they may live to themselves through the years while institutions care for their dependent relatives.

They may pour everything they have into living it up as they go along, or save all they can spare for the future; or they may budget for satisfactions both in the present and the near and distant future. They may bring up their children in traditional ways, or according to any of the fads or fancies that are proposed in our age, or try to gear into the developmental patterns that are emerging for childrearing. Any of these, and many, many more are possible for families today. They may choose what they will, both as families and as persons, and few there are who will either reward or punish them for their choices.

With so much freedom, is it any wonder that we are confused and bewildered? When family functions change as rapidly as they have, it takes time and effort to become familiar with the new expectations, and to assume the new roles involved. For members of transition generations, this means a period of uneasiness and instability, of innovation and exploration of new possibilities, until we can become more completely at home in these newly designed families of ours.

SUMMARY

Families in America have changed more rapidly and far more drastically in recent decades than ever before has been true of families anywhere. Family functions today are seen in terms of the personality development of their members. In underdeveloped countries today, as in our own not too distant past, we see the ways of life that are traditional for families everywhere down through history until the coming of modern industrialization. Some of the more significant of the changes American families have undergone in this century are: families have moved off farms and into cities, towns, and suburbs; they have shifted from an economy of scarcity to an economy of abundance; families have become smaller both in the number of children per couple and in the number of relatives who make their home with the family; families today work less and live better; they are established in larger numbers and at younger ages now; family roles are more complex and flexible today; family instability has increased along with freedom of family members to be themselves. These changes are seen as reflecting the family's need to adapt to industrialized, urbanized living. The full human potentials inherent in the emergent democratic ways of living together are still to be realized. These are all challenges for us as members of transitional generations.

SUGGESTED ACTIVITIES

1) Review one or more of the following sources on social change with special emphasis on how it effects family life:

> Frederick Lewis Allen, *The Big Change* (New York: Harper & Brothers, 1952).

> Frederick Lewis Allen, *Only Yesterday* (New York: Harper & Brothers, 1931).

Frederick Lewis Allen, "The Big Change: The Coming—and Disciplining—of Industrialism, 1850–1950," *Harper's Magazine*, October 1950, pp. 145–160.

Ruth Cavan, *The American Family* (New York: Thomas Y. Crowell Company, 1953), Part One, "The Present Status of the American Family."

Evelyn Duvall and Reuben Hill, *When You Marry* (Boston: D. C. Heath and Company, 1953), Chapter 20, "Marriage Isn't What It Used to Be."

Clifford Kirkpatrick, *The Family as Process and Institution* (New York: The Ronald Press, 1955), Part II, "Social Changes and the Family."

William Fielding Ogburn and Meyer F. Nimkoff, *Technology and the Changing Family* (Boston: Houghton Mifflin Company, 1955).

2) Develop Toynbee's thesis (*Woman's Home Companion*, March 1955, "We Must Pay for Freedom") in an essay on "What Price Freedom in the Family," touching on strains and stresses in the relationships between men and women, between the generations, and between the family and the community, that come with emancipation.

3) Select situations from Clarence Day's *Life with Father* or any other available source on family life as it was at the turn of the century. Role-play parallel and current family situations known to you, in "Then and Now" skits.

4) Document Peter F. Drucker's, "America's Next Twenty Years," *Harper's Magazine*, March 1955, pp. 27–32, as far as you have available data, and discuss the ways in which the trends he predicted have, have not, and may, or may not continue, and why.

5) View the kinescope on "Divorce" (No. 8 in the 1956 Marriage Series, produced by and available from The University of Michigan Television Center, Ann Arbor, Michigan), in which Professor William Goode is guest consultant. Discuss.

6) Write a paper on "The Family I Hope to Found" outlining your hopes, plans, and aspirations for your own home and family someday. Footnote it throughout with the items that would have been impossible to achieve in your father's or grandfather's time, and why.

READINGS

Allen, Frederick Lewis, *Only Yesterday* (New York: Harper & Brothers, 1931).

———, *Since Yesterday* (New York: Harper & Brothers, 1939).

———, *The Big Change* (New York: Harper & Brothers, 1952).

———, "The Big Change: The Coming—and Disciplining—of Industrialism," *Harper's Magazine*, October 1950, pp. 145–160.

Bossard, James H. S., and Boll, Eleanor S., *Ritual in Family Living* (Philadelphia: University of Pennsylvania Press, 1950), Chapters 5, 6, 7.

Burgess, Ernest W., and Locke, Harvey J., *The Family from Institution to Companionship* (New York: American Book Company, 1953), Chapter 16.

Calhoun, Arthur W., *A Social History of the American Family from Colonial Times to the Present* (Cleveland: Arthur H. Clark Company, 1917–1919).

Compton, Arthur, "Effect of the New Scientific Age of Family Life," *Journal of Home Economics*, September 1947, pp. 387–390.

Duvall, Evelyn Millis, and Hill, Reuben, *When You Marry* (Boston: D. C. Heath and Company, Revised Edition, 1953), Chapter 20.

Folsom, Joseph, *The Family and Democratic Society* (New York: Wiley, 1943), Chaps. 3 & 7.

Frank, Lawrence K., "Yes, Families Are Changing," *The Survey*, December 1949.

Furbay, John Harvey, "The One World Is Here," *National Parent-Teacher*, October 1950.

Linton, Ralph, *The Study of Man* (New York: D. Appleton-Century Company, 1936).

Kirkpatrick, Clifford, *The Family as Process and Institution* (New York: The Ronald Press Company, 1955), Part II, "Social Changes and the Family."

Kyrk, Hazel, "Economic Responsibilities of Families—Increasing or Diminishing?" *Journal of Home Economics*, Vol. 44, No. 8, October 1952, pp. 616–619.

Manikam, Rajah B., and Highbaugh, Irma, Co-editors, *The Christian Family in Changing East Asia.* (Report of the East Asia Christian Family Life Seminar–Conference, Manila, November 1954. [Manila: Philippine Federation of Christian Churches, 1955, 199 pp.]) Available through the International Missionary Council, 156 Fifth Avenue, New York City 10.

Mead, Margaret, "What Is Happening to the American Family?" *Journal of Social Casework*, Vol. 28, No. 9, November 1947, p. 327.

Ogburn, William Fielding, and Nimkoff, Meyer, *Technology and the Changing Family* (New York: Houghton Mifflin Company, 1955), 329 pp.

Toynbee, Arnold, "We Must Pay for Freedom," *Woman's Home Companion*, March 1955.

The hickory stick is obsolete
Discipline has long been on the
*   skids*
Everything in the modern home
Is controlled by a switch—but the
*   kids!*
AUTHOR UNKNOWN

He who stops being better
*   stops being good.*
OLIVER CROMWELL

CHAPTER THREE

Changing patterns in childrearing

As ways of life change, our ideas about what we expect of one another in our families shift. In few areas is this more dramatic than in the ways in which we see our children and perceive our roles in relation to them. Throughout history when families were busy with the production of a multitude of goods for family consumption, children were trained as assistant-apprentices from the earliest possible moment. Even a little child could help out on the farm by bringing in firewood and water, gathering eggs, weeding, running errands, and innumerable other chores that made him a useful member of his family. By the time a boy had reached adolescence, he was able to perform most of the tasks around the farm, and often took pride in being able to do "a man's work." His sister worked along side by side with her mother, where she learned to cook and bake and sew and mind the baby as well as any grown woman by the time she reached her teens.

Boys and girls traditionally learned how to be men and women through active apprenticeship throughout their childhood. This system of education-by-doing was effective in training each succeeding generation as long as life remained substantially constant and stable. In present-day rapid social change, children now are no longer prepared in childhood for their roles as adults.

RECENT CHANGES IN WAYS OF THINKING ABOUT CHILDREN

Today's children cannot be brought up in their father's and mother's image because they are not going to live in their parents' world. None can foretell what the future will require of our children. All we know is that it surely will be different than the present, and that it will require a high level of creativity in tomorrow's citizens to effect the innovations that will be needed. Innovation is the real frontier of a rapidly developing culture like ours. Technological advances resulting in new products and processes must be matched by social progress and improved human relationships.[1] So our need today is for the kind of healthy flexible personality that has what it takes to survive and flourish in the modern world.

Such basic changes in point of view are evident in trends in childrearing concepts and practices in recent decades. In the old-fashioned farm family children were expected to obey and honor their parents, hold their tongues, and respect their elders. The youngster who did not conform was promptly punished in ways that would impress him. Through the years, our notions about childrearing and discipline have changed rapidly toward more flexible developmental methods and conceptions. These new approaches are based upon adult desire to know and to meet each child's needs, and to help children develop into the kinds of persons they have the potentials for becoming.

This drastic shift in point of view, in values, and in practice has not come all at once to parents everywhere. There are significant differences in methods of discipline accepted as adequate and put into use among families in a given community or neighborhood, or even within the same family. In general, the changes in families tend to reflect the new climate of opinion that has swept over the entire culture through the later part of the nineteenth and the first half of the twentieth centuries. Certain individuals and movements have played prominent roles in opening windows and letting the fresh winds of freedom and developmentalism into our schools, our colleges, and our families. The trends from the traditional to the newer approaches in discipline are seen in the following summary outline that traces trends in discipline decade by decade from the later part of the nineteenth century to the middle of the twentieth century.

[1] Peter F. Drucker, "America's Next Twenty Years," *Harper's Magazine,* March 1955, pp. 27–32.

HOW DISCIPLINE CHANGED FROM THE 1880's TO THE 1950's [1]

1880's—Discipline was based upon authority with instant, unquestioning obedience expected.

Training was directed toward "uprooting the evil in human nature" at a time when widespread belief was that children are "conceived in sin and born in iniquity," and the clear duty of parents was to "whale the devil out of them."

Society for the Prevention of Cruelty to Children was organized "to resolutely and persistently attack cruel ways of treating children." Articles on prevention of cruelty to children mention: "whippings until bruised and sore," "shutting in dark closets until ill with fright," and "depriving of food until emaciated and feeble."

Seeds of the future planted by Frances Parker, G. Stanley Hall, William James, and Felix Adler who during this decade started respectively the Cook County Normal School, studies in child development, psychology based on experience at Harvard, and the Society for the Study of Child Nature in New York.

1890's—Authority still firmly established as basic point of view. For example, Larkin Donton, of the Boston Normal School expected "instantaneous obedience, with no sulkers, no laggards, no guerrillas, no independents, and the movement of all uniformly, quietly and instantly."

John Dewey founded Laboratory School, and Frances Parker founded an independent institute which was to become the School of Education, both at the University of Chicago.

The National Congress of Parents and Teachers had its beginning in the founding of the National Congress of Mothers in Washington in 1897.

1900's—Discipline is a major issue. Sixteen out of eighteen schools investigated reported corporal punishment in use, one in primary grades only, another "seldom" and others "good as a last resort," "cannot be dispensed with but might be reduced." The reporter of the study prophesied, "the birch and rattan will surely disappear into the limbo of a final oblivion."

Guidance begins to replace "training" in the literature. G. Stanley Hall published *Adolescence* (1904), the first work on the older child. William James in his *Talks to Teachers* set the theme for the decade in stressing the importance of habits. A child's independence being considered as implicit obedience is under question.

1910's—William Bagley in *School Discipline* (1915) admonished never to punish in anger, to use switch on legs or ruler on palm of hands but

[1] Adapted from Grace Langdon and Irving Stout, *The Discipline of Well-Adjusted Children* (New York: John Day Company, 1952), Chap. 1; and "Parents Welcome New Edition of Infant Care," *The Child*, Children's Bureau, Washington, D. C., January 1952, pp. 66, 67, 76.

never box over the ears, and asserted, "the discipline of the unpleasant and disagreeable can be much more certainly relied upon
to secure desired results than the pleasant and agreeable."

First Edition of *Infant Care* published by the Children's Bureau, established in 1912, recommended to stop thumb-sucking, pinning
sleeve of baby's jacket down over "fingers of offending hand for
several days and nights."

Freud, Montessori, John Dewey, and William H. Kilpatrick mentioned
frequently in popular literature. The Progressive Education Association founded in 1918–1919 with emphasis on "freedom for children
to develop."

1920's—Emphasis on objectivity and in "the scientific" rather than sentimental
approach to children under the stimulus of John B. Watson who
recommended kissing child on the forehead if at all, shaking hands
with the child in the morning, never hug, kiss or let child sit on
your lap. His *Behaviorism,* and *Psychological Care of Infant and
Young Child* widely discussed and followed. The conditioned response, stimulus-response bonds, and the laws of learning all current
in this decade.

Child Development Institutes established in several universities and
the National Council on Parent Education founded, all with Laura
Spelman Rockefeller Memorial grants.

Teachers College, Columbia University announced a new course,
"Training for Leadership in Education of Parents" in cooperation
with the Child Study Association. *Parents Magazine* established
(1925). "The child" and "child-centered" appear freely in the literature.

1930's—Objectivity at its zenith with great emphasis on the importance of
routine, habit formation—*i.e.* "adhere without deviation to regular
habits for sleeping, eating, and toileting beginning in early infancy."
The parent is advised to be cool, detached and unperturbed. High
interest in specifics such as sex education, allowances and toilet
training.

National Council on Family Relations established (1938) as national
clearing house of persons with professional interests in family living.
Research in family life, child and adolescent development increases
markedly. Corporal discipline rare in schools that now are much
more relaxed. Discussion of place of spanking as discipline continues
among parents.

1940's—Emphasis of the child in his family setting comes in with family-
centered approach seen in the first National Conference on Family
Life held at the White House in May 1948. Gesell and colleagues
at Yale, Sheviakov, Redl, Baruch, Hymes, and Spock are articulate
advocates of acceptance of the child and his feelings without shame,
guilt or feelings of failure. Emphasis on developmental levels and
the readiness of the child for each new experience is furthered by

steady increase in child study and parent education groups. Spock's *The Common Sense Book of Baby and Child Care* becomes young mother's "bible" as permissive, "enjoy your youngster" attitude toward children becomes widely accepted.

1950's—Personality development is key concept of the Midcentury Whitehouse Conference on Children and Youth that brought together some 6,000 leaders who reviewed the current contributions of the various disciplines related to child development, care, education, and guidance. Wide discussion of the role of the services of the home, school, church, leisure-time agencies as well as vocational guidance, health, social services and law enforcement services, in healthy personality development.

The developmental task as a concept formulated over two decades by such workers as Frank, Prescott, Erikson, Havighurst, and others, introduces phrases frequently appearing through this decade in the literature and discussion of children: "the teachable moment," "readiness," "developmental level," etc.

Sibylle Escalona [1] has summarized changes in our ways of thinking about children in recent years:

Ten years ago and less, authoritative public opinion subscribed to sentiments and rules which may be characterized as follows: Bodily and mental health is based upon an orderly, strictly scheduled existence from early childhood onwards. Prescribed formulae are superior to breast feeding, chiefly because the ingredients are known and nutrition becomes therefore, a controlled process. When babies or children cry without recognized legitimate cause it is best to let them cry it out. It is the responsibility of adults to teach children what is 'right' and what is 'wrong' in regard to meal times, sleeping hours, play interests and most other activities.[2]

"It is now thought that it is up to us as adults to meet the needs of the younger child, rather than to expect early adaptation from him. To wit, self-demand schedules and all that goes with them. Among the needs of the young child we recognize the need for affection and for an intimate relationship with the mother as of very great importance, tending to evaluate it as more crucial than the need for good physical care. We prize self-expression, sincerity of feeling and spontaneous interest above good manners, self restraint or intellectual accomplishment."[3]

In such a drastic shift from traditional ideas and practices that have characterized people in centuries past to conceptions and ways new to our generation in very recent times, several hypotheses are proposed.

[1] Sibylle Escalona, "A Commentary upon Some Recent Changes in Child-Rearing Practices," *Child Development*, Vol. 20, No. 3, September 1949, pp. 157–162.

[2] *Ibid.*, p. 158.

[3] *Ibid.*, p. 160.

1) Changes do not come suddenly to all people at equal rates, but are worked out more rapidly and completely in some groups than in others.
2) Changes in conceptions of children occur concurrently with changes in conceptions of mothers, of fathers and in what is expected of every member of the family.
3) In shifting from traditional to developmental values, the older views hold over in part while the newer ones are being established.
4) Problems and consequences of shifting from the traditional to developmental approaches within families tend to be acute for members of transition generations.

The first formulation of the traditional-developmental dichotomy of conceptions of family member roles came out of the author's original study of differential conceptions of parenthood.[1] The data were the verbatim responses of 433 mothers to the questions, "What are five things a good mother does?" (2,010 responses), and "What are five things a good child does?" (1,847 responses). Keeping the original wording used by the subjects, the responses were grouped into twelve categories for conceptions of "a good mother," and thirteen categories for "a good child." Early in the formulation of the categories a distinction became evident, in the way they tended to cluster around one or the other of two orientations. One type of category was recognized as being predominately traditional in conceptual content: what a good mother traditionally expected of herself, usually in terms of what she was supposed to do *to* and *for* her family and her children, were recognized as traditional conceptions of motherhood. What used to be expected of a child, usually in terms of behaving in ways that please adults were seen as traditional conceptions of the good child. Traditional conceptions of both the good mother and the good child tended to be somewhat static, rigid and specific behavioral expectancies.

A nontraditional, emergent type of conception on the other hand, was recognized as dynamic, flexible, and growth-promoting. Its emphasis was on the development of the person rather than on any specific form or type of behavior.

The outstanding characteristic of the non-traditional or emergent type of category is that it emphasizes the development of the person, both of the child and of the parent. This developmental emphasis is so consistently strong in the non-traditional type of response that at the cost of some semantic purity, a dichotomy of *traditional* and *developmental* (the nontraditional emergent emphasis) was recognized in the data . . . The distinction between

[1] Evelyn Millis Duvall, "Conceptions of Parenthood," *The American Journal of Sociology*, Vol. LII, No. 3, November 1946, pp. 193–203.

the two types of response is one of emphasis, an important factor in concept study.[1]

The responses in the mother's own words were grouped under "traditional" when they reflected older, previously accepted ideologies; and as "developmental" when the roles defined for either mother or child were dynamic, flexible, and primarily in terms of growth and development, rather than as specific behavioral conformities. Illustrative categories for traditional and developmental conceptions of a good child, and of a good mother, with typical responses in the original wording follow.

TRADITIONAL—DEVELOPMENTAL CONCEPTIONS [2]

A Good Child— Traditional Conception

1) "Keeps clean and neat." (Is orderly, is clean, keeps self neat.)

2) "Obeys and respects adults." (Minds parents, no back talk, respects adults.)

3) "Pleases adults." (Has good character traits, is honest, truthful, polite, kind, fair, courteous at all times.)

4) "Respects property." (Takes care of his things, is not destructive, hangs up his clothes.)

5) "Is religious." (Goes to Sunday School, loves God, prays, follows Jesus.)

6) "Works well." (Studies, goes to school, is reliable, takes responsibility, is dependable in his work.)

7) "Fits into the family program." (Has an interest in his home, does his share, runs errands willingly, helps out at home.)

A Good Child— Developmental Conception

1) "Is healthy and well." (Eats and sleeps well, grows a good body, has good habits.)

2) "Shares and cooperates with others." (Gets along with people, likes others, is developing socially, tries to help, plays with other children.)

3) "Is happy and contented." (Keeps in good humor, is a cheerful child, is happy, is emotionally well adjusted.)

4) "Loves and confides in parents." (Responds with affection, loves his parents, has confidence in his parents, trusts and confides in them.)

5) "Is eager to learn." (Shows initiative, asks questions, accepts help, expresses himself, likes to learn.)

6) "Grows as a person." (Progresses in his ability to handle himself and different situations, enjoys growing up.)

[1] Evelyn Millis Duvall, "Differential Concepts of Parenthood," Ph.D. Thesis, (Chicago: University of Chicago, 1946), p. 40.
[2] Evelyn Millis Duvall, op. cit. pp. 195, 196.

A Good Mother— Traditional Conception	A Good Mother— Developmental Conception
1) "Keeps house." (Washes, cooks, cleans, mends, sews, manages the household.)	1) "Trains for self-reliance and citizenship." (Trains for self-help, encourages independence, teaches how to be a good citizen, how to adjust to life, teaches concentration.)
2) "Takes care of child physically." (Keeps child healthy, guards child's safety, feeds, clothes, bathes, sees that child rests.)	2) "Sees to emotional well-being." (Keeps child happy and contented, makes a happy home, makes child welcome, helps child feel secure, helps child overcome fears.)
3) "Trains child to regularity." (Establishes regular habits, provides schedule, sees to regular hours for important functions.)	3) "Helps child develop socially." (Provides toys, companions, plays with child, supervises child's play.)
4) "Disciplines." (Corrects child, demands obedience, rewards good behavior, is firm, is consistent, keeps promises.)	4) "Provides for child's mental growth." (Gives educational opportunities, provides stimulation to read, reads to child, tells stories, guides reading, sends child to school.)
5) "Makes the child good." (Teaches obedience, instructs in morals, builds character, prays for, sees to religious instruction.)	5) "Guides with understanding." (Sees child's point of view, gears life to child's level, answers questions freely and frankly, gives child freedom to grow, interprets, offers positive suggestions.)
	6) "Relates self lovingly to child." (Shows love and affection, enjoys child, spends time with child, shares with child, is interested in what child does and tells, listens.)
	7) "Is a calm, cheerful, growing person one's self." (Has more outside interests, is calm and gentle, has a sense of humor, laughs, smiles, gets enough recreation.)

"Taking care of the child physically" (traditional conception) is mentioned consistently more often than other responses to the question "What are five things a good mother does?" by all the mothers in this study re-

These two little girls are obviously enjoying their joint task of washing dishes. They appear to be behaving according to developmental conceptions which picture a good child as one who shares and cooperates with others, tries to help, is eager to learn, and enjoys growing up.

gardless of their social class, experience (as gauged by the age of the eldest child), racial background, or religious affiliation.

The good child is defined as one who obeys and respects his parents and pleases adults, more frequently than in other role conceptions by all the mothers who participated in this study. This is a traditional conception of the child as defined here.

Differences in the percentage of traditional and developmental responses are significant in the following ways:

1) Traditional conceptions are significantly more frequent among mothers of the lower socio-economic class levels than among mothers of higher social class levels (equivalent to upper middle-class). This is a simple trend with the highest percentages of traditional responses at the lowest levels, and the greatest number of developmental responses at the upper levels. These class level differences remain for each age group, religious group, and racial stock studied and for conceptions of both the good mother and the good child.

2) Traditional conceptions of the good mother and the good child are consistently more frequent among Negro than among white mothers at every level studied.

3) Traditional conceptions are more frequent among mothers of older children (over five) than among mothers of younger children.

4) Developmental conceptions of both the good mother and the good child are significantly more frequent among mothers of higher social class levels, among white mothers, and among mothers of young children than among mothers of lower social classes, Negro mothers, and mothers of older children.

These findings are interpreted as follows:

In its transition from the traditional institution type of family to the person-centered unit of companionship that it is becoming, conceptions of the role of the parent and the child are shifting. These changes do not appear all at once and with equal force throughout the total society but are evidenced first in little islands of the new that break off from the mass of tradition and become established in subgroups within the culture. These developmental islands are characterized by such concepts as respect for the person (both child and adult), satisfaction in personal interaction, pride in growth and development, and a permissive, growth-promoting type of guidance as opposed to the more traditional attempts to "make" children conform to patterns of being neat and clean, obedient and respectful, polite and socially acceptable.

"Taking care of the child physically" is mentioned by the majority of mothers in the study mentioned as the principal responsibility in childrearing.

Traditional conceptions of parenthood remain in the lower-middle and upper-lower class levels, where recent migration, household drudgery, cramped living, and infrequency of opportunity to meet with other modes of adjustment keep both parents and children in line with traditional conceptions of role. The effort to achieve respectability so evident in the two lower class levels and among the minority racial group tends further to perpetuate conformity.

The tendency for mothers of younger children toward more developmental replies may be interpreted in a number of ways. The evidence points to the possibility that conformity is demanded of families with children old enough to have some life outside the family circle. As children become old enough to go to school and to range further afield in the community, the social pressures toward conformity are felt both by them and by their mothers.

Thus, we hypothesize a seesaw progress even within the more advanced groups. Some inexperienced mothers view their roles along new lines and break with the past in their efforts to make a more adequate adjustment to a changed social situation. As their children grow older and begin to represent them in the larger world, the earlier flexibility is modified by the demands of the more traditional mass.[1]

This study of shifting conceptions of roles of family members has been followed by a number of subsequent studies which generally tend to corroborate the thesis as originally proposed, and to carry the investigation out into new dimensions.

Rachel Ann Elder interviewed 32 Des Moines, Iowa, veteran fathers soon after World War II, in an effort to discover in what ways conceptions of the roles of fathers are changing as those of mothers and of children shift. She is humble in stating, "the limitations of this study, the relative small number of fathers interviewed, and the exploratory nature of its techniques must be recognized." [2] Yet hers marks the first investigation of fathers' conceptions of the roles of family members, and is especially provocative in the formulation of developmental and traditional father types as charted below.

CONSTRUCTED FATHER TYPES [3]

Traditional Father	*Developmental Father*
Father is a strong individual, always right, and child is his ward	Father and child are both individuals (therefore)
Father "knows" what child "should" be so does not seek to understand child as an individual	Father seeks to understand the child and himself
Father is interested only in activities which he determines are his responsibility for the child's "good"	Father concerns himself with all activities and needs of the child
Father places emphasis on giving things to and doing things for the child	Father places emphasis on the growth of child and of himself
Father is interested in child's accepting and attaining goals set by father	Father is interested in child's determining and attaining child's own goals

[1] Evelyn Millis Duvall, "Conceptions of Parenthood," *The American Journal of Sociology*, Vol. LII, No. 3, November 1946, pp. 202–203, copyright 1946, University of Chicago.

[2] Rachel Ann Elder, "Traditional and Developmental Conceptions of Fatherhood," *Marriage and Family Living*, Vol. XI, No. 3, Summer, 1949, p. 106.

[3] Rachel Ann Elder, *Traditional and Developmental Conceptions of Fatherhood*, Iowa State College Master's thesis, Ames, Iowa, 1947, p. 21.

CONSTRUCTED FATHER TYPES (*Continued*)

Traditional Father	*Developmental Father*
Father finds satisfaction in child's owing father a debt which can be repaid by the child's obedience and by bringing honor to the father by achieving goals established by the father	Father finds satisfaction in child's becoming a mature individual and in the child's contribution to father's growth as an individual
Father feels that parenthood is a duty which the church, the family, and/or society expect him to discharge, or which is forced on him as a biological function	Father feels that parenthood is a privilege which he has chosen to assume

Developmentally oriented fathers tend to differ from traditional fathers in the following ways that parallel differences between developmental and traditional mothers.

DEVELOPMENTAL FATHERS AS COMPARED WITH TRADITIONAL FATHERS—

tend to be skilled rather than semiskilled or unskilled workers
tend to enjoy more mutual father-child activities
are more apt to believe in frankness with their children
are more likely to express interested, expectant attitudes toward children's maturation and marriage
are more likely to help with housework regularly
are more likely to feel fatherhood and motherhood equally fun
tend to discipline children less, for fewer offenses, with less extreme severity, and with a greater variety of kinds of discipline
find PTA and parents' literature valuable
more often expect their children to finish high school, and attend college if they want to go
less frequently mention providing for the family their greatest satisfaction
less frequently find children's questions irritating.

HOW CHANGING ROLES LOOK TO CHILDREN

There are some indications that conceptions of parents' roles vary with the age of the child. One reason seems to be that parents' roles change as children grow up. We have already seen that mothers of children over five years of age tend to be more traditional than mothers

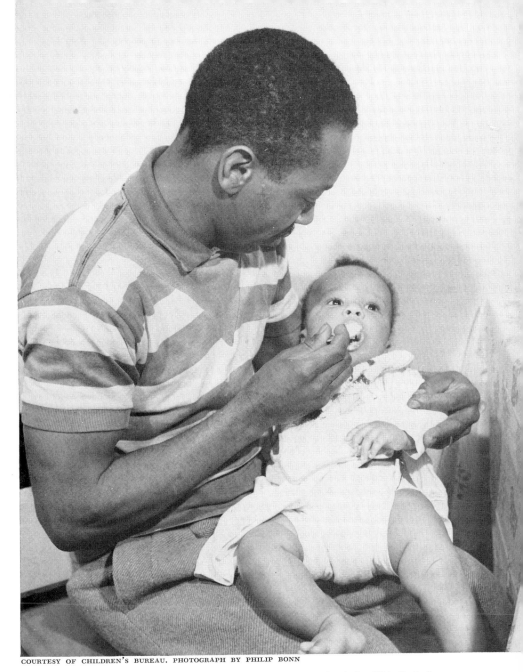

A developmental father concerns himself with all activities and needs of the child. He feels that parenthood is a privilege which he has chosen to assume. And so, we find him active in child-care procedures that a traditional father would not consider as part of his role.

with children under five.[1] Tasch [2] reporting interviews with fathers finds that from birth to four years of age, fathers tend to conceive of their roles in terms of the daily routine care and safety of the child; while fathers of children ranging from five to eight years of age, see their roles as helping the child develop intellectual abilities and interests and helping the child develop social standards, conduct, and control.

Helen Finch [3] studied children of 20 professional men in Tallahassee, Florida, whose wives were full-time homemakers, in an effort to identify the conceptions of parental roles held by children between the ages of three and seven years. Using a variety of projective methods, she found that the children tend to consider the mother as performing more roles related to the care of children and housekeeping, and that children see father helping in the performing of both of these roles.

Concurrently, Dr. Connor and others [4] at the same university analyzed the responses of 26 fathers, mothers, and college age daughters to the three questions: "What are five things a good father does?" "What are five things a good mother does?" and "What are five things a good child does?"

Using the categories of traditional and developmental conceptions devised by Duvall, the Florida State University team found responses in each role conception remarkably similar to those in previous studies.

Generally speaking, the traditional type of good father was defined in terms of providing for the family financially, disciplining and advising the children, and setting a good example . . . the traditional good mother as one who cares for the home and cooks, teaches religious values, and is a good example. The traditional good child is one who respects and obeys parents . . .

The developmental good father fosters the growth and development of the child and other family members, including himself in the home situation. The respondents viewed the developmental mother in much the same way as they saw the developmental father but added the concept of having outside interests such as the PTA. The developmental child responses centered about growing in all areas of personality and social development.[5]

[1] Duvall, op. cit., pp. 202–203.

[2] R. J. Tasch, "The Role of the Father in the Family." Journal of Experimental Education, 20, 1952, pp. 319–362.

[3] Helen M. Finch, "Young Children's Concepts of Parent Roles," Journal of Home Economics, Vol. 47, No. 2, February 1955, pp. 99–103.

[4] Ruth Connor, Theodore B. Johannis, Jr., and James Walters, "Intra-familial Conceptions of the Good Father, Good Mother and Good Child," Journal of Home Economics, Vol. 46, No. 3, March 1954, pp. 187–191.

[5] Connor et al., ibid., p. 190.

When the role conceptions were scored for developmentalism by simple ratio of developmental responses to total responses for each person participating, the adolescents' mean scores were found to be consistently more developmental than either fathers or mothers, for all three family roles, as is shown in the table below. The authors suggest that this quite possibly indicates greater acceptance of the developmental point of view among young people than there is among their parents.

TABLE 4. *Mean Developmental Scores of Conceptions of Good Father, Good Mother, and Good Child by Fathers, Mothers, and Adolescents* [1]

Respondent	Good Father	Good Mother	Good Child
Father	51.2	39.6	20.6
Mother	51.1	31.5	24.5
Adolescent	65.1	62.8	34.6

In the same trend is the finding that "children" with experience as parents are significantly less authoritarian than are their own mothers. Staples and Smith,[2] exploring the hypothesis that attitudes of grandmothers differ from those of mothers with respect to childrearing practices, found the grandmothers significantly more authoritarian and less permissive than the mothers of the same children.

This study of 87 grandmother-mother pairs in the same urban community elaborates and extends earlier findings [3] that the degree of permissiveness bears a positive relationship to the number of years of formal education.

In general then, we find that members of the younger generations, as adolescents, as well as parents themselves, are more permissive and developmental, and less authoritarian and traditional than are their own parents. There are strong indications that developmental attitudes are more frequent among family members with the advantages of education and the privileges of middle social class status than they are among less well educated and less privileged men and women.

[1] Connor *et al., ibid.,* p. 190.
[2] Ruth Staples and June Warden Smith, "Attitudes of Grandmothers and Mothers toward Child-Rearing Practices," *Child Development,* Vol. 25, 1954, pp. 91–97.
[3] Evelyn Millis Duvall, *Differential Concepts of Parenthood,* University of Chicago Ph.D. thesis, Chicago, Illinois, 1946.

THE CONSEQUENCES OF PERMISSIVENESS AND DEVELOPMENTAL CHILDREARING PRACTICES

Holding a developmental ideology about children is no guarantee that a parent will be more flexible with them. The general assumption is that developmental conceptions of parenthood and childhood would be related to less demanding childrearing practices, while traditional conceptions would be related to restrictive practices. Robert Blood's study of 40 middle-class families with preschool children living in similar dwellings in Chapel Hill, North Carolina, confirms the general observation in the finding that "parents with a developmental ideology were more permissive with their children than parents holding traditional conceptions of what constitutes 'a good child.' " [1]

Using the parents' "pick-up policy" with regard to children's clutter allowed in the living room, and the number of types of children's activities permitted indoors, as variables indicating the relative permissiveness of the practices, Dr. Blood [2] found that permissive parents reported consequences that fell into an unmistakable pattern, that contrasted with those of more restrictive parents in the following ways.

THE PRICE OF PERMISSIVENESS

Permissive parents report (as compared with restrictive parents):
1) Parents' lives more disrupted by children's behavior
2) Parents' activities more often disturbed by children's noisiness
3) Parents' privacy more difficult to achieve
4) Parents have greater difficulty controlling children's activities
5) Living room furnishings more often damaged by children
6) Living rooms more frequently cluttered with children's things

With such a high cost of permissive childrearing practices, one might expect that developmentally oriented parents might be envious of their more traditional neighbors. However, this does not seem to be the case. The developmental ideologies themselves serve as a buffer in keeping the parents from being too sorely bruised or too often irritated by children's free behavior. Interpreting the interviews with the eighty parents in his study Dr. Blood reports,

The developmental ideology and its associated attitudes apparently function as a prophylactic for permissive parents against the full force of the disorganiz-

[1] Robert O. Blood, Jr., "A Situational Approach to the Study of Permissiveness in Child-Rearing," *American Sociological Review*, Vol. 18, No. 1, February 1953, p. 86.

[2] Robert O. Blood, Jr., "Consequences of Permissiveness for Parents of Young Children," *Marriage and Family Living*, Vol. XV, No. 3, August 1953, pp. 209–212.

ing consequences of their children's behavior. As a result, such parents may be even less tense and anxiety-ridden than restrictive parents with their picture-book homes.

One attitude which makes it easier for developmental parents to "take it" is the frequently-expressed view that their furniture is "expendable." Rather than something whose polished newness should be preserved for the sake of guests, living room furniture is meant to be used by all the members of the family—young as well as old. From this perspective, wear and tear are a normal part of living. With damage thus incorporated in the expectations for life-with-children, its prospect and its occurrence become less terrifying even for families on a limited budget.

In line with this expectation of damage, developmental parents are especially apt to take steps to render their living rooms "invulnerable." Rather than expecting the child to adapt himself to the fragility of the room, such parents adapt the room to the boisterousness of the child. Decorative vases and figurines are placed out of reach or stored away for a few years. Furniture is slip-covered or reupholstered in plastic. In such ways, developmental parents make their living rooms suitable locales for permissive child-rearing.

As with damage, so clutter, too, is both expected and accepted as an inevitable part of living with children—by developmental parents, that is. For most of the traditional parents, the living room's crucial function is to provide an attractive setting for the entertainment of visitors. Since one never knows when a neighbor may drop in, this requires keeping the room presentable at all times. By contrast, developmental parents place their own family's present welfare above that of the uninvited guest. Just as furniture is expendable, so the living room should be used by the whole family, not excluding the children. And if the children are to be happy there, they will want to bring their blocks, coloring books, and dolls with them.

If an unexpected visitor arrives under such circumstances, he will be welcomed by developmental parents into the home and expected to take a place as pretty much a member of the family. A common definition of the situation by developmental Chapel Hill families went like this: "If the visitor understands children, he won't mind the mess. If he doesn't, that's his tough luck!" In this way, concern about one's own social status is discounted and the emphasis is placed on personality interaction rather than on the symbolic or representational function of the living room. Developmental parents can thus experience with a minimum of embarrassment or guilt a situation which would "precipitate a traditionally-oriented parent into a frenzy of apology and attempted remedy." [1]

Developmental parents apparently can take the immediate consequences of their childrearing practices, because they put their children's growth and developmental progress high in their value systems, because they do not expect to have a model picture-book home while their chil-

[1] *Ibid.*, pp. 210, 211.

dren are small, because they "child-proof" the house by adapting to what reasonably can be expected of little children, because they realize that the sacrifice of some of their adult values (for neatness, quiet, *etc.*) is only for awhile, and that as children grow older there will be less of a discrepancy between the values of the generations.

Fundamentally, developmental parents tend to be the kind of people who, by personality and life history, are inclined to accept the growing body of evidence (from child development research, nursery school experience, and clinical evidence) that supports their inner predispositions to encourage development in their children and themselves.[1]

FACTORS ASSOCIATED WITH THE RISE OF DEVELOPMENTALISM

Social change in recent decades has favored the swing from traditional conceptions of fathers, mothers, and children toward more developmental ideologies on the roles of family members, discipline, childrearing, and family interaction generally.

The rise of industrialization has relieved the family of the burden of the production of goods, and so freed it for more emphasis on the personality development of its members (see Chapter Two).

The increase in the number of women in the labor force in this century has accelerated the emancipation of women as wives and mothers as well as citizens. Such a modern woman has forsaken traditional roles of womanhood and is free to explore new possibilities as a mother as well as to develop as a person in her own right.[2]

The mechanization of the family home attracts the active participation of the husband-father in the everyday routines of family living in ways new in the roles of men. The popular do-it-yourself movement is based on man's initiation of and cooperation in family projects. Today's fathers work along with their wives and children in meal preparation, cleaning up, home refurbishing, entertaining, gardening, and child care—most of which traditionally were woman's work.[3]

The shorter working week; the increase in leisure time; the move to the suburbs; the increase in emphasis in children's toys, play equipment and play space; the decline in the size of the family; the increase in the

[1] Lawrence K. Frank, personal communication, May 31, 1956.

[2] Sidonie M. Gruenberg and Hilda S. Krech, *The Many Lives of Modern Women* (New York: Doubleday and Company, 1952).

[3] Alice C. Thorpe, "How Married Students Manage," *Marriage and Family Living*, Vol. XIII, No. 3, August, 1951, pp. 104–105, 130.

use of the family automobile with the subsequent increase in family trips and vacations—these are but a few of the factors that are in some measure related to the heightened emphases on human growth and development.

The rise of mental hygiene, preventive psychiatry, child development research, child study groups, parent education, nursery schools, family life education, marriage and family counseling are all associated with the general increase in man's interest in understanding himself and others, and in providing an emotional climate suitable for human development.

The kinds of advice given to parents by professional and lay writers clearly reflects the changing climate of opinion in childrearing practices. A survey of all articles appearing in three women's magazines at ten year intervals from 1890 to 1948, shows 100 per cent of the childrearing articles published in 1920 advising the mother to put her child on a tight schedule and to let the child "cry it out" if necessary; but in 1948, all of the articles advocated "mothering" the infant, and letting the child regulate his own schedule.[1] Another worker analyzing 644 articles on childtraining, written by both professional and lay writers between 1890 and 1949, finds a clear trend away from dogmatism, which he interprets as possibly indicative of the increased prestige and acceptance of child-care writers.[2] The wide acceptance of child-care literature and of other forms of parent education, family life education, mental hygiene teachings, dissemination of human development research findings, and preventive psychiatry emphases as active agents in accelerating the trends toward developmentalism needs to be explored. It is possible that these widespread recommendations become incorporated in some measure into the cultural expectancies that form one origin of the developmental tasks (Chapter Five). An educated guess is that they not only reflect, but actively effect the acceleration and the direction of changing patterns in childrearing.

The awakening of the masses of the world, so dramatically a part of our times, has its counterparts in the family with the recognition that even "little people" have certain rights that must be recognized. As more and more of the population enjoys the privilege of education, and be-

---

[1] Celia B. Stendler, "Sixty Years of Child Training Practices," *Journal of Pediatrics,* Vol. 36, 1950, page 126.

[2] Clark E. Vincent, "Trends in Infant Care Ideas," *Child Development,* Vol. 22, No. 3, September 1941, p. 207.

comes familiar with the great ideas of freedom, democracy, brotherhood, and the importance of love in all human relationships, the essence of the developmental point of view will become more and more acceptable. It is no accident that we find developmental conceptions appearing first in the better educated parts of the population, while traditional ideologies tend to cluster among the less privileged. Increases in the standard of living, in general education, as well as specific family life education may be expected to narrow the gap between the haves and have-nots as well as to make the developmental "traditional" in the times to come.

. . . Within another generation the new ways of bringing up children may themselves become traditional . . . If this happens, young parents' confidence should increase, since they will not feel so alone and so much in disagreement with the older generation.[1]

SUMMARY

The big difference between the developmental and the traditional approaches to children is in the focus of attention. The traditional emphasis was on peace and quiet, neatness and orderliness, and "Hush now, here comes father," insistence on the parents' comfort and values. The developmental orientation is that of giving first place to the developing personalities in the situation, and letting the things, the symbols, the outward appearances slide into a comfortable collection of resources to be used as the various persons in the family see fit. The traditional approach can be relatively static and rigid, for things stay put, especially if you insist upon it. The developmental orientation is dynamic, for people are everchanging and growing. Parents who put developing persons first in their concerns tend to be flexibly capable of change, ready to adapt and readapt as both their children and they themselves develop through the months and years. This point of view is of the twentieth century. It is the thesis of this book and will be elaborated stage by stage through the family life cycle.

SUGGESTED ACTIVITIES

1) Review the novel, *Craig's Wife*, with particular reference to the ways in which a home may serve to alienate rather than to satisfy the members of a family. List the situations as they occur throughout the book in which things take precedence over persons.

[1] Helen Witmer and Ruth Kotinsky, *Personality in the Making* (New York: Harper & Brothers, 1952), p. 102.

2) Outline and analyze Louis Bromfield's novel, *A Good Woman* (New York: Grosset and Dunlap, 1922), in terms of the principal character's concept of herself as a woman, and how she played out her role as "a good woman." What effect did she have on her son and family? Why?

3) Conduct a study of the ideologies of the members of your class and their parents, by providing each of them with cards on which to write, a) five things a good mother does, b) five things a good father does, and c) five things a good child does. Tabulate the statements as developmental or traditional according to the criteria in this chapter. Compare the developmental and traditional scores of males and females in the class, and of student and parent generations. Report your findings to the class with your interpretations of the data.

4) Plan a symposium of members of at least three generations—a student, a parent, a grandparent—on childrearing practices as they remember them when they were young. Try to match the participants for social class and educational backgrounds as closely as possible.

5) Write a letter to yourself as a parent (actual or potential), reminding yourself of the policies and practices that you feel are best in childrearing. Summarize briefly at the close the ways in which your recommendations for the rearing of your children differ from the ways in which you yourself were reared. In what ways are they similar?

6) Outline procedures for "child-proofing" the home of a young couple who want to be flexible with their young children and who are comfortable in the developmental point of view both for themselves and for their children. Itemize in detail the changes that should be made in every room of the home in order to meet the child's needs and still maintain comfort and pleasure for the parents.

7) Review Dr. Brim's paper (See *Readings*, below), and write a reaction paper of your own on the major points that are covered in this study.

READINGS

Blood, Robert O., Jr., "A Situational Approach to the Study of Permissiveness in Child-Rearing," *American Sociological Review,* Vol. 18, No. 1, February 1953, pp. 84–87.

———, "Consequences of Permissiveness for Parents of Young Children," *Marriage and Family Living,* Vol. XV, No. 3, August 1953, pp. 209–212.

———, "Developmental and Traditional Child Rearing Philosophies and Their Family Situational Consequences," Ph.D. Thesis, University of North Carolint, Chapel Hill, N. C., 1952.

Bossard, James H. S., *The Sociology of Child Development* (New York: Harper & Brothers, 1948), revised 1954, Part VII, "The Changing Status of Childhood."

Brim, Orville G., Jr., "The Parent-Child Relation as a Social System: Part I. Parent and Child Roles," mimeographed paper, July 1956. (Russell Sage Foundation and the Child Study Association of America.)

Children's Bureau, "Parents Welcome New Edition of Infant Care," *The Child*, Children's Bureau, Washington, D.C., January 1952, pp. 66, 67, 76.

Child Study Association of America, "Living and Growing with Our Children: Impact on Parents of Children's Growth Phases," *Child Study*, Vol. XXXII, No. 3, Summer 1955.

Connor, Ruth; Johannis, Theodore B., Jr.; and Walters, James, "Intra-familial Conceptions of the Good Father, Good Mother and Good Child," *Journal of Home Economics*, Vol. 46, No. 3, March 1954, pp. 187–191.

Duvall, Evelyn Millis, "Conceptions of Parenthood," *The American Journal of Sociology*, Vol. LII, No. 3, November 1946, pp. 193–203.

Duvall, Evelyn Millis, "Differential Concepts of Parenthood," Ph.D. thesis, University of Chicago, Chicago, Illinois, 1946.

Elder, Rachel Ann, "Traditional and Developmental Conceptions of Fatherhood," *Marriage and Family Living*, Vol. XI, No. 3, Summer 1949, pp. 98–100, 106.

Elder, Rachel Ann, "Traditional and Developmental Conceptions of Fatherhood," Masters thesis, Iowa State College, Ames, Iowa, 1947.

Escalona, Sibylle, "A Commentary upon Some Recent Changes in Child Rearing Practices," *Child Development*, Vol. 20, No. 3, September 1949, pp. 157–162.

Gruenberg, Sidonie, and Krech, Hilda, *The Many Lives of Modern Woman* (New York: Doubleday and Company, 1952).

Langdon, Grace, and Stout, Irving, *The Discipline of Well-Adjusted Children* (New York: John Day Company, 1952).

Sewell, William; Mussen, Paul; and Harris, Chester, "Relationships among Child Training Practices," *American Sociological Review*, Vol. 20, No. 2, April 1955, pp. 137–148.

Staples, Ruth, and Smith, June Warden, "Attitudes of Grandmothers and Mothers toward Child Rearing Practices," *Child Development*, Vol. 25, 1954, pp. 91–97.

Stendler, Celia B., "Sixty Years of Child Training Practices," *Journal of Pediatrics*, Vol. 36, 1950, pp. 122–134.

Thorpe, Alice C., "How Married Students Manage," *Marriage and Family Living*, Vol. XIII, No. 3, August 1951, pp. 104–105, 130.

Underwood, Virginia Van Meter, "Activities of a Selected Group of Student Fathers with Their Children," Department of Child Welfare and Euthenics, Kansas State College Master's thesis, Manhattan, Kansas, 1949.

Vincent, Clark E., "Trends in Infant Care Ideas," *Child Development*, Vol. 22, No. 3, September 1951, pp. 199–209.

Witmer, Helen, and Kotinsky, Ruth, *Personality in the Making*—The Fact-Finding Report of the Midcentury White House Conference on Children and Youth. (New York: Harper & Brothers, 1952.)

Vincent, Clark E. "Trends in Infant Care Ideas" Child
Development Vol 22, No 3, September 1951, pp. 99-202.

This article deals with an analysis of trends contained in
literature on infant care. It consisted of two parts. Part I
Critical Feeding Controversy and Part II Infant
Care discipline. The literature analyzed were articles
contained in the Cooley's Index to Periodical Literature from
1890 to 1899, Readers Guide to Periodical Literature from
1900 to 1949, the Journal of the American Medical Association
from 1890 to 1948, and the books listed in the University of
California Library Card Index File under the subject "Infant Care."
The literature under Part I shows a shift from constantly written
infant mortality & health to a concern with psychological
factors and a shift from predominantly medical writers around
the turn of the century to more non-medical writers in the midcentury's approach. In Part II of the study it was found that
there was appreciable change in infant care advice since 1890 as

Literature favored broad categorizations but by 1900 the
trend toward tightly detailed definitions was developing. This
trend toward detailed ... Plate in 1908 and in 1938 the trend toward regu-
regulations in regard numbers had begun.

The article also documented trends in degree of dogmatism in
the literature on breast vs artificial feeding from 1920-1949.
It was found that dogmatism increased up to 1930-1934
when it began to decline in favor of offering alternatives.

Inferiors revolt in order that they
may be equal, and equals that
they may be superior.
ARISTOTLE

I have to live for others
and not for myself:
That's middle-class morality.
GEORGE BERNARD SHAW

CHAPTER FOUR

Social class and family differences

The American Revolution resulted in part as a reaction against inherited titles and unjust discriminations based upon the accident of birth. As a result, there has been a strong feeling that "class differences" have no place in American life. Actually, more than a hundred studies have shown conclusively that the recognition of social class is not limited to a few "snobs," but is generally found in all segments and areas of American life. Between the lower, middle and upper classes there are real and identifiable differences, not only in social acceptance, but in attitudes, outlook, ideas, ideals, responsibility, mores, morals and general social behavior. Such differences necessarily affect family life profoundly.

Every family is aware of the other people in the community who are like itself, the people in the community "who think they are better than we are," and the people whom they in turn look down upon as "not the kind of people we want to associate with." Those families who have social access to each other belong to the same general social class. Those whom they consider above them in social position occupy a higher social class status. Those whom they do not consider good enough for them to mingle with socially occupy a lower social class position.

Communities of various sizes and kinds have been intensively studied in recent years in an effort to discover what determines social class, how many people are to be found in each social class position, how much movement there is from one social class to another, and how the way of life of a person or a family is influenced by social class.

Some communities are predominantly one class or another. A factory town may be made up almost entirely of working class people. The wealthy suburbs, and even wealthier "exurbs"[1] that circle our great metropolitan areas tend to be those where families of the upper class make their homes. Most communities have several social classes that range all the way from the families that live in humble dwellings "across the tracks," to those who live in mansions "on the hill."

THE SIX SOCIAL CLASSES

The United States as a whole has six well-defined social classes that may be characterized as follows. The *upper-upper* class consists of the established old families who live in the most exclusive sections of the community in homes built by their ancestors. Upper-upper families live upon inherited wealth and upon the income of the heads of the household who are usually professional men or business executives. Members of upper-upper families tend to associate with each other in exclusive clubs, to send their children to private schools, to marry within their social class, and to maintain a strong feeling of family solidarity.

The *lower-upper* class is made up of the well-to-do families whose wealth has been too recently acquired for them to be completely accepted socially by the old established families in the best sections of town. Members of the lower-upper classes belong to the less exclusive "good" clubs, send their children to the best colleges, and live as much as they can like the upper-uppers.

The *upper-middle* class consists of the families who are "the backbone of the community." These families live in the better, but not the most exclusive sections of the community. They earn a comfortable living by professional service or business activity. They send their children to college and encourage them to make friends with "nice people" (of their own or higher status), and make a "good marriage" preferably with a member of the upper class. Upper-middle class families are active in social service organizations, churches, and do what they can to improve standards of living for themselves and others.

The *lower-middle* class is made up of skilled workmen, clerks, small

[1] A. C. Spectorsky, *The Exurbanites* (Philadelphia: J. B. Lippincott Company, 1955).

shopkeepers, and some professional men and women who live in respectable sections of town in nice comfortable homes. Lower-middle class parents try to give their children a good education and some of the advantages of life that they may have lacked. They work hard, and put great stress on honesty, fair-dealing, and decency.

The *upper-lower* class with the lower-middle class just described is "the level of the common man." Families in the upper-lower class live in rented houses or apartments or simple, family dwellings not very far from the slums. The father and sometimes the mother and/or grown children earn the family income as semiskilled workers in factories, mills, mines, or in civil service jobs. These families work hard to keep up a respectable, independent life that is not to be confused with those at the bottom of the social ladder.

The *lower-lower* class is made up of families who live in the least desirable parts of town, in slums or slum-like dwellings. The family income comes from wages earned by the father, and usually the mother, at unskilled jobs that alternate with unemployment and being on relief. There is not always enough money to go around, and the family lives from day to day. Children of lower-lower class families drop out of school earlier than do members of other classes and are sooner in the labor force.

Although there are real differences in the proportions of the various social classes by communities and by regions in this country, in general, the population is divided into the six social classes in about the following percentages.

TABLE 5. *Social Class Percentages in the United States* [1]

Social Class		*Percentage of Population*
Upper-upper	(Old established families)	1% plus
Lower-upper	(Newly rich families)	2% minus
Upper-middle	(Civic leaders of the community)	10%
Lower-middle	(Good respectable families)	28%
Upper-lower	(Families of honest workingmen)	34%
Lower-lower	(Families at bottom of social ladder)	25%
		100%

[1] Adapted from: W. Lloyd Warner, *American Life: Dream and Reality* (Chicago: University of Chicago Press, 1953), Chapter 3; and W. Lloyd Warner and Mildred Hall Warner, *What You Should Know about Social Class* (Chicago: Science Research Associates, 1953).

HOW A FAMILY'S SOCIAL CLASS IS DETERMINED

Research studies tell us that a family's social class is determined by a number of factors: occupation, source of income, neighborhood, and type of house lived in. The *Index of Status Characteristics*, popularly known as the I.S.C., has been developed as a way of objectively determining the social class of a given family. The ratings have been derived from social science research findings of actual families in a number of communities. The simplified version in Table 6 generally applies.

TABLE 6. *Chart for Determining Social Class* [1]

Characteristics	Score
OCCUPATION	
Professionals and proprietors of large businesses (such as doctors and factory owners)	4
Semiprofessionals and smaller officials of large businesses (such as lab technicians or managers)	8
Clerks and similar workers (secretaries, bookkeepers, etc.)	12
Skilled workers (bakers, carpenters, etc.)	16
Proprietors of small businesses (owners of small groceries, restaurants, etc.)	20
Semiskilled workers (bus drivers, cannery workers, etc.)	24
Unskilled workers (such as warehousemen or ditch diggers)	28
SOURCE OF INCOME	
Inherited wealth	3
Earned wealth	6
Profits and fees	9
Salary	12
Wages	15
Private relief	18
Public relief and "nonrespectable" incomes (e.g., gambling)	21
HOUSE TYPE	
Large houses in good condition	3
Large houses in medium condition; medium-sized houses in good condition	6
Large houses in bad condition	9
Medium-sized houses in medium condition; apartments in regular apartment buildings	12
Small houses in good condition; small houses in medium condition; dwellings over stores	15
Medium-sized houses in bad condition; small houses in bad condition	18
All houses in very bad condition; dwellings in structures not originally intended for homes	21
AREA LIVED IN	
Very exclusive; Gold Coast, etc.	2
The better suburbs and apartment house areas, houses with spacious yards, etc.	4
Above average; areas all residential, larger than average space around house; apartment areas in good condition, etc.	6
Average; residential neighborhoods, no deterioration in the area	8
Below average; area not quite holding its own, beginning to deteriorate, business entering, etc.	10
Low; considerably deteriorated, run-down, and semislum	12
Very low; slum	14

[1] From W. Lloyd and Mildred Hall Warner, *What You Should Know about Social Class* (Chicago: Science Research Associates, 1953), pp. 22, 25.

Characteristics (Continued)	*Score*

Social Class	*Total Score*
Upper class	12–17
Upper class probably, with some possibility of upper-middle class	18–22
Indeterminate: either upper or upper-middle class	23–24
Upper-middle class	25–33
Indeterminate: either upper-middle or lower-middle class	34–37
Lower-middle class	38–50
Indeterminate: either lower-middle or upper-lower class	51–53
Upper-lower class	54–62
Indeterminate: either upper-lower or lower-lower class	63–66
Lower-lower class probably, with some possibility of upper-lower class	67–69
Lower-lower class	70–84

Putting the scoring device for determining social class into practice, let us take family A as an example. Mr. A manages the local plant (score 8), and has earned his present wealth (score 6). The A's live in a medium-sized house in good condition (score 6), in an above average residential community (score 6). The total I.S.C. score is 26, which puts the A family into the upper part of the upper-middle class. Family B, on the other hand lives in an apartment building (score 12) in an area that is rapidly changing and not quite holding its own (score 10). The B's income is derived entirely from profits (score 9) from their fruit store (score 20). Totaling their score, we get 51, an indeterminate score between lower-middle and upper-lower social classes, which means the B's could be either depending upon how their neighbors rate them.

Social status is on a continuum. The indeterminate scores between each of the six social classes indicates that there are no rigid categories into which all families must fit. But rather, as Cuber and Kenkel [1] suggest, we have a continuum of social status from the bottom to the top of the social ladder. In this continuum, some characteristics loom larger than others in the minds of people. Among the items used in the I. S. C. scale, occupation is felt to be most important by the people studied. Source of income and type of house lived in rank second in people's thinking, with the area of the community lived in falling into fourth place. Other factors such as the amount and type of education, church attended, style of clothing worn, clubs belonged to, and activities participated in, are all part of the status reputation a family member enjoys. This

[1] John F. Cuber and William F. Kenkel, *Social Stratification in the United States,* (New York: Appleton-Century-Crofts, Inc., 1954).

multiplicity of factors determining one's social status is related to the ease with which one can move up and down the social ladder.

SOCIAL MOBILITY

The family determines the social class into which one is born. But whether or not a person remains in the social class of his family of orientation depends on many factors. A person may conform to his or her family standards and patterns and be "a chip off the old block," remaining static in the same social status all his life. Or, he or she may, by any of many available means (education, occupational success, sports, beauty, "a good marriage," fortunate investment of earned or inherited money, special talent, etc.) move up out of the social status in which he or she was born, so that his (her) family of procreation established upon marriage is a notch or so higher than the family of orientation in which he or she was brought up. This is called upward mobility. Downward mobility occurs when the person slides down the social ladder by lack of education, dissipation, ill-fortune, delinquency, incompetence, or whatever—losing his place in the social scene for one farther down the social scale.

Generally speaking, one of every four or five persons moves upward at least one social class level during his lifetime in the United States today.[1] The greatest amount of upward mobility occurs in the lower-middle and the upper-lower class levels, with nearly 30 per cent mobility from the status below reported at these levels. The lowest percentage of upward mobility is found at the upper-class levels, in which there is less than 8 per cent of mobility from the class below. The great American Dream of "doing better than your parents did" is possible for the boy or girl from a lower-class family who gets an education, learns a salable skill, makes a good marriage, and establishes a nice home in a good neighborhood. The part of the promise that says "there is plenty of room at the top" is realized by few of those who strive for upper-class status. It takes time to accumulate the necessary wealth, to gain acceptance into upper-class circles, and gain the reputation needed for upper-class placement, as many a social climber has learned the hard way. Families oriented toward upward mobility tend to carry their children along with

[1] Carson McGuire, "Social Stratification and Mobility Patterns," *American Sociological Review*, Vol. 15, No. 2, April 1950, pp. 195–204.

Middle-class families live in the better, but not the most exclusive, sections of the community, in good-sized homes that are in good condition.

them and to encourage their young people to climb.[1] While more static families in which mother and father accept the way of life that is theirs tend to have nonmobile children (85 per cent).[2]

Women generally tend to rise in social status, more than do men, especially in the later decades of life.[3] A person of either sex who spends his teens in a large community is more apt to be upward mobile than is an individual who grows up in a small community.[4] The rising standard of living, the increase in the assimilation of ethnic groups, the differential birth rate that creates a middle-class vacuum to be filled with lower-class children, the high valuation of education, the growth of labor unions— all seem to be associated with upward social mobility in the United States generally. A study of adults between the ages of 40 and 60 in Kansas City, Missouri, reveals more than a third as upwardly mobile

---

[1] Carson McGuire, "Conforming, Mobile, and Divergent Families," *Marriage and Family Living*, Vol. XIV, No. 2, May 1952, pp. 109–115.

[2] *Ibid.*, p. 113.

[3] Robert J. Havighurst and Ruth Albrecht, *Older People* (New York: Longmans Green and Company, 1953), Chap. 19.

[4] Seymour Martin Lipset, "Social Mobility and Urbanization," *Rural Sociology*, Vol. 20, Nos. 3 and 4, September–December, 1955, pp. 220–228.

Lower-class families live in the less desirable parts of town, in simple family dwellings or slum-like apartments that are apt to be crowded.

(33.6 per cent), and 12.5 per cent downwardly mobile, yielding a net upward mobility of 21.1 per cent.[1]

Here then, we have a picture of the open social class system in the United States: a pyramid of status levels with the lower classes claiming the greatest number of families, with a large and growing middle class, and a small but influential upper class. Each social class has distinguishing characteristics that tend to be general for the families within it. The social class of a given family is determined by the associations and evaluations of its members and those who know the family. Social science investigation has eventuated in a standardized scale by which the social class placement of a person or a family may be determined. Most families are content with their way of life and bring up their children to conform to the ways of their social class. Some lose status and decline as families from their social class to one below. Twenty per cent, or more, for discernible personal-social reasons, rise up out of their original class into one above. Whatever the social class or the mobility pattern, it greatly affects every area of the life of every member of the family and determines in large measure the strivings and values, routines and rituals, practices and policies of the family itself.

[1] Richard Coleman, Research paper on Social Mobility for the Committee on Human Development, University of Chicago, May 1956, unpublished material, p. 2.

CLASS DIFFERENTIALS IN FAMILY ROUTINES AND RITUALS

Social class differences in the routines and rituals of family living around the clock and through the calendar, are to be found in everyday and special family celebrations of upper-, middle- and lower-class families.[1] Daily routines from awakening, through bathroom procedures, mealtime practices, and the ways in which the day is spent and ended, differ from class to class. The lower-class family, crowded for space scatters into the neighborhood and makes out as best it can on a hand-to-mouth basis. The middle-class family tends to do more together as a family unit through the day and so establishes relatively rigid routines for getting things done efficiently. The upper class offers more privacy and physical resources to the members of the family and at the same time it demands a greater loyalty to family tradition and custom than do either of the other classes. All these tend to make for characteristic ways of living among families within the three major classes.

Religious practices differ among the families of upper, middle and lower classes; in church affiliation, church attendance, religious rituals within the home, and in use of the church for christenings, confirmation, weddings, funerals, and other rites.

The money habits of families of different classes differ widely. Allowances are not expected by lower-class children as they are in both middle- and upper-class families. Neither upper- nor lower-class children participate in family councils on budgeting of family expenditures as is common in middle-class families. Contributing to the family income, expected of lower-class children, is rare in middle-class families and found not at all among upper-class families.

The giving of presents for a wide variety of reasons and occasions is more frequent among middle-class family members than in the other social classes. Upper-class families tend to treasure and build rituals around their family heirlooms. Generally lower-class families do not value their past and have few valuable heirlooms to treasure.

Family pictures may be works of art in an upper-class family, objects of fond amusement among middle-class family members, and rare within the lower-class home. Special occasions like christenings, gradua-

[1] James H. S. Bossard and Eleanor S. Boll, *Ritual in Family Living* (Philadelphia: University of Pennsylvania Press, 1950), Chap. 6, "Class Differentials in Family Rituals," pp. 105–134.

tion, and weddings are usually photographed by middle- and upper-class families. A recent custom of sending a family picture on a Christmas card to friends and relatives has become established among middle-class families. Lower-class families occasionally take pictures of their babies. Their teenagers often get snapshots of themselves and their friends. But they rarely treasure old family photographs as do higher placed families who are proud of their background and antecedents.

Upper-class families tend to remain rooted on the old family place through the years from generation to generation. Their financial interests, their friends, their family traditions—all make staying on the thing to do. The lower-class family has little to keep it from moving on as soon as a more attractive possibility opens up somewhere else. When times are bad, streams of "Okies" flee the drought-hit areas for more promising possibilities on the coast. When times are good (during World War II, for instance), and good jobs open up in the metropolitan areas, hundreds of thousands of workers migrate from South to North, from farm to city, and to both coasts in search of "good money." In recent years with the growing industrialization and militarization of life, professional and business men have followed openings across the country and around the world taking their families with them to make a new life in a new place with astonishing frequency. Even more amazing is the way in which these millions of families tend to remain within their class customs as they move from place to place: in the ways in which they work and play, make love, marry, bear and rear and educate their children; and weather or go down under the crises that hit them from time to time.

CLASS PATTERNS IN FAMILY WORK AND PLAY

The husband-father of the upper-class family goes regularly to his office, where he oversees the family investments, carries on the family business, or pursues his profession. His wife customarily is not gainfully employed, but follows the social life, serves the charities, and pursues the hobbies traditional in her family and among upper-class people in her area. The children, away at private schools or busy at home with their lessons in school and cultural subjects (music, art, dancing, etc.), are not expected to get or hold a job until they are adult. The young women "come out" as debutantes and, soon after, marry, leaving the protection of the father's home for that of the husband. These young women have little or no work experience save that gained as a volunteer or possibly a part-time position in some temporary connection. The young men may serve as apprentices in the family business or as interns in the profession they have chosen with the active assistance of the elder members of the family. Work in the upper-class home is done by servants under the supervision of the wife and mother, who may perform certain tasks as her privilege as lady of the house. The family gets together but rarely to do household tasks, play games, or listen to the radio (each has his own radio in his room). They assemble for family celebrations, visits to grandparents, regular opera-going, and (depending upon the area) for participation in horse shows, theatre, orchestral concerts, high status sports events, charity bazaars, and balls. The upper-class family "summers" in the same place year after year, to which many of their family friends traditionally go, for pleasant climate, change of pace, and a variety of exclusive activities.[1]

In the middle-class family, the husband-father works hard at his business or profession, for which he has prepared himself, with the encouragement of his parents, but without their rigid expectation that he will follow in his father's footsteps, a pattern more characteristic of the upper-class family. The wife and mother of the middle-class family may or may not be gainfully employed, depending upon the age of the children, her husband's attitudes, her abilities, and other personal and family considerations. Teenage children are often encouraged to get and hold part-time jobs designed to help them develop responsible work habits. The money they earn is considered their own for present or future use. There are few employed helpers in the middle-class home today—a cleaning woman by the day or a handy man by the hour for the heavier menial tasks of washing floors and windows is about all that is usual. Middle-class families pride themselves on their do-it-yourself skills and accomplishments, and get together for all sorts of family work projects—from the regular daily dishwashing, through weekly car washing, house cleaning and marketing, to the special building of a barbeque, or the finishing of an extra room in basement or attic.

Middle-class families enjoy a wide variety of vacations and are not bound to returning to the same summer spot year after year. They may tour as a family to visit places of interest in their car; they may go to a summer cottage for the season with father commuting out for weekends; they may decide to stay home and complete some family project with

[1] Cleveland Amory, "Newport: There She Sits," *Harper's Magazine*, February 1948.

only occasional excursions to the library,[1] the beach, or the country. Through the year Saturday and Sunday are special days in the middle-class home with Saturdays given over to trips into town for shopping, lunch, and a show; Sunday the day for going to church and being together as a family with a Sunday afternoon ride, on pleasant days, or the TV set or favorite games in inclement weather.

The lower-class family encourages its members to work as soon as they are able to supplement the family income. The earnings of children (paper routes, house or yard work for more affluent neighbors, work by the hour as errand boy, babysitter, etc.) are considered primarily the property of the family. The woman of the house works as she can around her responsibilities of bearing and rearing the children. The lower-class family is too busy making ends meet to have much time, money, or energy for whole family activities in either work or play. Even church attendance is on an individual basis, with some members of the family needed to care for the too young and too old or ailing family members at home, while others go off one by one or two by two to Mass and other church functions.

In summertime, lower-class parents can rarely get away except possibly for a few days to visit relatives or attend a workers' camp. The children may get a week or two at a low-cost or free camp or may participate in the stay-at-home-camp programs available in many communities. Teenagers as well as adults slip off to the local hangout, tavern, and other commercial amusement whenever time and money allow. Parks, playground, community chest agencies, and museums are all more frequently used by members of lower-class families than by those higher in social status.[2] Home is too crowded and too noisy for games, entertainment, or even favorite radio programs for the rank and file of lower-class family members studied.[3]

SOCIAL CLASS DIFFERENCES IN EDUCATION

There are striking differences according to social level in both the type and the amount of schooling among America's children.[4] These differences are due to a complex of factors in which the family's financial

[1] R. Clyde White, "Social Class Differences in the Uses of Leisure," *The American Journal of Sociology*, Vol. LXI, No. 2, September 1955, pp. 145–150.
[2] *Ibid.*
[3] Bossard and Boll, *op. cit.*, p. 119.
[4] James S. Davie, "Social Class Factors and School Attendance," *Harvard Educational Review*, Vol. 23, 1953, pp. 175–185.

circumstances, customs, beliefs, values, and attitudes are significant. The child of the working-class family receives little encouragement in his studies from home; at the same time, he feels rejected by his teacher who, being middle class, may not understand the behavior of the lower-class child.

In the words of Dr. Allison Davis, who has spent many years of work on this problem,

From the time that these children begin school—and more than 70 out of every 100 of our elementary school children come from these lower-socio-economic groups—most of their ability is misdirected, or wasted . . . because their teachers do not understand the basic cultural habits of the working groups.

The slum child, whose own parents curse as a routine method of communication, fight, and consider the school unimportant in their futures, lives in a physical, economic, and cultural reality basically unlike that in which the middle-class child is trained. Therefore, if the slum child is to be realistic, many of the habits and attitudes which he learns will inevitably differ from those of the more sheltered, intimidated, and highly supervised middle-class child . . .

On the other hand, the middle-class child is pressed by parents to learn too early and fast. Contrary to popular belief, the middle-class child is required to help with chores earlier, and to assume responsibility for other children earlier. . . . he has to come in earlier in the evening, and to work longer on school lessons. Middle-class children are more worried—they suck their thumbs and show other anxiety-symptoms much more (3 to 1) than do lower-class children. But their family's insistent pressure upon them for early and rapid attainment, and for conscientious work habits, makes middle-class children work much harder in school. Thus they please the teacher much more than do lower-class children . . .[1]

Still another factor that Dr. Davis and his colleagues have found discriminating against the lower-class child's progress in school is the culturally biased "standard" intelligence test using middle-class ideologies and experiences. The lower-class child does not speak the language (literally) of the test and so rates significantly lower than his native capacity warrants. This means that he is often placed in so-called "slow" groups and given inferior equipment and curricula where his achievement remains low, quite understandably. The emergence of culturally fair tests is one practical result of these studies through the years.

A child's reputation and acceptance among his classmates in school is strongly influenced by the status level of his family. Children from lower-

---

[1] Allison Davis, "Socio-Economic Influences upon Children's Learning," *School Life*, Vol. 33, No. 6, March 1951, p. 87.

class families are less often wanted as friends (even by other children of their own social class), while children of middle-class families are desired as friends by children of all social levels represented in the fifth and sixth grades of a school studied.[1] The same study tells us that children from middle-class homes are considered by fifth and sixth grade children to be better looking than their lower-class classmates, in significant percentages. The lower-class child feels that school is not for him, and often drops out as soon as the law allows.

Length of schooling is directly related to the family's social class, with children of the higher classes getting more years of formal education than do the lower-class children. The best "educated guess" of these national averages is that the members of the upper-middle and upper classes average 16 years in school (graduating from college), the lower-middle class child averages 12 plus years of schooling (equivalent to completing high school), the upper-lower class child averages 11 years of formal education (attending, but not graduating from high school), while the lower-lower class youngster averages 10 plus or minus years of schooling (dropping out of school as soon as the law allows in his state).[2]

Social class differences in school attendance are apparent from the beginning. The evidence is that children from the lower social classes attend preschool in significantly smaller percentages than do those from the middle and upper social classes: A study of parents of five social classes (Warner, Meeker and Eels classification) whose children were in school or were to enter first grade in the fall shows marked differences by social class in the preschool attendance of the children:

> Results showed that a child's chances of attending preschool decrease as one goes down the social ladder; almost 100 per cent of uppers and upper-middles send their children to preschool, while only 14 per cent of lower-lowers send theirs. Results cannot be explained solely in terms of the economic factor but may be due to differences in the way in which different social classes regard the school.[3]

School drop-outs during the elementary and high school years show sharp social class differences. An extensive study of the social class

[1] Bernice L. Neugarten, "The Relation between Family Social Position and the Social Development of the Child," Doctoral dissertation, University of Chicago, 1943.

[2] Robert J. Havighurst, Committee on Human Development, University of Chicago, personal communication, June 1956.

[3] Celia Burns Stendler, "Social Class Differences in Parental Attitude toward School at Grade I Level," *Child Development*, Vol. 22, No. 1, March 1951, p. 45.

system in one Midwestern community [1] presents the percentages of the members of the two social classes at the bottom of the social ladder who dropped out of school by school grades completed. These findings, detailed in Table 7, indicate clearly that lower-class children start dropping out of school before the seventh grade, and that the period when the largest percentage of children of the lower classes drop out of school comes at the interval between elementary and high schools, between the eighth and ninth grades.

TABLE 7. *Percentages of School Children Dropping Out of School by School Grade Completed in the Two Lower Social Classes in a Midwestern Community* [2]

Grade Completed	Upper-Lower Social Class	Lower-Lower Social Class
Fifth	100.0%	100.0%
Sixth	99.2	97.6
Seventh	96.1	78.9
Eighth	92.2	57.4
Ninth	45.7	23.0
Tenth	31.0	14.7
Eleventh	12.4	6.4
Eleventh plus	3.9	0.0

These findings indicate that three-fourths of the children at the lowest social class level and more than half of the upper-lower class pupils do not complete the ninth grade. For a member of the lower class to graduate from high school in this community is apparently a rarity. The poor family heritage (as measured by the neighborhood, broken homes, rented homes, low and sporadic family income, mother's absence from the home in outside work) correlated significantly with the lower-class child's dropping out of school in the community studied.

FAMILY HEALTH DIFFERENTIALS BY SOCIAL CLASS

An intensive study of the 2,168 illnesses reported by 1,256 individuals in a community in the hill country of New York State,[3] indicates that

[1] August B. Hollingshead, *Elmtown's Youth* (New York: John Wiley & Sons, Inc., 1949).
[2] Adapted by permission from A. B. Hollingshead, *Elmtown's Youth,* copyright 1949, John Wiley & Sons, Inc., p. 332.
[3] Earl Lomon Koos, *The Health of Regionville* (New York: Columbia University Press, 1954).

members of the lower classes have a higher percentage of both disabling and nondisabling illnesses and lose significantly more time from the job, especially in illnesses costing more than twenty days of time lost, than do members of the middle and upper social classes. A significantly smaller percentage of lower-class families in this study have a family doctor, and a higher percentage are dissatisfied with the medical care they receive for reasons that range from: "doctor prescribed too-expensive drugs," to "doctor not interested in caring for us."

Dental attention in terms of prophylaxis and emergency repair among members of the lower classes is considerably less than that received by persons who are better off in the community studied. This is reflected vividly in the percentage of extractions due to neglect: none at the top social class studied, 8.8 per cent of the social class members in the middle of the population studied, and 57.1 per cent of the lowest class placement. The reasons for such a high percentage of teeth lost through neglect in the lower classes are suggested by a public health worker in the community who says,

That percentage may seem high, but most of the poor grown-ups—especially those who live away from the towns and cities—let their teeth go until there isn't anything to do but have them pulled. I wonder sometimes how they can have any teeth left in their heads. Oil of cloves or some other pain killer is used in almost every low-class home in my district. So far as I am concerned, this is the biggest single over-all health problem there is.[1]

Preventive health examinations are practically nonexistent and health insurance significantly less in the lower social classes than among the middle and upper social classes. Lower-class families rely on the druggist for their health needs and stock an exceptional quantity of "kidney pills," "stomach medicines," and "liver pills" in an effort to ease discomfort and to keep well through self-medication. As several lower-class interviews report,

"My husband and I take C—— Liver Pills regular. We get to feeling stuffy if we don't, and keeping your liver flushed out gets rid of the stuffiness . . . Once in a while I take S—— Kidney Pills too. It's good to flush out your kidneys once in a while . . . If I do this, I don't get sick."

"I always take S—— Compound every fall. It thickens my blood, and gets me ready for cold weather."

[1] *Ibid.*, p. 122.

"We take H—— Tonic (alcohol 16 per cent) all the time during the winter when we aren't outdoors much. It keeps us fit; we don't have hardly any sickness since we've been doing this for three years now." [1]

This and other studies point to markedly different patterns of health and sickness, health care, and use of medical facilities among the social classes in a given community. The members of the middle and upper classes know more of the dynamics of illness and health and are more aware of the resources to be tapped for prevention and treatment of sickness. They live in a climate of social acceptance of the services of physicians, specialists (gynecologists, obstetricians, pediatricians, psychiatrists, and the rest), dentists, orthodontists, plastic surgeons, and the other professions whose services make life safer and more pleasant for human beings. The men and women of the lower classes, on the contrary, are not as aware of the nature of sickness and health. They do not feel that the health resources and facilities of a community are for "our kind of folks," so they tend to live in a heritage of bravely "getting along and making do." Self-medication and the use of nonmedical personnel are patterns that are transmitted to the children as the thing to do in everyday family living.

SOCIAL CLASS FACTORS IN DATING AND COURTSHIP

"Birds of a feather flock together" in the adolescent clique as in the adult community. This is clearly seen in examining the findings of studies of dating and courtship behavior among young people. Hollingshead's classic study of the high school students of one community reveals the fact that from 49 to 70 per cent of all clique ties are with those of the same social class. [2] The one-third of the boys and girls who associate closely in a clique with a member of another social class do so with a member of the class adjacent to his or her own. When a member of the highest social class associates with someone other than his own, it is with the next below; the lowest social class member establishes close associations within his own group, or more rarely the social class next higher in the social ladder. Bridging over more than one social class position is infrequent both in cliquing and in dating; the social distance is just too great.

Table 8 is an actual representation of the dating partner patterns of

[1] *Ibid.*, pp. 89 and 90.
[2] Hollingshead, *op. cit.*, p. 213.

TABLE 8. *Intra- and Interclass Dating Patterns of High School Students* [1]

Social Class of Person Dated	Boys				Girls			
	I and II	III	IV	V	I and II	III	IV	V
Classes I and II	54%	38%	8%	——	50%	35%	15%	——
Class III	18%	53%	27%	2%	15%	58%	27%	——
Class IV	3%	11%	79%	7%	4%	16%	74%	6%
Class V	——	2%	28%	70%	——	9%	33%	58%

the high school students of Elmtown by social classes. In this study Classes I and II are at the highest social class level, roughly equivalent to upper and upper-middle classes in other studies. Class V is the lowest social class level, roughly similar to lower-lower social class, while Classes III and IV approximate lower-middle and upper-lower class levels. There are interesting sex differences in interclass dating: when a boy crosses a class line, the chances are two to one that he dates a girl from a class below himself, while a girl, conversely, usually dates above herself when she leaves her own social class.

Boys and girls at the higher social class levels report more dates with more persons than do teenagers at the other social class levels. Higher placed girls are considered popular because of the number of dates they have and the number of boys they date. Going steady in this community tends to be frowned upon by many parents and teachers because of the emotional and sexual involvements that often result for members of the pair.

Young people from working-class families are more direct in expressing sex interest and response and indulge less in extended petting than do young people from middle-class families.[2] The better educated the young person is, the less premarital sex experience he or she has. This association of educational level achieved to incidence of premarital sex is in a straight-line relationship age for age and grade for grade with the greater incidence at the lower educational levels, and the highest percentage least at the higher educational levels (see in Table 9).

Remembering that the majority of lower-class young people do not go

[1] Data drawn with permission from A. B. Hollingshead, *Elmtown's Youth*, copyright 1949 John Wiley & Sons, Inc., page 231, excerpts from Chart I.

[2] Alfred C. Kinsey *et al.*, *Sexual Behavior in the Human Male* (Philadelphia: Saunders, 1948); and *Sexual Behavior in the Human Female* (Philadelphia: Saunders, 1953), p. 368.

TABLE 9. *Pre-Marital Sex Relations by Educational Level Experienced by Girls and Boys in Age Group 16–20* [1]

Educational Level	Girls	Boys
Grade School	38%	85%
High School	32%	76%
College and Graduate	17–19%	42%

far beyond grade school (Table 7), we can now picture them as out of school youth doing little of the "playing around" and postponing of serious involvements so characteristic of middle-class boys and girls. In the middle class, educational and vocational plans call for less direct sex expression and for conformance to the code of chastity before marriage.

MARRIAGE AND DIVORCE PATTERNS IN THE SOCIAL CLASSES

Just as young people tend to make friends with, date, and run in cliques with members of their own social class, so too they tend to marry within their class. This holds generally true of men and women of all class levels and is known as the principle of *homogamy*, the tendency for like to marry like.

Members of lower-class families marry at younger ages than do young people of the middle-class level, in ways consistent with their way of life. They are usually out of school in their middle teens, active in direct sex experience with their heterosexual partners; burdened neither by social pressures for supporting the sex code, nor by urgent reasons for postponing pregnancy and marriage such as restrain members of middle-class families. Early marriage follows as the inevitable next step for the majority of boys and girls of the lower classes. These are the young people who miss out on what family-life education is offered in the high schools of their community;[2] they are not welcomed in the "nice respectable" social clubs and activities of the area, nor do they have the clothes and money for them even if they were invited to participate. Their homes are crowded; their parents are burdened with the problems of making ends meet; their mothers are out of the home in tiring, non-

[1] Alfred C. Kinsey *et al., Sexual Behavior in the Human Female* (Philadelphia: Saunders, 1953), p. 331.

[2] Robert J. Havighurst, "Social Class Differences and Family Life Education at the Secondary Level," *Marriage and Family Living,* Vol. XII, No. 4, Fall 1950, pp. 133–135.

gratifying but necessary labor; thus the family is hardly capable of launching its young people into a way of life vastly different from its own.

Young people of the lower classes more frequently come from broken homes than do the more privileged young men and women of the higher social class levels. There are many factors related to this tendency for more instability of family life at the lower levels than among the higher social classes. Age at marriage is related to success in marriage, with the teenage marriages significantly more risky than those of more mature persons. Educational level is related to stability of the family, with the better-educated men and women making the more stable unions. Income level and occupation are both significantly related to proneness to divorce, as we see in the rank order below taken from a scholarly analysis of census data on divorce in America today.

TABLE 10. *Occupational Groupings in the United States by "Proneness to Divorce" Indices* [1]

Occupational Group	Proneness to Divorce Index *
Professional, semiprofessional	67.7
Proprietors, managers, officials	68.6
Clerical, sales	71.8
Craftsmen, foremen	86.6
Operatives (semiskilled)	94.5
Laborers (except farm and mine)	180.3
Service workers	254.7

* The proneness to divorce index expresses the relationship between the proportion or percentage of "Other Marital Status" (than single or married) in any given occupational category, to the proportion of "Married, Wife Present" in that same category. The index is a way of stating whether the number of broken homes in any given group is as much as, or more than, expected, in view of the proportion which that group is of the total population which could divorce (*i.e.*, the married). For the data from which these calculations were made see *Current Population Reports, Labor Force*, Series, P-50, No. 22, April 19, 1950, Table 5.

The lower-income levels and less skilled occupational groupings have the highest proneness to divorce, while significantly less proneness to divorce is found among the skilled workers and professional and proprietary occupations and at the higher-income levels. The reasons for these tendencies are complex and challenging to the serious student of

[1] William J. Goode, *After Divorce* (Glencoe, Illinois: The Free Press, 1956), p. 46.

family stability.[1] The striking differences between the marriage and divorce patterns in the various status levels in our society are clearly evident to even the casual reader.

CHILDBEARING AND CHILDREARING AMONG FAMILIES OF DIFFERENT SOCIAL CLASSES

Low-income families have more children per family than do high-income families in the United States. Most of America's children are in low and moderate income families as is vividly portrayed by Chart 6, in which we see that (as of 1948) 69 per cent of America's children are in families with incomes under $4,000, while at the other end of the economic ladder only 3 per cent of our children are in families with incomes over $10,000.

Middle-class mothers tend to have their babies in a hospital, while lower-class mothers, especially in the lower-lower class families, are delivered at home.[2] Some of the comments of lower-class mothers about the births of their babies in the study quoted indicate who attends the birth of the lower-class baby, as well as the emotional climate of the mothers' attitudes toward their deliveries.

"My babies wuz all borned at home."

"All my babies but one was born at home."

"Ma was here and helped when the first two came. My sister, sister-in-law, and neighbors helped when the others were delivered . . ."

"There's nothing like a good midwife to 'catch' the babies when they come." [3]

Punishment of children seems to differ from class to class in form, amount, offenses dealt with, and in the person responsible for punishing children for misbehavior. In the words of one research report,

Punishment in the lower-class home tends to be inconsistent, at least from the field workers' points of view. One group of observers has included this summary, "For a thing that is funny one time, the lower-class child may be whipped the next. They are whipped so much, they lose their fear of it and come to expect it for almost anything . . ."

[1] A provocative summary is to be found in August B. Hollingshead, "Class Differences in Family Stability," *The Annals of the American Academy of Political and Social Science*, Vol. 272, November 1950, pp. 39–46; as well as in the Goode Study, *ibid.*, pp. 43–55.

[2] Carson McGuire, "Family Life in the Lower and Middle Class Homes," *Marriage and Family Living*, Vol. XIV, No. 1, February 1952, p. 4.

[3] *Ibid.*, p. 4.

Out of every
100 children   Are in families with incomes

25	Under $2,000
22	$2,000 – 2,999
22	$ 3,000 - 3,999
13	$4,000 – 4,999
7	$5,000 – 5,999
4	$6,000 – 6,999
4	$7,000 – 7,999
3	$ 10,000 and over

CHART 6.   Most Children Are in Low and Moderate Income Families [1]

Alternate loving and "fazing," that is, petting and then slapping a child "to toughen him up," are not infrequent mechanisms which go along with shaming, ridiculing, and whipping in the lower-class home. Passages such as the following are to be found in lower-class interviews.

"I whup 'em with a belt when they git out of hand." "Whipping's the best way. I usually save up until they need it bad and then give 'em a good one." "They usually build up to one." "I jest got through whippin' that one. She jest needed a good strapping." [2]

Middle-class mothers are more frequently opposed to physical punishment, and so they use a variety of methods of control including disap-

[1] Midcentury White House Conference on Children and Youth, *Children and Youth at the Midcentury: A Chart Book,* (Raleigh, North Carolina: Health Publications Institute, Inc., 1951), Chart 22.
[2] Carson McGuire, *op. cit.,* p. 5.

proval, deprivation of some privilege, isolation from other members of the family by being sent to one's room, and "talking to the child," in an effort to explain why what he had done is wrong, and discussing what are better ways of behaving.

Two intensive studies of social class differences in childrearing practices have been conducted in recent years, one in the Chicago area,[1] and the other by social scientists at Harvard.[2] There were differences in the samples of children and families studied, in the methods employed, in the items explored, and in the comparable findings of the two studies. In spite of these variations, the two studies agreed on a number of items that are summarized simply as follows:

Lower class families are more severe in punishment in toilet-training.
Middle class families have higher educational expectations of their children.
No class difference in amount of care given children by father.
No class difference in display of aggression by children in the home (excluding aggression toward siblings) . . .
Middle-class children allowed more freedom of movement away from home during the day.[3]

The outline below reflects the research of the Committee on Human Development of the University of Chicago contrasting the training environments of the middle-class and the lower-class child in America.

CLASS DIFFERENCES IN SOCIALIZATION PATTERNS [4]

Child Training and Child Behavior in a Middle Class Family	*Child Training and Child Behavior in a Lower-class Slum Family*
"Slow" socialization; child not pushed toward adult roles. Much parental shielding of child from world.	"Fast" socialization; child pushed into adult roles rapidly, owing to economic pressures and less parental protection.

[1] Allison Davis and Robert J. Havighurst, "Social Class and Color Differences in Child-Rearing," *American Sociological Review*, Vol. 11, 1946, pp. 698–710.

[2] Robert R. Sears, Eleanor E. Macoby and Harry Levin, *Patterns of Child-Rearing*, in press; see also, Eleanor E. Macoby and Patricia K. Gibbs and the staff of the Laboratory of Human Development, Harvard University, "Methods of Child-Rearing in Two Social Classes," in *Readings in Child Development* by William E. Martin and Celia Burns Stendler (New York: Harcourt, Brace and Company, 1954).

[3] Robert J. Havighurst and Allison Davis, "A Comparison of the Chicago and Harvard Studies of Social Class Differences in Child-Rearing," *American Sociological Review*, Vol. 20, No. 4, August 1955, p. 441.

[4] Reproduced by permission from John W. Bennett and Melvin M. Tumin, *Social Life* (New York: Alfred A. Knopf, Inc., 1948), pp. 669–671, using basic data from Allison Davis and Robert J. Havighurst, *Father of the Man* (New York: Houghton Mifflin, 1947).

CLASS DIFFERENCES IN SOCIALIZATION PATTERNS (*Cont.*)

Child Training and Child Behavior in a Middle Class Family

Child encouraged in later years to "succeed," often to "do better" than father in achievement and status. Child-training methods in general develop a desire in child for achievement.

Parents habitually stress conformity to group norms as well as individualistic achievement. Success of child often measured against neighborhood paragon. Child often unsure of what standards he must adopt.

Sexual roles distinct: Boys should be "masculine but gentlemanly"; "sissy" stigma fairly strong; varies by age group. Girls should be "feminine" and attractive to boys. Variation with respect to issue of equal education, right to earn own living, etc.

Training teaches the virtue of competition and cooperation in the "fair play" sense ("get ahead, but do it fairly"). Playing down of aggressive methods and of aggression in general, at least in overt forms. Middle-class child in school with lower-class pupils is often labeled "sissy." Middle-class child gangs compete, but do not follow regular aggressive pattern.

Training methods use parental love systematically as a reward for obedience and achievement, thus stimulating anxiety. Guilt on part of parents arises, and sympathy characteristically and inconsistently follows severe withholding of love, breeding further anxiety.

Child Training and Child Behavior in a Lower-class Slum Family

Same goals often present, but played down. More acceptance of fact that child will probably follow status of father. Training methods do not usually develop desire for achievement.

Much less stress on conformity. Group norms less rigid, more informal. No "living up to the Joneses" pattern. Rare stress on measuring up to standard set by neighbor child. Child freer to set own standards.

Sexual roles distinct, but different: Boys should be hypermasculine, aggressive, anti-gentlemanly. "Sissy" stigma very pronounced. Girls should be feminine, but also greater aggressiveness is accepted. More acceptance of right of girl to earn own living, etc.

Training teaches the virtue of aggressive defense and attack-as-defense. Aggression in general less tabooed, more accepted. "Fair play" unstressed or absent in home, but child encounters it in school. Leads to conflict with school authorities, who are middle-class-minded. Lower-class child gangs very aggressive and combative.

Training methods do not use love as reward systematically. Rewards more usually in material sphere. "Obedience" not stressed beyond basic adjustment to somewhat informal family routine. Love more freely given. Hostility between parents and child more readily accepted. System probably less anxiety-producing.

Child Training and Child Behavior in a Middle Class Family	*Child Training and Child Behavior in a Lower-class Slum Family*
Sibling rivalries usually intense; center around competition for parental love and attention.	Sibling rivalries probably equally intense, but are more open and aggressive. Center on competition in social relationships outside family to some extent.
Family and home environment more complex in material sense: more restrictions required to maintain routine and order.	Family and home environment simpler, fewer restrictions required.
Punishment inconsistent. Parents tend to have much guilt over punishment, and do not sustain practices. More emphasis on "humanitarian" treatment of child, alternating with severe punishment. Child learns more complex and variable patterns of love and hostility. *Situational* punishment stressed ("go stand in the corner and feel ashamed").	Punishment, like love, given more freely and more consistently. Child learns simpler, more clear-cut patterns of love and hostility. *Physical* punishment stressed.
Considerable restriction and repression of organic functions of body. Elimination viewed as "dirty"; toilet training early and rigid (usually earlier than physical maturation of child can assimilate). Sex tabooed; introduction to sexual knowledge occurs late in childhood. Whole system introduces anxieties and tensions over organic functions.	Less restriction and repression of organic pleasures and functions. Partly due to such physical factors as more crowded living conditions, partly due to more relaxed attitudes. Earlier exposure to sexual functions, often within home. Children permitted to "get dirty"; fewer taboos on dirt; more likely to be seen as a practical rather than a moral issue. Probably less anxiety-producing. Some conflicts with school authorities over system.
Routinized feeding of child in infancy; carried over into later childhood in form of rigid three-meals-a-day system. Children in general show more anxieties of a basic sort over food.	Feeding not routinized in infancy; rigid meal schedules not adhered to later. Family tends to "eat when there's food." Anxieties over food more realistic—based on hunger.

CLASS DIFFERENCES IN SOCIALIZATION PATTERNS (*Cont.*)

Child Training and Child Behavior in a Middle Class Family	*Child Training and Child Behavior in a Lower-class Slum Family*
Children's fears seem to center in symbolic areas (as in the fear of not being loved, of not living up to the neighborhood paragon, or to parent's goals for child).	Fears seem to center in environmental areas (as in the fear of going hungry, being dispossessed, and the like). Some symbolic fears develop in school, when awareness of deprivation develops.
Training in the use of language stresses the symbolic expression of ideas. Literacy stressed greatly, because it is a large factor in "success."	Training in the use of language stresses emotional expression (e.g., profanity), and in utilitarian control over environment, rather than in the expression of ideas. Literacy not stressed. Leads to school difficulties.

It is generally agreed that a great deal more exploration is needed both on the question of comparative methods of rearing children in lower-, middle- and upper-class families, and on the conceptions of motherhood, fatherhood, and childhood held by family members at the various class levels, as explored in Chapter Three, "Changing Patterns in Childrearing." In the meantime, there has been enough initial opening up of these fields of research investigation to hypothesize safely that families differ significantly in both their expectations and conceptions of themselves as families and as family members, as well as in their ways of putting their conceptions into actual practice in the rearing of their children.

SOCIAL CLASS DIFFERENCES IN FAMILY REACTIONS TO CRISIS

Families differ by the social class level they occupy, in the number of crises they go through, what they consider a family crisis, the severity of their reaction to family troubles, and in the ways in which they weather family crises. In his study of his own and others' investigations of family crises, Dr. Earl Koos concludes that "middle-class families more often react more severely to crisis than do low-income families, but they recover their earlier interaction patterns more readily, and . . . they are more likely to come out of the crisis with some benefit to themselves . . . the middle-class family has far more to lose in the way of *morale* than does its counterpart in the low-income group; in general, too, it has much more opportunity, and much more with which to reestablish itself after the crisis is over."[1]

SUMMARY

This chapter does not attempt to exhaust the vast amount of original research and social theory on the effect of social class on family life. Rather, an effort has been made to introduce some of the highlights and the dark shadows that are to be seen in the ways families differ by their social class placement. These differences are to be found in the everyday patterns of living within the family—in rituals and routines, work and play, education, health, dating and court-

COURTESY OF DOROTHEA LANGE: "FAMILY OF MAN"

The lower-class family has few resources for meeting its crises and often suffers permanent damage as each recurring trouble leaves the family unit more vulnerable and less well integrated.

ship, marriage and divorce, childbearing and childrearing, and in type and frequency of family troubles.

Looking at this chapter in relationship to those that have gone before, we must recognize that social class is an important factor to be taken into account in understanding family life and intrafamily interaction at every stage of the family life cycle, in seeing family life through history, and in tracing the ways in which the philosophy of family relationships and child nurture and training are changing within our dynamic culture. These social class variables have been summarized briefly early in this volume so that they may influence all that is yet to come and implicitly play a significant part in clearly seeing flesh and blood families at every stage of the family life cycle.

SUGGESTED ACTIVITIES

1) Review one of the following works of fiction, identifying (1) the social class level of the principal family portrayed, (2) the extent of the social

[1] Earl L. Koos, "Class Differences in Family Reactions to Crisis," *Marriage and Family Living*, Vol. XII, No. 3, Spring 1950, p. 78.

mobility exhibited by the main character, (3) the stage(s) of the family life cycle in which the action takes place. Document your decisions on all three points with direct quotations from the book and primary research sources for the criteria you employ.

Farrell, James T., *Father and Son* (New York: Vanguard Press, 1940).

Fitzgerald, F. Scott, *The Great Gatsby* (New York: Charles Scribner's Sons, 1925).

Gilbreth, Frank B. and Carey, Ernestine, *Cheaper by the Dozen* (New York: Thomas Y. Crowell Company, 1948).

Lewis, Sinclair, *Babbitt* (New York: Harcourt, Brace and Co., 1922).

MacDonald, Betty, *Onions in the Stew* (Philadelphia: J. B. Lippincott Company, 1954).

Marquand, John P., *The Late George Apley* (New York: P. F. Collier and Son, 1936).

McConnell, Raymond A., Jr., *Trampled Terraces* (Lincoln: University of Nebraska Press, 1950).

Morley, Christopher, *Kitty Foyle* (Philadelphia: J. B. Lippincott Company, 1939).

Schulberg, Budd, *What Makes Sammy Run?* (New York: Random House, 1941).

Smith, Betty, *A Tree Grows in Brooklyn* (New York: Harper & Brothers, 1943).

Streeter, Edward, *Father of the Bride* (New York: Simon and Schuster, Inc., 1948).

Wouk, Herman, *Marjorie Morningstar* (New York: Doubleday and Company, Inc., 1955).

2) Plot on an area map of your locality the residences of the families mentioned in the society columns of one of your local papers for the period of one week. Discuss your findings in the light of what you know about social class and membership of families in the "social set."

3) Using the simplified version of the Index of Status Characteristics (Table 6) given early in this chapter, determine your own social class placement as seen in your family of orientation and in your plans for your family of procreation. Discuss the mobility evidences apparent in any discrepancies between the two scores, with indications of their possible sources in your developmental experience.

4) Write a paper on the social class origins of the men who are the controlling voices in large industrial organizations in contemporary America using as your primary source the material found in the original study by W. Lloyd Warner and James Abegglen in *Big Business Leaders in America* (New York: Harper & Brothers, 1955).

5) Discuss the most likely reasons for the recent popularity of the do-it-yourself movement among American families in terms of the question:

Why has the movement arisen at this point in history? (Review pertinent aspects of Chapter Two for relevant data.)

6) Make a simple survey of the school drop-outs in your community for the past year. Try to find out from the school authorities which children dropped out (in terms of occupation and income of the father, area lived in, probable social class placement, etc.), percentages of children leaving school by grade levels, and attitudes of representative teachers toward the boys and girls who have left school.

7) Graph the divorces granted in your area during the past year by income and occupation of the man and by the section of the community the couples had lived in just prior to the granting of their divorce. To what extent do these findings corroborate those on the national level that divorce is more frequent among the unskilled and low income families than among the more privileged and skilled (Table 10)?

8) Review six to ten of the popular works on child development and guidance in your library with particular notice of the general class levels from which findings have been gathered, and the social class placement of the anticipated audience of parents and teachers expected to use the book. Is such material primarily slanted to middle-class orientation? If so, why? What possible difference does this make in the tendencies of middle-class families to be more developmentally oriented than families of the lower classes (Chapter Three)?

READINGS

Bossard, James H. S., *Ritual in Family Living* (Philadelphia: University of Pennsylvania Press, 1950), Chapter 6, "Class Differentials in Family Rituals," pp. 105–185.

Cavan, Ruth S., *The American Family* (New York: Thomas Y. Crowell Company, 1953), Part Two, "Social Configurations of the American Family," pp. 119–258.

Christensen, Harold T., "Studies in Child Spacing: I—Premarital Pregnancy as Measured by the Spacing of the First Birth from Marriage," *American Sociological Review*, Vol. 18, No. 1, February 1953, pp. 53–59.

Cuber, John F., and Kenkel, William F., *Social Stratification in the United States* (New York: Appleton-Century-Crofts, Inc., 1954).

Davie, James S., "Social Class Factors and School Attendance," *Harvard Educational Review*, Vol. 23, 1953.

Davis, Allison, "Socio-Economic Influences upon Children's Learning," *School Life*, Vol. 33, No. 6, March 1951, pp. 87, 93, 94.

Goode, William J., *After Divorce* (Glencoe, Illinois: The Free Press, 1956), Chapters IV and V.

Havighurst, Robert J., and Davis, Allison, "A Comparison of the Chicago and Harvard Studies of Social Class Differences in Child Rearing," *American Sociological Review*, Vol. 20, No. 4, August 1955, pp. 438–442.

Havighurst, Robert J., "Social Class Differences and Family Life Education at the Secondary Level," *Marriage and Family Living,* Vol. XII, No. 4, Fall 1950, pp. 133–135.

Hollingshead, August B., "Class and Kinship in a Middle Western Community," *American Sociological Review,* Vol. 14, No. 4, August 1949, pp. 469–475.

——, "Class Differences in Family Stability," *The Annals of the American Academy of Political and Social Science,* Vol. 272, November 1950, pp. 39–46.

——, *Elmtown's Youth* (New York: John Wiley and Sons, Inc., 1949).

Koos, Earl L., "Class Differences in Family Reactions to Crisis," *Marriage and Family Living,* Vol. XII, No. 3, Summer 1950, pp. 77, 78, 99.

——, *The Health of Regionville* (New York: Columbia University Press, 1954).

Maas, Henry S., "Some Social Class Differences in the Family Systems and Group Relations of Pre- and Early Adolescents," *Child Development,* Vol. 22, No. 2, June 1951, pp. 145–152.

McGuire, Carson, "Family Backgrounds and Community Patterns," *Marriage and Family Living,* Vol. XIII, No. 4, November 1951, pp. 160–164.

——, "Family Life in Lower and Middle Class Homes," *Marriage and Family Living,* Vol. XIV, No. 1, February 1952, pp. 1–6.

Seeley, John R.; Sim, R. Alexander; and Loosley, Elizabeth W., *Crestwood Heights* (New York: Basic Books, Inc., 1956).

Stendler, Celia Burns, "Social Class Differences in Parental Attitude toward School at Grade I Level," *Child Development,* Vol. 22, No. 1, March 1951, pp. 37–46.

Warner, W. Lloyd, *American Life: Dream and Reality* (Chicago: The University of Chicago Press, 1953).

Warner, W. Lloyd, and Lunt, Paul S., *The Social Life of a Modern Community,* Vol. I, Yankee City Series, (New Haven: Yale University Press, 1941).

Warner, W. Lloyd, and Warner, Mildred Hall, *What You Should Know about Social Class* (Chicago: Science Research Associated, Inc., 1953).

The proper study of mankind is man.

ALEXANDER POPE

Growth is the only evidence of life.
JOHN HENRY, CARDINAL NEWMAN

CHAPTER FIVE

Family developmental tasks

E thel Merman may sing, "Doin' What Comes Nacherally," implying that all that is necessary in marriage, or in life, is to follow one's impulses. Grandmother, puzzled over some misbehavior in the family, may sigh and comment that "bad blood will out" as she remembers old Uncle Ned, the black sheep on her husband's side of the family. Seeing no other immediate explanation, she jumps to the conclusion that heredity accounts for everything she cannot understand.

Heredity, of course, is a force in human development. Each of us is born with forty-eight chromosomes (24 pairs) that carry to each new individual the particular assortment of tendencies that are to be his from both lines of forebears. Certain specifics can be easily identified as hereditary: [1] eye color, hair form, body stature, musical genius, certain anomalies, and so forth. These factors cannot be changed no matter what the individual possessing them does. A girl may put a "permanent wave" in her hair, but as soon as it grows out, her hair form returns to its natural state. She may "make up" her face to call attention to her eyes, but their shape and size and color remain the same. A man may wear elevator-

---

[1] Amram Scheinfeld, *The New You and Heredity* (Philadelphia: J. B. Lippincott Company, 1950).

shoes, or slouch down as he walks to give the illusion of being taller or shorter than he really is, but he cannot by willing "add one cubit to his stature," as old words of wisdom remind us. A person may develop or ignore his special talents, but they are still his whatever he does about them. An individual may correct, or refuse to recognize, or learn to live with, the particular atypicalities that are natively his or hers; but the individuality remains.

Among many of the lower forms of life, heredity plays a major role in what the individual is and does throughout its life span. Bees swarm, collect honey, and attend the queen because of inherited instincts that regulate even the smallest details of the individual bee's behavior. The coyote prowls at night and howls and hunts in response to instinct. The domesticated dog or cat may learn a great deal about how to live with humans, but it remains forever driven by the instinctual canine or feline forces that are inherited from generations to generations of dogs and cats.

Not so with humans. Ethel Merman's song is misleading. Grandmother did not have the correct answer when she credited heredity with all behavior she did not understand. Man behaves as he does, primarily because of what he has learned to do in various situations throughout his life.

Studies of humans who grew up away from contact with other human beings indicate clearly that most of what we consider as basically human behavior is *learned*.[1] With only a few latent inherited tendencies to guide him, man must learn how to function in a vast number of situations that change as he grows, and shift as he develops throughout the weeks, months, years, and decades of his lifetime. This flexibility and capacity for learning and unlearning is man's unique inheritance. In understanding what this looks like at various stages of human development, the concept of the developmental task has proven to be helpful.

A BRIEF WORD ABOUT CONCEPTS

All of us use concepts. A concept is a tool to think with, a way that helps us make sense of our many-faceted experiences. Illustrations of some simple concepts that men everywhere use are: food, color, friend,

[1] Read Arnold Gesell, "Biography of a Wolf-Child," *Harper's Magazine*, January 1941; and Kingsley Davis, "Extreme Social Isolation in a Child," *American Journal of Sociology*, Vol. 45, pp. 554–565.

A child learns to know what is good to eat within the food habits of his own family.

time, space, roundness. Such things are so elemental that we pick them up as we grow, from those around us who use them. The baby learns that certain things are good to eat and that other things are forbidden as "bad." The American learns to think of food as consisting of the variety of fruits, vegetables, meats, and sweets that are eaten in his area —cow peas, chitterlings and yams in one section of the country; clam chowder, apple pie, and beans in another region; or rare steak and green salad in still another subculture. Many of us learn so well what is good to eat in terms of the food habits of our own families that we have difficulty being fully nourished when we are plunged into another culture where foods are differently defined. We are repelled from eating dried octopus or fried locusts or snails because our concept of food does not include such items of diet. The sophisticated person, who has "been around," has a broad concept of food that includes a great many edible items not considered as food by a more provincial person.

We all need concepts with which to handle our perpetual particulars. As long as we live we must make sense of our world and our place in it.

To use the food concept as illustrative again, let us take the baby just beginning to crawl around the house. Then anything and everything goes into his mouth—a piece of mud, a crumb of cake, a marble, an old shoe, the cat's tail—all those and more might be food, and he learns what is and what is not by trying them out as well as by being admonished by his mother either to "eat it up, like a good boy," or to "spit it out, this instant." Only as he learns what to eat, and how and when, is he ready for independent existence away from his mother's supervising eye.

All of us are in danger of being snowed under by a multitude of particulars in every area of life. In any new situation we are like the baby who must sample and listen and learn until we find the groupings of objects, people, and ideas that make sense. The mother juggling in her mind the tumbling array of memories of what her son has done and not done in recent hours or days may wail, "What has gotten into Junior?" What she is seeking is some plausible concept that will help her make sense of the wide variety of conflicting and confusing behaviors that represent Junior right now. What she does reflects the concept she chooses for understanding Junior's behavior. She may "give him a good licking," or "flush out his system with a cathartic," or "have his father give him a talking to when he gets home," or complain to her neighbors that she "doesn't know what modern kids are coming to," or call in expert help; but whatever she does, she is acting on the basis of her concept of what all Junior's many actions add up to in her mind.

The teacher with twenty or thirty or forty pupils in her classroom has the mother's need for a conceptual framework for understanding children's behavior, multiplied many times over. The businessman must make sense of what is happening among his workers. The politician must categorize what builds up as public opinion. In order to understand any phenomenon, each of us must first collect and organize the data of experience. As Kant emphasized in his *Critique of Pure Reason*, the human mind is equipped to interpret what we see and hear and experience by developing certain categories that are fundamental to the gaining of knowledge.

THE DEVELOPMENTAL TASK CONCEPT

"A developmental task is a task which arises at or about a certain period in the life of an individual, successful achievement of which

leads to his happiness and to success with later tasks, while failure leads to unhappiness in the individual, disapproval by the society, and difficulty with later tasks." [1] So the developmental task is defined by Robert J. Havighurst, who speaks for the members of the faculty and many others who participated in the workshops through more than a dozen years when the concept was being explored and elaborated at the University of Chicago. The case history of the concept is one of interest to students in the field. [2] In order to learn how to use this intellectual tool, let us look at the phrases that make up the definition, so that the meanings may become clear.

"*A developmental task is a task . . .*" implies that a developmental task is a job-to-be-done, something he should achieve, a responsibility the individual assumes for his development. This puts the burden of development upon the individual in tasks he himself assumes for growing up at any period in his life in his culture.

The next phrase—"*. . . which arises at or about a certain period in the life of the individual—*" recognizes that at some periods of an individual's life certain developmental tasks are especially important because of what is happening in the organism, and in what his world expects of him. At other times, other facets of his personality surge ahead, and the developmental tasks associated with their emergence gain ascendency. A parallel can be drawn between the emergence of developmental tasks and the pattern of development of the physical organs of the embryo. Erik Erikson calls our attention to the point when he says, quoting C. H. Stockard, *The Physical Basis of Personality* (New York: W. W. Norton and Company, Inc., 1931),

In this sequence of development each organ has its time of origin. This time factor is as important as the place of origin. If the eye, for example, does not arise at the appointed time, "it will never be able to express itself fully, since the moment for the rapid outgrowth of some other part will have arrived, and this will tend to dominate the less active region and suppress the belated tendency for eye expression.". . .

The organ which misses its time of ascendency is not only doomed as an entity; it endangers at the same time the whole hierarchy of organs. "Not only does the arrest of a rapidly budding part, therefore, tend to suppress its development temporarily, but the premature loss of supremacy to some other organ

[1] Robert J. Havighurst, *Human Development and Education* (Longmans, Green and Company, 1953), p. 2.
[2] *Ibid.*, pp. 328–332.

renders it impossible for the suppressed part to come again into dominance so that it is permanently modified . . ." The result of normal development is proper relationship of size and function among the body organs: the liver adjusted in size to the stomach and intestine, the heart and lungs properly balanced, and the capacity of the vascular system accurately proportioned to the body as a whole. Through developmental arrest one or more organs may become disproportionally small: this upsets functional harmony and produces a defective person.[1]

The physiological development of the organism suggests the way in which development of the individual-as-a-whole takes place. If a developmental task is not satisfactorily accomplished at its appointed time, it may not be achieved as well later, and its failure may be reflected not only in itself, but in the incomplete fulfillment of related aspects of development.

Illustrations of developmental task failures are numerous. The child that is isolated from other humans at the time it should be learning to talk, never learns to speak as other children do, as the studies already quoted [2] show so clearly. The adolescent who does not establish his autonomy and free himself from his childish dependence on his parents may have difficulty in his social development as a teenager, and may continue to be tied to his parents as a "Mama's boy" even as an adult. The newly wedded man or woman who fails to make an adequate adjustment as husband or wife not only fails to find happiness in the marriage, but finds difficulty also in accomplishing the developmental tasks as a parent in the years that follow.

The phrase—"*successful achievement of which leads to his happiness*" —indicates the bright side of the developmental task concept in the satisfactions that accrue to the individual when he is successful in accomplishing a developmental task. To use the illustrations above in their positive aspects: the little child who learns to talk at the proper time is happy in his ability to communicate and finds pleasure in practicing his speech at every opportunity; the teenager who learns to make his own decisions, to stand on his own feet and to develop more mature forms of affection for his parents finds satisfaction in becoming a man; the young married couple who succeed in achieving their developmental

---

[1] Erik H. Erikson, *Childhood and Society* (New York: W. W. Norton and Company, Inc., 1950), pp. 61–62.
[2] Arnold Gesell, *op. cit.*, and Kingsley Davis, *op. cit.*

tasks as husband and wife find happiness in their marriage, and as parents and grandparents and as persons throughout life.

The phrase—*"and to success with later tasks"*—has been anticipated in our treatment of the ways in which failures to achieve a developmental task at its appointed time leads to difficulties later on. Conversely, successful accomplishment of a developmental task paves the way for the emergence and effective achievement of future developmental tasks. A ready example is that of the girl who learns as an adolescent how to be an autonomous person. Because she has learned to be comfortable with her parents on a mature basis, she is free to love and to be loved. She can win the affection of a suitable mate (granted that she has achieved success in the other developmental tasks that are relevant), and finds fulfillment in marriage as a woman.

The phrase—*"while failure leads to unhappiness of the individual"*— may be illustrated with the plight opposite that of the above illustration. This girl, for one or more reasons, does not successfully accomplish the developmental task of freeing herself from her infantile dependence on her parents. She is unhappy because she has not found herself as a person. She feels that she does not belong to her own generation as do the other young people who achieve more success in this task.

The phrase—*"disapproval by the society"*—indicates the cultural basis of the developmental task in the rewards for success in achievement, and the penalties for failure to accomplish a given developmental task. A common example is found in the child who fails to learn to read with the others of his age and grade. Such a boy or girl feels the disapproval of his teacher, his father, mother and siblings with intensity that depends upon his cultural group. The middle-class family that makes much of educational achievement may be especially anxious about, and severe with, the child who seems to fail in such a basic intellectual accomplishment as reading. A child in such a family may feel rejected by them at this time because of the threat of the conditional love [1] (receiving love only when achieving something desired by parents) that seems to be withdrawn when he does not measure up to their expectations of him.

---

[1] Carson McGuire, "Family Life in Lower and Middle Class Homes," *Marriage and Family Living*, Vol. XIV, No. 1, February 1952, says in discussing this factor, "A conditional element in giving and withholding affection seems to serve to foster striving behavior in members of middle class families . . . It is perpetuated because the 'conditional love' of the parent . . . usually reinforces learning to be responsible, to achieve . . ." (p. 3).

The meaning of the final phrase—*"and difficulty with later tasks"*—should be clear by now. If, for some reason, a developmental task is not satisfactorily achieved at its proper time, the individual presumably will have difficulty with developmental tasks later on. Let us take as an illustration the child who does not satisfactorily learn to read in the first or second grades when his peers are learning this task. Not only does he fail to learn to read competently, but also in so doing, he does not master the basic tool for accomplishing such future tasks as are involved in learning history, literature, social studies, and all such educational and personal areas of life dependent upon reading ability. Furthermore, the feeling of failure engendered in his inadequate efforts to achieve mastery of reading fundamentals quite likely carries over into other tasks with the unfortunate overtones of lack of self-confidence, and proneness to failure, that add further to his difficulties.

ORIGINS OF DEVELOPMENTAL TASKS

Developmental tasks have two primary origins: (1) physical maturation, and (2) cultural pressures and privileges. A secondary origin derived from the first two is found in the aspirations and values of the individual.

As the individual grows, he matures. Growth is much more than just added stature and bulk. It involves the elaboration and maturation of muscle, organ, bone, and neural systems of the organism that develop according to a predictable sequence within the individual. Certain developmental tasks come primarily from the maturation of one or more aspects of the organism. Examples are many. As the infant's leg and back muscles develop strength enough, and the neural connections mature to the place where the child has conscious control over their movement, he faces the developmental task of learning to walk. When the adolescent girl's body develops into one resembling that of a woman and she begins to menstruate, she must come to terms with her femaleness and develop a wholesome acceptance of herself as a woman. Later, when she is in her forties, menopause is a reality that must be met with the new developmental task of accepting the termination of her reproductive life and facing the challenge of aging. And so it is with many other developmental tasks throughout the life of both men and women.

Cultural pressures are seen in the many rewards and penalities the individual receives (and anticipates) for his various behaviors. Society, in

Society in the form of peers, associates, parents, teachers, and all "the significant others" of his life, expects and often puts pressures upon the person to conform to the prescribed ways of behaving within that culture.

the form of peers, associates, parents, teachers, and all "the significant others" of his life, expects and often puts pressures upon the person to conform to the prescribed ways of behaving within that culture. These expectations and pressures emerge at the times believed appropriate in the culture for the individual to function in the roles and statuses assigned to him. Unfortunately they may be too soon or too late for an individual.

By the time a child reaches a certain age, he is expected to eat solid foods, at another age to be toilet trained, at another to walk, at another age to talk, at another to respect property rights, at another to mingle socially with members of the other sex, at another to marry and "settle down," and so on through his entire life span. Regardless of what they are and when they come into effect, these expectancies exert pressures upon the individuals of the culture to behave in certain ways and so are an important origin of his developmental tasks. Examples in our society are: learning to read, learning to handle money responsibly, learning how to gain a place for oneself with one's age-mates, establishing

The child who is loved and knows it has the inner security needed to keep working on his or her developmental tasks.

oneself as an acceptable member of a dating crowd as a teenager, and among the young married set as a husband or wife.

Developmental tasks differ from culture to culture. Each cultural group has its own developmental definitions and expectations. They also vary from region to region in our country, even from class to class in the same area, resulting in many persistent problems among children of different ethnic and cultural backgrounds.

Encouragement and support by family and friends are often essential in achieving developmental tasks that the individual alone might find too difficult. As cultural pressures play upon the maturing organism, the emergent personality is formed with all of its idiosyncratic values and aspirations which themselves then influence greatly the direction and form of future developmental tasks. Two examples of developmental tasks derived primarily from the personal aspirations and values of the individual are choosing a vocation and achieving a personal philosophy of life, which of course are always responsive to the life around the person.

Basically, a developmental task is a thrust from within the individual to develop in such a way as to narrow the discrepancy between his present behavior and what he might achieve. The push to change usually comes from inside the person but may be evoked by others' demands and expectations. It receives its direction from the cultural definition of what is expected of such an individual at his stage of development. A developmental task, while culturally defined, is neither a chore nor a duty, in the sense that it is externally imposed. It is rather a growth responsibility the individual assumes for his own development as he relates himself to his life situation.

The individual's assumption of a given developmental task consists of at least four interrelated operations: (1) perceiving new possibilities for his behavior in what is expected of him or in what he sees others, more mature than he, accomplishing, (2) forming new conceptions of himself (identity formation), (3) coping effectively with conflicting demands upon him, and (4) wanting to achieve the next step in his development enough to work toward it (motivation). To illustrate: a small boy sees somewhat bigger boys riding their bicycles (operation 1—perception); he conceives of himself as a potential bicycle rider (operation 2—identity formation); he resolves the conflicts between his mother's protests that he might get hurt and his own fears of failure with the expectancies of his peers, and the demands of his father that he become "a big boy" (operation 3—coping with conflicting demands); and finally, he wants to learn to ride a bike enough to practice what it takes to become proficient in it (operation 4—motivation).

Most of the growth responsibilities the individual is faced with result from the combined impact of his biologic maturing, the environmental forces that play upon him, and his own personal drives, ambitions, and value orientation. Thus, being weaned results from his physiological maturation (teething, etc.), as well as from the cultural pressures in the form of maternal insistence that he take solid foods and his own desire to be a "big boy" and eat as the others in the family do. Teenage dating emerges partly from the biologic maturing of puberty, partly from the cultural pressures of friends and family to have a girl or boy friend and go out to young people's activities in the community, and partly from the person's own aspiration to belong, to be accepted, to be a recognized member of the younger set in the neighborhood.

THE TEACHABLE MOMENT

When the time comes that the body is ripe for, culture is pressing for, and the individual is striving for some achievement, the teachable moment has arrived. It is at the convergence of the several origins of the developmental task that its accomplishment is most highly motivated, when the individual is most truly *ready for* the next step in his development. Before that the person is not mature enough for the desired outcome, and so efforts to push him through a premature accomplishment may be largely wasted. Readiness also implies that the person has lived fully at his present stage and so is not being hurried into the next stage.

An illustration is found in the early efforts to toilet train an infant. In the 1920's and 1930's, this training was often attempted while the baby was but a few weeks old. At that age, his sphincters were not ready for such control, his neural connections were not matured enough to make possible his cooperation, and his own aspirations were in quite another direction. It is not surprising to find that these precocious demands of the parent upon the child met with failure and often created persistent conflict. Knowledge of child development has modified these expectancies, and today good practice is to wait for signs that the baby is ready for toilet training before assisting him to achieve the task. This concept of readiness is well established in the field of human development.

The concept of the teachable moment goes a bit deeper in indicating specifically the three dimensions in which readiness emerges—in the physical organism, in the social pressures, and in the personal values of the individual. It has importance for anyone responsible for the growth, development, and guidance of others: teachers, supervisors, parents, indeed anyone who works with, or cares about, other people. For it gives a gauge of what we expect of given persons and at what time we may anticipate change. This ability to predict what persons at various stages of development are, or soon will be, ready for is of paramount importance to curriculum formulators, and educators in general. If we assume that the general purpose of both family life and education is to assist the individual to grow up to his own best potential, we see that some knowledge of developmental tasks and especially of the teachable moments at which these tasks arise is highly relevant.

There is a tide in the affairs of men,
Which, taken at the flood, leads on to fortune;
Omitted, all the voyage of their life
Is bound in shallows and in miseries.
SHAKESPEARE, *Julius Caesar*, IV, 3.

Let us review quickly the concept *developmental task*, by indicating specifically just what is and what is not included. Teething is not a developmental task because it occurs automatically without the participation of the person. Learning to eat solid food *is* a developmental task, because it involves the active assumption of responsibility for eating on the part of the child. Menstruating is a purely biological phenomenon, while learning what it means to be a woman is a developmental task. In other words, the developmental task implies the assumption of responsibility for accomplishment on the part of the person. His talents, his biologic machinery, and his inheritance, are all part of his "givens" with which he attempts to achieve the tasks of growing up.

PRINCIPLES WHICH MAY BE DERIVED FROM THE DEVELOPMENTAL TASK CONCEPT

1) Every growing person faces certain responsibilities of growing up at every stage of his life as man or woman, adult or child.
2) A person must accomplish the developmental tasks of any given period in his development if he is to grow on to the next level of his maturation.
3) Growth responsibilities are so urgent and insistent, they take precedence over outside pressures.
4) No one else can accomplish for the individual the developmental tasks that he faces.
5) Very few developmental tasks can be mastered in isolation.
6) A teacher or parent who encourages and assists a child accomplish his developmental tasks, helps to promote the child's development.

The developmental task concept is helpful in understanding a given individual's behavior by indicating fruitful aspects for investigation in his success or failure in the tasks of his developmental level, as well as the contributing factors. Furthermore, the developmental task concept enables prediction of behavior in general by foretelling the readiness of groups and of individuals of certain developmental levels living within certain cultural settings, and functioning within certain general value orientations.

CHART 7.   Developmental Tasks in 10 Categories

	INFANCY (Birth to 1 or 2)	EARLY CHILDHOOD (2–3 to 5–6–7)	LATE CHILDHOOD (5–6–7 to pubescence)
I *Achieving an appropriate dependence-independence pattern*	1. Establishing one's self as a very dependent being 2. Beginning the establishment of self-awareness	1. Adjusting to less private attention; becoming independent physically (while remaining strongly dependent emotionally)	1. Freeing one's self from primary identification with adults
II *Achieving an appropriate giving-receiving pattern of affection*	1. Developing a feeling for affection	1. Developing the ability to give affection 2. Learning to share affection	1. Learning to give as much love as one receives; forming friendships with peers
III *Relating to changing social groups*	1. Becoming aware of the alive as against the inanimate, and the familiar as against the unfamiliar 2. Developing rudimentary social-interaction	1. Beginning to develop the ability to interact with age-mates 2. Adjusting in the family to expectations it has for the child as a member of the social unit	1. Clarifying the adult world as over against the child's world 2. Establishing peer group-ness and learning to belong
IV *Developing a conscience*	1. Beginning to adjust to the expectations of others	1. Developing the ability to take directions and to be obedient in the presence of authority 2. Developing the ability to be obedient in the absence of authority where conscience substitutes for authority	1. Learning more rules and developing true morality
V *Learning one's psycho-socio-biological sex role*		1. Learning to identify with male adult and female adult roles	1. Beginning to identify with one's social contemporaries of the same sex
VI *Accepting and Adjusting to a changing body*	1. Adjusting to adult feeding demands 2. Adjusting to adult cleanliness demands 3. Adjusting to adult attitudes toward genital manipulation	1. Adjusting to expectations resulting from one's improving muscular abilities 2. Developing sex modesty	
VII *Managing a changing body and learning new motor patterns*	1. Developing physiological equilibrium 2. Developing eye-hand co-ordination 3. Establishing satisfactory rhythms of rest and activity	1. Developing large muscle control 2. Learning to co-ordinate large muscles and small muscles	1. Refining and elaborating skill in the use of small muscles
VIII *Learning to understand and control the physical world*	1. Exploring the physical world	1. Meeting adult expectations for restrictive exploration and manipulation of an expanding environment	1. Learning more realistic ways of studying and controlling the physical world
IX *Developing an appropriate symbol system and conceptual abilities*	1. Developing preverbal communication 2. Developing verbal communication 3. Rudimentary concept formation	1. Improving one's use of the symbol system 2. Enormous elaboration of the concept pattern	1. Learning to use language actually to exchange ideas or to influence one's hearers 2. Beginning understanding of real causal relations 3. Making finer conceptual distinctions and thinking reflectively
X *Relating one's self to the cosmos*		1. Developing a genuine, tho uncritical, notion about one's place in the cosmos	1. Developing a scientific approach

of Behavior of the Individual from Birth to Death

EARLY ADOLESCENCE (pubescence to puberty)	LATE ADOLESCENCE (puberty to early maturity)	MATURITY (early to late active adulthood)	AGING (beyond full powers of adulthood through senility)
1. Establishing one's independence from adults in all areas of behavior	1. Establishing one's self as an independent individual in an adult manner	1. Learning to be interdependent—now leaning, now succoring others as need arises. 2. Assisting one's children to become gradually independent and autonomous beings	1. Accepting graciously and comfortably the help needed from others as powers fail, and dependence becomes necessary
1. Accepting one's self as a worthwhile person really worthy of love	1. Building a strong mutual affectional bond with a (possible) marriage partner	1. Building and maintaining a strong and mutually satisfying marriage relationship 2. Establishing wholesome affectional bonds with one's children and grandchildren 3. Meeting wisely the new needs for affection of one's own aging parents 4. Cultivating meaningfully warm friendships with members of one's own generation	1. Facing loss of one's spouse, and finding some satisfactory sources of affection previously received from mate 2. Learning new affectional roles with own children, now mature adults 3. Establishing ongoing satisfying affectional patterns with grandchildren, and other members of the extended family 4. Finding and preserving mutually satisfying friendships outside the family circle
1. Behaving according to a shifting peer code	1. Adopting an adult-patterned set of social values by learning a new peer code	1. Keeping within reasonable balance activities in the various social, service, political, and community groups and causes that make demands upon mature adults 2. Establishing and maintaining mutually satisfactory relationships with the in-law families of spouse and married children	1. Choosing and maintaining ongoing social activities and functions appropriate to health, energy, and interests
	1. Learning to verbalize contradictions in moral codes, as well as discrepancies between principle and practice, and resolving these problems in a responsible manner	1. Coming to terms with the violations of moral codes in the larger as well as in the more intimate social scene, and developing some constructive philosophy and method of operation. 2. Helping children adjust to the expectations of others and to conform to the moral demands of the culture	1. Maintaining a sense of moral integrity in the face of disappointments and disillusionments in life's hopes and dreams
1. Strong identification with one's own sex mates 2. Learning one's role in heterosexual relationships	1. Exploring possibilities for a future mate and acquiring "desirability" 2. Choosing an occupation 3. Preparing to accept one's future role in manhood or womanhood as a responsible citizen of the larger community	1. Learning to be a competent husband or wife, and building a good marriage 2. Carrying a socially adequate role as citizen and worker in the community 3. Becoming a good parent and grandparent as children arrive and develop	1. Learning to live on a retirement income 2. Being a good companion to an aging spouse 3. Meeting bereavement of spouse adequately
1. Reorganizing one's thoughts and feelings about one's self in the face of significant bodily changes and their concomitants 2. Accepting the reality of one's appearance	1. Learning appropriate outlets for sexual drives	1. Making a good sex adjustment within marriage 2. Establishing healthful routines of eating, resting, working, playing within the pressures of adult world	1. Making a good adjustment to failing powers as aging diminishes strengths and abilities
1. Controlling and using a "new" body		1. Learning the new motor skills involved in housekeeping, gardening, sports, and other activities expected of adults in the community	1. Adapting interests and activities to reserves of vitality and energy of the aging body
		1. Gaining intelligent understanding of new horizons of medicine and science sufficient for personal well-being and social competence	1. Mastering new awareness and methods of dealing with physical surroundings as an individual with occasional or permanent disabilities
1. Using language to express and to clarify more complex concepts 2. Moving from the concrete to the abstract and applying general principles to the particular	1. Achieving the level of reasoning of which one is capable	1. Mastering technical symbol systems involved in income tax, social security, complex financial dealings and other contexts familiar to Western man	1. Keeping mentally alert and effective as long as is possible through the later years
	1. Formulating a workable belief and value system	1. Formulating and implementing a rational philosophy of life on the basis of adult experience 2. Cultivating a satisfactory religious climate in the home as the spiritual soil for development of family members	1. Preparing for eventual and inevitable cessation of life by building a set of beliefs that one can live and die with, in peace

Source: An elaboration of Caroline Tryon and Jesse W. Lilienthal III, "Guideposts in Child Growth and Development," *NEA Journal*, March 1950, p., 189.

DEVELOPMENTAL TASKS OF THE INDIVIDUAL
THROUGH HIS LIFE HISTORY

The developmental tasks an individual faces through the years of his life from birth to death are innumerable. It would be impossible to completely list all of the growth responsibilities to be achieved by any one person. Yet, there are certain general categories of tasks that make possible a cataloging of the more common developmental tasks within our culture. Such a formulation is found on pages 108 and 109 in an elaboration of one developed originally by Caroline Tryon and Jesse W. Lilienthal III.

This outline is used as being illustrative of the kind of developmental tasks to be achieved by individuals in the various periods of the life history. It is not a catalog of those to be considered in more detail in the chapters that follow but is rather one frame of reference that may prove to be of value to those students interested in further elaborating the development of the conceptual tool. Study of this outline of the individual's developmental tasks from birth to death in ten categories of human behavior perhaps best summarizes the discussion of the nature of developmental tasks.

Such a listing of the individual's developmental tasks is not all-inclusive, nor is it universally applicable. Different cultures and subcultures make different demands upon their members. In most of the cultures of the world today, the general expectancies change from time to time, so that the developmental tasks of one generation differ somewhat from those of the preceding or of the succeeding one.

Whatever the society in which the individual grows up, he faces the developmental tasks peculiar to it at every stage of his life span. The successful achievement of his developmental tasks brings the individual from a state of helpless dependence as an infant, through varying dimensions of independence as an adolescent, to a mature level of interdependence with his fellowman that lasts through the greater part of adulthood.

INTERACTING DEVELOPMENTAL TASKS OF FAMILY MEMBERS

This progression is not regular and all-of-a-piece. At any moment, children are striving to meet their growth needs, parents to reconcile conflicting demands, and each individual to find himself within the security and threats of his world.

At times members of the family mutually support and sustain one another. During certain stages of the family life cycle, the developmental tasks of both children and parents call for the same general direction of energies, so that the family moves as a unit toward the meeting of the developmental requirements of each member. Such a time comes when the children are established in school and daily bring home to their parents the stimuli and broadened horizons that both mother and father are striving for as mature adults at the school-age stage of the family life cycle.

Just as "naturally," upon occasion, the goals, needs, strivings, and developmental tasks of family members are in conflict. If we hold the entire family in focus, we see that many of the normal tangles of members during the family's life cycle are due to incompatibility of the diverse developmental strivings of family members at critical points of growth.

From time to time the developmental tasks of the husband may conflict with those of his wife. A simple illustration is found in the young husband's developmental tasks of developing competency with his do-it-yourself projects that clutter up the house at the time when his wife is trying to maintain a pleasant, attractive home amid the already heavy demands of infants and small children.

Developmental tasks of children conflict with those of their parents at several stages in the family life cycle. In adolescence the young person is struggling to emancipate himself or herself from the authority of the parents, whose own developmental tasks as parents call for sustained guidance and supervision of the not-yet-adult child. At such a time, storms brew and break within the family as normally as they do in the weather, when two or more energy systems moving in opposite directions collide.

Now unified, now atomized, each family lives out its own unique history in pulsing, throbbing rhythms and everchanging tempos. Each family is an arena of interacting personalities, each trying to achieve his own developmental tasks within the pattern of family life that in turn is evolving in interaction with the larger society of which it is a part.

Most developmental tasks of most persons, as children and as adults, are worked out within the family through their lifetimes. The modern family assumes as one of its primary functions that of becoming a place that is good to grow in for its several members. So families, as families,

The mother, father, and son that we see pictured here appear to be enjoying together the musical interest that they share in common. Such experiences are growth-promoting for each member of the family.

can be seen to have responsibilities, goals and developmental tasks that are specifically related to the development of their members. All these developmental tasks of both family members and families-as-a-whole shift as the family changes and are constantly being modified by the interplay of forces both within and without the family in every society, in every age.

FAMILY DEVELOPMENTAL TASKS

What the developmental tasks of any given family are, is difficult to enumerate. Families differ one from another in many, many ways as we have already seen in preceding chapters. However, just as it is possible to predict, in general, the developmental tasks of an individual at any given developmental level, so too, we can describe, in general, the family developmental tasks of American families through the family life cycle.

In much the same way that developmental tasks of the individual change as he grows and develops, so families face the developmental tasks required for each stage of the family life cycle. According to structure-function theory,[1] every group must achieve certain cultural prerequisites in order to survive, continue, and grow. The family as a human group is seen to be faced with nine such central urgencies, which are listed and elaborated in the chapters that follow as family developmental tasks—those predictable growth responsibilities faced by the family-as-a-whole at every stage of its development.

As the family grows, each member must assume additional roles in order to relate and communicate with each other member who expects such individualized recognition, response, and opportunity for specific interpersonal relations. For instance, loving means investing others with meaning and lovableness, which operates to evoke more lovableness, thereby creating a virtuous circle of mutual generosity.[2]

The size of the family increases by arithmetic progression: first two persons as husband and wife marry and settle down to establish a family, then three as the first baby comes, then four with the second sibling, and so on as long as the family grows in size. The complexity of family

[1] See Chapter Fifteen and p. 521 of the Historical Footnote.
[2] Lawrence K. Frank, "On Loving," Ashley Montagu, ed., *The Meaning of Love* (New York: The Julian Press, Inc., 1953), pp. 25–45.

relationships increases much more rapidly, according to the "Law of Family Interaction." Bossard states the law as follows:

> With the addition of each person to a family or primary group, the number of persons increases in the simplest arithmetical progression in whole numbers, while the number of personal interrelationships within the group increases in the order of triangular numbers.[1]

To find the number of interpersonal relationships within a family, the following formula is used (x equals number of interpersonal relationships, and y equals the number of persons):

$$x = \frac{y^2 - y}{2}$$

Applying this formula to a specific family, the following series emerges:

Number of persons in the family	2	3	4	5	6	7	8	9	and so forth
Number of relationships in the family	1	3	6	10	15	21	28	36	and so forth

Thus we see that a family consisting of a father, mother, and three children, has a total of five individuals, with a total of ten interpersonal relationships: father with mother, father with first child, father with second child, father with third child; mother with first child, mother with second child, mother with third child; first child with second child, first child with third child; second child with third child. Dynamically, the number of interrelationships within that family may be even more in the coalitions that form from time to time with small inner groups seeing themselves as a unit as opposed to all other members of the family. It is common, for instance, in a three-child family for two children to form a tight little dyad that functions almost as another entity within the family group. Not infrequently, the children line up as opposed to the parents in still another interrelationship along generational lines. The conclusion to be drawn is that as the family grows in size its interpersonal relationships multiply even more rapidly; and conversely, when the family contracts in size in the launching stage of the family life cycle, the number of persons leaving the home is not as large as the decrease in the number of interrelationships.

This phenomenon was seen graphically by the Work Group on Family Development Research, of the Interdisciplinary Workshop on

---

[1] James H. S. Bossard, "The Law of Family Interaction," *American Journal of Sociology*," January, 1945, p. 292, copyright 1945, University of Chicago.

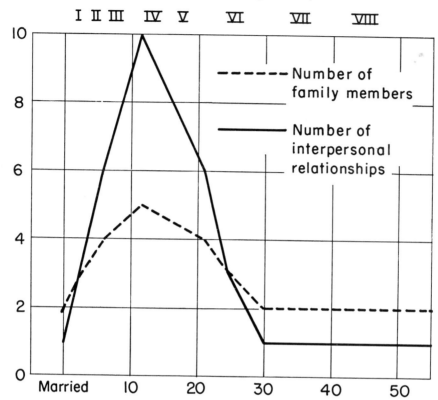

CHART 8. Schematic Profile of Complexity of Family Interaction through Life of a Three-Child Family (*The horizontal columns indicate Stages in the Family Life Cycle and the number of years married. The vertical column indicates the number of family members and interpersonal relationships.*) [1]

Marriage and Family Research, under the direction of the author, at the University of Chicago in 1950.[2] Chart 8, an adaptation of the graph prepared by that Work Group, shows the complexity of intrafamily interaction by stages in the family life cycle. The ordinate of the graph shows the complexity of intrafamily interaction measured by the formula

[1] P. K. Whelpton and Clyde V. Kiser, *Social and Psychological Factors Affecting Fertility*, (New York: Milbank Memorial-Fund, 1950), Table 6, p. 224; and Gerald R. Leslie, Harold T. Christensen and Glenn L. Pearman, "Studies in Child Spacing: IV. The Time-Interval Separating all Children in Completed Families of Purdue University Graduates," *Social Forces*, Vol. 34, No. 1, October, 1955, p. 80.
[2] Reuben Hill, "Interdisciplinary Workshop on Marriage and Family Research," *Marriage and Family Living*, Vol. XIII, No. 1, February 1951, pp. 21 and 22.

$x = \dfrac{y^2 - y}{2}$, in which x equals the number of interpersonal relationships,

and y equals the number of persons. The graph is designed to serve as a bold outline of the changing profile of complexity of interaction in the family through its life cycle.

SUCCESSFUL FAMILIES

Successful families may be defined as those that (1) encourage and assist their members in the achievement of their individual developmental tasks, and (2) effectively accomplish the appropriate family developmental tasks at every stage of the family life cycle.

According to this definition, a family is succeeding when its members, adult and child, male and female, are getting the support, the acceptance, and the opportunities for working through the developmental tasks they each must achieve in order to move on competently into the next stage of their development; and when the family-as-a-whole is meeting effectively the developmental tasks of its present developmental level.

Just as individuals sometimes succeed and sometimes fail in accomplishing one or more of their developmental tasks, so families too at times move smoothly and effectively and at other times find the going rough. In much the same way that individuals find their developmental tasks more easily achieved when success has met their efforts in the past, so families too, find that success leads to further success, while failure tends to increase the difficulty of the tasks that lie ahead.

No one expects perfection either in an individual or a family. Even a champion ballplayer does not bat a thousand. Moving through a complete life cycle with its many confusing, sometimes conflicting, and always complex developmental task patterns within a family poses a persistent challenge to families everywhere. For families in America today, in the midst of revolutionary social change, where the ways of the past no longer are completely appropriate, there are hazards that greatly increase the difficulties of successful developmental task achievement. No wonder so many families taste the bitter bread of failure from time to time.

The successful family today is a flexible group of persons with the courage to innovate and the willingness to explore new possibilities in the accomplishment of its growth responsibilities and those of its members. When the family functions are in terms of raising sturdy mature personalities, capable of withstanding the stresses and strains of modern living and contributing creatively to society, the developmental task concept has special relevance. Families that competently achieve their developmental tasks today find life deep-down good as they tap a new dimension of the human spirit.

SUMMARY

Concepts help us categorize experience and to make sense of a multitude of particulars. The developmental task concept is especially helpful to the person who must make sense of human behavior. A developmental task is defined as a responsibility for growing up that arises at or about a certain period in the life of an individual, successful achievement of which leads to his happiness and to success with later tasks, while failure leads to unhappiness in the individual, disapproval by the society, and difficulty with other tasks.

Developmental tasks originate in the biologic maturing of the individual, and the cultural pressures and opportunities that play upon him. As cultural pressures play upon the maturing individual, his personality emerges with the personal aspirations and values that further influence and give direction to his developmental tasks. A developmental task is a thrust from within the individual to narrow the discrepancy between his present behavior and what he might achieve. Operationally, the individual's assumption of a given developmental task consists of (1) perception of new possibilities, (2) identity formation in the new direction, (3) coping with conflicting demands, and (4) motivation sufficient to assume the task. The developmental tasks of the individual have been outlined from birth to death in ten major categories of human behavior. The developmental tasks of the various members of the family interact so that sometimes they are in conflict and sometimes they mutually support each other.

Family developmental tasks are those responsibilities for survival, growth, and development assumed by the family as a whole as it moves stage by stage through the family life cycle. The intensity of family interaction increases more rapidly than does family size, according to the law of family interaction. Thus we see graphically the bulging profile of family member interaction through the family life cycle, as complexity builds up as the family grows, and diminishes as the family ages. Successful families are those which encourage their members in the achievement

No one expects a perfect score either for the individual or the family. The game of life is well played when both the family and its various members find satisfaction in growth and development.

of their individual developmental tasks, and effectively are accomplishing their family developmental tasks. This is a big order today in which many families fail. Its challenge is so important and its rewards so sweet, it may be seen as the new frontier of twentieth century mankind.

SUGGESTED ACTIVITIES

1) Write a paper outlining several of the developmental tasks that you are attempting to accomplish at this period of your life. Document each developmental task with comments on its origins in terms of biologic maturation, cultural pressure and personal aspirations. Illustrate with anecdotal material and appraise roughly the degrees of success and failure you are finding in each developmental task.

2) Compare the concept of "the principle of readiness" with that of "the teachable moment." In what ways do the two support one another? What are the differences between the two concepts?

3) Write a review of some book of family fiction, biography, or drama with special attention to the ways in which the developmental tasks of the several family members depicted mutually support or conflict with each other.

4) Make a chart outline of *The Fourposter* by Jan de Hartog (Random House, 1952) indicating developmental tasks of various family members by stages of the family life cycle depicted. Illustrate with quotations, and document when needed from primary sources.

5) Using the Law of Family Interaction, calculate the number of interpersonal relationships of your family of orientation, list each by name, and illustrate the types of interaction usual in each combination, as you remember it.

6) Role play a situation illustrating the phrase, "Each family may be seen as an arena of interacting personalities, each trying to meet his own basic needs within the pattern of family life."

7) Support or refute the statement, "Parents, who themselves have urgent needs, make most of the adjustments in building complementary roles between themselves and their children." Would your conclusion be the same at an earlier stage in the family life cycle? In a later stage?

8) Write a paper on the ways in which social class differences manifest themselves in developmental task differences at various stages of the family life cycle.

READINGS

Bennett, John W., and Tumin, Melvin M., *Social Life* (New York: Alfred Knopf, 1948), Chapter 4, "Functional Prerequisites."

Blalock, Ann, "Introduction to a Study of the Theory of Family Development," Master's thesis, University of North Carolina, Chapel Hill, N. C., 1955, Chapter 1, "A Conceptual Scheme for Looking at the Family as a Small Group."

Blood, Robert O., Jr., "Contributions from Structure Function Sociology to a Conceptual Framework for Family Analysis," unpublished manuscript.

Bossard, James H. S., and Boll, Eleanor S., *Family Situations* (Philadelphia: University of Pennsylvania Press, 1943).

Bossard, James H. S., and Boll, Eleanor S., "Personality Roles in the Large Family," *Child Development*, Vol. 26, No. 1, March 1955, pp. 71–78.

Bossard, James H. S., *The Sociology of Child Development* (New York: Harper & Brothers, Revised Edition, 1954).

Child Study Association of America, "Living and Growing with Our Children: Impact on Parents of Children's Growth Phases," *Child Study*, Vol. XXXII, No. 3, Summer 1955 issue.

Duvall, Evelyn Millis, "Changing Roles in the Family Life Cycle," *Journal of Home Economics*, Vol. 42, No. 6, June 1950, pp. 435–436.

Duvall, Evelyn Millis, and Hill, Reuben, eds., *The Dynamics of Family Interaction*. Mimeographed materials for the National Conference on Family Life, Washington, 1948.

Erikson, Erik H., *Childhood and Society* (New York: W. W. Norton, Inc., 1950), especially Chapter 7, "Eight Stages of Man."

Erikson, Erik H., "Growth and Crises of the Healthy Personality," *Symposium on the Healthy Personality*, M. J. E. Senn, ed. (New York: The Josiah Macy, Jr., Foundation, 1950).

Frank, Lawrence K., *Nature and Human Nature* (New Brunswick, New Jersey: Rutgers University Press, 1951).

Godfrey, Eleanor, "A Construction of Family Typologies and Their Initial Verification," Ph.D. dissertation, Radcliffe College, June 1951.

Havighurst, Robert J., *Developmental Tasks and Education* (Chicago: The University of Chicago Press, 1948).

————, *Human Development and Education* (New York: Longmans, Green and Co., 1953).

Hill, Reuben, "Interdisciplinary Workshop on Marriage and Family Research," *Marriage and Family Living*, Vol. XIII, No. 1, February 1951, pp. 13–28.

Parsons, Talcott, and Bales, Robert F., *Family, Socialization and Interaction Process* (Glencoe, Illinois: The Free Press, 1955).

Prescott, Daniel A., *Emotion and the Educative Process* (Washington, D. C.: American Council on Education, 1938).

Stott, Leland H., "The Problem of Evaluating Family Success," *Marriage and Family Living*, Vol. XIII, No. 4, Fall 1951, pp. 149–153.

Tryon, Caroline, and Lilienthal, Jesse W., III, "Guideposts in Child Growth and Development," *NEA Journal*, March 1950, pp. 188–189.

PART 2

Expanding families

Families begin at marriage and with the coming of children, families grow both in size and in complexity of interaction. What are children trying to accomplish—as infants, as preschoolers, as schoolagers, and as teenagers? How do families change as children grow up? And, in what ways do family members sometimes complement and sometimes conflict with each other in what they are trying to become?

To have and to hold from this day
*   forward,*
For better, for worse, for richer,
*   for poorer,*
In sickness, and in health, to love
*   and to cherish,*
Till death us do part.
      Book of Common Prayer

Beginning families: establishment phase

From the time a couple marries until their first baby is born is Stage I of the family life cycle as defined in Chapter One. For the sake of clarity in discussion of the many developmental tasks, Stage I is divided into the Establishment Phase (Chapter Six) and the Expectant Phase (Chapter Seven).

The establishment phase of the beginning family starts with the couple at marriage and continues until they become aware of the fact that the wife is pregnant. This may be a period of some months or years. It may last for the duration of the marriage as in the home of childless couples. It may be a brief phase of only a few weeks. Or, it may completely overlap the expectant phase as happens when the woman is already pregnant at marriage. Although premarital pregnancy is not in keeping with the mores, it occurs not infrequently, as Christensen finds in his study of the spacing of the first birth from marriage in a sample of 1,531 families in Tippecanoe County, Indiana, where he reports a conservative estimate of about one-fifth of all first births conceived before marriage.[1] When marriage occurs after the first pregnancy is already begun, the couple faces the developmental tasks of both the establishment and the expectant phase of Stage I concurrently.

[1] Harold T. Christensen, "Studies in Child Spacing: I—Premarital Pregnancy as Measured by the Spacing of the First Birth from Marriage," *American Sociological Review*, Vol. 18, No. 1, February 1953, pp. 53–59.

ORIGINS OF DEVELOPMENTAL TASKS
OF THE EARLY-MARRIED COUPLE

The developmental tasks of the newly married couple arise in both the husband and wife first out of their physiological maturation, with its adult drives for ongoing sexual fulfillment. The second origin of the developmental tasks of the newly married couple is found in the cultural expectations and pressures for the married pair to settle down and behave as married couples are supposed to in the given community. Thirdly, the man and woman are moved by their own personal aspirations to establish their marriage according to the dreams that both of them have built through the years.

The multiple nature of the origins of the developmental tasks at this stage makes for some difficulties in itself. What the culture expects and what the young couple want do not always coincide, especially in this day and age. What the realities of the situation are and what the married pair dream of as right for them are rarely identical. The young woman who has built up extravagant ideas of what she must have at the time she marries may be disappointed when hers does not turn out to be a fashionable wedding or a modern home correct to the latest detail. The dreams of the husband and wife may mesh in many respects, but be miles apart in others. Being married first of all involves coming to terms with what is expected—by one's culture, by one's mate, by oneself, and as a couple.

COMPLEMENTARY AND CONFLICTING DEVELOPMENTAL
TASKS OF HUSBAND AND WIFE

At the time of their marriage, the husband is attempting to achieve his developmental tasks as a young adult male, while his wife is concurrently working out her growth responsibilities as a young adult female. The young man must learn what it means to be a young adult, with young adult responsibilities in his home and community. He must learn what is expected of him as a husband, and what it means to be a married man. By the time his first baby is on the way, he is faced with the task of defining his role as a father and of becoming a parent. Simultaneously, the young wife is learning what it means to be a wife, a young married woman both in her home and in the community, and what becoming a mother involves. Sometimes the developmental tasks of husband and wife complement and mutually support each other. At other times the efforts

The bride and groom each have personal aspirations to establish their marriage according to the dreams that both of them have built through the years.

of one conflict with those of the other. This is the nature of the dynamics of interaction in marriage and family living, as is suggested in the following items.

Some Contemporary Developmental Tasks of the Young Husband	*Some Contemporary Developmental Tasks of the Young Wife*	*Complementary and Conflicting Possibilities*
Becoming established in an occupation Getting specialized training Assuming responsibility for getting and holding a job. Working toward security and advancement in his work	Making a home and managing the household Getting settled in a home Establishing and maintaining household routines Learning the many skills of homemaking and housework	Complementary (Shared responsibility in homemaking) Conflicting (Husband engrossed in work away from home, while wife tries to elicit his active cooperation in homemaking)

Some Contemporary Developmental Tasks of the Young Husband	*Some Contemporary Developmental Tasks of the Young Wife*	*Complementary and Conflicting Possibilities*
Assuming responsibility for the support of his family Earning the family income Planning for the long pull of family support through the years	Becoming a financial helpmate in establishing the home Working until her husband is established Seeing her work as secondary and temporary	Complementary (Both are economic partners through establishment phase) Conflicting (Her work threatens his status as bread winner)
Fulfilling his military service requirements Choosing the time for service Juggling educational, marital, occupational plans with the demands of military service Absenting himself from home for the duration of his service	Maintaining a home base with her husband in service Deciding where and how to live while he is away Keeping a sense of being married during her husband's absence Continuing educational, vocational, and family activities after her marriage	Conflicting (Husband is pulled away from home, while wife's efforts are in maintaining unity and integrity of home through their separation)
Establishing mutually satisfying sex relationships Awakening his wife sexually Developing competency as a husband	Becoming a satisfactory sex partner Learning her sex role as wife Responding effectively and participating in their mutual fulfillment	Complementary (Each has the task of communicating intimately with the other)
Becoming "domesticated" as a married man Sharing leisure time with his wife Developing mutual interests Cultivating joint activities Getting into the young married set	Assuming hostess and companionship roles as a married woman Planning for recreational activities as a couple Accepting and refusing social invitations Entertaining their friends and associates	Complementary (Both husband and wife are learning to move in tandem in their social life as a couple)

The distinction should be made between the conflict of developmental tasks of the husband and wife and conflict arising out of the couple's difficulties in accomplishing their tasks. The young wife may be ineffectual as a sex partner at first, experiencing some degree of sex conflict with her husband. But, in such a case, it is not the developmental tasks of the husband and wife that conflict. It is rather the husband's inexpertness or the wife's difficulties in working through the complementarity of sex roles that result in their conflict as sex partners. The husband may find it hard to become socially "domesticated," involving some marital conflict, but his task in this direction complements his wife's.

There are some complementary and some conflicting aspects in many of the developmental tasks of husband and wife. When the two people are drawn together in mutually supportive ways as they work on their individual developmental tasks, we see those tasks as complementary. When the working through of their tasks as husband and wife tend to pull the couple in opposite directions, the tasks are conflicting. The difference is in the lines of force, in the pull toward or away from the other. In conflicting developmental tasks the lines of force between the pair oppose and repel. In complementary tasks the lines of force pull the two together and operate toward unity, as we see in Chart 9.

Conflicting developmental tasks:

Complementary developmental tasks:

Developmental tasks with both conflicting and complementary aspects:

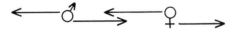

CHART 9. Conflicting and Complementary Developmental Tasks

GOALS OF THE DEVELOPMENTAL TASKS OF
RECENTLY MARRIED COUPLES

No matter how adequate the courtship and the engagement period (see Chapter Twelve), the two people who come together in marriage have much to learn about each other, and about what it means to be married. The primary goal of the period is to make of the two persons a married couple in the many aspects of living. At the end of this phase, the marriage should be relatively well established as a working and workable unit.

Adjusting to living as a married couple involves many secondary goals in terms of fulfilling the basic requirements for housing; money; sexual, emotional and intellectual communication; division of responsibilities; relationships both as individuals and as a couple, with both families, friends, job associates, community organizations and religious affiliations; the anticipation of children; and the development of a workable philosophy of life. These goals must be satisfactorily met in the establishment phase if the family is to become a stable ongoing unit. The meeting of these goals requires the accomplishment of the developmental tasks of the period.

THE DEVELOPMENTAL TASKS OF THE
ESTABLISHMENT PHASE

The developmental tasks of beginning families are basic for the establishment of the family. Although they differ from family to family, from class to class, and from culture to culture, they may be listed in their more general aspects as follows:

1) establishing a home base in a place to call their own
2) establishing mutually satisfactory systems for getting and spending money
3) establishing mutually acceptable patterns of who does what and who is accountable to whom
4) establishing a continuity of mutually satisfying sex relationships
5) establishing systems of intellectual and emotional communication
6) establishing workable relationships with relatives
7) establishing ways of interacting with friends, associates, and community organizations
8) facing the possibility of children and planning for their coming
9) establishing a workable philosophy of life as a couple.

How couples go about accomplishing these developmental tasks is a long and interesting story that never can be completely told. Some of the variables in our society, found in working through the developmental tasks of the establishment phase, are discussed in the sections that follow.

ESTABLISHING A HOME BASE TO CALL THEIR OWN

One of the first questions a couple considering the possibilities of marriage faces is, "Where will we live?" If they are still in school or college, they may explore the resources for married students living near the campus. If the boy is soon to leave for military service, they consider where the wife will live while the husband puts in his time for Uncle Sam. The girl may remain at home with her parents, seeing her service-bound husband only on furloughs and leaves. She may make her home with his parents. She may follow her man, going from camp community to camp community and making a home base as best she can close to her husband for as long as she can. "Home" may be a dozen different spots in the first year or two of marriage, in any of the places they call their own during the period.

Couples with both schooling and military service out of the way find more stability in their home base as they choose the place where they can settle down and invest themselves and their resources in making a real home. At first this probably will be a rented place near their work and possibly near friends and family. It may be a furnished room or two for the couple marrying "on a shoe string," or a commodious house or apartment for the more affluent. Newly married members of the upper class sometimes move into a new house completely furnished for them by one or both of their families, but this is rare. Most couples must together puzzle out their homemaking plans from the possibilities at hand and the promises ahead.

ESTABLISHING MUTUALLY SATISFACTORY SYSTEMS
FOR GETTING AND SPENDING MONEY

At the time of first marriage, the husband is usually young, inexperienced, and so relatively poorly paid. Yet the needs and wants and dreams of the young couple call for more money than will be available to them for some time. A successful family in the eyes of the midtwentieth century man or woman, is one able to buy not only the necessities of life in terms of shelter, food, and clothing but also such important "extras" as education, preventive medical care, leisure time activities, and cultural opportunities. The source of much of the trouble in "making ends meet" among young married couples stems from the incongruity between the sales pressures they are under and the realities in the nature of things. Few newly married couples can meet the magazine advertisement standards for the modern American kitchen, living room, or neighborhood. Today's high-priced household equipment is either inaccessible to the vast majority of young married couples or can be made available only at the sacrifice of more children, future financial security, and peace of mind.

Everybody accuses everybody else of "keeping up with the Joneses," but despite protestations almost no one wholly escapes it. For the young married pair in America most financial problems do not involve a struggle to secure the bare biological essentials of life or even the conventional comforts. The "squeeze" comes in trying to get those things which one is almost forced to want, not to meet his own needs but to meet those superimposed desires related to what is usually called one's "social position." Husband and wife feel they *need* a car, club membership, or a home in the "better part" of town, not so much because they need these things intrinsically, but rather that they are under pressure to display evidence of their success to their friends, business associates, and in-laws, who may be better established or simply more lucky.

Trouble arises from the tempting expedients the family is induced to use in its sometimes frantic efforts "to live beyond its means." Radio, newspapers, television, and neon signs remind one hourly that everything he wants can be bought for a fraction down and a ridiculously small amount per week. There are no singing commercials to remind the family novitiate that these ridiculously small weekly payments on home, car, dental fees, fur coat, radio, bedroom suite, and dream kitchen quickly add up what the hard-headed New England forefather would call "paying for a dead horse."

To be sure, some people do escape the "rat race" of pecuniary rivalry, whether the majority or the minority is difficult to say. Some couples endure their privations with grace and the determination to "put first things first." Others develop skills for home production of goods and services, new ways for noncommercial leisure, and cooperative purchasing in order to make savings by quantity orders. Their inventiveness is impressive.

The young husband and wife may augment their income in a number of ways. Some couples accept financial help from their parents in any of the various forms of subsidy current today. This is not unusual, especially among those who marry before they have completed their educational plans in which the parents already have an investment. Many parents would rather help out the young married couple for awhile, than have their son or daughter drop out of school upon marriage. This is not always an easy arrangement, and many couples avoid it if at all possible. Some young husbands carry a part-time job in addition to their full-time employment or school load. This makes strains in the establishment phase when relaxed time together is so important for the building of the marriage.

The most frequent solution is found in the wife's ability and willingness to work during the establishment phase of the marriage. During the first year of marriage some 40 per cent of all wives work outside the home.[1] Unforeseen problems often arise in this connection. Not all women have the salable skills that will net them enough to be worthwhile. Not all women have health and energy enough to handle both a job and a home, however abbreviated the latter may be. Not all men either know how or feel constrained to share the household responsibilities with their working wives.

The more optimistic side of the picture is found in the many men and women who are learning the new roles required for a real partnership in getting and spending the family income. As more and more married women enter the working force and bring home their pay checks, decisions about the spending of the family income tend to become cooperative, democratic, and based on joint planning of husband and wife.

One study of married students indicates that an overwhelming majority (86.8 per cent) of the couples made their financial plans jointly. Some 84.1 per cent of them budgeted their money, and nearly three-fourths of the couples who used financial plans (74.2 per cent), kept records of their expenditures.[2] This is in sharp contrast to older patterns of handling money where the woman often did not know how much income there was or how it was spent, but like Vinnie Day[3] cajoled what sums she could from her reluctant mate who held the purse strings with a firm hand.

With both husband and wife increasingly responsible for getting and

[1] Paul C. Glick, "The Life Cycle of the Family," *Marriage and Family Living*, February 1955, Vol. XVII, No. 1, p. 8.

[2] Alice C. Thorpe, "How Married Students Manage," *Marriage and Family Living*, Vol. XIII, No. 3, Summer 1951, pp. 104–105, 130.

[3] Clarence Day, *Life with Father* (New York: Alfred A. Knopf, 1935).

By reading labels and intelligently comparing values, young married couples stretch their money as far as it will go.

spending the family income, there arises more consideration of the principles of wise purchasing. When both have planned for the purchase of some new item, they both are concerned with "getting the best buy." Courses, classes, units, and single lecturers in consumer buying; and subscriptions to such guides as *Consumer Reports* and *Consumers' Research Bulletins* have greatly increased in recent years. Today one sees an occasional young couple reading labels on packaged products and intelligently comparing the values of competing commodities. With a limited amount of money and a large number of needs, today's early married couple wants to know how to stretch the family dollars as far as they will go.

Establishing mutually satisfactory systems for getting and spending money as a developmental task involves at least four specific challenges: 1) coming to terms with the realities of one's own financial situation in the face of the appealing claims of modern advertising, high pressure salesmanship, and "keeping up with the Joneses" pressures, 2) finding mutually comfortable sources of income for the immediate and the distant future, 3) establishing ways of deciding how the money will be spent, for what and by whom, and 4) developing sound financial plans and buying methods. These challenges must be met in some way during the early days of the marriage. Successful methods express the values of the couple (see section "Establishing a Workable Philosophy of Life as a Couple"), and are based upon the realities of their situation. Upon the successful accomplishment of this developmental task rests the future financial health of the family.

ESTABLISHING MUTUALLY ACCEPTABLE PATTERNS OF WHO DOES WHAT AND WHO IS ACCOUNTABLE TO WHOM

Traditionally the roles of husband and wife were rigidly defined and underwent little variation by the individual couple. There was man's work and woman's work, and each knew which was which. The man was the head of the house, and his wife and children respected his authority and bowed to it. Today's newly married couples have no such definite outlines to follow in the division of responsibilities and the assignment of the roles within the union. They must work them out for themselves within the new patterns of freedom characteristic of the modern age.

Couples are free to define their interlocking roles as husband and wife along traditional lines if they wish. One frequently finds a couple in which the man is the sole breadwinner and authority figure, while the woman makes her life within the four walls of her home. But, the trend is toward more democratic, flexible roles (Chapters Two and Three).

Nowadays more women find a place for themselves outside the home in remunerative work and volunteer service within the larger community. Concurrently men are becoming increasingly familiar with the household and its operation. Thus we find that among the married students already cited,[1] most of the husbands regularly help with the housework (77.2 per cent). Husbands as well as wives are found taking the laundry to the nearby laundromat and casually enjoying menu-planning as foods are bought for the week ahead. Men as well as women today engage in meal preparation with the help of packaged products, quick-frozen foods, modern kitchen equipment, and outdoor grills and barbeques. Merchandising that directly appeals to the male food handler (men's aprons, chef-outfits, etc.) both represents and facilitates this trend.

[1] Alice C. Thorpe, *op. cit.*, pp. 104–105.

The young couple today continues the mutual exploration of each other's interests and skills begun during the courtship and engagement periods, in the experimentation that becomes a major challenge in early marriage. Together they work out their own system of who will do what on the basis of individual preference, work schedules, time and strength, and a sense of fairness. One young husband says, "Sure I mop the kitchen floor and help clean house on Saturdays. It's the least I can do when she has so many other things to do all week."

Accountability in terms of who checks up on whom works itself out either along the older lines of male domination and authority, or along the newer approaches of the authority resting in the one who is taking the more responsibility for the activity, with each accountable to the other for his stewardship. The first pattern is familiar. The wife accounts to her husband of what she did with her time and their money during the day. He approves or corrects as he deems wise, and the household runs along on the principle of coming up to the expectations of the man of the house. The current trend is in the direction of responsibility for a project being assumed by the one who does the work on it, with joint consultation and planning as the source of general direction. Thus, the couple together decides to paint the kitchen, what color to use, and when it can best be done. Either the man or the woman, or both of them together may do the actual painting with its related decisions, problems, and rewards accruing to the worker(s). Both are accountable to their common budget and to each other in their decision-making and performance.

Modern equalitarian principles do not always work out happily in the new marriage. Both husband and wife bring to their marriage not only their desires to be flexible and intelligent about these things, but also their previous conditionings and emotional sets that are very much a part of the picture. A man may agree intellectually that he should carry some of the load of work around the house while his wife is working quite as hard as is he at remunerative work. But, if he has been brought up by a mother who has dominated the household with her efficiency, driving her sons from the kitchen with her insistence that they wait until they are called to dinner, he may find it hard to know how to start being helpful, what to do as his part of the responsibility, or even to accept emotionally the idea that he too is a partner in the housekeeping.

Similarly, if the wife has grown accustomed to seeing her mother ac-

Young couples today work out their own systems of who does what; they enjoy joint planning, consultation, and working together on mutually agreed projects.

count to her father in all things, she may *need* to report to her young husband many a detail that neither he nor she intellectually accept as necessary in their relationship. These things have to be worked out in the day by day association of the married pair in the many varied situations that make up their life together.

ESTABLISHING A CONTINUITY OF MUTUALLY SATISFYING SEX RELATIONSHIPS

Part of the enigma of marriage stems from the fact that American codes have not yet reached agreement concerning the eternally troublesome questions of sex and love.[1] Being in love is presumed by most people to be a sufficient answer in itself to any questioning of an adequate reason for a marriage. Elders, generally speaking, think that love is not enough to marry on and they make a good case for their point of view. But to Joe and Jane in their teens or early twenties, the principal and impelling fact which stimulates them to marry, and to marry each other, is the unanswerable imperative that "it *is* love."

[1] See Sylvanus M. Duvall, *Men, Women, and Morals* (New York: Association Press, 1952). For abundant statistical data see Alfred C. Kinsey, Wardell B. Pomeroy, and Clyde E. Martin, *Sexual Behavior in the Human Male* (Philadelphia: W. B. Saunders, 1948); and Kinsey *et al.*, *Sexual Behavior in the Human Female* (Philadelphia: W. B. Saunders, 1953).

Probably most people assume that sex is, at its best, one of life's great fulfillments, and there is evidence in many marriages that the assumption is a sound one. But it is not always fully recognized that this blessing is unequally distributed among married couples in America and that frustration is experienced by many in their search for such fulfillment.

Sexual maladjustments of one sort or another are confusing and irksome to many couples, especially during the first few years of marriage. Generally speaking, much of the trouble stems from the contradictions between the couple's expectations for pleasant experience, on the one hand, and the inaccuracy of their knowledge regarding the subtleties of "the facts of life."[1] The problem is not, of course, wholly a matter of knowledge and intent. It is greatly complicated by the fact that husbands and wives both bring to marriage numerous and significant unconscious needs and wants.[2] At best we perceive our true selves only dimly, as if through a dense mist into which we can occasionally peer, with distortions and mirages common. But the illusion persists that we really know ourselves, our needs, our desires, and also those of our mates.

Individual needs growing out of different hereditary makeup, different background of experience, and differing conceptions of the purpose of sex, create barriers to mutual gratification. Accumulating frustrations bring forth angered epithets like "prude," "cold," "sensual," "beastly," "oversexed," and the like. It requires time,[3] more patience than some people have, more information than many can get, and skills of a specific nature to find mutual fulfillment. The almost innumerable avenues of sex satisfaction present further difficulties. Intimate personal acts which embellish the sexual experience for one mate may offend the fastidiousness of the other. Guilt, shame, indecision, and, many times, deep and abiding hostility become ingrained in the very fabric of sex in marriage. More than that, hostilities which were unnecessary in the first place, may over a long time grow and fester into an impairment of the whole marital structure.

[1] Inadequacies in knowledge in this area may be met in part by reading such books as Eustace Chesser, *Love Without Fear* (New York: Signet Books, 1949); Evelyn Duvall and Reuben Hill, *When You Marry* (New York: Association Press, 1953 edition); and Hannah and Abraham Stone, *A Marriage Manual* (New York: Simon and Schuster, 1952 edition).

[2] John Levy and Ruth Monroe, *The Happy Family* (New York: Alfred A. Knopf, 1938).

[3] Judson T. Landis, "Length of Time Required to Achieve Adjustment in Marriage," *American Sociological Review*, Vol. 11, No. 6, December 1946, pp. 666–677.

There are often painful discoveries such as lack of sexual response of the wife, the "insatiability" of the husband, jealousies with or without foundation in fact, or inabilities to forgive indiscretions in the past. These may have been confessed by the spouse in the frantic attempt to relieve guilt feelings, only to find his or her marriage bond threatened by candor.

In time, sexual difficulties like other conflicts and disappointments work out one way or another. The nature of this accomplishment is indeed varied. Failure is seen in resignation to one's fate, chronic frustration concealed (or ill-concealed), overt hostility to the mate, or generalized irritability. Progress is found in discovery of unexpected strength in self or mate, realization that success is worth working for and that the race for it can be fun, selective forgetting of earlier frustrated goals, and learning the knowledges, skills, and attitudes that make for mutual fulfillment.

The husband and wife who work out together a continuity of mutually satisfying sex relationships early in their marriage not only find a source of deep satisfaction for the present, but they also have established a firm foundation upon which other tasks can be undertaken, and future happiness built.

ESTABLISHING SYSTEMS OF INTELLECTUAL AND EMOTIONAL COMMUNICATION

One of the biggest jobs facing the recently married couple is that of communicating with each other. Two people may live in the same house, they may share the same bed and board, but unless they establish effective systems of communication between them, they might as well be miles apart. She may live through the days in tight-lipped silence, he may pout and mope through the evenings, with no awareness of what "is eating" either of them, unless and until they have developed the signs and signals, the words and the gestures that keep the state of affairs open to them both.

Human beings do not live in emotional vacuums, but in a climate of feeling that changes quite as often as the weather. Each of us as men and as women at times feel loving and at times feel hateful; at times are high and at other times low; are sometimes mad and sometimes sad. Mental hygiene findings have indicated without question that the healthful way to live is to recognize emotional states for what they are, as they arise, and to deal with them realistically and honestly. Pretending that all is well while one seethes inside is not only hypocrisy, it is corrosive even to the point of gastric ulcers if it becomes habitual.

If two people are to live intimately together in marriage, they must learn to express their real feelings in ways that are acceptable and healthful. They must develop ways of communicating for the mutual planning and for the furtherance of mutual services; and for the sheer necessity of sharing the meanings of a moment in the sense we mean by true companionship—two people understanding and being understood in a system of mutual identification that is deeply satisfying.

The young husband who has been brought up in a home where his father communicated with his wife by asking one of the children to "tell your mother" this or that, may have problems when he marries, in learning to be as open with his wife as she may desire. Such a wife tries to share her husband's day by little inquiries upon his return home: "How did your day go, dear?" or "Did you have a nice lunch?" only to have her efforts met with either a mumbled grunt or an annoyed, don't-bother-me-now response that does little to further the communication between the two.

Communication is a two-way task and a mutual achievement. Just as the husband may have difficulties in getting out of himself at times, so too the wife may find it hard to project herself into enough of her husband's interests to get much beyond the homey superficial levels of their life together. One young bride took lessons in photography in order to be able to share more intelligently her husband's interest in taking and showing his Kodachrome slides. Another wife found that her part-time job in her husband's plant one rush season added a great deal to the level of communication between them. This may be one reason why we find that women with some regular work experience make better adjustments after marriage than those who move from the protection of their father's home to that of their husband's with no opportunity to learn by experience how a man spends his day at work.[1]

Communication is an intricate complex of words, gestures, signs, and symbolic actions that have meanings to the communicating people. Some of these words and meanings are universal. Some are peculiar to the language and cultural group. More subtle systems are highly individ-

[1] Ernest W. Burgess and Leonard S. Cottrell, *Predicting Success or Failure in Marriage* (New York: Prentice-Hall, 1939), pp. 136–158.

ual and must be built up within the new relationship. One of the joys of courtship, engagement, and the honeymoon is found in the development and the practice of intimate, personal gestures and symbols that have meaning only for the two persons. They identify "our song," they walk by "our house" through "our park," and they repeat little ceremonies that convey more than words could the special significance each has for the other. Special gestures of affection become their own language of love that channel love feelings and add immeasurably to the satisfaction they get in each other's company.

It may be relatively easy to get through to each other with love and affection. But learning how to handle the inevitable negative feelings that arise from time to time is a difficult assignment for many couples. No two people see eye to eye about all things. No two people feel the same way about everything they share in life together. So some conflict is to be expected in marriage, especially during the establishment phase when the two people are learning to mesh their former ways of living into a unity of habits, aspirations, and values.

The romantic illusion prevalent in America calls for two people in love living "happily ever after" in a state of perpetual bliss that offers no room for the disagreements and differences that two normal people inevitably find cropping up between them. So, when the first quarrels occur, one or both of the pair mistakenly may feel that the marriage is failing, their love is not lasting, or they were not "made for each other" after all. The couple that is able to see conflict as a part of the close, intimate marriage relationship, accepts its reality and assumes the responsibility for meeting constructively the differences that arise.

One of the critical tests of the adequacy of the communication established within a marriage is found in the way in which the two people meet a conflict situation. As long as they keep silent and pretend that they have no problems, little progress can be made in getting through to each other. When one person leaves the conflict situation in anger or in tears, or in patient martyrdom, communication between the partners is poor. As the husband and wife make a real effort to share their true feelings and to accept without anxiety or fear the fact that their feelings and values do differ, they are able to learn to bridge their differences.

The outline, "A Pattern for Problem Solving" has evolved in family life education classes at Oklahoma A & M College as a guide for the development of skills in solving interpersonal problems.

A PATTERN FOR PROBLEM SOLVING *

Stillwater, Oklahoma By permission, Department of Family
Oklahoma A & M College Relations and Child Development,
Division of Home Economics Girdie Ware

STEPS	KEY QUESTIONS	PURPOSE
1 FACE THE PROBLEM	What is the matter? Why do I/we think it is a problem?	To get problem into words. To uncover the fear involved.
2 LOOK AT THE CAUSES	What has been happening? What has made it a problem now?	To get the build-up of the problem. To get a clear statement of what is bringing it to a head.
3. SET SOME GOALS	What do I want to accomplish for myself? For the other person? What do we/I want the situation to be?	To be sure of desires for self. To be sure that decisions will benefit others as well as self. To set a definite change to work toward.
4. GET MORE KNOWLEDGE AND UNDERSTANDING	What knowledge from the biological, psychological and social sciences are applicable? Have I found all the available material in technical and popular literature? What has been the experience of other people in similar situations?	To increase understanding. To gain insight.
5. BE THE OTHER PERSON (Try to be each of the other persons or groups of persons involved in the problem)	Just how would I, as this other person, think about it? And as this other person what does he or she feel?	To get the other person's point of view and emotional slant. To allow thinking and feelings of others be a framework for the next step.
6. CONSIDER WHAT TO DO	What could we/I do about it? Will that bring me to my goals? Will it fit the thoughts and feelings of the other person?	To get a list of possible actions. To be sure they lead to the goals To be sure they will be acceptable to other person.
7. MAKE A PLAN OF ACTION	Just how can this be done? Who will do each part? How will I do it? Who will help me?	To plan how to do it. To develop a 1, 2, 3, plan. To select the person to help at each point if needed.
8. CHECK THE PLAN WITH THE GOALS	Will this plan lead you to your goals? Does it provide for each goal?	To be sure the plan is really directed at the desired solution. To be sure it covers all the goals set.
9. PLAN THE FOLLOW-UP	What shall I/we watch for to be sure the plan is working?	To encourage watchfulness in using the plan. To encourage abandonment if it seems to be failing.

* An adaption of "A Pattern for Counseling" by L. A. Lynde, Extension Specialist in Parent Education, Jan. 30, 1947.

It takes time to learn to live constructively with differences in ways that increase the harmony of the marriage and the understanding of each other. It may not be fully accomplished during the first establishment phase of the marriage, but it should be begun well enough so that further tasks will not be rendered more complicated by failure to communicate effectively in moments of strain and tension. The husband and wife who establish good systems of communication for handling the hot spot areas of their relationship find real satisfaction in knowing "if we can handle this, we can weather anything that comes."

Unity as a couple is established by the network of bonds that weave the two into two-in-one. The bonds are not ties in the sense of fetters. There are open systems of communication through which each gets across to the other for the comfort, the love, the understanding, the sympathy, the loyalty and the sense of purpose a man or woman needs to feel truly married. Without such communication a person may ache with loneliness even while beside the mate. With a well-established communication system, the husband and wife feel united even though they may be separated by many months and miles.

ESTABLISHING WORKABLE RELATIONSHIPS WITH RELATIVES

When a man and woman marry they are plunged into membership in three families: (1) the family they are founding together as their family of procreation, (2) his family of orientation (his mother and father and siblings and all his other relatives), and (3) her family of orientation, made up of all her close and distant relations. In an effort to encourage the autonomy of the young couple, the general feeling is that the biblical injunction, "Forsaking all others, keep Ye only to him/her as long as Ye both shall live," should be closely followed. The woman who marries a man with the conviction that she is not marrying his family is apt to be in for a rude awakening. Comes the first Christmas or the first baby, she will discover that his family as well as hers is in the inner circle of the family and must be taken into account.

Relationships with in-laws are generally dreaded before marriage, and avoided as much as possible thereafter, in the stereotyped fear of intrusion that forms the basis of the universal mother-in-law joke and general mother-in-law avoidance. Yet actual investigation of in-law relationships turns up many satisfactory, mutually helpful in-law relationships. Many a mother-in-law turns out to be an angel in disguise rather than the ogre she is often painted to be.[1]

After marriage it is sometimes difficult for the husband and wife to establish workable relationships with their relatives, because they find that they cannot discuss each other's family as objectively and as easily as they can work through other issues and problems. Both husband and wife may feel the other would suspect jealousy as the real motive behind in-law misunderstandings. So the issues are not met and resentments toward the relatives build up. Probably the mother-in-law gets more than her share of the criticism because it is almost "socially acceptable" to have mother-in-law trouble early in marriage.

The families of both the husband and the wife cannot merge their value systems as easily as can the couple in love, and therefore there is reason for misunderstanding and conflict from time to time. In the mixed marriage—spanning the chasms of race, religion, nationality, social class, or socio-economic levels—friction with the in-laws on both sides of the family may be expected to be greater than in the marriage of persons from similar backgrounds. Not only are the ways of life different in different cultures, but in-law rejection of the young couple is more common when a son or daughter marries outside "our own kind."[2]

When both sets of parents and the young couple recognize that it is normal for parents as well as grown children to go through a "weaning" process when the young people marry, their interrelationships are less troublesome. In the physical weaning of the child, the mother is involved more than is the father; so too in the psychological weaning, the mother is usually the more emotionally involved. Mothers who are encouraged to develop lives of their own find it easier to let their children go and grow. Those who are appreciated as individuals by their married children frequently can be counted on as friendly allies in ways that are mutually appreciated as the years roll by.[3]

Although it is the members of the immediate family that most often have to be dealt with in the establishment phase of marriage, there are many others who may affect the lives of the young adult today,

[1] Evelyn Millis Duvall, *In-Laws: Pro and Con* (New York: Association Press, 1954), Chapters 6, 7, and 8.

[2] *Ibid.*, Chapter 5

[3] *Ibid.*, Chapters 15 and 16

as Dr. Albrecht points out (see Chapter One). A relative may need a home for awhile. A younger sister or brother may call upon the young couple for help. An accident may befall a cousin or an aunt or uncle rallying the whole family and its resources to the assistance of the stricken ones. Disgrace can hit the young couple through a relative, as can sudden wealth or any public notice. One never can completely cut off one's roots. The larger family circle surrounds each newly married couple and some sort of relationship must be established that will carry through the years.

ESTABLISHING WAYS OF INTERACTING WITH FRIENDS, ASSOCIATES, AND COMMUNITY ORGANIZATIONS

"With someone like you, a pal so good and true, I'd like to leave it all behind, and go and find, somewhere that's known to God alone, just a place to call our own . . . and let the rest of the World go by," are words of a popular song that are often repeated in one way or another by the newly married pair desiring nothing so much as to be let alone. Being alone together is expected during the engagement and the honeymoon periods. But there comes a time when the married pair is ready for social activities. Friends, associates, and the larger community expect the couple to be active as a young married pair in the married set.

Getting into the young married set of the neighborhood is a developmental task that comes easily to the couple that settles down in the home community. It may pose problems for large numbers of young husbands and wives who move into a new area where they know no one and must find for themselves the companions and the social activities that interest both of them.[1] The mixed marriage may require redefinitions of who is considered a pleasant companion and what is an acceptable social activity. Different experiences bring different definitions of how home is used. Jane, a minister's daughter, sees her home almost as a social center and expects neighbors and friends to drop in unannounced; while Jane's Joe sees their home as a refuge with privacy and undisturbed quiet as prime values.

The demands upon the married couple made by the husband's job

---

[1] "About four-fifths of the persons who marry change residences at the time of marriage or within the ensuing year." Paul C. Glick, "The Life Cycle of the Family," *Marriage and Family Living*, February 1955, Vol. XVII, No. 1, p. 8.

vary from the annual picnic of the plant to which workers and their families are invited, to the exacting pressures made upon the corporation wife by the young executive's boss. The amount of business entertaining a young couple is expected to do depends upon his job, their social standing, and their social mobility. "Having the boss to dinner" has become a stereotyped problem situation in popular thinking that not incorrectly describes the anxiety and effort involved in becoming established as a socially acceptable married pair.

The extent to which the young husband and wife participate in community organizations depends on their previous involvements, on their social status, and on the length of time married. Lower-class families tend to be much less active in community work than are members of the middle and upper classes. Young married couples are not as active in the community as are families established a number of years. The young husband and wife are highly mobile and busy getting themselves established, a task already achieved by longer married couples. The children of the established family bring father and mother out to participate in neighborhood, school, church, and political projects that do not appeal as personally to the couple without children. The previous involvements of the young man or woman in union affairs, social activities, political campaigns, or church functions may continue to absorb the individual, especially if these interests are shared with the mate.

There may be some problems over the religious affiliations of the couple, especially if theirs is an interfaith marriage. Generally, there is more instability in mixed marriages than in those within the same faith. Three studies in various regions of the country (populations totaling 24,184) agree in finding significantly higher percentages of mixed marriages ending in divorce than do those in which the husband and wife share the same religious faith, as is summarized in Table 11.

Sylvanus M. Duvall suggests several questions to be examined by two people attempting to establish a mixed marriage:

1) How intense is the loyalty of each to his own religious group?
2) How many complicating factors are there, such as relatives and influential friends?
3) What aspects of religion does each feel most strongly about?
4) Is there danger that religious differences will be used as a means by which one can dominate the other?
5) Are there other strong bonds to compensate for the religious differences?
6) What compromises are both willing to make to solve the problem?

7) What specific decisions can be made in regard to:
   a) Who, if either, will change his church relationship?
   b) If each retains his separate faith, where will they attend church, if at all?
   c) In what faith, if any, will the children be brought up? [1]

TABLE 11. *Percentage of Marriages of Mixed and Non-Mixed Religious Faiths Ending in Divorce or Separation as Revealed by Studies of Marriages in Michigan, Maryland, and Washington* [2]

Religious Categories	Landis Study * in Michigan (N = 4,108)	Bell Study † in Maryland (N = 13,528)	Weeks Study § in Washington (N = 6,548)
	Per cent	Per cent	Per cent
Both Catholic	4.4	6.4	3.8
Both Jewish	5.2	4.6	—
Both Protestant	6.0	6.8	10.0
Mixed, Catholic-Protestant	14.1	15.2	17.4

* Judson T. Landis, "Marriages of Mixed and Non-Mixed Religious Faith," *American Sociological Review*, Vol. 14, No. 3, 1949, pp. 401–407.
† Howard M. Bell, *Youth Tell Their Story* (Washington, D. C.: American Council on Education, 1938), p. 21.
§ H. Ashley Weeks, "Differential Divorce Rates by Occupation," *Social Forces*, Vol. 21, No. 3, March 1943, p. 336.

Even in marriages within the same faith there often are difficulties over the degree of interest in religious activities. A common conflict occurs when the wife wants to go to church regularly with her husband, while he prefers to sleep late on the one morning of the week when that is possible. The patterns a couple develops for resolving such differences and expressing their own wishes, desires, values, and beliefs take time to work out. These accomplishments are greatly aided by discussing the possible problems and their solutions in the premarital period, and then being willing to rethink and rework the tentative working agreements as needed during the establishment phase of the marriage.

FACING THE POSSIBILITY OF CHILDREN AND PLANNING FOR THEIR COMING

The modern American couple marry with the anticipation of having children. Many of them have their first baby within the first year, some

[1] Evelyn M. Duvall and Reuben Hill with chapters in collaboration with Sylvanus M. Duvall, *When You Marry* (Boston, D. C. Heath and Company, Revised 1953), pp. 391–394.
[2] Data excerpted from Judson T. Landis, "Marriages of Mixed and Non-Mixed Religious Faith," *American Sociological Review*, Vol. 14, No. 3, June 1949, p. 403.

almost too soon.[1] Most young husbands and wives, especially among the college-educated, expect that they will have a period together as a young couple before the first baby is on the way. The concept of planning for children is part of the *modus operandi* of young marriage. These plans are not isolated, arbitrary notions, but are related to other marital objectives, such as completing the husband's or the wife's education, securing a house or apartment where children are permitted, getting out of debt, building up a nest-egg in the bank before the wife stops work to have a baby, and so forth.

Evidence indicates that a majority of American married women (84.9 per cent of all women and 69.0 per cent of Catholic women in a nationwide representative sample) believe that birth control information should be available to married couples.[2] There is greater approval of the propriety of birth control than there is knowledge of approved methods and the psychological subtleties connected with their practice.

Unplanned pregnancies may be a crisis for the couple, for either member of the pair, as well as for the child-to-be. Coming within the establishment phase of the newly founded family, a pregnancy may make it difficult if not impossible for the wife to go with her husband as he completes his military service; it may necessitate the wife's cutting short her educational plans; it may pull the young husband from long-range professional plans, and into some vocation where money is quicker and advancement sooner; it may mean the bringing in of one or both sets of parents for financial and personal help; or it may, if the couple is ready for a child, cement the marriage as nothing else can do.

Inability to conceive a child is another challenge to be faced. Infertility is encountered by something less than fifteen per cent of all married couples. During Bible days when a married woman did not become pregnant she was considered "barren." This term is no longer used by informed people for two reasons. First, because the condition is often caused by some inadequacy in the male, most frequently insufficiently motile sperm; and, second, because the inability to have a child is frequently a temporary condition that responds well to treatment, or even to time. Infertility clinics in connection with hospitals in many communities, as well as private physicians in recent years, have greatly increased the number of young married couples who want

[1] Christensen, *op. cit.*, pp. 53–59.
[2] *Fortune*, Vol. 28, August 1943, pp. 24, 30.

to become parents. Couples who have been married more than one year without conceiving a child are wise to go for examinations of both husband and wife and to accept treatment as indicated before becoming discouraged or jumping to the conclusion that theirs is a sterile union.

Adoption is an increasing possibility for otherwise childless couples. Between 1944 and 1954, there was an 80 per cent increase in the number of adoptions in the United States (50,000 in 1944; 90,000 in 1954). Adoption of children by non-relatives increased by 90 per cent in that decade, while adoption of children by relatives increased by 69 per cent. Happily, the placements by social agencies have increased more, proportionally, than independent placements.[1]

The developmental task of the establishment phase of the marriage is in terms of anticipating having children, controlling conception by whatever means are acceptable to one's group until time to start the baby, planning positively for the coming of the first baby, building up a financial reserve that will allow the young mother to drop out of gainful employment while she is having and rearing the baby and its siblings yet to come, accepting the fact of pregnancy when it comes whether planned or not, and getting psychologically set for the roles as parents that lie ahead. In many marriages today, the establishment phase flows quickly into the pregnant phase of marriage with an overlapping of the roles and developmental tasks of each phase in the beginning family stage.

ESTABLISHING A WORKABLE PHILOSOPHY OF LIFE AS A COUPLE

Presumably the young adult has some kind of philosophy of life by the time he or she is old enough to marry. Yet with marriage comes the weaving of one's own convictions and values with those of the partner into a philosophical whole that gives unity to the marriage. Marriage provides for the young husband and wife many opportunities for testing previous orientations and situations that challenge former conclusions. Together the two people in marriage must choose those alternatives that best represent their present positions. Together over a period of time they develop a philosophy of life by which they can live.

[1] Children's Bureau, *Children,* Vol. 3, No. 6, November–December 1956, p. 238.

Pressures during the early establishment phase of marriage push the young married couple into taking one stand or another on a good many issues. As a married pair they must decide what church they will attend or if they will affiliate with any religious group. As a married couple they face the current political situation with either indifference or with dedicating loyalties. As soon as they are married they meet the question of the filing of joint or individual income tax returns with temptations for "saving" as much as they can on their tax, on the one hand, or submitting a completely honest statement on the other. These are the decisions that make up a philosophy-of-life.

As a newly established unit of society they find themselves forced to take some kind of position—in their social groups, in the neighborhood, at work, as they read the daily paper, listen to the news reports over the radio, and fall into casual conversations—on the widely discussed issues of the day. In a hundred different weekly situations they are testing and establishing the philosophy by which they are to live—in the attitudes they take toward the new family, from another ethnic background, recently moved into the neighborhood; in the way they feel and talk about an incident of aggression in the central square; in the position they take on the new zoning law that is being voted upon; in the way they behave when given too much change for a purchase; in the way they act toward the man who carries away their trash, or the deference they show the people above them in the community; in the degree of perfection they expect of themselves, of each other, and of others. In all these situations, and more, they are weaving the philosophy of life by which they as a couple are to live.

Establishing a philosophy of life for the average couple does not involve writing out a personal family creed. Few families come to that degree of explicit awareness of the philosophies by which they live. But whether it becomes explicit or not, the philosophy of life is there, worked out in everyday life together.

This does not imply that the couple must come to exactly the same stand on every issue of life. In some areas they may agree to disagree, each recognizing the other's right to feel as he or she must, believe what makes sense, and act according to his or her own convictions. But over and beyond the personal philosophy that moves each person to be himself is the philosophy of life-as-a-couple that must be established explicitly or implicitly in early marriage.

SUCCESS DOES NOT COME ALL AT ONCE IN EARLY MARRIAGE

With so many developmental tasks clamoring for the attention of the newly married couple, it is no wonder that not all couples succeed. Many marriages fail to make the grade during the early establishment phase. The evidence is that divorce frequency is highest in the early period of married life, reaches its peak in the third year of marriage, and from there on declines with each additional year of marriage.[1]

Many happily married couples, whose marriages have lasted for twenty years or more, report that satisfaction did not come from the beginning in all areas of their life together. More succeeded from the first in some developmental tasks than in others. We see, for instance, that fewer couples found satisfaction from the beginning in their sex relations than in any other area (Chart 10).

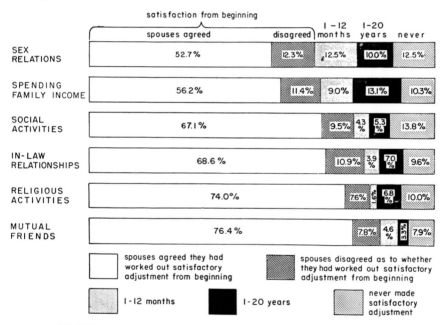

CHART 10. Percentage of 409 Couples Reporting Various Periods of Time after Marriage to Achieve Adjustments.[2]

[1] Paul H. Jacobson, "Differentials in Divorce by Duration of Marriage and Size of Family," *American Sociological Review*, Vol. 15, No. 2, April 1950, pp. 235–244.
[2] Judson T. Landis, "Adjustments After Marriage," *Marriage and Family Living*, Vol. IX, No. 2, May 1947, p. 33.

In all cases studied success in achieving satisfaction in the various areas of life together brought happiness in the reported marriages; while failure to achieve satisfaction in three or more areas led couples to estimate their marriages as only average or unhappy. Such findings corroborate the developmental task assumption that success in a task brings happiness, while failure leads to unhappiness.

Leland Stott suggests research possibilities for exploring degrees of success and failure in achieving developmental tasks of husband, of wife, and of the young married couple at the establishment phase when he says:

At the newly married or establishment phase of family life, for example, the man must accomplish certain developmental tasks as a prerequisite to satisfactory functioning in the role of husband. One such functional prerequisite, more or less prescribed by our American middle-class culture, is that he become a "domesticated man." He must now be concerned less with his own gratifications and inclinations in regard to recreation and amusement and more with staying at home or going out with his wife and learning to share various activities with her. Certain indications of progress or retrogression in this developmental task could be observed more or less directly. Check lists of activities the husband enjoys and of activities he enjoys sharing with his wife could be applied "before and after," thus giving a measure of progress. A sense of progress in becoming a good husband would normally be a satisfying experience.

Comparable individual developmental tasks are assumed by the woman at marriage. The middle-class expectation is that she be devoted to her husband, that she grow in ability to function as his confidante and refuge from the strains and strife of the world without, and that she make a comfortable home. Direct observation, interviews, questionnaires, and attitude scales are possible means of evaluating her progress in achieving these developmental tasks.

One functional prerequisite (developmental task) common to the roles of husband and wife is the achievement of the mature and exclusive love for mate which is so important for a stable and lasting marriage. This achievement usually involves the working out of personal adjustments in several areas. One promising method of measuring progress in this developmental task was used by Kelley some years ago and has been used more recently by Stewart. In this method ratings of self and spouse on attitude scales or personality inventories are analyzed in various ways in relation to each other. Stewart used the MMPI (Minnesota Multi-Phasic Inventory) in his study. He found that a tendency in either spouse to rate the mate as superior to or better adjusted than himself was one of the surest indicators of happiness in marriage so far discovered. This tendency to idealize the mate, to magnify the good, the positive in him, might well be regarded as an indicator of progress in the development of a substantial and mature love.

It is true that such methods do not reveal the sequential appearance of fixed, universal maturity indicators such as those we look for in the child's achievement of locomotion, for example. They do, however, provide some basis for evaluating individual change in effectiveness in fulfilling family roles.[1]

In marriage, as in the life of an individual, success or failure in one developmental task influences success or failure in others. For instance, difficulties in establishing satisfactory systems for earning and spending money may adversely effect efforts to establish good sex relationships. Failure to find fulfillment in sex life may carry over into additional bickering over in-law relations, social activities, and going to church together, to name a few. Success in any one developmental task often brings the glow of achievement, and the feeling that "we are getting along all right" that seems to predispose the couple to further success in other tasks. Getting off to a good start in marriage involves the achievement of many highly complicated and difficult tasks important for the happiness of the couple, for the present and in the future.

RESOURCES FOR THE MARRIED COUPLE IN THE ESTABLISHMENT PHASE

The honeymoon period is generally recognized as important in offering the newly married couple the privacy needed for the mutual exploration and establishment of the intimate, personal side of living together as man and wife. Whether the couple take an extended trip or move at once into their new little place, they usually may count upon being protected from the too-interested supervision of friends and family as long as they themselves wish during the honeymoon period.

Newlyweds may "put on an act" for the benefit of one of their families, when storms brew in their relationship. For, the expectation of family and friends that they will work it out keeps them at it when otherwise they might give up. In time the husband may be reassured by his associates that his wife is acting "just like a woman," while she gets comfort from "the other girls" that other men are thoughtless too. Resentments and disappointments gradually drain off in socially accepted

---

[1] Leland H. Stott, "The Problem of Evaluating Family Success," *Marriage and Family Living*, Vol. XIII, No. 4, Fall, 1951, pp. 151–152.

ways. While through it all, the two are thrown together with the expectation of success by all who know them.

The climate of opinion today that accepts some of the realities of early marriage is more helpful than the older romantic illusions that built rosy pictures of newlyweds living together in unending bliss. Newspaper and magazine articles and stories, TV and radio portrayals, and some movies on the dynamics of marriage suggest insights, offer recommendations, and even imply to many a couple, "we aren't as badly off as those people, anyway." This may not be romantic, or even very scientific, but it may provide a breather in which the couple can remobilize for the next task ahead in building their marriage together.

There is wide recognition of the importance of the establishment phase of family life in a variety of services and resources available to couples. Physicians called upon to make routine premarital blood tests are increasingly establishing the kind of helpful contact with the members of the couple that includes adequate premarital examinations and postmarital conferences that clear up many difficulties before they become either chronic or critical. Ministers consulted about wedding plans nowadays often go the next mile of counseling the couple about their marriage and maintaining a relationship with the pair that makes marital counseling a natural thing to do when further questions arise. Members of other professions (budget counselors, home economists, psychologists, sociologists, social workers, marriage counselors, and others) make helpful services available to young people on the threshold of marriage.

Churches, YMCA's, YWCA's, and other youth and family serving agencies have established themselves in most communities as agencies interested in helping young men and women get a good start in marriage. Their services often include classes for engaged couples and young married couples, premarital and marital counseling services, special consultants in various aspects of marriage, films, books, pamphlets, and not infrequently some types of group discussion and therapy.

Schools and colleges in rapidly increasing numbers offer courses in Family Life Education, Preparation for Marriage, Marriage and Family Living, and related subjects designed to acquaint the student with the knowledges, skills, attitudes, and values that make for success in marriage. Unfortunately, most of these offerings are at the senior high school and college levels, and so are not available for the less privileged lower-class youngster who drops out of school.

Colleges and university centers in recent decades have greatly increased their research studies in marriage and family life. The implications of marriage research findings and clinical evidence are a substantial part of the many marriage texts now available for the young husband, wife, or couple interested in becoming informed in any of the various areas involved in the establishment of their marriage.

SUMMARY

The establishment phase of the beginning family takes the couple from their marriage to the time when they become aware of the wife's pregnancy. The period is one full of developmental tasks of great importance as the couple satisfy their need for ongoing adult sex fulfillment within marriage (biologic origin), as they attempt to measure up to what is expected of them as a young married couple (origin in cultural pressures), and as they try to make their dreams come true in the merging of their aspirations and values as a couple (origin in personal aspirations).

The developmental tasks of this phase of the family life cycle may be summarized as (1) establishing a home base in a place they can call their own, (2) establishing mutually satisfying systems for getting and spending money, (3) establishing mutually acceptable patterns of who does what and who is accountable to whom, (4) establishing a continuity of mutually satisfying sex relationships, (5) establishing systems of intellectual and emotional communication, (6) establishing workable relationships with relatives, (7) establishing ways of interacting with friends, associates, and community organizations, (8) facing the possibility of children and planning for their coming, and (9) establishing a workable philosophy of life as a couple.

Each of the developmental tasks involved in establishing a marriage has hazards and challenges that must be met successfully if the couple is to develop and grow satisfactorily. Success in developmental tasks does not come all at once but must be achieved if the couple is to find happiness together. Upon the accomplishment of the developmental tasks of the establishment phase rests the future success of the developmental tasks still to come in the stages ahead for the couple in the family life cycle.

Resources available to help couples satisfactorily achieve the developmental tasks of the establishment phase are: the honeymoon period that protects the young couple in a circle of privacy in which the first intimate, personal adjustments to married living may be made; the encouragement and support from family, friends, and community in becoming a married couple and learning to live as a married pair; family life education in schools, churches, and community settings that prepare young people for marriage responsibilities ahead; premarital counseling; marriage and family research with its implications for mate selection and preparation for marriage; marriage and family books that translate research and clinical evidence into discussions and recommendations that are functionally most relevant for the couple.

SUGGESTED ACTIVITIES

1) Review any five of the marriage texts listed in the *Readings* with special attention to the amount of space given the various tasks of the establishment phase of the beginning family. Count the number of pages in each text devoted to each of the developmental tasks (as described in this chapter) and make a chart by texts and tasks of the coverage of each. Discuss your findings.

2) Write a letter to your sister who is to be married soon, suggesting the resources she may want to avail herself of as her wedding date approaches, as well as after the ceremony. Tell her why you recommend the services you do.

3) Investigate the living units available in your community for a young married couple by answering a representative sampling of the advertisements in your local paper for rooms, apartments, and homes available for rent. How much rent will a young married couple have to pay for various types of housing in your area? In what condition are the available places?

4) Survey the married students in your area in terms of (a) working wives, (b) part-time employment of student-husbands, (c) other sources of income, and (d) use of budgets or other financial plans by the couple. Write up your findings in a report on "How Married Students Get and Spend Their Money."

5) Explore the factors discussed in the literature on sex adjustments in marriage for possible reasons why the task of achieving a mutually satisfying sex relationship is less often accomplished from the beginning than other aspects in building a marriage. Review your findings with an experienced physician, marriage counselor, or worker in a marriage counseling service in your community for further interpretation of the nature of this developmental task. Summarize your material in a short report.

6) Find out what research studies have to say about which in-law is the most difficult, what husbands and wives report as objectionable behavior on

the part of in-laws, and what makes for good in-law relationships. *In-Laws: Pro and Con* in your *Readings* may be a helpful resource in this assignment.

7) View the kinescope "In-Laws" (No. 11 in the 1956 Marriage Series), produced by and available from The University of Michigan Television Center, Ann Arbor, Michigan, in which Robert O. Blood, Jr. and Evelyn Millis Duvall discuss in-law relationships in marriage. Discuss.

8) Consider the importance of emotional maturity in the accomplishment of the developmental tasks of early marriage in a series of psychodramas illustrating immature and relatively mature ways of meeting one or more of the usual early marriage challenges.

9) Practice problem solving approaches to husband-wife differences in a series of "talk-out" sessions as developed by Dr. Hazel Ingersoll, Department of Home Life, Oklahoma A&M College, Stillwater, Oklahoma. She divides the class into couples (man and woman preferably, or a pair of men or of women). Each pair takes roles of husband and wife, chooses a problem from such a list as is given below, and practices talking out differences. Stress is placed on considering feelings and attitudes of individuals as well as the facts of the case. Talk-out sessions go on simultaneously for a while, then volunteer pairs do spontaneous demonstration "talk-outs" before the entire group. Problem situations such as the following are suggested:

    a) Who will manage the money—husband or wife?

    b) Working wife versus wife as a fulltime homemaker?

   ✓ c) Simple small town life versus living in a large city?

    d) He thinks entertaining is a waste of money. She thinks it is important.

    e) She wants a large church wedding but he wants a simple family ceremony.

    f) He wants to accept a job in a foreign country; she wants to stay close home.

    g) She insists on going to church and Sunday school; he likes to stay home and sleep late on Sunday.

    h) He expects her to move into a large ranch house with his father; she objects.

READINGS

Becker, Howard, and Hill, Reuben, eds., *Family, Marriage and Parenthood* (Boston: D. C. Heath and Company, 1955), Part Three, "Marriage Interaction."

Bigelow, Howard F., *Family Finance* (Philadelphia: J. B. Lippincott Company, Revised 1953).

Blood, Robert O., Jr., *Anticipating Your Marriage* (Glencoe, Illinois: The Free Press, 1955), Part II, "Marriage."

Bowman, Henry A., *Marriage for Moderns* (New York: McGraw-Hill Book Company, Revised 1953).

Burgess, Ernest W., and Wallin, Paul, with Shultz, Gladys Denny, *Courtship, Engagement and Marriage* (Philadelphia: J. B. Lippincott Company, 1954).

Christensen, Harold T., *Marriage Analysis* (New York: The Ronald Press Co., 1950).

Duvall, Evelyn Millis, *In-Laws: Pro and Con* (New York: Association Press, 1954).

Duvall, Evelyn Millis, and Hill, Reuben, *When You Marry* (Boston: D. C. Heath and Company, Revised 1953), Part 2, "What It Means to Be Married."

Fishbein, Morris, and Burgess, Ernest W., eds., *Successful Marriage* (Garden City, New Jersey: Doubleday and Company, Revised 1955), Part Two, "The Marriage."

Havighurst, Robert J., *Human Development and Education* (New York: Longmans, Green and Co., 1953), Chapter 16, "Developmental Tasks of Early Adulthood."

Himes, Norman E., *Your Marriage* (New York: Rinehart and Company, Revised and enlarged by Donald L. Taylor, 1955), Part Two, "Now that You're Married."

Koos, Earl Lomon, *Marriage* (New York: Henry Holt and Co., 1953), Chapters 8–15.

Landis, Judson T., and Landis, Mary G., *Building a Successful Marriage* (New York: Prentice-Hall, Inc., 1948), Chapters 10–17.

Landis, Paul H., *Making the Most of Marriage* (New York: Appleton-Century-Crofts, 1955).

Levy, John, and Munroe, Ruth, *The Happy Family* (New York: Alfred A. Knopf, 1938).

Magoun, F. Alexander, *Love and Marriage* (New York: Harper & Brothers, 1948), Chapters 8, 9, 10.

Pike, James A., *If You Marry Outside Your Faith* (New York: Harper & Brothers, 1954).

Rock, John, and Loth, David, *Voluntary Parenthood* (New York: Random House, 1949).

Stone, Abraham, and Stone, Hannah, *A Marriage Manual* (New York: Simon and Schuster, 1952).

Van de Velde, Th. H., *Ideal Marriage: Its Physiology and Technique* (New York: Convici-Friede Publishers, 1937).

Waller, Willard, *The Family, a Dynamic Interpretation* (New York: The Dryden Press, Revised by Reuben Hill, 1951), Part Four, "Marriage: the Established Status."

*Age is not all decay, it is the ripen-
ing, the swelling of fresh life
within, that withers and bursts
the husks.*

GEORGE MACDONALD

CHAPTER SEVEN

Beginning families: expectant phase

The expectant phase of the beginning family starts with the awareness that the wife is pregnant and continues until the birth of
the first child. This phase is no longer than nine months, and may be
considerably shorter than that if the pregnancy is not confirmed immediately or if the woman is already pregnant at marriage. Short in length,
the pregnant family phase is long on tasks and responsibilities. How
husband and wife assume their nesting roles varies greatly depending
largely on their readiness for this step in their development.

Many young couples marry just because they love each other, with
little conscious intent of raising a family. As one woman puts it, "If I
get pregnant right away, that's all right, and if I don't, I will sooner or
later; my sister did." For other couples it is not as matter-of-fact as that.
It depends on many things: how they both feel about children, whether
other goals of the couple conflict with having a baby (education, travel,
money for a house, a car, or other things may mean a great deal), how
ready they are for parenthood, and what pressures are exerted by their
friends and family for having a baby. In such factors as these are the
origins of the developmental tasks of the phase of expectancy in beginning families.

COMPLEMENTARY AND CONFLICTING DEVELOPMENTAL TASKS
DURING PREGNANCY

As the young couple go through the first pregnancy, there are times
when their individual tasks complement each other in shared accom-

plishment as parents-to-be. Just as naturally there are times when their individual developmental tasks conflict and husband and wife are pulled in opposite directions. Illustrative instances of some of the opposing and complementary forces at work in today's developmental tasks of husband and wife at the expectant stage are outlined below.

Some Contemporary Developmental Tasks of the Expectant Father	Some Contemporary Developmental Tasks of the Expectant Mother	Complementary and Conflicting Possibilities
Starting a family. Planning the first child's arrival. Learning what it means to become a father. Giving his wife his support through her pregnancy and childbirth.	Starting a family. Planning the first child's arrival. Learning what it means to be a mother. Proceeding successfully through the pregnancy and childbirth experience.	Complementary (both work together in the common task of becoming parents for the first time).
Becoming a man in a man's world. Finding himself among his fellow workers and male colleagues. Taking jeers and taunts of other men good naturedly as his wife's condition becomes apparent. Continuing some activities with "the boys" that do not include their wives necessarily.	Becoming a woman in a woman's world. Identifying with her women friends and neighbors in personal special female ways. Participating in baby showers and other "women only" affairs. Borrowing and lending, sharing and being shared within the feminine fellowship of her relationship with "the girls."	Conflicting (the husband is pulled into male circles and his wife is being absorbed in feminine interests and functions).
Being responsible as the main support of the family. Getting to work on time. Carrying a full load as a breadwinner.	Seeing her chief jobs as mother-to-be as well as wife. Letting up on her outside interests as the pregnancy advances. Becoming content to be wife and mother primarily.	Complementary (common task of nest-building). Conflicting (he is pulled outward, and she is pulled inward in her childbearing.

There is no one pattern of response when she misses that first menstruation. Rather there are four possible responses: (1) they both accept the fact that they have become an expectant family, (2) they both reject the baby months before he/she is due, (3) the husband accepts the pregnancy while the wife does not, and (4) she is delighted while he grouses about it. The first reaction is most typical today, when babies tend to be highly valued, but the other three reactions do occur.

DEVELOPMENTAL TASKS OF THE EXPECTANT FAMILY

If the married couple is to find a comfortable adjustment to pregnancy and have their first baby with more of a sense of fulfillment than distress, creating along with the child a climate good for its well-being, they must accomplish a number of developmental tasks inherent in the period. These are briefly:

1) reorganizing housing arrangements to provide for the expected baby
2) developing new patterns for getting and spending income
3) revaluating procedures for determining who does what and where authority rests
4) adapting patterns of sexual relationships to pregnancy
5) expanding communication systems for present and anticipated emotional constellations
6) reorienting relationships with relatives
7) adapting relationships with friends, associates, and community activities to the realities of pregnancy
8) acquiring knowledge about and planning for the specifics of pregnancy, childbirth, and parenthood
9) testing and maintaining a workable philosophy of life.

REORGANIZING HOUSING ARRANGEMENTS TO PROVIDE FOR THE EXPECTED BABY

No one has to teach birds their nesting rites and responsibilities. Their instincts guide them through the whole process. Not so with humans. They must learn their nesting tasks, step by step through the expectant phase.

Some husbands and wives take the coming of their first baby casually and do very little in providing a place for it before its arrival. The story is told of the young parents who simply dumped the contents of a dresser drawer in a box and plopped the new baby in the drawer which served as a bed until the infant was big enough to sleep with its brothers. A maternity hospital reports that occasionally a baby arrives with no clothes to wear, no blankets, and no home to go to. But this is not the usual story, especially for the first baby. Later siblings may "make do" with provisions dating back to the arrival of their elder brothers and sisters. But some special provision is usually made for the first baby.

There are young couples who must make drastic shifts in their housing in order to make way for the expected first baby. Many modern apartment houses rule against children. A married couple whose first home has been in such a building must search out a more hospitable home base before their baby arrives. The husband and wife who have been floating from place to place in a series of rented rooms now want to settle down in something more permanent because of the expected arrival of their first baby. The couple who has found satisfaction in living with one set of parents, quite likely now desire to find a place of their own when they expect to become three. There are couples who must find something less expensive than they have been enjoying in housing as soon as a baby is expected. Even more numerous are the young families-in-the-making who move to more desirable neighborhoods, sensing the importance of suitable neighbors, congenial companions, adequate play space, and good schools.

The husband and wife who stay on where they have been living make some rearrangements in their living space when a baby is expected. Room is cleared and provided for the baby's sleeping, eating, bathing, and playing. This may be a separate nursery complete with new baby furniture and sundry equipment. Or it may be a corner that is equipped for baby care, away from the main household traffic. The differences in spatial arrangements are not important as long as husband and wife see eye to eye on them. Trouble comes when the definition of the demands of expectant parenthood differs greatly between the husband and wife.

The most frequent problem arising in reorganizing the household for the first baby is that of the wife wanting more elaborate preparations and expensive rearrangements than the husband deems necessary. The wife who wants to move to a new place that she considers much more suitable for them now that the baby is on the way may be distressed that her husband flatly balks or obviously does not share her enthusiasm for the shift. When her husband fails to back up her plans for the new family home, she may feel that he is rejecting not only her ideas, but her and the baby as well. The man defines the situation from his point of view as husband quite differently at times. As a man, he may tend to feel that his wife's plans are so much feminine falderal. As the principal breadwinner, he is aware of the new responsibilities that will fall on him as father and so is reluctant to undertake any unnecessary expenditures. How the two resolve their dilemma is dependent in part upon how well they achieve the other developmental tasks they face as expectant parents.

DEVELOPING NEW PATTERNS FOR GETTING AND SPENDING INCOME

"It isn't the initial cost, it's the upkeep" that mounts in having a baby. The cost of having a baby was relatively low in the days when a family's children were born in the master bedroom with only the family doctor, midwife, neighbor, or female member of the family in attendance. Today most babies are born in hospitals where the initial costs necessarily are higher, even for low-income families. The cost of rearing a child to maturity was relatively low in the days when the family home was on the farm where food and clothing were made or raised and one more mouth to feed made little economic difference. In contrast, since the Industrial Revolution, rearing a child has become a costly investment for a family. One careful study shows clearly that in families with annual incomes averaging $2,500, the cost of raising a child to maturity was $7,766 in 1935–36 price levels. Families with annual incomes in the $5,000 to $10,000 bracket spent on the average $16,337 on each child raised to 18 years of age, as is shown in Table 12. In present-day figures these amounts would be considerably greater, as of course would be the family incomes. Proportionally, the cost of having a child now is a considerable investment by the family—not only for the bare essentials but also for what is involved in education, recreation, transportation, culture, medical care, and all the "sundries" purchased over the years.

The costs of rearing a child do not descend upon the new family all at once, but their anticipation may. Many a young wife makes her first visit to the physician to ascertain whether or not she is pregnant. She returns not only with the happy news that a baby is on the way but also with the dismaying array of costs that have been outlined for her: so much for the doctor, such and such an amount for the hospital, the use of the delivery room, the bed she will occupy for her lying-in period, recommended nursing service, and all the rest. She may stop

TABLE 12. *Costs of Bringing Up a Child to Age 18 by Two Income Groups (Price Levels of 1935–1936)* [1]

Expenditure Item	Annual Family Income	
	$2,500	$5,000 to $10,000
Total	$7,766	$16,337
Cost of being born	300	750
Food	2,275	3,628
Clothing	711	1,697
Medical care	299	846
Shelter	2,647	5,774
Education	82	283
Transportation and recreation	1,126	2,787
Sundries	326	572

in at a baby shop on her way home and be further impressed with the amount of money charged for the tiny garments that go into making up the layette. Not knowing whether hers will be a girl or a boy, she fingers little dresses and is startled to realize they cost almost as much as a dress for herself, while clothing for little boys is priced nearly as high as her husband's items. By the time she and her husband get their pencils out to figure what it will cost to have the baby, they are sobered by the realization that family expenses from now on will be appreciably higher.

Even more of a jolt comes when the couple realizes that with the coming of the first baby, the wife's income will stop and the family will have to live on the husband's income alone. Today, many young wives work until the first baby is about to arrive and then drop out of gainful employment until the children are old enough so that full-time mothering is no longer necessary. Some couples are smart enough to anticipate the decrease in the family income when the wife no longer contributes her earnings to it. These couples live on the husband's income from the beginning, saving wife's earnings against the time when there will be need for special outlay for a baby, a car, a down payment on a home, furniture, and other equipment. The husband and wife who have been living up all their joint income while both were working get

[1] Louis I. Dublin, and Alfred J. Lotka, *The Money Value of Man* (New York: The Ronald Press Company, Revised Edition, 1946), page 55.

a shock, when suddenly, with the coming of the first baby, they must live on only one set of earnings at the very time that they face big increases in their expenditures.

Difficult too are the tasks of the young couple facing pregnancy early in the marriage, before there has been time to accumulate a backlog of savings or even to meet the initial costs of being married.

Insurance plans help defray the initial costs of childbirth. David Treat reports that in Flint, Michigan, Blue Cross pays for three-fourths of all births.[1] Life insurance now becomes a necessity as never before. As long as both the husband and wife were working and able to work, life insurance might or might not have been an item to consider. Now, with a baby on the way, a woman needs and will continue to need the protection of life insurance on the husband until the childrearing period is over.

Savings take on more meaning when children appear in the family. Starting a savings account for the children's education, for the medical expenses, and for the other needs that are inevitable in the expanding stage of the family life cycle makes sense to young husband and wife as never before.

Where is all the money coming from for initial costs of having the baby, its upkeep through the years, the many new needs as a family, the insurance, the savings, and all the rest at the very time that the wife stops work to give her time entirely to having and raising children? The answer varies from couple to couple, from social class to social class.

Depending upon its orientation, resources, and values, the young family may decide from among a variety of solutions to their financial problems. The young family may float a loan, or dip into savings, or look to their parents for help, or go into debt or into an orgy of installment buying. But whatever it does, the decision is there to be made in the beginning stage of the family life cycle.

REVALUATING PROCEDURES FOR DETERMINING WHO DOES WHAT AND WHERE AUTHORITY RESTS

Today's young mother-to-be assumes a multiplicity of roles. She carries on the responsibilities of her household; she works as long as her physician allows throughout the pregnancy; she is at home in classroom and

[1] David B. Treat, Director, The Clara Elizabeth Fund for Maternal Health, Flint, Michigan, personal communication, June 27, 1956.

laboratory as she tries to finish her education before maternity is upon her; she is found in her smart maternity garments as hostess or play-mate along with her husband at neighborhood gatherings in the com-panionship roles so important today. Any one of these roles has been a full-time job for some woman in the past—housewife, worker, mother-to-be, school-girl, hostess-companion. The modern young woman carries them all, with the help of her husband.

Now that men have a reasonably short working week (as compared with the 60 or more hours in the nineteenth-century work week), they have more time at home. Household tasks in the modern home, with its electrified equipment and packaged goods, are less arduous, more fun, and require less technical knowledge. Any man who wants to can whip up a tasty meal in today's kitchen. And many of them do. Now with wives out of the home carrying the variety of roles characteristic of modern woman, husbands are finding a new place for themselves in the family.

During the first trimester of pregnancy when many expectant mothers feel nauseated upon awakening in the morning, a husband may get breakfast and bring his wife something to eat that will ease the dis-comfort of her arising, before he leaves for work. During pregnancy, heavy mopping and cleaning may be forbidden the pregnant woman by her doctor; her figure enlarges making stooping over uncomfortable and so other tasks may be reassigned the husband. By the time the first baby is born many couples have rearranged their previous defini-tions of who does what to make way for the new roles and realities of parenthood.

Outsiders become a new source of authority in many an expectant family's home. What the doctor has prescribed or proscribed is taken as law, more conscientiously now than it will be for further pregnancies, in many homes. The elder women of the family may come into the picture in many ways that are threatening to the authority of the young husband. One of the hazards of this phase of family living lies in the ego-shattering experience he goes through in being low man in the hier-archy of influence in his own home:

It's foolish I know, but I'm jealous of my own obstetrician.

I hate to admit that I don't know all there is to know, but frankly, I'm lost with all this gobbledegook the wife talks over with the Doc.

Many young couples make their first trip to the obstetrician or family doctor together. There they bring up as a couple the questions they want answered and together establish the relationship with the doctor that makes carrying out the prescribed regimen of pregnancy and birth a cooperative enterprise in which doctor, wife, and husband participate. Such a mutual assumption of responsibility provides effective ways of achieving the developmental tasks involved for the couple and is to be recommended wherever possible.

ADAPTING PATTERNS OF SEXUAL RELATIONSHIPS TO PREGNANCY

When a woman becomes pregnant there are obvious changes in her body that remind both her and her husband that she is something much more than just a sexual being for the pleasures of marriage. One of the first of these changes is the filling out of her breasts early in pregnancy. In recent generations, a woman's breasts have become powerful sex symbols, almost to the point of fetishism.[1] In premarital petting, as well as during the foreplay in marriage, love-play involving the breasts is prominent in heterosexual lovemaking. But with the rounding out of the mammary glands in pregnancy, comes the realization that these organs are soon to be shared with the little newcomer already on the way. For some husbands this means an abrupt change in types of sex play. As the pregnancy progresses, both husband and wife shift earlier patterns of sexual relationships to accommodate to the realities of the physical situation. They may or may not adversely effect the sexual relationship of the marriage.

One study of married college students indicates that for the majority, pregnancy has no effect on the sexual relationship, about one in four report unfavorable effects, and nearly one in every five husbands and wives find pregnancy effecting their sex adjustment for the better, as is shown in Table 13.

Wives generally report that their husbands are more thoughtful and considerate during pregnancy than they were before with such comments as these usual:

He became more affectionate and closer to me.

More gentle in manner and speech.

[1] Betsy Marvin McKinney, "The Sexual Aspects of Breast Feeding," *Child-Family Digest,* 5320 Danneel Street, New Orleans, La., December 1955, pp. 45–57.

He babied me a lot especially towards the last part of pregnancy.

He thought and acted as if I were now a woman, no longer a child.[1]

TABLE 13. *Percentages of Husbands and Wives Reporting How First Pregnancy Effected Their Sexual Adjustment* [2]

Reported Effect	Per cent of Husbands Reporting	Per cent of Wives Reporting
No effect	58	58
Unfavorable	23	25
Favorable	19	17
	100	100

Both husband and wife tend to report decreasing sexual desire as the pregnancy progresses, suggesting that both men and women are influenced by psychological as well as physiological factors during the expectant period, at least among married college students. There is a strong tendency for husbands to identify with their wives during the first pregnancy. Such a spirit is evident in the young father-to-be who says, "We are pregnant at our house." When both husband and wife can jointly accept the pregnancy in this way, the husband suffers less of the sense of deprivation of sexual response from and access to his wife when it becomes indicated as the pregnancy progresses. Reasons for stopping sexual intercourse during pregnancy are several, with physician's advice against it most common (usually in the last six weeks of pregnancy—see Table 14).

In general, couples who have a mutually satisfying sex life before pregnancy make a good sex adjustment during pregnancy.

EXPANDING COMMUNICATION SYSTEMS FOR PRESENT AND ANTICIPATED EMOTIONAL CONSTELLATIONS

Pregnancy is an emotional adventure for most couples. Long before the baby actually arrives fantasy makes him a member of the family.

[1] *Ibid.* p. 770.
[2] Adapted from Judson T. Landis, Thomas Poffenberger and Shirley Poffenberger, "The Effects of First Pregnancy upon the Sexual Adjustment of 212 Couples," *American Sociological Review*, Vol. 15, No. 6, December 1950, pp. 767–772.

TABLE 14. *Percentages of Husbands and Wives Giving Reasons for Cessation of Sexual Intercourse during Pregnancy* [1]

Reasons	Wives (N = 184) *	Husbands (N = 191) †
Doctor ordered it	38.0%	29.9%
Painful for wife	16.5	18.3
Fear of hurting baby	15.6	18.8
I didn't enjoy it	14.6	3.2
Fear of miscarriage	5.4	9.9
Nauseated wife	4.4	2.6
It didn't seem right	3.3	6.8
Spouse didn't enjoy it	2.2	10.5

* Wives, 28 no response.
† Husbands, 21 no response (some gave multiple responses).

One young husband set a place at the table for the baby: cup, plate, spoon, and high chair, as soon as the doctor confirmed the pregnancy. His wife interpreted, "He's crazy just a little, but you see we've waited for seven long years. I've dreamt about his sitting there at the table too."

Fears of "going through the shadow of death" still haunt an occasional expectant mother. Although the dangers of childbearing are dramatically less now than a generation or two ago, the memory lingers on. As one experienced gynecologist observes:

Young people still reflect the association of childbearing with illness: the doctor, the nurse, many days of hospitalization, infants in the sterile nursery —all fear-inducing thoughts.

. . . The morbidity which resulted from the poor obstetrics of years ago was very real. There was reason enough for fear. Lacerations which were unrepaired from one pregnancy to another resulted in cystoceles, prolapse, and relaxed vaginal canals. Intercourse was painful when the tears were left to heal spontaneously. The profuse leucorrheal discharges from lacerated or infected cervices overlubricated the vaginal canal. In many, repeated deliveries occurring so rapidly that the patient hadn't recovered from one before the next pregnancy was started, resulted in very flabby, large vaginal canals. All these factors prevented many husbands and wives from enjoying intercourse after the first pregnancy. In addition to the poor approximation of the sex organs, the wife lacked desire for coitus. She was either pregnant, nursing, or in pain.[2]

[1] *Ibid.* p. 771.
[2] Nadina R. Kavinoky, "Marital Adjustments During Pregnancy and the Year After," *Medical Woman's Journal*, October 1949, pp. 1–2.

The expectant fathers' pacing room in today's maternity hospital occasionally reflects many second-hand memories locked in the minds of impressionable boys until the time when they become fathers themselves. These hand-me-down memories are prime forces in making a man feel guilty about his wife's pregnancy and childbirth. As one young expectant father put it, "If she comes through this OK, I swear, I'll never get her pregnant again." Even before the actual birth a man may be haunted by anxieties, uncertainties, and guilts:

I feel so guilty seeing her so miserable mornings, and knowing that I got her into this, and that the worst is yet to come too.

Is it normal to be so blamed scared? I get so worried about what might happen that I'm not even pleasant around the house . . . what if she has a miscarriage? what if she has the baby before I can get her to the hospital? what if she has to have a Caesarean?

Pride over his proven virility, satisfaction in his wife's prenatal care and progress, plans for his child's future, and the sense of fulfillment as fatherhood approaches are but a few of the positive emotions that the expectant father needs to learn to express. One of his developmental tasks involves developing the channels for communicating both the negative and the positive feelings that have their genesis in his first experience as a father-to-be.

Some men and women learn to express their feelings about the pregnancy, about the birth experience, and about their forthcoming relationship with their first child relatively easily. These are usually the persons whose positive acceptance of their roles as men and women overweighs their negative feelings. An investigation of the way new mothers feel about menstruation, pregnancy, childbirth, breast feeding, rooming-in, and satisfaction with woman's role in life, indicates that women who complain about pregnancy, childbirth, and breast feeding tend to be those who find it hard to accept their feminine role in life.[1]

Now, when many women attempt to carry a number of responsibilities concurrently (home, school, work, etc.), problems over conflicting roles may be expected. A study of young wives of married students reports,

Those wives who were enrolled in school or employed outside the home were to a greater extent represented among those wives who had tried to

[1] Niles Newton, *Maternal Emotions* (Philadelphia: Paul Hoeber, 1955).

avoid pregnancy than were those wives whose role was confined to home-making alone. The latter were more represented among the wives who planned their pregnancies. This relationship suggests that scholarly pursuits or a vocation outside the home may influence plans for children in the early period of marriage. The comments of wives whose pregnancies interrupted the completion of a college degree were more often indicative of deep regret than were those of working wives whose remarks for the most part reflected their willingness to quit wage-earning and be full-time homemakers.[1]

Clinical as well as statistical evidence indicates that those young wives and husbands who most comfortably achieve the developmental task of getting through to each other on the decisional and emotional realities of pregnancy and childbirth are those who have already accomplished previous developmental tasks of accepting feminine or masculine sex roles and so are ready for the experience of parenthood.

When the multiple roles of the sexes are as flexible as they are today, some problems in defining them are inevitable. To the extent to which the two people can learn to establish the communication systems necessary for making the decisions and handling the feelings involved in having a baby, and learning to be parents, to that extent will they find their new roles with confidence.

REORIENTING RELATIONSHIPS WITH RELATIVES

For every new baby born there is not only a new mother and a new father, but also new grandparents, new aunts and uncles, and many other new constellations in the family circle. Mothers and mothers-in-law who have been relatively successful in "keeping hands off" the new couple during their honeymoon and establishment periods feel more closely involved with the new household as soon as a baby is expected.

Relatives sometimes vie with each other in showering gifts for the new baby upon the expectant parents. These often reflect their own unfulfilled desires rather than the needs of the baby. Even more hazardous are the tales of their own experiences in childbearing with the well-meaning advice that too often is in conflict with that of the attending physician.

There is a positive side to the picture. Nowadays when nurses are hard to come by, and the new mother and tiny baby return from the

---

[1] Shirley Poffenberger, Thomas Poffenberger, and Judson T. Landis, "Intent Toward Conception and the Pregnancy Experience," *American Sociological Review*, Vol. 17, No. 5, October 1952, p. 617.

COURTESY OF THE ALBUM

The expectant husband and wife who learn to establish good communication systems for making the decisions and handling the feelings involved in becoming parents, find their new roles with confidence.

hospital soon after the birth, a young couple is fortunate in having the willing hands of a mother or mother-in-law to help them through the lying-in period until the young mother can fully take over. A recent study turned up many appreciative comments:

When our daughter was born, who but Mom-in-law would have come and stayed to cook, clean, care for a baby and mother, keep a household running smoothly, and yet have unbounded love and sheer joy in doing all this? (*Mrs. M., Indiana.*)

Last month we added a daughter to our family and we asked Tom's Mom to lend us a helping hand for a while. She immediately took a month's leave of absence from her work and home duties, to give us her time during the busiest of everyone's life—the Holiday Season. (*Mrs. T., Indiana.*)

When my child was born my own mother could not be with me and although my mother-in-law, who is in business for herself and finds it hard to get away, was at time needed at home, she came to me and saw me through it all. (*Mrs. J., Illinois.*)

My husband and I have been married five and a half years. At first I resented my mother-in-law. Our first baby was born a year after we were married. She came five hundred miles to help care for me and the baby. (*Mrs. L., Kansas.*) [1]

Reorienting relationships with relatives of both sides of the family is an important developmental task during the expectant phase. Its success contributes a sense of accord and belonging to the parents-to-be, and paves the way for many helpful mutually supportive relationships in the years to come. Grandparents and other relatives can be liabilities or assets to the young family, depending in large part upon the accomplishment of this developmental task before the first child arrives.

ADAPTING RELATIONSHIPS WITH FRIENDS, ASSOCIATES, AND COMMUNITY ACTIVITIES TO THE REALITIES OF PREGNANCY

As the pregnancy progresses the recreational and social life of the couple has to be readapted to the realities of the situation. Some activities are sharply curtailed, and others stop altogether, while a regimen more suitable for the expectant mother is put into effect. Instead of gay nights out on the town, the couple may find more of their evenings given to a game of cards with old friends, or taking walks together, or reading aloud some of the current literature on bringing up Baby.

Some couples find such adaptive procedures difficult. This one did, who says, "He just does not dare go north fishing while I'm carrying this baby for him. If he does, I'll—I'll leave him and he knows I'm not fooling." Or this one, a young veteran reflects, "You have to grow up fast when you get out of the Army and your wife is pregnant, and you aren't through school yet. I almost lost my wife in the process. She went back home to her mother and our son was two months old before I even saw him. We finally got together as a family again, but we almost didn't make it."

If the wife's insecurity in her pregnancy makes her jealous of her husband's night out with the boys, or his bowling league, or his educational and vocational projects, or any of his leisure-time pursuits that are not specifically related to the pregnancy, something will have to give. The husband may give in and defer to his wife through the period. Or, the wife may weather it on her own with either immature resentment or determination to grow up and be a woman through it all. Usu-

---

[1] Evelyn Millis Duvall, *In-Laws: Pro and Con* (New York: Association Press, 1954), pp. 94–95.

ally outside loyalties and involvements with friends, and associates, tend to drop off in importance as the pregnancy progresses. They possibly will never return to their former state. For with parenthood comes even more confining days and nights.

New associations become a part of the expectant phase as the young mother-to-be is inducted into the women's clubs and organizations for which her new status makes her eligible. She may attend expectant mothers' classes or join a sewing circle where she will have congenial companionship while she makes maternity clothes and the wee garments for the layette. In general, she is now drawn more into feminine association than before. And if she has learned to enjoy being a woman, she will like the new woman's world that her baby and she enter together.

The hazard lies in the husband's being left out of it all as the pregnancy continues. His wife, who before shared everything with him, now shares her physical problems with the doctor and her practical plans for the baby with friends whose personal experience parallels hers. Baby showers are given for HER to which HE is not invited. If he puts on his hat and coat and goes out for the evening, it is understandable. It takes a wise young husband and wife to work out a mutually acceptable social life that gives each of them freedom for the associations that are most personally meaningful, at the same time that they pursue enough joint activities to continue to enjoy life as a couple. A comfortable balance of their individual autonomy and integration as a couple forms a basis for their life together for the years ahead.

ACQUIRING KNOWLEDGE ABOUT AND PLANNING FOR THE SPECIFICS OF PREGNANCY, CHILDBIRTH, AND PARENTHOOD

The old taboos about refusing to talk about sex and reproduction have broken down in recent decades. Today a husband and wife facing their first pregnancy want to know what is happening, and they both are learning to put their questions into words. This is harder for some than for others; more difficult for men than for women, perhaps, but it is being done.

One of the reasons why men find their wife's first pregnancy difficult is that in the areas of sex and reproduction a man hates to admit that he doesn't know all there is to be known. Up to now we have been rearing our sons that way. Parents tell sons less about reproduction than they tell daughters. The earthy and vulgar jokes about sex and

The Men's Forum of the Clara Elizabeth Fund for Maternal Health in Flint, Michigan, considers expectant fathers' questions under the professional leadership of William Genné.

pregnancy of locker room and tavern are difficult to reconcile with the tenderness a man feels for his wife when she feels miserable in her pregnancy. Didn't he "get her that way?" Along with the pride he feels over his proven virility is more than a little guilt that he is causing her distress.

Unless the wife, at this point, understands her man and begins to talk about what THEY can do to prepare the home for the baby, his emotional "valley of the shadows" may be even deeper than hers. Unless he can find some satisfactory answers to the questions that are his at this time, he is apt to be an unhappy man, a gloomy husband, and a reluctant father. He may be fortunate in being one of the thousands of men who through the years have attended expectant fathers' classes. For instance the Men's Forum, of the Clara Elizabeth Fund for Maternal Health in Flint, Michigan, considers expectant father's questions of which these are only a few:

Who is responsible for the sex of our baby?

How is the baby fed before he's born?

Is my reproductive system as complicated as my wife's?

Why are some babies marked?

Can childbirth be easier because there isn't fear and tension?

Are twins hereditary?

What is the rabbit test?

When can there be sexual relations during pregnancy?

Why are doctors letting women get up so early after childbirth?

How long does a woman have to be in labor?

What does it cost in dollars to have a baby? [1]

Meanwhile, an expectant mother is getting answers to her questions from her doctor, the prenatal clinic, or the preparation for motherhood classes she attends. She wants to understand the normal process of bearing and giving birth to a child. She wants to know how she can best cooperate in what she eats, what she does, and how she feels about it.

Social class differences in the expectant phase are many. In general, members of the middle and upper classes seek out more earnestly, take more seriously, and follow more conscientiously the advice of physicians and other experts than do members of the lower class, for whom childbearing tends to be taken for granted as another part of life to be endured. A recent comparative study of 401 women pregnant for the first time concludes that women of higher intelligence and higher social status tend to (1) be more careful in planning their first pregnancy and adjusting to it, (2) have better diet, (3) be more eager to breast-feed the baby, and (4) use birth control more effectively than do mothers of the lower classes. [2]

The middle- or upper-class woman may bombard her doctor with questions about his plans for her delivery, his preference for anesthetic, his opinion of "natural childbirth," rooming-in, and breast-feeding. She

[1] David Treat in "Preliminary Report, Committee on Dynamics of Family Interaction," Evelyn Duvall and Reuben Hill, eds., Washington, D. C., National Conference on Family Life, 1948, p. 18.

[2] D. Baird and Eileen Scott, "Intelligence and Childbearing," *Eugenic Review,* Vol. 45, 1953, pp. 139–154.

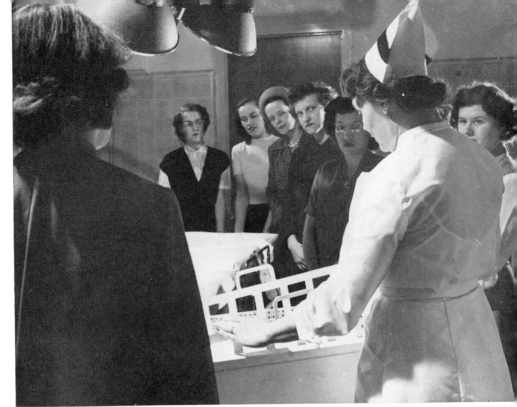

Expectant mothers get answers to their questions from the preparation for motherhood classes they attend, sometimes in the hospital where the deliveries will take place.

may need to be reassured about the possibilities of birth anomalies, or the incidence of trouble with incompatability of *Rh* blood types in pregnancy, or any of the other difficulties with which she has had some personal or vicarious experience.

If anything happens and she loses this first baby, she needs more help than ever. Disappointed potential motherhood can be a terrifying thing, even if she is assured that she can have another baby someday. If the couple faces the possibility of remaining childless, they must come to terms with what they are going to do about it.

Adoption is a possibility some husbands and wives consider if they find that they cannot have children of their own. One study indicates that 89 per cent of a college population (93.7 per cent of the women, and 84.7 per cent of the men) would be willing to adopt a child if they could have none of their own.[1] Child-placing agencies have re-

[1] Lemo D. Rockwood and Mary E. N. Ford, *Youth, Marriage and Parenthood* (New York: John Wiley and Sons, Inc., 1945), p. 156.

quirements that necessitate patient cooperation on the part of expectant adoptive parents. Black-market procedures are too hazardous to consider seriously.[1]

TESTING AND MAINTAINING A PHILOSOPHY OF LIFE

"Our children should have a better chance than we had," is a common goal of American families. The desire is to provide children with the opportunities and the resources that will assure them of more desirable living than their parents have been able to attain. This is especially true of upward-mobile families, while even among the relatively static, some elements of it are taken for granted today.

With the coming of children comes a highly motivated thrust for reworking the couple's way of life to provide a better setting for the little newcomer. Lucy decides that Ricky's English is not good enough for the expected baby, so she signs them up for a series of language lessons in an hilarious episode in the popular "I Love Lucy" television show. In real life, examples can be found that are quite as revealing. Tom and Mary return to church-going when their first baby is on the way, their motive is "it just seems the right thing for parents to do so the kid will get a good start." Elsie visits the art museum, not in a belief in prenatal impressions, but to become a more "cultured" mother worthy of the child-in-the-making. Nick gives up gambling, Tony stops smoking, Albert sends his first contribution to the orphans home—all during the first expectant period. Why? Because the approach of parenthood means for many men and women the revaluation of their ways of living and the deliberate attempt to test and rework their philosophies of life.

At few other times in the whole life cycle do men and women become more self-conscious about such questions as: Who are we? What is our way of life? Is this the kind of life we want to bring our children up in? What kind of parents will we be? What can we do to make ourselves the persons our children can be proud of? In this sense the expectant phase is a critical period in the life of the couple. For it means that the life style is now seen not only through the eyes of each of the pair as persons or from the point of view of the couple, but also from the view-

[1] See F. G. Brown, and others, *Adoption Principles and Services* (New York: Family Service Association, 1952); also H. L. Gordon, *Adoption Practices, Procedures, and Problems* (New York: Child Welfare League of America, 1952); and Ernest and Frances Cady, *How to Adopt a Child* (New York: William Morrow and Co., 1956).

point of the unborn generation, their children. This testing, evaluating, and maintaining of a workable philosophy of life runs through all other decisions and developmental tasks of the period. The beginning family successful in achieving this task is well on the way to family integration and a sense of identity upon which future periods and stages may be built.

HAZARDS AND DIFFICULTIES FACING THE FAMILY IN THE EXPECTANT PHASE

The danger of losing the wife and mother in childbirth is now dramatically less than it has been in earlier decades as we see clearly in Chart 11. Former hazards in childbearing have been greatly reduced by the increase in the number of births in hospitals, advances in medical knowledge and maternal care, as well as increases in prenatal services. Despite the great decline in maternal mortality there still remain

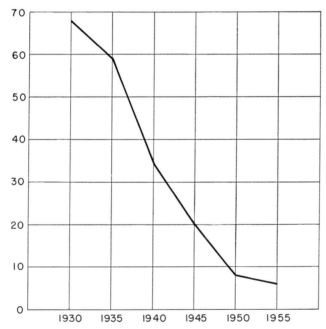

CHART 11.   Decrease in Maternal Mortality 1930–1955 [1]
(Maternal Deaths per 10,000 Live Births)

[1] Compiled from Metropolitan Life Insurance Company, *Statistical Bulletin:* June 1947, p. 5; July 1951, p. 2; and February 1954, pp. 8 and 9.

difficulties and problems of the expectant family that may be summarized briefly as follows:

PRESENT-DAY DIFFICULTIES OF THE EXPECTANT FAMILY

1) Modern housing must be drastically adapted for the coming of the first baby. Many places do not allow children, others have inadequate facilities for babies and so major rearrangements for coming of children must be made.

2) Double family income shrinks to one at a time when costs balloon. Wife drops out of work to have and raise her baby at a time when expenditures rise rapidly, putting strains on the family budget, and necessitating careful financial and family planning.

3) Husband or wife is not ready to assume new role as parent-to-be. Immature husband cannot accept sharing wife or adapt to changes in schedule too well. Infantile wife is not ready to settle down and have a family.

4) There is an increase in emotional instability in early pregnancy. ". . . wives as a whole experienced some heightened emotional tension in the early part of pregnancy as compared with their previous emotional stability."[1]

5) Married couples often are isolated from the supporting help of parental families. Modern marriages are often established far from families of orientation making it more difficult for members of the family to rally their resources and services to aid the new family at the birth of the baby.

6) Ignorance and superstition increase the difficulties of being expectant parents. Fallacies and current fictions about pregnancy, reproduction, and childbirth confuse the husband and wife and make their following healthful regimens more difficult.

7) There is fear of labor and childbirth experience. "Some anxiety is generally experienced" is the conclusion of one study of married college students in which 63.2 per cent of the wives studied indicated they feared the labor and childbirth.[2]

8) The pregnancy is unplanned and the baby unwanted. Difficulties occur in working through the developmental tasks of the period and accepting the baby when it comes.

[1] Shirley Poffenberger *et al.*, *op. cit.*, p. 618.
[2] *Ibid.*, p. 620.

RESOURCES AND SERVICES FOR EXPECTANT FAMILIES

Preparation for parenthood begins in childhood. As boys and girls are brought up by parents who want children, who love them, and who let them know it, they get a good feeling about having children that strongly influences their own attitudes toward parenthood. As children have their questions answered by their parents, teachers, and leaders in an ongoing integrated program of sex education, they are not as influenced by unfounded fears, superstitions, and ignorance and are better prepared for pregnancy, childbirth, and parenthood. Classes in preparation for marriage give both man and woman some idea of what to expect in marriage and family life as well as a chance to clarify their values and develop the positive attitudes that go a long way toward paving the way for the realities of living together as a family.

As the period of expectant parenthood approaches there are specific services available in some communities that help beginning families accomplish their developmental tasks. In Flint, Michigan, where series of classes for expectant parents (both husbands and wives) have been held continuously since January 1939, records show that women are now seeking medical care earlier in their pregnancies than was formerly the case. The emphasis of the classes ("You need early, regular, and complete obstetrical care") frequently sends a pregnant woman to her doctor much earlier than she would otherwise have gone. Once she is under professional guidance, and in the classes for expectant mothers, her emotional health as well as her physical condition improves.

It is easier to accept the physical inconveniences that go with pregnancy if there are from a dozen to fifty others in class in various stages of expectancy who have, or will have experiences paralleling one's own. Just to see that many women together who are listening to an explanation of childbirth, makes childbearing seem to be the very normal experience it is.

Many a man enjoys the celebration with cigars that accompanies the announcement, "It's a boy! Hey, Fellows! He's a boy!" And he may be quite as proud of being responsible for the pregnancy. Privately he confides to her, "By golly, Sweetheart, I am all right, I can start a baby." Even while publicly he shuns the kidding of his fellow office workers or the men on the assembly line at the plant.

The expectant father goes to Fathers' Forum a bit sheepishly and finds to his surprise that there are more than thirty-five other men there. Perhaps the fellow in the shop with whom he eats lunch is also "expecting." The informal discussion that starts out about understanding a wife's tears and occasional temper outbursts leads the fellow in the seat ahead of him to exclaim, "Tell you what I do when my wife blows her top—I just keep my hat near the door." Whereupon another fellow blurts out, "Keep your hat near the door? Hell! I keep mine on my head." The roar of understanding laughter rips the last shred of tension away as three dozen men realize that they individually are going through some of the same experiences in trying to understand the emotional disturbances that often accompany pregnancy. So it goes, too, for answering their inevitable questions about what is happening in pregnancy and what their roles as husbands and fathers are.[1]

Modern obstetrics, nursing, and hospital care now more frequently take into account the emotional and familial factors of having a baby that, in older more rigid systems, unnecessarily increased the woman's panic in childbirth. Her physician now wins her confidence not only in his skill, but also in herself as a woman who understands what is happening. He instructs her on how to cooperate in a comfortable pregnancy and a good delivery.[2] The nurse who sees her patient not just as another light to be answered, but as a flesh-and-blood person with feelings to be considered and new responsibilities to learn, can be very helpful in giving the support that is needed during labor. She offers instruction that may be needed to get breast-feeding off to a good start and baby and mother comfortable in each other's company.

Films on the progress of pregnancy, prenatal development and care, the nature of labor, the birth of a baby, and postnatal care are used widely by many agencies, *i.e.*, the Louisiana Association for Mental Health, and the American Institute of Family Relations' series on Parentcraft (for Husbands and Wives Who Are Expecting). The Dickinson-Belskie models of prenatal development and childbirth are extensively used, as are also a wide assortment of books and pamphlets on marriage, family relations, and the specific aspects of beginning families of greatest interest to parents-to-be.

Young couples themselves are ingenious in innovating ways of helping each other through expectant parenthood. One consumers' cooperative

[1] David Treat, *op. cit.*, pp. 16–18.
[2] Nadina R. Kavinoky, *op. cit.*, p. 5.

The Dickinson-Belskie models of prenatal development and childbirth are effectively used in classes for expectant parents.

has a clearing house for the exchange of maternity garments and infant furnishings by which these expensive items can be loaned from one expectant family to another with only the repair, cleaning, and replenishing costs involved for any one family. Other neighbors get together in their planning of social activities that fit the needs of young families. Potluck suppers, beach parties, community sings, and evenings around a campfire take the place of the dancing and night-clubbing that once occupied the same younger set in their courting and early marriage days. Now they are "settling down" to equally enjoyable activities that can carry through the expectant family phase into the childbearing periods just ahead.

We need have no fear that young couples are floored by the developmental tasks and hazards of childbearing. More families are having babies (two or three) today than ever before. Couples expecting their first baby are at the threshold of a great adventure. As they move from being a married couple to becoming a family "with baby makes three," they find new joys and satisfactions out of the successful accomplishment of the new tasks and responsibilities that are inherent in being in the expectant phase of family living.

SUMMARY

The expectant phase of the beginning family stage covers the period of the first pregnancy. It begins with the first awareness that a baby is on the way and carries through to the birth of the first child. There are four possible responses to the knowledge that husband and wife have become an expectant family: (1) they both accept their new status, (2) both reject the pregnancy and the unborn child, (3) he is pleased while she is unhappy about it, and (4) she is delighted but he grouses about it.

Developmental tasks of the expectant family are (1) reorganizing housing arrangements to provide for the expected baby, (2) developing new patterns for getting and spending income, (3) evaluating procedures for determining who does what and where authority rests, (4) adapting patterns of sexual relationships to pregnancy, (5) expanding communication systems for present and anticipated emotional constellations, (6) reorienting relationships with relatives, (7) adapting relationships with friends, associates, and community activities to the realities of pregnancy, (8) acquiring knowledge about and planning for the specifics of pregnancy, childbirth, and parenthood, and (9) testing and maintaining a workable philosophy of life.

In our present-day society the expectant family faces a number of difficulties in the successful accomplishment of its various developmental tasks. Promising new services and greatly improved established resources increase the chances of the survival of mother and baby in childbirth and the neonatal period and of the effective achievement of the family developmental tasks during the expectant phase.

SUGGESTED ACTIVITIES

1) Compute the costs of having a baby in your neighborhood on the basis of prevailing rates for the doctor's services, hospital costs, basic layette, infant furnishings, etc.
2) Interview a practicing obstetrician in your community on the common complaints of pregnant women and of women in labor and childbirth, with special emphasis on the kinds of supportive therapy he finds most generally helpful. Relate his experience to what you now know about the developmental tasks of women in first pregnancy and childbirth.

3) Prepare a scrapbook of announcements of offerings of agencies with special services for expectant parents, including those in your area as well as such ones as:

> American Institute on Family Relations
> 5287 Sunset Boulevard
> Los Angeles 27, California
>
> Clara Elizabeth Fund for Maternal Health
> 302 West Second Avenue
> Flint, Michigan
>
> Louisiana Association for Mental Health
> 816 Hibernia Building
> New Orleans 12, Louisiana
>
> Maternity Center Association
> 654 Madison Avenue
> New York 21, N. Y.

4) Review the series of *Pierre the Pelican* bulletins sent to expectant mothers by the Louisiana Association for Mental Health, 816 Hibernia Building, New Orleans, 12, Louisiana, on the explicit and implicit hazards and challenges of each trimester of pregnancy.

5) Go through Dickinson and Belskie's *Birth Atlas* (available through the Maternity Center Association, 654 Madison Avenue, New York 21), of photographs of the growth of the fetus and the birth of a baby with an expectant couple with whom you have offered to share the pictures in exchange for the privilege of recording verbatim their questions, page by page. Discuss these questions in terms of what is revealed in the interest in and knowledge about pregnancy, fetal growth, and birth by married men and women typical of the couple you studied.

6) Visit the library of your county medical association or local maternity hospital and list the films, pamphlets, and books available for expectant parents. According to their records, how many individuals availed themselves of these services during the current year? From what social class levels did these expectant parents come? Write an interpretive comment on your findings.

7) Send for *Natural Childbirth* a documentary recording (LP, 53 min.) of childbirth, available from Westminister Recording Sales Corp., 275 Seventh Ave., New York 1, N. Y. The recording was supervised by Dr. Grantly Dick Read, author of *Childbirth Without Fear*. Prepare your group for listening to this record by reading aloud the commentary provided with the recording and written by Aileen Hogan, Consultant in Maternity Nursing, The Maternity Center Association, New York, N. Y. Then, play the recording and allow time for comments and questions. Request papers to be written on reactions to the recording, describing feelings experi-

enced upon hearing the recording and subsequent feelings upon thinking
about the recording.

READINGS

Becker, Howard, and Hill, Reuben, eds., *Family, Marriage and Parenthood*
(Boston: D. C. Heath and Company, 1955 Revision), Chap. 15.

Bigelow, Howard F., *Family Finance* (Philadelphia: J. B. Lippincott Company, 1953 Revision), Chap. 16.

Biskind, Leonard, "Alleviation of Anxiety during Pregnancy," *Modern Medicine*, May 1946, pp. 3–11.

Blood, Robert O., Jr., *Anticipating Your Marriage* (Glencoe, Illinois: The Free
Press, 1955), Chaps. 15 and 16.

Corbin, Hazel, *Getting Ready to Be a Father* (New York: Macmillan, 1939).

Davis, M. Edward, *Natural Child Spacing* (Garden City, New York: Hanover
House, 1953).

Duvall, Evelyn Millis, *In-Laws: Pro and Con* (New York: Association Press,
1954), Chaps. 6 and 16.

Duvall, Evelyn Millis, and Hill, Reuben, *When You Marry* (Boston: D. C.
Heath and Company, 1953 Revision), Chaps. 16 and 17.

Fishbein, Morris, and Burgess, Ernest, eds., *Successful Marriage* (Garden
City, New York: Doubleday and Company, Inc., 1955 Revision), Part
Three.

Genné, William, *Husbands and Pregnancy: The Handbook for Expectant
Fathers* (New York: Association Press, 1956).

Himes, Norman, and Taylor, Donald, *Your Marriage* (New York: Rinehart &
Company, 1955 Revision), Chaps. 20, 21, 22.

Jackson, Edith B. and Trainham, Genevieve, eds., *Family Centered Maternity
and Infant Care* (New York: Josiah Macy, Jr., Foundation, 1950).

Koos, Earl Lomon, *Marriage* (New York: Henry Holt and Company, 1953),
Chap. 10.

Landis, Judson, and Landis, Mary, *Building a Successful Marriage* (New
York: Prentice-Hall, 1953 Revision), Chaps. 17, 18, 19.

Landis, Judson T.; Poffenberger, Thomas; and Poffenberger, Shirley, "The Effects of First Pregnancy upon the Sexual Adjustment of 212 Couples," *American Sociological Review*, Vol. 15, December 1950, pp. 767–772.

Lewis, Abigail, *An Interesting Condition: The Diary of a Pregnant Woman*
(Garden City, New York: Doubleday and Company, 1950).

Louisiana Association for Mental Health, *Pierre the Pelican, Prenatal Series*
(New Orleans: Louisiana Association for Mental Health, 816 Hibernia
Building, New Orleans 12, La.).

Merrill, Frances, *Courtship and Marriage* (New York: William Sloane Associates, Inc., 1949), Chap. 11.

Newton, Niles, *Maternal Emotions* (New York: Paul Hoeber, 1955).

Poffenberger, Shirley; Poffenberger, Thomas; and Landis, Judson T., "Intent toward Conception and the Pregnancy Experience," *American Sociological Review,* Vol. 15, December 1950, pp. 767–772.

Potter, Edith L., *Fundamentals of Human Reproduction* (New York: McGraw-Hill Book Company, Inc., 1948).

Superintendent of Documents, *So You Are Expecting a Baby* (Washington, D. C.: Government Printing Office, 1947).

Superintendent of Documents, *Prenatal Care* (Washington, D. C.: Government Printing Office, 1949).

Van Blarcom, Carolyn, and Corbin, Hazel, *Getting Ready to Be a Mother* (New York: Macmillan, 1940).

Waller, Willard, and Hill, Reuben, *The Family: A Dynamic Interpretation* (New York: The Dryden Press, 1951), Chap. 18.

Wasson, Valentina, *The Chosen Baby* (Philadelphia: J. B. Lippincott Company, 1939).

Zabriskie, Louise, *Mother and Baby Care in Pictures* (Philadelphia: J. B. Lippincott Company, 1946).

*You are the bows from which your
children as living arrows are
sent forth*

Kahlil Gibran

CHAPTER EIGHT

Childbearing families

The childbearing stage of the family life cycle begins with the birth of the first baby and continues until the firstborn is thirty months of age. During this period the husband and wife have their first experience as parents. They enter the stage as a married couple and leave it as established parents with one or more children. This stage of family life proceeds at a rapid pace through a series of overlapping phases. These involve the changing nature of the parents' roles and tasks of settling down as parents, the child's developmental progress, and the parade of family developmental tasks that appear, are satisfied or left incomplete, and are replaced by other urgencies that demand the attention of the young family.

THREE PHASES IN SETTLING DOWN AS A FAMILY

The first phase of the childbearing family is one of exaltation and rejoicing. The man has come through the crisis of the birth of his first child with a sense of relief and satisfaction. He throws out his chest as he passes cigars and announces the coming of his firstborn. The woman emerges from the first fatigue of childbirth with a glorious sense of accomplishment, a sensation of being in on the process of creation itself. She puts a ribbon in her hair and relaxes in the luxury of bedcare and postpartum attention, replete with telephone calls from wellwishers, congratulations from her friends, beaming pride of her parents, and her husband's family. There is a new tenderness from her mate. There are flowers, gifts for the baby, and a general spirit of celebration.

By the end of the first week mother and baby have made their first efforts to learn to live together. The mother has already taken the step that leads her into, or away from, active nursing of her baby. The baby has made his first adjustment to nursing and is either succeeding well or having trouble at his mother's breast. The new father's visits to the hospital are full of detailed accounts of what the baby is doing, how the nurses love him, how much handsomer, or brighter, or bigger, or quieter he is than the others in the nursery, and speculations as to which relative he resembles most closely. While mother and baby have been confined at the hospital through the lying-in period, the young father has been "baching it" alone at home or has been "farmed out" for his meals among neighbors and relatives. In the relatively few families where the first baby is delivered at home (see Chart 12), parents and baby are hosts to visitors who drop in with some tasty dish to congratulate the new parents, to see the new baby, and perhaps to lend a hand with the housework until the young mother is again able to take over completely.

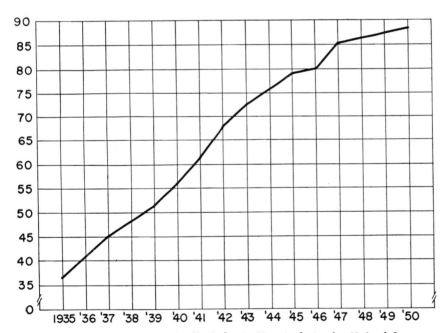

CHART 12. Percentage of All Births in Hospitals in the United States 1935–1950.[1]

[1] Compiled from Metropolitan Life Insurance Company; *Statistical Bulletins:* December 1947, Vol. 28, No. 12, p. 8; July 1951, Vol. 32, No. 7, pp. 1 and 2; February 1954, Vol. 35, No. 2, p. 9.

This first phase of parenthood we have described as the "flowers and pink ribbons stage:"

There are at least three stages in getting used to a new baby. The first is the flowers and pink ribbons stage. Mother is in her glory bedecked in her best bed jacket, with roses on her table and solicitous friends and family asking after her and the little newcomer. Father, who has felt like a fifth wheel during the long days of the pregnancy and the interminable hours of labor and birth, now comes into his own as exuberant herald to all the world of the miracle that has happened. He passes out cigars to all the boys and showers this wonderful woman of his with tokens of his undying affection. Everybody is happy. The parents are thrilled. Life is wonderful—too wonderful to last.[1]

With the homecoming of mother and baby from the hospital comes the end of the first flush of elation and the realization that parenthood is a strenuous responsibility. Now the care of the newborn is no longer in the capable hands of the nursing staff, but becomes a round-the-clock task of the young family. Baby's feeding schedule has to be worked out in ways that satisfy him and make sense in terms of the household. His bath-time at first is marked by the nervous fumbles of the new mother whose experiences in handling a tiny baby are limited, especially now when families are small and a girl has little opportunity to practice on younger brothers and sisters who used to keep on arriving until she had a baby herself. Keeping the baby clean and dry seems to be an everpresent challenge at first, and the diaper pail fills up at an alarming rate, or so it seems to the young mother who assumes as one of her responsibilities the daily laundry connected with infant care. Discouragement is so common at this time that it is known professionally as "involutional melancolia." Even in her weakened condition, she might manage all this if only she could get a good night's sleep. But many a newborn takes time to adjust to day and night schedules at home, and his howls between 2:00 and 4:00 A.M. not only rob his parents of sleep, but also increase their insecurity about their competence in caring for him.

There usually is some much-needed assistance at this stage to help the young couple through these first hectic days of establishing the new baby in the family. A nurse for the baby in the upper-class family takes over the care of the infant and keeps him from disturbing the rest of the household. In the middle-class and lower-class home, some female rela-

---

[1] Evelyn Millis Duvall and Reuben Hill, *When You Marry* (Boston, D. C. Heath and Company, Revised 1953), p. 363.

When the baby becomes stabilized, and the mother's strength returns, the daily outing becomes a satisfying experience for both of them.

tive, generally one of the baby's grandmothers, comes in for awhile and does the housework and the baby's laundry, gets the meals, and tries to keep things together until the mother regains her strength and has made some progress in caring for her baby.

Where such a willing relative cannot be drafted, the young husband may bear the brunt of the new burden, hurrying home from work to pitch in and help his wife with all she couldn't accomplish around the edges of baby care through the day. The strain of double duty for them both on a day and night basis may take its toll in frayed nerves and a kind of chronic fatigue that is characteristic of the period in many a young family.

After a while, the baby becomes stabilized around a predictable schedule and sleeps through the night most of the time. The mother's strength returns, and she becomes more skilled in caring for the baby as a normal part of her day's work. Now bathtime is fun for both. The daily outing becomes a lark and shopping an outing. The outsiders who have helped out during the baby's first days at home have departed and father, mother, and baby settle down to the sweet peace of domesticity. Thus begins the long pull of parenthood, with its alternating phases of pride, pressure, and pleasure.

Throughout the childbearing stage of the family life cycle, the infant is attempting to achieve his developmental tasks, the father and the mother are trying to accomplish their developmental tasks as mates, as parents, as persons, and the family is facing a series of developmental tasks characteristic of the stage that must be accomplished if the family is to move successfully into its next stage of development. What these various developmental tasks are for each member of the family and for the family as a whole, and how these individual developmental tasks fuse and fractionate the family, meeting in complementary or conflicting ways within the dynamics of the family interaction, is a story that varies from family to family, from class to class, and from culture to culture, and yet can be reliably predicted in their universal aspects.

DEVELOPMENTAL TASKS OF INFANCY AND EARLY CHILDHOOD (BIRTH TO THIRTY MONTHS) [1]

This first period of life takes the infant from birth, when he emerges as a helpless bundle of potentials, to the place where he is somewhat independent of others. At the end of this period, the child has acquired a measure of autonomy, is taking solid foods, has achieved independent locomotion, and has mastered the first steps in a complex system of communication. Each of these accomplishments represents many hours of practice in real efforts on the part of the child to achieve the developmental tasks involved. These developmental tasks can be summarized as follows:

1) *Achieving physiological equilibrium following birth:*
    Learning to sleep at appropriate times.
    Maintaining a healthful balance of rest and activity.
2) *Learning to take food satisfactorily:*
    Developing ability to nurse—to suck, swallow, and adjust to nipple comfortably.

---

[1] Freely adapted from Loyd W. Rowland, "II. Child Bearing Family Stage," Evelyn Millis Duvall and Reuben Hill, co-chairmen, Report of the Committee on the Dynamics of Family Interaction, the National Conference on Family Life, Washington, D. C., 1948, and the University of Chicago workshop materials through several years.

Learning to take solid foods, to enjoy new textures, tastes, and temperatures, to use cup, spoon, and dishes competently in ways appropriate to his age.

3) *Learning the know-how and the where-when of elimination:*
Finding satisfaction in early eliminative processes.
Wanting to adapt to expectations of time and place of functioning as developmental readiness and parental pressures indicate.
Participating cooperatively and effectively as ready in the training program.

4) *Learning to manage one's body effectively:*
Developing coordination (eye-hand, hand-mouth, reach, grasp, handle, manipulate, put and take).
Acquiring skills in locomotion through kicking, creeping, walking, and running.
Gaining assurance and competence in handling oneself in a variety of situations.

5) *Learning to adjust to other people:*
Responding discriminatingly to others' expectations.
Recognizing parental authority and controls.
Learning the dos and the don'ts of his world.
Reacting positively to both familiar and strange persons within his orbit.

6) *Learning to love and be loved:*
Responding affectionally to others through cuddling, smiling, loving.
Meeting emotional needs through widening spheres and varieties of contact.
Beginning to give self spontaneously and trustfully to others.

7) *Developing systems of communication:*
Learning patterns of recognition and response.
Establishing nonverbal, preverbal and verbal communicative systems.
Acquiring basic concepts ("Yes," "No," "Up," "Down," "Come," "Go," "Hot," etc.).
Mastering basic language fundamentals in interaction with others.

8) *Learning to express and control feelings:*
Managing feelings of fear and anxiety in healthful ways.

Developing a sense of trust and confidence in one's world.

Handling feelings of frustration, disappointment and anger effectively in accordance with his development.

Moderating demanding attitudes as time goes on.

9) *Laying foundations for self-awareness:*

Seeing oneself as a separate entity.

Exploring rights and privileges of being a person.

Finding personal fulfillment with and without others.

THUS A CHILD LEARNS

Thus a child learns: by wiggling skills through his fingers and toes into himself, by soaking up habits and attitudes of those around him, by pushing and pulling his own world.

Thus a child learns: More through trial than error, more through pleasure than pain, more through experience than suggestion, more through suggestion than direction.

Thus a child learns: through affection, through love, through patience, through understanding, through belonging, through doing, through being.

Day by day the child comes to know a little bit of what you know, to think a little bit of what you think, to understand your understanding. That which you dream and believe and are, in truth, becomes the child.

As you perceive clearly or dully, as you think fuzzily or sharply, as you believe foolishly or wisely, as you dream drably or goldenly, as you are unworthy or sincere—thus a child learns.

FREDERICK J. MOFFITT
Associate Commissioner for
Elementary, Secondary and Adult Education
New York State Education Department

DEVELOPMENTAL TASKS OF THE MOTHER OF THE INFANT AND YOUNG CHILD

The first baby arrives in most families when the husband and wife are still working to establish their relationship as a married couple. Therefore, there is an inevitable overlapping of the developmental tasks of the young wife with those of the young mother during the baby's infancy. The young woman carries concurrently the unfinished business of being a competent and happy wife with that of becoming an effective and fulfilled mother. She masters many new skills during the infancy of her firstborn as she adjusts to the realities of motherhood and comes eventually toward the end of the period to a feeling of being established as a mother and settled as a family. At the end of this stage of the family life cycle, the young mother has begun to discover her own strengths and weaknesses and to establish the attitudes, values, and procedures that make sense for her as wife, mother, and a person. This progress is successful to the extent to which she has effectively achieved the developmental tasks of this stage in her development which, outlined in summary form, include:

1) *Reconciling conflicting conceptions of roles:*

Clarifying her role as a wife-mother-person.

Reconciling differences in conceptions of roles held by herself, her husband, and the various relatives, friends, and significant others.

Developing a sound workable conception of what she expects of her child.

Coming to comfortable understanding of her husband's role as a young father.

2) *Accepting and adjusting to the strains and pressures of young motherhood:*

Gearing activity to the lessened physical vigor in the periods of involution and lactation.

Cooperating in the processes involved in effective infant feeding.

Balancing the demands of the child, the expectations of the husband, and her commitments as a person with the limits of her abilities.

3) *Learning how to care for her infant with competence and assurance:*

Assuming responsibility for the care of the child.

Mastering the skills of feeding, bathing, protecting, and maintaining a healthy happy baby.

Learning how to anticipate and to recognize the needs of the baby.

Becoming increasingly able to enjoy caring for the young child.

4) *Establishing and maintaining healthful routines for the young family:*

Learning how to choose, prepare, and serve nutritious foods for both adult and infant needs.

Reorganizing family routines to meet the changing needs of the growing child within the family context.

Assuring a sufficiency of rest, relaxation, and sleep for the baby, the young husband, and herself.

Readjusting time schedules to make way for the necessities and for some purely pleasurable activities within the young family.

5) *Providing full opportunities for the child's development:*

Enriching the physical situation within the limits of family resources.

Providing plentiful varieties of experiences in exploring, manipulating, and learning for the infant and small child.

Protecting the furnishings and equipment in ways that keep to a minimum the physical restraint of the growing child (child-proofing the home).

Learning to enjoy and to wholeheartedly encourage the child's development and progress.

Accepting the child as himself without undue pressure, disappointment, or comparison.

6) *Sharing the responsibilities of parenthood with her husband:*

Recognizing the importance of the father-child relationship from the beginning.

Encouraging the participation of the young father in the care of the baby and small child in appropriate ways.

Bringing the young father into the planning, decision-making, evaluating processes that make him feel that his wishes and values are being respected and appreciated.

Establishing the habits of thinking of the child as "ours" rather than "mine".

7) *Maintaining a satisfying relationship with her husband:*

Protecting her husband's values as a person through the demanding pressures of young parenthood.

Reestablishing ways of being a couple with the unique values of husband-wife companionship throughout the infancy of first child.

Maintaining the joys of being a wife in the sexual, recreational, emotional, intellectual, and spiritual aspects of married living.

8) *Making satisfactory adjustments to the practical realities of life:*

Assisting her husband in the financial and housing planning for the family.

Adapting happily to the limitations of space and resources of the family.

Innovating ways of enriching the family experience by new use of available facilities and resources.

Supplementing the family income when it seems wise or necessary in ways that safeguard the well-being of all members of the family.

9) *Keeping alive some sense of personal autonomy through young motherhood:*

Retaining some satisfying contacts with personal interests and stimuli.

Continuing some aspect of personal development that is especially meaningful within the realities of the present family situation.

Utilizing the unique experiences of young motherhood for the fulfillment inherent within it.

Following her child's growth experiences out into new horizons of personal insight and growth.

10) *Exploring and developing the satisfying sense of being a family:*

Initiating family recreation in which the whole family may participate with pleasure—picnics, trips to zoo and beach, music, automobile trips, etc.

Participating with other young families in community functions.

Joining with other young wives and mothers in cooperative endeavors.

Providing for whole-family participation in church, neighborhood, and community activities suitable to this stage in family development.

Maintaining mutually supportive contacts with parental families.

This is quite an assignment for the young wife and mother. No wonder so many young women feel so overwhelmed during this phase of their lives. In the big, old-fashioned family (in which the young couple lived near, or sometimes with, their parental families), there was a sharing of functions and responsibilities of childbearing and rearing with the support of other members of the extended family that lessened the burden on the young mother. In the simple folk-society, infants and young children are cooperatively cared for by any conveniently located adult.

Margaret Mead reports that in some primitive cultures today a little child may be nursed by any lactating female at hand and that all women of the village assume responsibility for all the young children.

Not so today in contemporary American families. Our young families are usually removed from either parental homes or from the many other mutually supportive relationships of the extended family. The young mother is alone with her baby for most of the waking day and shares with her mate the child's care around the rest of the clock and calendar. Only an occasional respite comes with the expensive baby-sitter (a new institution in recent years). In such a situation the young wife and mother is free to develop her own ways and to work out her developmental tasks as best she can on her own. To the extent to which she has been prepared for the multiple responsibilities of young motherhood, to the extent to which she is encouraged to make use of the resources that might be tapped, and to the extent to which society is aware of and concerned about the burden placed upon the young mother, to that extent will she be helped to succeed in the singularly important tasks that are hers today.

DEVELOPMENTAL TASKS OF THE FATHER OF THE INFANT AND YOUNG CHILD

The young father is not as directly responsible for his baby as is his wife, and yet he faces certain inevitable developmental tasks arising directly out of his new status as father. The very fact that it is his wife rather than himself who is most intimately related to the child's birth, nursing, and early care, gives rise to some unique developmental tasks. Of course, it is humanly possible, as it is among other species, for the father to escape entirely the experiences of living intimately with his own young offspring. There are men, especially among the lower classes, who are home enough to impregnate the wife but who thereafter take little or no responsibility for the bearing and rearing of the child. In earlier times in the Western world, a man had little to do with the baby or very small child. The care of the young child was relegated to the women of the household almost entirely. A father began his active role when his youngster could handle himself well enough to go along on hunting, fishing, or short treks near home. Until then, or at least until the child was "housebroken," the father's life was relatively undisturbed by the baby.

Today's pattern is for the young husband-father to assume jointly the responsibilities and privileges of parenthood with his wife. These expectations are in conflict with the more traditional system in which the children were told, "Hush now, here comes Father," in the wife's sincere effort to protect the man from any noise or disturbance normal to young children. Modern fathers no longer can make all the rules, and only occasionally sit in judgment on wife and children as was once the case. Nowadays, a man improvises along with his wife as both of them attempt to live with the disturbing little newcomer in ways that will be mutually

COURTESY OF THE LIBRARY OF CONGRESS

Nowadays, the young husband-father assumes the responsibilities and privileges of parenthood along with his wife.

pleasant and satisfying. Now as always, a man is expected to be the primary breadwinner and set up his little family in the style to which he wants them to become accustomed. But here too, there are puzzling variations from the older norms. All in all, the young husband-father has quite a surprising number of developmental tasks during the childbearing stage of the family life cycle, as we see in the summary of them here:

1) *Reconciling conflicting conceptions of role:*

Settling upon a satisfactory role for himself as father out of the many conflicting possibilities in conceptions in himself, his wife, both families, friends, and others of influence.

Coming to terms with what he expects of his wife, now mother of his child, out of the conflicting expectations in each of them and in their significant other responsibilities.

Reconciling conflicting conceptions of childhood to a point of assurance in what to expect in his own child.

2) *Making way for the new pressures made upon him as young father:*

Accepting a reasonable share of responsibility for the care of the child, compatible with the realities of the situation at home and on his job.

Being willing to accept without undue stress, or complaint, his wife's increased emotional and physical need of him during the time when she is not yet functioning at peak effectiveness.

Assuming his share of responsibilities in representing the new family in the community in appropriate ways.

3) *Learning the basic essentials of baby and child care:*

Acquiring enough of the knowledges and skills of early child care to be able to function effectively in the baby's personal life, as indicated.

Practicing the fundamentals required in caring for a tiny baby and small child to serve as first lieutenant both alone and with the mother present.

Learning enough about early child development to know what to expect and understand what is relatively normal at a given stage of development.

Becoming increasingly able to enjoy intimate personal interaction with the baby.

4) *Conforming to the new regimens designed as most healthful for the young family:*

Adapting his eating habits to facilitate the new food intake patterns of mother, baby, and young family as a whole.

Working out ways of getting enough sleep and rest around the edges of the young child's needs and disturbances.

Designing new approaches in recreation that will fit in with the needs and limitations now operating in the family.

Being willing to experiment with any promising possibilities that seem worth trying, rather than insisting that "life go on as usual" in all instances.

5) *Encouraging the child's full development:*

Investing in the equipment and resources that will be most helpful and useful.

Cooperating in child-proofing the home for the period of young childhood.

Planning with his wife for the enriching experiences that will

provide opportunities for the child's well-rounded development.
Encouraging the child as it is, or may become, rather than as a
"chip off the old block" or a vessel for unfulfilled personal ambitions and dreams.

6) *Maintaining a mutually satisfying companionship with his wife:*

Wooing her back into tender sweetheart and intense lover roles
as she recovers from childbirth and the arduousness of the first
mothering responsibilities.

Seeing to it that the husband-wife relationship is neither chronically nor critically submerged beneath new parenting responsibilities.

Taking the initiative, when necessary, in renewing satisfying activities as a couple that may have been suspended during the pregnancy, childbirth and lying-in periods.

7) *Assuming the major responsibility for earning the family income:*

Carrying breadwinner responsibilities willingly.

Augmenting the family income, in ways that are appropriate, as
may become necessary.

Being willing to accept assistance, as it may be required, from either set of parents, from the wife's supplemental earnings, from
savings, from loans or other mortgages on the future, at this time
of relatively high needs and low income.

Assisting in financial planning that will keep expenditures within
available resources.

8) *Maintaining a satisfying sense of self as a man:*

Continuing personal interests and pursuits compatible with childbearing responsibilities and limitations.

Finding new levels of fulfillment in the new experiences of fatherhood.

Growing as a person in the maturing experiences of sharing fully
with his developing baby and with the full-bloom of womanhood in his wife.

Mastering the infantile, jealousy-provoking impulses that might
alienate him from his little family at the very times when they
need each other most.

9) *Representing the family within the wider community:*

Serving as chief representative of his family in the workaday
world.

Recognizing that he is the one to whom his wife looks for adult stimulus, interest, and activities while she is confined with baby care.

Bringing home the ideas, the people, the projects that will keep the young family in touch with the larger community during childbearing days.

Carrying on the community participation compatible with the pressures at home and on the job.

10) *Becoming a family man in the fullest sense of the term:*

Finding satisfactions in whole family activities.

Cooperating with his wife and baby in the new pursuits that appeal to them.

Initiating experiences for the whole family that will broaden horizons and enrich their life together as a family unit.

Enjoying the new dimensions of life with other relatives now rekindled with the new roles as aunts, uncles, cousins, and grandparents of the new baby.

Needless to say, all this is more than the average man bargained for when he fell in love and got married. As Frederick Lewis Allen used to say, "Everything is easier to get into than out of." And parenthood is surely a good example. It is so easy for most people to conceive, and so hard to deliver, so easy to dream of settling down and having a family, and so hard to meet the realities of family life when they flood in upon one.

Few men have been adequately prepared for what to expect when children come. They only rarely go through schools where boys as well as girls receive an educational program in preparation for marriage and family life. They come up in homes where little has been expected of them in direct child care. Until a man's first child appears, he usually has had very little first-hand experience with a baby. He doesn't know what to expect. He finds that his fingers are all thumbs in his first attempts to change or bathe or dress a baby. He tenses in fear that he will drop the baby or that it will be hurt while in his care.

Most difficult of all may be the intimate sharing of his wife with the intrusive little rival that now claims so much of her attention. The husband has had his wife all to himself during their courting and honeymoon days and has learned to take her for granted as his partner and companion during the establishment phase of marriage. He now must see her time, energy, and love directed to the demanding baby in ways that may fill him with intense feelings of being left out and neglected. It is a mature husband indeed who can early feel enough centrally involved in the new relationships to get the deep sense of belonging necessary for his security as a husband and father. One of the usual to-be-expected hazards in this stage of the family life cycle is for the mother to devote herself disproportionally to the new baby, and for the young father to retreat emotionally to a doghouse of his own making. Until he can share his wife maturely and participate with her in the experiences of parenthood he may feel like little more than a fifth wheel around the place.

How well the young husband juggles the conflicting loyalties and expectations and manages the multiplicity of roles opening up to him depends in large measure on how ready he is for fatherhood and how successful he is in accomplishing the developmental tasks inherent in the childbearing stage of family life. As he succeeds in achieving his own developmental tasks, he will be able to participate effectively in working through the family developmental tasks necessary for the survival, continuation, and growth of the family as a unit.

DEVELOPMENTAL TASKS OF THE CHILDBEARING FAMILY

With the coming of the first baby, the couple now becomes a family of three persons: mother, father, and baby. At the same time the interrelationships within the family have jumped from one (husband-wife) to three (husband-wife, father-child, and mother-child) as we saw in Chapter Five, in the discussion of the law of interpersonal relationships within the family.

The developmental tasks of the family in the childbearing stage are basically concerned with establishing the young family as a stable unit, reconciling conflicting developmental tasks of the various members, and mutually supporting the developmental needs of mother, father and baby in ways that strengthen each one and the family as a whole.

With the coming of the first baby, there appears for the first time a new mother, in the sense that this woman has never been a mother before, a new father who must learn what it means to function as a father, and a new family that must find its own way of being a family. While the baby is learning what it means to become a human being by growing, developing, and achieving his developmental tasks, his mother is learning how to be a mother, his father is practicing what it means to be a father, and the new family is settling itself into family patterns for the first time in its history. This involves the simultaneous working out of the developmental tasks of the baby, the mother, the father, and the family-as-a-whole. The basic developmental tasks of the childbearing family are discussed briefly in the sections that follow.

ADAPTING HOUSING ARRANGEMENTS FOR THE LIFE OF THE LITTLE CHILD

In millions of families around the world, no special provisions are made for the infant and little child. He or she is carried about by the mother or an older sibling, either in arms, or in some kind of shawl, or sling or even wrapped tightly on a board. The baby sleeps with the parents until he is old enough to fend for himself with the other children of the household. There are many homes in the United States where a child never knows a bed of his own, where everything is "share and share alike" within the home from the baby's first appearance until he is grown and leaves for a home of his own.

As the standard of living improves among American families, giving the baby a special place of his own and readapting the family housing for the comfort and convenience of the little child has become the norm.

In traditionally oriented homes (Chapter Three), the goal in making these special arrangements is to keep the baby from annoying and disturbing adults, as well as to assure its comfort. In more developmental families, there is a conscious effort to provide the kind of facilities in which the child may grow at his best, be free to roam as he becomes ready, explore without hurt or restraint, and to learn from active manipulation how to master his environment and develop his own skills. This kind of family life involves adapting the home so that the normal destructiveness of the little child will not violate the parents' values of a pleasant comfortable home in which they as adults may continue to find satisfaction.

Developmental parents accept the fact that a little child is born with ten hungry fingers that must "get into things." They know that the rough and tumble of the baby's early exploration, soiling, and fumbling must be allowed for in the home they share with him. Rather than cooping him up indefinitely or forbid him access to their living quarters, they so arrange the household that he may enjoy it with them with a minimum of restraint. To avoid the continual "NO!" and to protect their belongings as well as their child, they child-proof the home.

CHILD-PROOFING THE HOME DURING THE CHILDBEARING STAGE
(Outlined suggestions for keeping little children from getting hurt or destroying property)

Item	Danger	Child-Proofing Suggestions
Furniture	Tipping over on child	Select big-bottomed, heavy, plain pieces (esp. lamps and tables)
	Painful bumps	Rounded corners better than sharp
	Drawers dumped	Safety catch on all drawers (catch pegs at back hold them)
	Breaking treasured items	Pack away breakables or put in inaccessible places—use wall or hanging lamps instead of table and floor lamps wherever possible
	Soiling upholstery	Choose expendable items, or slip cover with washable fabrics, or upholster in durable, easily cleaned figured patterns that can take it (feet, sticky fingers, moist surfaces, etc.)
Floors and floor coverings	Chilling in drafts and cold surfaces	Weatherstrip under outside doors in cold weather, supplement heating at floor level, cover with rugs
	Slipping and falling	Avoid hazardous waxing, discard throw rugs, keep traffic lanes as clear as possible
	Soiling rugs	Choose colors that do not show dirt, in patterns rather than plain, select washable or reversible rugs, plan to discard after childbearing stage is over
	Marring floors	Cover with relatively indestructible surface, plan to refinish after heavy duty phases of family living pass
Walls	Marking and scratching	Choose washable papers or paints, or spray with washable plastic, convert a sizable section into blackboard (paint or large strips of paper) where child may mark, supply child with washable crayons, plan to redecorate when children are older.
Table tops	Scarring and staining	Cover with Formica, linoleum, terrazo, marble, or other surface not harmed by wetting, soiling, and pounding—use second hand items at first

The National Safety Council recommends putting gates at the top and bottom of stairs. Until the child has mastered the skills of going up and down safely, such a precaution allows the toddler to roam freely about the house without the danger of falling down stairs.

CHILD-PROOFING THE HOME DURING THE CHILDBEARING STAGE (*Continued*)
(Outlined suggestions for keeping little children from getting hurt
or destroying property)

Item	*Danger*	*Child-Proofing Suggestions*
Toys	Littered	Provide low shelves, and accessible storage places
	Harmful paints and surfaces	Select things child can suck and chew without harm
	Sharp edges and corners	Choose toys that will not hurt child in bangs and bumps
	Swallowing	Nothing smaller than a plum for baby
	Breaking	Give child sturdy things he cannot easily break (frustrating him, and you)
Bathroom fixtures	Falling baby	Provide convenient bathing, changing and toileting facilities for care of baby and little child
	Clinging child	Encourage child's independence as he becomes ready by low steps by wash bowl, low hooks for his towel, wash cloth and cup
	Training problems	Supply equipment he can manage himself when he is ready to care for his needs
	Running water	Allow for child's joy in water play by providing time and place for it with some supervision
Locked cupboards	Breaking treasures	Hang key high for door of good dish cabinet, etc.
	Swallowing poisons	Lock up paints, varnish, cleaning compounds, ammonia, lye, medicines, insecticides
	Inflicting wounds	Keep tools, guns, knives, and all other such objects locked away
Stairs and windows	Falling	Put gates at top and bottom of all stairways, give time to child as he learns to go up and down stairs, bar or tightly screen windows
Electric outlets	Shocking child	Cap low outlets, protect cords and keep to reasonable lengths, fence off with heavy furniture so child cannot introduce his finger, tongue or object into outlet
Entranceways	Cluttering	Provide shelves for rubbers, mittens, and other small objects; make room for baby buggy, sled, stroller, etc.

CHILD-PROOFING THE HOME DURING THE CHILDBEARING STAGE (*Continued*)
(Outlined suggestions for keeping little children from getting hurt
or destroying property)

Item	*Danger*	*Child-Proofing Suggestions*
	Soiling	Supply washable mats at outside doors to keep dirt from being tracked in, keep rubbers, boots, and wheeled objects near door
	Falling	Keep doorway gated or door closed, or screen locked when baby begins to get around
Kitchen	Burning	Provide play space near but not at the stove, keep handles of pans turned in rather than out
	Lighting gas	Make burner knobs one of the "No-Nos" that baby may not touch
	Lighting matches	Keep matches on high shelves, establish firm "No-No" policy on them
	Tripping workers	Fence off child's play area from main traffic lanes in kitchen, or provide high chair play during meal preparation
	Cutting	Hang knives high on wall
General	Hurting baby	Minor cuts, bruises, bangs, burns, etc., are taken in stride; major ones are turned over immediately to medical attention (keep doctor's number, and other resources on telephone pad)
	Damaging the house	Keep perspective of child being more important than things, use temporary, expendable things while children are small, plan to redo the place as youngsters near the teen years (they'll push for that anyway)

MEETING THE COSTS OF FAMILY LIVING AT THE CHILDBEARING STAGE

A baby born into a typical American family is fortunate. He will enjoy a higher standard of living than a child born in any other culture. His family will have a higher income year by year than would be average in any other country. The median family income in the United States was estimated at $4,200 in 1954, as we see in Table 15.

Even in a country of high income, and at a time of prosperity char-

TABLE 15. *Number of Families by Family Income,*
for the United States, 1954

Family Income	Number of Families
Under $1,000	3,700,000
$1,000–$1,999	4,600,000
$2,000–$2,999	5,000,000
$3,000–$3,999	6,400,000
$4,000–$4,999	6,500,000
$5,000–$5,999	5,000,000
$6,000–$6,999	3,600,000
$7,000–$9,999	4,700,000
$10,000–$14,999	1,800,000
$15,000 and over	600,000
Median: $4,200	Total 41,900,000

FROM: *Current Population Reports: Consumer Income,* Series P-60, No. 18, October 7, 1955.

acteristic of this period in the American economy, we see from Table 15 that 13,300,000 families in 1954 had an annual income of less than $3,000. At current prices, and at the highly advertised living standards, such an income would hardly be considered affluent in most American communities. Yet, nearly half (47 per cent) of all children at midcentury were born into families with incomes under $3,000 (Chart 6, Chapter Four).

Pertinent to our discussion is the fact that the first baby comes into a family still struggling to establish itself financially. If we take 25 as the age of the father at the birth of his firstborn, we see from Chart 13 that the likelihood is that the family income then will be under $3,000, with the peak of annual earnings still ahead for the family at any one of the eight economic levels. The figures in Chart 13, are estimates of average earnings of groups of men with maximum earnings of various amounts after deduction of personal income taxes. They are intended to show the relative earning power of men of different ages.

The costs of the family at the childbearing stage tend to balloon because it is then that the past, present, and future needs of the family are simultaneously part of the family budget. The first baby comes on the heels of the establishment stage of the family, when payments for furniture, equipment, house, car, and other high-cost items are still being made. The first child represents current costs in terms of doctor and hospital bills, baby furnishings, layette, special foods and medicines,

Annual Earnings, Dollars

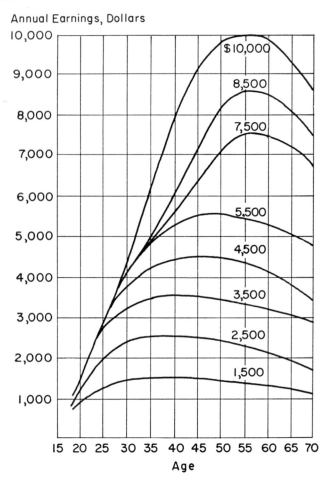

CHART 13.   Annual Earnings, According to Age, Corresponding to
Eight Specified Maximum Levels [1]

baby-sitter fees, and at least some new clothing for the mother after
nine months of pregnancy. With the coming of the first child the future is sharply focused by realization of the importance of insurance.
Such protection means safeguarding the mother and children during the
childbearing and rearing stages, saving for the rainy days when sickness,
accident, or other crisis drain the family purse, or put the breadwinner

[1] Louis I. Dublin and Alfred J. Lotka, *The Money Value of a Man* (New York:
The Ronald Press Company, copyright, 1946, Revised Edition), Figure 4, p. 65.

out of work, as well as financing dreams for education, cultural advantages, and a comfortable future for the family members.

As we have seen, this meeting of past, present, and future financial needs in the childbearing family stage spirals costs when family income is relatively low and when the wife is likely to be no longer gainfully employed. Therefore, the pinch is on, and making ends meet is a real challenge to the young family. Families each with its own problems and possibilities meet this developmental task in many ways.

The young father may get a part-time job in an effort to make ends meet. This will supply more income but at the cost of his time with his family, and possibly in fatigue, irritability, and strain. The young mother may go back to full-time employment soon after the baby is born. This will maintain the family income at the previous level, but it sacrifices the mother's full-time care of the child, their early hour by hour companionship with its satisfactions both for the baby and for the mother. Actually, if the mother has to replace herself in the home with a paid household helper, her work may not net the family much. If her mother, or his, is available for the early childcare and housework, the employment of the young mother may make financial sense, as it does in many lower-class homes.

Some young mothers have the kinds of salable skills that continue to supplement the family income even with a small child in the home. The young woman who can type, tutor, sew, or do specialized crafts (baking or cooking, or other money-making projects), can often continue to earn some money even during the active childbearing and rearing stages. Some young women can do such things easily and well. Others find extra activities beyond those of caring for the children and the household an added strain that cannot be comfortably handled.

The couple may borrow money for some high-cost purchases—mortgaging their future by that much but having the equipment when they need it most. Installment buying may be of this sort, with payments over a period of years for such things as the car, the refrigerator, the washing machine, and the other items that mean much when children are small. The danger is in loading up on installment purchases beyond the ability to pay comfortably over the months and years to come. Borrowing is feasible only if the family can see enough income in the foreseeable future to take care of the payment of the loan, with its accumulated interest charges, within a reasonable length of time. "Borrowing early in a period of financial strain is unwise, for it only serves to add interest charges to the already too heavy expenditures," is the counsel of one authority in family finance.[1]

Savings laid away earlier may be used for such items as the automobile, the first baby, or the furniture. Or, in some families, the grandparents pitch in with gifts that assure the young family of what they need as they need it. Some families can do these things well. Where there are tendencies to jealousy or rivalry between the two in-law families, or emotional immaturity and dependency on the part of one or both of the young parents, expensive gifts from grandparents may be hazardous.

"Making do" is one way of balancing the budget during this stage in the family life cycle. Many young families recognize that the household can be kept simple and inexpensive while the children are coming and growing, with furnishings that are expendable and with little importance put on appearance. Later, when the children are old enough to appreciate nice things and to share in their care, the old, inexpensive, beat-up things may be replaced.

Which course the young family follows in accomplishing this developmental task of meeting the costs of the family at the childbearing stage depends upon how they are approaching and meeting a number of their other developmental tasks of the period, especially those having to do with the allocation of responsibility, developing systems of communication, adapting relationships with relatives and friends, and working through a philosophy of life.

REWORKING PATTERNS OF MUTUAL RESPONSIBILITY AND ACCOUNTABILITY

The first child brings with him/her new responsibilities in terms of round the clock care, including the intricacies of feeding, bathing, soothing, and diagnosing distress signals. Daily laundry of baby clothing is a new responsibility. Making formula for the bottle-fed baby is a daily job. Cleaning up the household swollen by the new activities incident to child care is an everpresent responsibility. At the same time the former responsibilities of earning the family income, shopping, cooking,

[1] Howard F. Bigelow, *Family Finance* (Chicago: J. B. Lippincott Company, Revised Edition, 1953), p. 345.

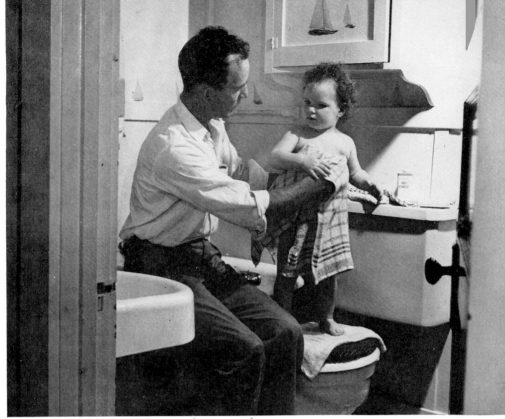

Baby's bath may be scheduled for the evening hours when the father is available for this and other intimate person-to-person responsibilities.

dishwashing, housecleaning, mopping, bedmaking, and all the rest continue as before.

There are some responsibilities that will be automatically allocated to one or the other of the parents: the father assumes the role of primary breadwinner, the mother of nursing the baby. Everything else that must be done in the young family may become the responsibility of either partner on either a short-term or a long-term basis. The usual pattern in the American family is for the wife to assume responsibility for child care, housework, laundry, and food preparation for both the baby and the adults, with the assistance of the husband in those chores in which he is particularly interested or capable. For instance, now that the young mother is confined with the care of the baby, the husband may assume more responsibility for marketing and other errands that he can take care of on his way home from work.

There is an increase in the number of families that define the father's role in terms of relating intimately to his children (Chapter Three, discussion of developmental fathers and families). In such homes the baby's bath may be scheduled for the evening hours when father as well as mother may actively participate. Similarly, changing the baby, airing the baby in leisurely Saturday afternoon walks, playing with the little child, putting the youngster to bed, feeding the baby, burping, cuddling, comforting, and all the other intimate person-to-person responsibilities of parent for child are being shared by the father as well as the mother in modern day families.

As both parents increasingly share the responsibilities for the family's welfare, certain chores may be relegated to the husband and others to the wife on a basis of individual strength. An example is found in the number of young husbands who take over some of the heavy cleaning and carrying jobs until the young mother has regained her strength and has the time and energy for all the housework again. It works the other way too. In some beginning families the shopping is done by both members of the pair in weekly marketing excursions. With the coming of the first baby, the wife now enjoys getting out of the house and taking the baby for a daily airing, and so now shops more often while she is out with the baby. Groceries are wheeled home in the carriage at the baby's feet and are no longer part of the weekend routines.

The wife, who is home most of the time with the baby, relates to the husband at his return home what has transpired through the day and how she and the child have fared. She brings up for his approval purchases made or contemplated and decisions that must be made one way or the other in the immediate and distant future. The husband in turn tells his wife of progress and problems on the job and goes over with her alternatives that may be theirs for improving their financial or vocational position.

As the baby grows he becomes accountable to his parents for the behavior that is expected. This has its beginnings long before the thirty-month age when the child is well launched into a set of expectancies of what to do when and how. What constitutes good behavior and what is "being bad" varies enormously by families, by cultural groups, and by developmental-traditional orientation. But in every home the child soon learns that he must assume certain responsibilties for himself and his conduct and that he is accountable to his parents for what he is and does. These responsibilities increase as the child grows; are least when he is a tiny infant; and grow as he develops more and more toward the "age of responsibility."

RE-ESTABLISHING MUTUALLY SATISFYING SEXUAL RELATIONSHIPS

It is usual for the sex life of the couple to decrease during the periods of pregnancy, childbirth, and postnatal days (Chapter Seven). By six weeks after the birth of the baby, the woman's pelvis is back to normal, the postnatal discharge has ceased, involution is complete, and normally she is physically able to enjoy an active sex life again. The re-establishment of their sex relationships is not a simple physiological problem; it has many intricate psychological aspects for both the wife and her mate.

Many a young mother experiencing for the first time the challenges of motherhood, becomes absorbed in its responsibilities and satisfactions so much that the husband is pushed into the background, unless he or she takes the initiative in keeping their mate-love central in the family. It may be the man of the house who re-establishes some of the wooing and courtship processes that will get them both occasionally out of the house with its constant reminders of the baby. The renewal of sweetheart roles will often rekindle the banked fires of desire in both of them. It may be the wife who takes the initiative in re-establishing full marital relationships as soon as she is ready. One of the first steps the wife takes in this direction is that of making herself attractive for her man again.

Throughout the pregnancy she may have felt the loss of her sexual attractiveness, as her body became swollen with child and the maternal functions gained ascendancy. Now that the baby has safely arrived and is well on the way to healthy infancy, the young mother is free to take an interest in becoming attractive to her husband again. She may get some stylish new clothes to fit this new slim silhouette of hers. She may get a new hairdo and pay new attention to her figure and skin care. Quite likely she will watch her diet to keep her weight in line during lactation at the same time that she assures her baby of sufficient milk.

Medically and emotionally there may be some specific problems. It is usual in most hospitals to perform an episiotomy, cutting the perineum enough to let the baby through without the danger of tearing maternal tissue. The stitches are removed in a few days, but the itching of the healing tissues continues a while. For some time afterwards, the memory of the pain in the sensitive area may make the re-establishment of sexual relations difficult. A young mother may complain that "the doctor sewed me up too tight," when the main trouble is the tightening of the tissues as she involuntarily tenses during stimulation of the area. Patient thoughtfulness on the husband's part, and active cooperation of the wife are usually all that is necessary for those who previously have known a good sex adjustment.

For couples whose early sex life has been frustratingly inadequate, the nursing period may be used as a protective device by the young mother. In some societies, and in some families here and now, the mother has been known to prolong the nursing of the infant as a way of protecting herself from the sexual advances of her husband. In still others, the young mother may complain of fatigue, ill-health, or pain as a way of avoiding the re-establishment of active sex life as long as possible.

Happy families soon find their way through the emotional and physical problems involved. The best of them find that the infant's call for attention may interrupt the most tender embrace from time to time. It is at such times that the couple's communication systems and philosophy of life stand them in good stead as they meet the baby's need and return to each other in good humor without the overtones of frustrated, disgruntled impulses spoiling their relationship one with another.

REFINING INTELLECTUAL AND EMOTIONAL COMMUNICATION SYSTEMS FOR CHILDBEARING AND REARING

Something new is added to family intercommunication when a baby comes into the household. The newborn makes his needs known through a series of signals and distress calls that have to be "received" by his parents with appropriate responses if he or they are to be comfortable. As he is able to communicate his wishes and feelings, and as his parents become increasingly skillful in understanding his communicative efforts, both baby and parents get a feeling of satisfaction in their interrelationship. When this developmental task is difficult, the baby and the parents find each other unsatisfying, even to the point of mutual frustration.

As the mother and father cuddle and fondle the baby, expressing their love for him in close person-to-person contacts, the baby learns to respond. He smiles when his mother or father comes near. He gurgles when they pick him up. He pats them when they care for him. He soon learns to hug, nestle, kiss, snuggle, and to express in the ways of

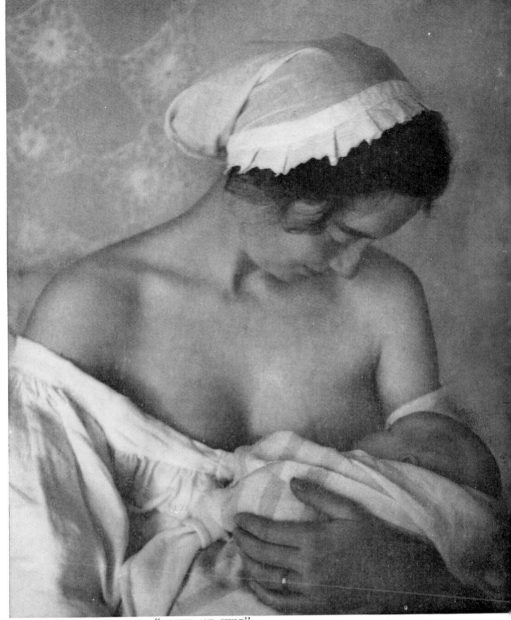

As a mother nurses her baby, she expresses her love by cuddling and holding him close—communication that even the littlest infant can "understand."

his particular family the love he feels in response to those who love him.

Long before the child is two years old, he has learned the basic response patterns appropriate for his little world. He has learned a degree of trust and confidence in his parents. He has learned how to express his annoyance and impatience with those around him. He has laid down the foundation of his emotional being in the loves and hates, fears and anxieties, joys and satisfactions that he has experienced and expressed during his early life with his family. His basic security as a personality rests upon the faith that he early develops in his world through his trust in his parents and his feeling that he is able to communicate, to be understood, and to have his needs met as they arise. By the time the family leaves the childbearing stage of the family cycle, the baby has learned the fundamentals of language and is talking in ways that may be understood not only by his parents, but also by others outside the family. He uses a growing number of concepts accurately and is fast becoming a fully communicating member of his family.

Mother and father must re-establish communication systems between each other as they become parents. A new dimension to their shared living is added with the coming of their first child. Now they live together not only as husband and wife, but also as father and mother of their firstborn. They now must learn how to communicate their new feelings as parents—the anxieties, the prides, the insecurities and the assurances, the loves and the annoyances of early parenthood. They may be bewildered by the ambivalence of young parenthood. It may be dismaying to find one's mate or oneself grumbling at the helpless infant who howls at two in the morning, or shouting at the well-meaning mate who does not quickly enough silence the baby's howls when the telephone rings. Protective roles learned earlier in family living become manifest now in this otherwise frustrating period. In time, the young adults will be able to take in stride the full repertoire of parental emotions. But these are new to young parents of the first child, and may not be as easily expressed, as comfortably recognized, or as speedily handled as they will be later.

Sharing one's mate with the newcomer involves still other communication systems in which there is mutual recognition of the multiple involvements of both the man and the woman as mates, as parents, and as persons. The young father now must recognize his wife as also "Mother" with the coming of their first baby. She must become accustomed to seeing her husband as also "Father" as soon as children come. Sometimes these terms are actually employed and continue throughout the life of the family. In other families, these designations are used only occasionally in jest but they serve their purpose of assisting the partners to accept, express, and internalize the new roles as parents that both of the partners face.

The young family is successful in accomplishing the several-faceted developmental task of refining communication systems to accommodate the new constellation of emotional interactions when it emerges from the childbearing stage with a well-knit sense of being a family. When difficulties in achieving the task are unresolved, the family may emerge from the stage with problems of poor integration that carry over to complicate further stages in its development.

RE-ESTABLISHING WORKING RELATIONSHIPS WITH RELATIVES

With the coming of the first baby, grandmother comes into her own in many a home. She is welcomed as the one who holds things together during the baby's first days at home while the mother is fully absorbed in the baby's care and in regaining her strength. As the young mother is increasingly able to take over the full responsibility for her household with the assistance of the baby's father, the grandmother's role recedes in importance. About that time, other relatives begin to come by to see the new baby, call on the new mother, and bring gifts, advice, and warnings that have to be absorbed and dealt with one way or another.

In-law jealousies and juggling for power not infrequently emerge with the coming of the first baby. One parental family gives more, does more, demands more, or expects more of the little new family than does the other. If one or both of the parents is immature or on the defensive, the imbalance of grandparental interest may fan the flames of envy, jealousy, and insecurity to a white heat of passionate resistance.

In the mixed marriage, the interest of the grandparents in seeing that the new baby is baptized in the church of their faith rather than that of the other mate may become a battle royal, involving both grandparental families in armed camps in which "anything is fair in love and war." This may take the form of anything from covert hints and maneuvers to open aggression and abuse, as we saw in the many cases of in-law relationships both pro and con analyzed earlier.[1] Even if the home is of one faith there may be, with the coming of the first baby, inter-

---

[1] Evelyn Millis Duvall, *In-Laws: Pro and Con* (New York: Association Press, 1954), Chaps. 5 and 8.

ference in religious practices, financial plans, household routines, social activities, and so on until the young family finds its own autonomy as a family unit.

The childbearing family is now a unit in the larger family circle, with all the problems and promises appertaining thereto. As the young family establishes itself as a comfortably interdependent unit within the larger whole, giving and receiving in ways that are mutually satisfying, it is ready for the years of interlocking family interrelationships that lie ahead. No man can live to himself alone. Few families, even today in our age of individualism, are entirely independent. Most of us profit by serving and being served by our own flesh and blood, the brothers and sisters, parents, uncles, aunts, and cousins that make up our larger families.

FITTING INTO COMMUNITY LIFE AS A YOUNG FAMILY

Families tend to keep to themselves during the nesting time. Young families are apt to be highly mobile during the period when the young husband is transferred from place to place as he gets established vocationally. Community contacts in any one location tend to be temporary at best. Old friends and family are left behind. Old interests and group ties may be weakened. After a man and his wife have become parents they have little in common with their childless friends. They are not as available for gadding about as they were before the baby came. When the cost of a baby-sitter must be considered with every social affair the couple is invited to, they think twice before accepting the invitation.

Baby-sitters not only charge for their services, but they run up other costs as well. The inexperienced high school girl may give the young parents a feeling of severe insecurity that rises to fever pitch when some adolescent indiscretion is discovered. The older available woman may lack the physical stamina, the point of view, or the mental poise for dealing with the active little child. There has been such a shift in ideologies about the care of children since the older woman was herself a young mother, that it may be extremely difficult to trust to her the type of child-care procedures that seem important now (Chapters Two and Three). Even if the ideal baby-sitter is found and groomed for her tasks, there still remain the scheduling problems inherent in trying to fit together the needs of the young family with the available time of the sitter. In the "good old days," parents were freed for life as a couple in neighborhood and community affairs by the resident adults, who accepted as one of their roles in the larger family the staying with children that was expected from time to time. Nowadays it is much harder for the little new family, more removed from the extended family, to keep active in community life while their children are small.

Young parents today have developed some ingenious ways of working through this developmental task. In some neighborhoods, parents take turns minding each other's children, thus freeing each other for more social life. There are examples of parents' sitter-pools, by which parents sign up as available for the care of their neighbors' children in exchange for like service in return. One such sitter-pool is operated among twenty families with a rotating secretary who keeps track of the sitting-bank in which parents sit for others a certain number of hours and are repaid a like number of hours of sitting time when they go out. Holidays and hours after midnight count double, otherwise the exchange is an hour for an hour. One advantage is that the sitters are experienced young parents themselves. Other reported satisfactions are in serving in each other's families, enjoying the resources of each other's homes, and realizing through practical experience that one's own child is no worse than his agemates in similar homes. A disadvantage is that, while the one parent is doing duty in sitting for another family, the other parent is home alone with his or her own children. Since this is usually at the quiet hours of the family day, when the children are asleep and the adults free for their life as a couple, there may be something of a problem.

Even church-going presents problems for the couple with their first baby. Few churches have nurseries equipped to care adequately for a small child during the church service, although some are experimenting in that direction. Taking the baby along to church, so widely practiced in other cultures, is not feasible in most American churches today. The practice of one parent going to church while the other remains home with the baby is not satisfactory for the couple who want to participate as a unit. Much more frequent, although generally frowned upon as inadequate, is the tendency of young families with a child or children too small for church attendance to remain away from church. Sunday then is spent together as a family, at home, in short trips to the country, to visit relatives, or in various ways that satisfy their needs as persons and as families.

Among lower-class families there generally is more of the old-world custom of taking the baby along in shawl or bundle to any of the community or church affairs that continue to interest the mother of the family. But since such families rarely participate actively in the wide variety of community activities, family participation as such does not increase during the childbearing stage.

Upper-class families frequently have a nurse whose responsibility it is to care for the baby from the time it comes home from the hospital until he or she is old enough to be sent away to school. The nurse frees the mother and father from the day by day and night by night care of the little child, and so they are more apt to continue their previous activities in work and play, clubs and charities, benefits and concerts less disturbed by their parenting responsibilities (except in times of emergency such as the child's serious illness) than is the middle-class parent.

PLANNING FOR FURTHER CHILDREN IN THE FAMIILY

Most young parents today want two, three or more children.[1] If no planning for further children is done, one baby follows another at yearly intervals in the fertile family. This interval is shorter than many parents find desirable. Some couples marry late and want their babies just as fast as they can have them until the family reaches the desired size. Most couples today marry at a young age and want to space their children so that they can take the best care of them in ways that are most appropriate for them as a family.

It is possible to conceive again as soon as marital relations are resumed after the birth of the first child. Some women, believing that lactation postpones pregnancy, continue to nurse the first baby as long as possible in an effort to delay the coming of the second child. Others refuse to resume sexual contact with their husbands until they are ready to accept the responsibility of the possibility of another pregnancy. More effective today is the medical assistance given the couple that allows them marital access at the same time that they are relieved of further parenting responsibilities until they are ready for their next child. The belief is that a child should be wanted before it is born, and that this is more readily assured if the parents are helped to plan their families.

The procedure is a simple one. When the woman goes for her check-up six weeks following the birth of her child, her physician advises her on the practice that will best meet her situation, taking into consideration

[1] Ronald Freedman, David Goldberg, and Harry Sharp, "Ideals' about Family Size in the Detroit Metropolitan Area: 1954," *The Milbank Memorial Fund Quarterly,* Vol. XXXIII, No. 2, April 1955, pp. 187–197.

her anatomical requirements, religious affiliation, attitudes, preferences, and values as the representative of her family. This may be (with the advice of an obstetrician) some form of the rhythm method. It may be a diaphragm fitted to the mother's new requirements following the birth of her child. Or, it may be any other method the physician advises out of his knowledge of the particular family and their needs. The method is important. But even more important for the well-being of the family is the philosophy underlying whatever is done.

REWORKING A SUITABLE PHILOSOPHY OF LIFE AS A FAMILY

There is a five-fold crisis in family living at the childbearing stage that is essentially philosophical in nature:

1) Seeing through the drudgeries to the fundamental satisfactions of parenthood.
2) Valuing persons above things.
3) Resolving the conflicts inherent in the contradictory developmental tasks of parents and young children, and of fathers and mothers.
4) Establishing healthy independence as a married couple.
5) Accepting help in a spirit of appreciation and growth.

Faced with the daily round of diapers, dishes, and distractions, a young mother may feel weighed down with drudgeries to the point where she loses her sense of perspective. The young father burdened with his new responsibilities and pressures to make ends meet, may become chronically harassed and under strain. The young couple who sense through their daily duties the deep-down satisfactions involved in having their own child to care for, find ways to shrug off needless worries and to adopt a light-hearted approach to their family life and with each other. They find joy in little everyday happenings. They delight in their youngster's development, as well as in his emerging skills and cute doings and sayings. They discover the spiritual meanings of their own family living as they free themselves for the fulfillments of parenthood.

Things are in the saddle in many a family at the childbearing stage. The parents have invested a great deal of themselves and their resources into equipping a home they can be proud of. Along comes Junior with none of the adult values of neatness and cleanliness in his make-up, but rather bent on active exploration of as much of his world as he can get into his mouth, or pound to a pulp, or sit on, or wet and mess. The family soon has its back to the wall in the struggle of values as to which comes first—persons or things. Put *things* first and you get an unhappy, fenced-in baby, a tense tight-lipped mother, and a semblance of peace and quiet on the surface, while beneath, emotions seethe. Put *people* first in family life and the whole jigsaw puzzle falls into place as the parents relax and enjoy their lusty little human animal and "to heck with too much concern about the stuff."

If one's philosophy of family life centers in feeling that a good family is one where everyone always agrees with everyone else, one in which no voice is ever raised in protest, but all is sweetness and light, the childbearing stage is apt to be pretty difficult. For inherent in the period are contradictory developmental tasks and needs of parents and little children. Example: the parents need rest, sleep, and time for tender moments with each other; while a little child may clamor for attention, food, or special care at any hour of the day or night. Somehow, some way the fact of conflicting interests and values has to be seen, accepted, and lived with, if the family is to prosper.

It is at this stage that a family works through the dynamics of its primary and secondary orbits. The basic conflict is between the mother-child and the wife-husband relationship. If the young mother is so absorbed in her new mother role that her husband plays second fiddle, the family revolves around the mother-child orbit, with all the unfortunate aspects so widely recognized today. Struggling through conflicting pressures to the full realization of the importance of keeping the husband-wife relationship primary, often involves some tears, not a few tense moments, and a young mother torn by conflicting loyalties within herself. Resolving such a basic conflict rests first of all upon the philosophy of family life that sees the husband-wife relationship as central for the stability and well-being of the entire family.

Establishing healthy independence as a young family means cutting loose from the dependencies of childhood and standing on one's own feet. Fears of sponging, of imposing, of being "beholden," or of exploiting operate in this direction. Yet if the feeling that "our lives are our own, and what we do is nobody's business" prevails, it may be exceedingly difficult to get the help that is needed for a sick child, an ailing marriage, or a failing family.

Accepting help in the form of assistance and gifts from relatives, professional guidance of physicians, marriage counselors, child-guidance

The current practice of taking the baby to the physician for regular physical check-ups, preventive "shots," and vaccinations, protects the little child from many illnesses. Such a young family accepts the professional help of physicians, child-guidance experts, and others as needed, in a spirit of humility and with the recognition of the interdependence of all humans.

experts, or whatever is needed, is dependent in large measure upon the philosophy of the family.

If the young family is developing the philosophy of humility in open recognition of the interdependence of all humans, then they as family members can accept help with appreciation. Maturing families, as well as persons, grow from serving and being served by those in whom they have confidence. Especially now, the young father and mother can learn a great deal from parent-education experiences, as well as family counseling opportunities in which they talk over their problems, evaluate their progress, and plan for their future as a family.

If each new day in the life of the childbearing family started out without reference to those that had preceded, life might be hectic indeed. Each new situation would be faced without the benefit of precedents and established procedures. Each person would be confronted with a multitude of possibilities that could be frighteningly confusing. Each new developmental task of individual or family would be borne by the persons involved with its full weight. Fortunately the tasks of family life are not that heavy upon anyone, partly because of the early establishment of family rituals that help routinize into familiar patterns many of the aspects of living together around the clock and calendar. Rituals that are commonly part of the childbearing stage of the family life cycle are outlined below.

COMMON RITUALS OF THE CHILDBEARING STAGE

Rituals of awakening in the morning.
> Little child comes into parents' bed.
> Ritualized games and language play.

Breakfast rituals.
> Eating from special dishes.
> Names for foods and functions given by the baby used within the family.

Naps for baby and mother ritualized.
> Special blankets and toys.
> Ceremonies and routines.

Shopping on daily outings.
> Baby takes special possessions.
> Child allowed certain privileges.

Father's homecoming.
> Child watches for father from window.
> Father brings home gifts and surprises for baby.
> Mother and child welcome returning father in own special ways.

Bedtime bath for child.
    Special toys and procedures.
    Father may participate in particular functions.
Bedtime routines and ceremonies.
    Stories, songs, prayers at child's bedtime.
    "Drink a water" demands for further attention.
    Special light or customs to give child assurance.
Special holidays.
    Birthday celebrations ritualized.
    Visits to see relatives.
    Vacations and trips with baby.
    Photographing baby in special holiday settings.
    Sitter routines when parents celebrate as a couple.

Rituals add a great deal to the life of the childbearing family. They provide the workable routines that ease the parents' days and nights. They give the little child a sense of reliable, secure expectations of what comes next. And, they provide the simple, sweet sources of satisfaction that come to mean most in family living.

SUMMARY

The childbearing family goes through three phases in settling down to being a family, marked by changing moods, tempos, and feelings. There are predictable developmental tasks of the infant and young child that must be achieved in the childbearing family. The mother of the young child has developmental tasks she must accomplish as a mother, as a wife, as a person. The father at the childbearing stage has a series of complicated developmental tasks as a father, husband, and man that he must work through as a person. The developmental tasks of the childbearing family as-a-whole are several: adapting housing arrangements for the life of the little child (child-proofing the home during the childbearing stage), meeting the costs of family living at the childbearing stage, reworking patterns of responsibility and accountability, re-establishing mutually satisfying sexual relationships, refining intellectual and emotional communication systems for childbearing and rearing, re-establishing working relationships with relatives, fitting into community life as a young family, planning for further children in the family, and reworking a suitable philosophy of life as a family. Rituals of family living at the childbearing stage ease the parent's job, give security to the youngster, and bring satisfactions to the family.

SUGGESTED ACTIVITIES

1) Consulting authoritative child development sources for norms of development from birth through thirty months, make a master chart of the step by step progress the normal infant makes from the period of restless dependency to relatively poised independence as a little child able to communicate, get around, and master many aspects of himself and his world.

2) Review one or both of the films, *Helping the Child Accept the Do's* and *Helping the Child Accept the Don'ts* (Encyclopedia Britannica Films, Inc.; black and white, ten minutes each), with especial emphasis on the ways in which a child learns what is expected of him in a variety of situations.

3) Take pad and pencil to a nearby park, tot-lot, or other place where young mothers congregate with their babies. Record everything that is done and said by both a selected mother and her child for a five minute interval. Write a paper incorporating your verbatim record and interpreting the behaviors included in terms of the developmental tasks of both mother and baby that might be inferred at this stage, and in this situation.

4) Interview four mothers whose first babies are two years old or younger, on the question, "What part of the daily routine with your baby do you find hardest to work out comfortably?" Capture in your recording of the interviews not only the areas in which the mothers report difficulties but also their attitudes and feelings about themselves, their babies, and their adequacy as mothers in childbearing families. Comment critically on your findings in terms of the hazards young mothers find in achieving their developmental tasks during the childbearing stage.

5) Review the first 85 pages of *Fathers Are Parents, Too*, by O. Spurgeon English and Constance Foster (New York: G. P. Putnam's Sons, 1951) for implicit and explicit factors relating to the developmental tasks of the young father during the childbearing stage.

6) Write a letter to your sister who has told you of her concern over her first child's thumbsucking, telling her what is considered good practice in dealing with thumbsucking today, the developmental basis for the recommendations, and readings that may be still further helpful to her.

7) Outline a course of study to be used for a "Grandmothers' Refresher Course in Child Care" that would help a present-day grandmother bring up to date her concepts, ideas, and understandings of child development and guidance through the first three years of a baby's life. Contrast throughout present-day practices with those prevalent twenty to thirty years ago (when she brought up her children) using such references as were generally current then as manuals of baby care, in books, magazines, and government bulletins and pamphlets.

8) Prepare a double chart through a day in the life of 1) a traditionally oriented childbearing family, and 2) a developmentally oriented child-bearing family making notations of all entries in which scheduling and procedures differ significantly between the two families.

9) Contrast expected family rituals at the childbearing stage for families at the lower-, middle-, and upper-class levels documenting your materials with quotations from James H. S. Bossard and Eleanor S. Boll, *Ritual in Family Living* (Philadelphia: University of Pennsylvania Press, 1950), Chap. 6, as well as excerpts from selected fiction and biography representative of the three class levels.

10) Chart the complementary and conflicting developmental tasks of the mother, the father, and the baby of the childbearing family, using the materials detailed in this chapter in the style developed in Chapters Six and Seven. Discuss the relative mutuality of this stage as compared with the previous two stages of the family life cycle.

READINGS

Aldrich, C. Anderson and Mary, *Babies Are Human Beings* (New York: Macmillan Company, 1938).

Baruch, Dorothy, *Parents Can Be People* (New York: Appleton-Century, 1944).

Baruch, Dorothy, *New Ways in Discipline* (New York: Whittlesey House, 1949).

Blood, Robert O., Jr. "Consequences of Permissiveness for Parents of Young Children," *Marriage and Family Living*, Vol. XV, No. 3, August 1953, pp. 209–212.

Bossard, James H. S., and Boll, Eleanor S., *Ritual in Family Living* (Philadelphia: University of Pennsylvania Press, 1950).

Brody, Sylvia, *Patterns of Mothering* (New York: Basic Book, Inc., 1956).

Davis, M. Edward, *Natural Child Spacing* (Garden City, New York: Hanover House, 1953).

Duvall, Evelyn Millis, *Family Living* (New York: Macmillan Company, Revised 1955), Unit V, "Children in Your Life."

Duvall, Evelyn Millis and Hill, Reuben, *When You Marry* (Boston: D. C. Heath and Company, Revised 1953), Chapter 18, "What It Means to Be Parents."

English, O. Spurgeon, and Foster, Constance J., *Fathers Are Parents, Too* (New York: G. P. Putnam's Sons, 1951).

Greenhill, J. P., "The Birth of the Baby," Chapter 5 in Part Three in Fishbein, Morris, and Burgess, Ernest (eds.), *Successful Marriage* (Garden City, New York: Doubleday and Company, Revised 1955).

Hymes, James L., *Enjoy Your Child—Ages 1, 2, and 3* (New York: Public Affairs Committee, 1948).

Levy, David M., *Maternal Overprotection* (New York: Columbia University, 1948).

Louisiana Association for Mental Health, *Pierre the Pelican, Post-Natal Series* (New Orleans, Louisiana Association for Mental Health, 816 Hibernia Building, New Orleans 12, La.).

McKinney, Betsy Marvin, "The Sexual Aspects of Breast Feeding," *Child-Family Digest*, 5320 Danneel Street, New Orleans 15, La., December 1955, pp. 45–60.

Ridenour, Nina, *Some Special Problems of Children* (Eight pamphlets published by the New York City Committee on Mental Hygiene, 105 East 22nd Street, New York, 10, New York, 1948).

Smart, Mollie Stevens, *Babe in a House* (New York: Scribner's, 1950).

Smart, Mollie Stevens and Russell, *Living and Learning with Children* (Boston: Houghton Mifflin, 1949).

Spock, Benjamin, *The Pocketbook of Baby and Child Care* (New York: Pocket Books, Inc., 1946).

Superintendent of Documents, Government Printing Office, Washington, D. C.:
   A Healthy Personality for Your Child (1952)
   Breast Feeding (1947)
   Foods Your Children Need (1953)
   Infant Care (1955)
   Your Well Baby (1949)
   Your Child from One to Six (1956)

Zabriskie, Louise, *Mother and Baby Care in Pictures* (Philadelphia: J. B. Lippincott Company, 1946).

The child is father of the man
WORDSWORTH

CHAPTER NINE

Families with preschool children

F amilies with preschool children are defined as those whose first children are of preschool age, from 2½ to 5 years old. By the end of this stage, the second baby is quite likely already on the scene, increasing the family to four members, and its interrelationships to six (Law of Family Interaction, Chapter Five). New developmental tasks are constantly arising in the young parents' relationships with their rapidly growing children, with each other, and with the changing culture around them.

DEVELOPMENTAL TASKS OF PRESCHOOL CHILDREN (2½ TO 5 YEARS)

From the preoccupation of babyhood, the preschool child is emerging as a social being who can share with others, who participates as a member of his family, and who is ready for school. His pace of physical growth is slowing down, and many of his body activities are becoming routine. Progress in his emotional and intellectual development is increasingly apparent in his growing ability to express himself in speech and in his greatly increased acquaintance with his environment. The preschool child's chief developmental tasks are outlined below:

1) *Settling into healthful daily routines of rest and activity:*

Going to bed and getting his needed rest without a struggle.

Taking his nap or rest, and learning to relax when he is weary.

Enjoying active play in a variety of situations and places.

Becoming increasingly flexible and able to accept changes happily.

2) *Mastering good eating habits:*

Becoming adequate in the use of the customary utensils for eating.

Accepting new flavors and textures in foods with interest.

Enjoying his food with lessening incidents of spilling, messing, and toying.

Learning the social as well as the sensual pleasures of eating.

3) *Mastering the basics of toilet training:*

Growing in his ability to indicate his needs for elimination.

Cooperating comfortably in the toilet training program.

Finding satisfaction in behaving appropriately as to time, place, and ways of toileting expected of boys/girls of his age in the culture.

Becoming flexible in his ability to use the variety of resources, places, and personnel available to him.

4) *Developing the physical skills appropriate to his stage of motor development:*

Learning to climb, balance, run, skip, push, pull, throw, and catch in whole body use of large muscle systems.

Developing manual skills for buttoning, zipping, cutting, drawing, coloring, modeling, and manipulating small objects deftly.

Becoming increasingly independent in his ability to handle himself effectively in a variety of physical situations and expectancies.

5) *Becoming a participating member of his family:*

Assuming responsibilities within the family happily and effectively.

Learning to give and receive affection and gifts freely within the family.

Identifying with parent of the same sex.

Developing ability to share his parents with another child and with others generally.

Recognizing his family's ways as compared with those of his friends and neighbors.

6) *Beginning to master his impulses and to conform to others' expectations:*

Outgrowing the impulsive, urgent outbursts of infancy.

Learning to share, take turns, hold his own, and enjoy the companionship of other children, and at times play happily alone.

Developing the sympathetic cooperative ways with others that insure his inclusion in groups.

Learning appropriate behavior for situations in which he is (times and places for noise, quiet, messing, nudity, etc.).

7) *Developing healthy emotional expressions for a wide variety of experiences:*

Learning to play out his feelings, frustrations, needs, and experiences.

Learning to postpone and to wait for satisfactions.

Expressing momentary hostility and making up readily afterwards.

Refining generalized joy or pain into discriminating expressions of pleasure, eagerness, tenderness, affection, sympathy, fear, anxiety, remorse, sorrow, etc.

8) *Learning to communicate effectively with an increasing number of others:*

Developing the vocabulary and ability to talk about a rapidly growing number of things, feelings, experiences, impressions, and curiosities.

Learning to listen, take in, follow directions, increase his attention span, and to respond intellectually to situations and to others.

Acquiring the social skills needed to get over feelings of shyness, self-consciousness, and awkwardness, and to participate with other people comfortably.

9) *Developing the ability to handle potentially dangerous situations:*

Learning to respect the dangers in fire, traffic, high places, bathing areas, poisons, animals, and the many other potential hazards.

Learning to handle himself effectively without undue fear in situations calling for caution and safety precautions (crossing streets, greeting strange dogs, responding to a stranger's offer of a ride, etc.).

Becoming willing to accept help in situations that are beyond him without undue dependence or too impulsive independence.

10) *Learning to be an autonomous person with initiative and a conscience of his own:*

Becoming increasingly responsible for making decisions in ways appropriate to his readiness.

Taking initiative for projecting himself into situations with innovations, experiments, trials, and original achievements.

Internalizing the expectancies and demands of his family and culture groups in his developing conscience.

Becoming reasonably self-sufficient in situations in accordance with his own make-up and stage of development.

11) *Laying foundations for understanding the meanings of life:*

Beginning to understand the origins of life, how the two sexes differ, and who he or she is as a member of his or her sex.

Trying to understand the nature of the physical world, what things are, how they work and why, and what they mean to him.

Accepting the religious faith of his parents, learning about the nature of God, and the spiritual nature of life.

The preschool boy or girl must achieve enough independence to be comfortable without his parents in a variety of situations. He or she must become reasonably self-sufficient both in the home and in outside settings, in keeping with his particular stage of development. The child who has preliminary practice in crossing streets, managing his outside garments, going to the toilet alone, washing his own hands, using his handkerchief, and in handling everyday routines, accidents and minor crises, will be ready to enter school feeling self-confident enough to be ready for its challenges. If his parents have introduced stories, songs, pictures, conversations, excursions, and creative play materials into his life, he will be able to enter school as a contributor as well as a recipient. When the preschool child has successfully accomplished the developmental tasks of this stage, he is ready to go to school. The check test on readiness for school attendance details some of the specific learnings derived from the preschooler's developmental tasks.

As a little girl "feeds her baby" she identifies with her mother by playing out what she sees as the feminine way to be. It is this identification with the parent of the same sex that is operating when a little girl trots around after her mother wanting "to help" in the things she sees her mother doing about the house. Similarly, the little boy frequently tags after his father, copying mannerisms, expressions, and ways of doing things down to the most meticulous detail.

CHECK TEST FOR THE CHILD'S READINESS FOR SCHOOL [1]

	Always	Usually	Sometimes	Rarely
1. The child knows his name, address, and father's name.				
2. He is free from those physical defects which can be corrected.				
3. He knows the way to school and can find his way home again.				
4. He has been taught how to cross streets.				
5. He recognizes policemen, is not afraid of them, and will follow their directions.				
6. He can go to the toilet, manage his clothing by himself, and conform to expected modesty patterns.				
7. He can hang up his coat, put on his outdoor clothing, and recognize his own belongings.				
8. He is content to stay with adults other than those he knows well.				
9. He has had opportunities to play with children his own age and gets along well with them.				
10. He is familiar with some of the places in the neighborhood which are of interest to children his age (post office, grocery store, fire house, a building under construction, etc.).				
11. He can entertain himself with constructive tasks for short periods of time.				
12. He is interested in books and will spend some time looking at them quietly.				
13. He attacks a new job willingly and welcomes new situations without fear.				

[1] Adapted freely from Fay Moeller, *Understanding Our Children*, Extension Service, University of Connecticut, Storrs, Connecticut, June 29, 1954 bulletin (mimeographed).

	Always	Usually	Sometimes	Rarely
14. He is in the habit of sharing certain household tasks with other members of the family.				
15. He is patient about waiting his turn and respecting property rights of others.				
16. He can keep his temper, his tears, and his other emotional outbursts under reasonably good control.				
17. He is curious about many things and, with a little help from an adult, can follow up his interests.				

DEVELOPMENTAL TASKS OF PARENTS OF PRESCHOOL CHILDREN [1]

Parents help the young child achieve his many developmental tasks by accepting his increasing range of skills and physical activity and by finding satisfactory roles in which physical help is gradually diminishing and other kinds of help gradually increasing. They must assume responsibility for supervising the child and yet avoid unnecessary worry and fear, whether in connection with a child's physical competence or growing social interests.

One of the perpetually surprising features of family life is the fact that it never stays put. No sooner has a fence been built to keep a 2-year-old out of the street than he is a 3-year-old, capable of understanding why he must keep to the sidewalk. The period of teaching the youngster to keep dry is succeeded by one of helping him to get used to sharing his parents with a new baby. Just as a child has reached a stage when his mental growth has made him an increasingly interesting companion, he is away at nursery school or kindergarten, and his parents begin to be outsiders, unaware of what is happening to him during a big share of his waking hours.

Parents who expect changes in themselves and in changing conditions will not find themselves washed up high and dry on the beach

[1] Freely adapted from Faegre, Marion L.; Hymes, James L., Jr.; Chandler, Caroline A., M.D.; and Work, Henry, M.D.; "Section III, Pre-School Family Stage," for the Committee on the Dynamics of Family Interaction, Preliminary Report, Evelyn Duvall and Reuben Hill, co-chairmen, National Conference on Family Life, February 1948 (mimeographed materials).

when their children are sailing merrily down the stream of life. They will have kept in the swim of things, will have found the necessary change and development exhilarating and enjoyable.

LOVING THE CHILD FOR WHAT HE REALLY IS

As their child enters a wider area of relationships and presses strongly for independence, parents need to maintain a sense of balance that recognizes helpfully that the child is still young, still dependent, and still in need of comfort and help in many areas.

He especially needs the comfort of being loved, appreciated, and enjoyed for himself. Both parents may need to check upon possible tendencies toward trying to make the child over, tweaking and pulling at him in little criticisms rather than giving encouraging and appreciative little pats. They must recognize that it is their job to help the child develop the capacities he has rather than to try to build up their self-esteem by pushing him beyond what he can do. Being aware of dangers in visiting "the curse of the norm" on any child and enjoying the unique individuality of each child are paired developmental tasks of prime importance.

CREATING TOGETHER AN ATMOSPHERE OF LOVE WITHIN THE HOME

Much of the parents' feeling about their child, and their attitudes toward him, reflect their own peace of mind and harmonious adjustment or lack of it. Their happiness with each other, and security in each other's love, is a major contribution to their child's emotional well-being. Unconsciously, the preschool child is forming attitudes that influence his own behavior toward, and expectations of, the opposite sex. The amount and kind of affection he receives tend to encourage his being warm, responsive, and outgoing, or stingy, fearful, and cold, unable to give freely of himself. This does not imply that parents can change the basic nature of their child's personality, but rather suggests the need of great sensitivity on their part to what the child is like, and what his needs are.

Agreement by his parents on reasonably similar ways of working with the child; standards, values and reactions that represent team-work rather than lack of interest in common goals—all give a child a comforting sense of the unity and solidarity underlying his home life.

At this stage the parents may need to strengthen their creative partnership and express their affection in ways that will keep their relationship from falling to a humdrum level. Expression of affection for each other may seem like an odd "task" to set up, but lack of such expression ranks high among the grievances husbands and wives list when trying to analyze their sources of unhappiness.[1] Apparently it is easy to fall into the habit of assuming that the other partner will take for granted the love each really wants and needs.

WHOLESOMELY ACCEPTING THE WEAKNESSES IN THEMSELVES AND IN EACH OTHER

Somehow parents have to learn to take their unavoidable failures, mistakes, and blunders without piling up feelings of guilt, blame, and recrimination. One way of doing this is to try to be sympathetic toward, instead of full of blame for, each other's faults in connection with dealing with the children. In a day when so much emphasis is placed on parent-child relations, while so little is known about how to keep from foisting one's own frustrations and insecurities on one's children, parents need each other's help in striking a balance between worry and nonchalance, between self-recrimination and indifference. We all make mistakes, but if our basic attitudes are wholesome, loving and friendly, the mistakes are going to be more than offset by good feelings.

CONTINUING TO DEVELOP AS INDIVIDUALS AND AS A MARRIED COUPLE

This is a time when a man and woman must learn to nourish mutual tastes, interests, and friendships as an aid to making the satisfactions of marriage permanent and enduring; and to provide for each other the satisfactions that strengthen their belief in themselves and give them status. The many demands and pressures upon each parent may tend to leave little time for them to enjoy each other and the hobbies or pursuits that may have been initially responsible for drawing them together. The mother may be so concerned with the demands of child care and homemaking that she gives little thought to her need for continuing to develop as a person. The father may be so taken up with his work and with earning a living that he neglects to enter, with sympathetic

[1] Lewis M. Terman et al., *Psychological Factors in Marital Happiness* (New York: McGraw-Hill Book Company, Inc., 1938), Chap. 5, "The Interpretation of Domestic Grievances."

interest, into discussions of the child's problems, the mother's concerns about household affairs, her reading, club work, or even fun for himself.

Making the partnership a fifty-fifty affair illustrates, for the children, the meaning of democratic family life. Parents need to be on the alert against falling back into acceptance of hand-me-down patterns of family life that no longer fit the changed conditions in which families now live. They need to share equally the enjoyments, the burdens, the ideals that give family life meaning. Each parent has his own special obligations, such as the husband's task to affirm his wife's possible need for outside interests and his obligation to keep abreast of his children's need of him as a man. The mother must accomplish such tasks as realizing the importance of progressively letting go of her child, in order that he may achieve independence, and of maintaining some sense of autonomy and development as a woman even while her children are young.

FAMILY DEVELOPMENTAL TASKS AT THE PRESCHOOL STAGE

While the preschool child is achieving his developmental tasks, and the parents are attempting to accomplish theirs as parents and as husband and wife, the family as-a-whole is concurrently faced with developmental tasks inherent in having a preschool child.

SUPPLYING ADEQUATE SPACE, FACILITIES, AND EQUIPMENT

Housing now should promote the growth of the preschooler, a good start for his younger sibling, and allow some privacy and comfort for the parents. Nothing can be a greater challenge to good family growth than inadequate room to work out the problems of group and individual maturation. When the entire neighborhood seems compressed and hemmed in through social barriers, the problem of full expression of the individual and the family is compounded. Play facilities, recreational areas, parks and their availability to all are important in providing an outlet for family tensions. Inefficient houses and inadequate household equipment complicate the mother's already onerous tasks of dividing her time between the needs of her children and the demands of the household. Many families achieve a high degree of family solidarity and goodwill by their ingenious collective use of too-tight quarters and too-limited facilities. But the fact that some families do well under severely limiting conditions does not thereby recommend the restrictions for general usage.

This is the stage when climbing, pulling, and hauling equipment gives the preschooler the large muscle exercise and skill development opportunities he needs, at the same time that it takes him out from under foot, assuring both his parents and his new sibling of some relief from his boisterous activity. Facilities adequate for the differential sleep and rest requirements of the several members of the family are a real asset. Parents now especially need privacy for their more intimate moments together without the everpresent interest of the inquiring preschooler, "Whatcha doing?" The child-proofing of the house mentioned earlier carries over into this stage with all its safeguards, especially now, when protecting the new baby without unduly restraining the preschool child, becomes an additional factor of importance.

MEETING PREDICTABLE AND UNEXPECTED COSTS OF FAMILY LIFE WITH SMALL CHILDREN

If the family income is fairly steady, it is possible to budget carefully for the normal expenditures of the growing family: so much for food, clothing, sitter fees, recreation, utilities, rent or house payments, and the rest. When the income fluctuates as it does with periods of unemployment or sickness or accident, major adjustments may need to be made.

The preschool stage is notorious for its unpredictabilities. The family may be getting along fine, with income matching outgo, when suddenly something happens that throws the whole financial picture out of focus. In early childhood there is a multiplicity of minor illnesses, any one of which can upset the family budget temporarily. Now when the older child ranges further afield in the neighborhood, to nursery school, kindergarten, play lot, park and beach, he comes in contact with many more children than he met as long as he was content in house and yard. These increased contacts multiply exposure to infections that make childhood diseases common for the preschooler and quite often for the baby sister or brother as well.

Accidents, falls, burns, and cuts are even more distressing because of the factor of suddenness that is added to the distress of actual incapacity. Children's accidents are frequently of great importance in the amount of guilt they arouse in the parents. When a long continued illness or an abrupt accident results in a deforming handicap or a crippling condition, it may necessitate critical shifts in the economic aspects as well as the emotional relationships of the family. Intelligent medical and social management are often necessary to keep the illness at the physical level from producing emotional maladjustment in its wake.

The high costs of medical care, continuing insurance drains, installment buying, debts, and mortgages complicate even well-planned family economics and are disastrous to those less carefully organized. Recent years have seen some advance in general recognition of such financial hazards facing young families with the development of such cushioning resources: group hospitalization and medical service plans, well-baby clinics, cooperative nurseries, child guidance clinics, mental hygiene services, family service facilities, parent education agencies, adult and child recreational programs, as well as special facilities for the care and education of all types of exceptional children. That such helpful resources are not yet generally available, or even known, to the rank and file of families who need them is all too true in most communities.

Nationally, grants-in-aid to the several states, funneled through the Children's Bureau, are available for maternal and child health, crippled children, child welfare services, etc., as is also the mental hygiene program under the United States Public Health Service.

The preschool family characteristically gets along on the single income of the husband. Only 15 per cent of all mothers of children under six are employed outside their homes.[1] This contrasts with 40 per cent of all wives working during the first year of marriage, and with 33 per cent of the wives in the labor force by the time all of the children have reached school age.[2] Now when little children must be cared for, it is the exceptional mother who leaves home to earn money, even at a time when family needs are great. This is the period when the family tightens its belt and tries to make ends meet on the husband's income alone.

SHARING RESPONSIBILITIES WITHIN THE EXPANDING FAMILY

Careful division of responsibility is needed at this time, when both mother and father may feel overworked. That the mother of young children is greatly overworked was publicly recognized in the widely discussed forum report, "The Plight of the Young Mother," in which the problem is introduced by these words:

[1] Paul C. Glick, "The Life Cycle of the Family," *Marriage and Family Living,* Vol. XVII, No. 1, February 1955, p. 8.
[2] *Ibid.,* p. 8.

Is our society asking too much of the young mother? Is it possible for her to give her children the best care when she must work as long as 100 hours a week—much more than is expected of people in business and industry—with no relief, even when her health is below par? Does this system produce the best results for the nation, for the community? [1]

Daily round-the-clock child care involving "chasing the children" who play in yard and neighborhood to properly supervise their play and protect them from danger, as well as attending to the needs of the infant, and doing the housework (marketing, cooking, baking, cleaning, dishwashing, sewing, washing, ironing), are generally assigned the young wife and mother in our society. In former days, these many responsibilities were divided among other grown and growing members of the family. In the old-fashioned farm family, there was always a pair of willing hands to mind the baby, or do an errand, or set the table. Margaret Mead reminds us that most primitive peoples recognize that it takes more than one adult to care for small helpless children and recommends that American families innovate ways of sharing small-child care more broadly today.

We have established a strange and lonely way of life, as grandmothers, aunts, grown daughters, and domestic help have progressively been banished from the home. We must devise new ways for real neighborhood sharing of the care of children, more cooperative nursery schools, more sharing of minor crises, so that the neighborhood takes over what the family used to do. And we need more generosity on the part of parents toward the grandparents, the childless aunts and uncles, all of whom could share a lot of the care of children if the parents were willing to really share their children. The present-day mother is alone in the house with her small children too much, and she has her hands too full. [2]

Until real help from the outside can be recruited, it may fall to the husband to share with his wife the tasks of childrearing and housekeeping through the preschool stage of the family life cycle. The young father returns home from work to find his wife busy with her end-of-the-day chores, the children irritably clinging to her while she tries to get the evening meal. He steps in and volunteers to take the children off her hands or to do some of the chores that she has not been able to finish through the hectic pace of the day. He may be tired but he comes in fresh from

[1] The Fifth Journal Forum, "The Plight of the Young Mother," *Ladies' Home Journal*, February 1956, p. 61.
[2] *Ibid.*, p. 62.

the outside without the mutual annoyance and frustration that is so often a part of the young mother's hour by hour life with active young children. He can whisk them off for a frolic, or give them their baths, or take over their feeding with a light touch just because he has been out of the home all day. The more strenuous tasks of floor mopping, window cleaning, washing, or trash dumping may be saved for the man of the house by the woman whose strength is barely adequate for the many other demands upon it.

The high cost of labor, coupled with the great increase in home ownership, means that more men are taking over the repair and development projects around their homes. One estimate [1] indicates that men spend from 22 to 30 hours a week at such tasks as plumbing, carpentry, yard work, gardening and lawn-care, helping out in a family crisis, and working at special improvements. As one householder put it:

> I come home from the office, shuck off my coat, and the wife tells me whether I must become plumber, mason, gardener, electrician, cook, or baby-sitter. Around our place there's always a crisis.[2]

The apartment dweller is not so burdened with household service nor is the man in the higher income brackets, as Table 16 indicates.

TABLE 16. *Annual Income and Household Responsibilities of the Man of the House, 1956* [3]

Annual Income	Responsibilities Assumed by the Householder
Up to $4,500	Virtually all home repair work
$4,500–$7,500	Remodeling and restyling done personally
$7,500–$10,000	Easier jobs with professional hired for big painting and construction projects
Above $10,000	Some chores personally done, the rest planned and supervised

Some young families have established such heavy allocations of responsibilities to the young husband and father that he may be severely exploited by a wife who reserves more and more of the day's work for him to do when his day's work is presumably finished. The young husband

---

[1] Bruce Lee, "Who Works Longer—Husband or Wife?" April 29, 1956, pp. 7, 21, 22. Reprinted from *This Week* Magazine, copyright 1956 by the United Newspapers Magazine Corporation.
[2] *Ibid.*, p. 21.
[3] *Ibid.*, p. 22.

is apt to be sorely pressed for time and energy at this stage of his life. This is the time when the man of the house is trying to get ahead on his job. He possibly is taking an evening course or two with an eye to advancement. He may be doing what overtime he can get to help make ends meet. Even if he is willing to help out at home there is a limit to what any one person can do comfortably and well.

This is a time when it is necessary to have an equitable division of responsibility between mother and father on the basis of time, strength, interest, ability, and mutual concern for the well-being of the family. The man of the house may prefer taking the laundry to the laundromat if that is where he can meet and chat with the other fathers of the neighborhood. In another household, the young mother may choose to assume full responsibility for the laundry at home where she can keep the baby's things done up and some portion of the household linen taken care of on a daily basis. One family may decide to invest in an automatic washer the money that another family pays out for diaper services and laundrying. Whatever the decision, the important thing is that the members of the family agree to it as appropriate for their situation.

The preschool child is old enough to assume some real responsibilities. He gradually takes over more and more of his own care in toileting, washing his face and hands, dressing and undressing, and picking up his toys, with help or supervision as needed. As he enters the preschool period, he or she has begun to take a real interest in what is going on in the household and wants to participate. The little girl of two and a half or three begs to help make beds, to sweep the floor and to wash dishes when her mother is occupied with these tasks. The child identifies with the parent of the same sex and likes nothing better than acting out the sex role. Parents are wise not to discourage these efforts on the part of the small child "to help." They share with the child the jobs he or she can join in, not so much in the interest of the child's labor, but especially because helping makes the youngster a real participant in his family. The child learns thus to internalize his or her sex role.

The parent's burden varies greatly according to social class, with families of the upper classes hiring more domestic help in the form of housekeepers, cooks, maids, and infant nurses. Middle-class families spend little on domestic help; and lower-class mothers hire no help, themselves often available for day labor. The middle-class family invests more in labor-saving devices and equipment: electric washers and dry-

The preschooler is old enough to assume some real responsibility, and parents are wise to encourage this "help" as the child's way of participating in the family.

ers, dishwashing machines, vacuum cleaners, waxers, steam irons, mangles and other "wife-savers," that tend to be lacking in the lower-class home. Some struggling farm families, with more children than in the higher social levels on the average, carry and heat their water, cut and carry in their fuel, and raise, gather and process much of their food-stuffs in a daily round of "chores."

Many a young family sails smoothly through the preschool family stage in these days. Modern equipment in kitchen and laundry eases the load that the young mother must carry. Miracle fabrics are easy to keep clean and need practically no ironing. Prepared baby foods and frozen prod-

Modern automatic washers and dryers ease the load the young mother must carry and make some provision for the preschool child to assist in collecting and sorting the laundry.

ucts that can be readied for use in a few moments are a God-send. The modern young mother's ability to plan her work, putting the essential tasks on the agenda and letting the relatively unimportant things slide, removes much of the strain from daily routines. Spacing the arrival of the children so that each is assured the care it needs without unduly taxing the mother's strength does much to keep the young family on an even keel during the preschool stage when life can so easily become pretty hectic.

Success in achieving this developmental task is not just a matter of how much or how little there is to be done, but rather of how decisions are made, how roles are assigned, and how the several family members feel about their responsibilities. If each family member feels pride and pleasure in doing his tasks, if each is accountable to the others for common concerns, if each feels needed and appreciated, the family is finding happiness and integration as a working unit.

MAINTAINING MUTUALLY SATISFYING SEXUAL RELATIONSHIPS AND PLANNING FOR FUTURE CHILDREN

At this stage of the family life cycle, the parents have been through the full process of conception, pregnancy, childbirth, and establishment as a family. They are able to take further pregnancies more in their stride than was possible when the first baby came. But the very fact that there is already one child in the family adds its increment of responsibility to the second period of "infanticipating."

When mother goes to the hospital for the delivery of subsequent babies, father usually maintains the equilibrium at home. He gets his first youngster up in the morning and off to a good start in the day before he goes off to work. Not infrequently the young father takes his "vacation" from his job so that he can be at home to care for his firstborn while his wife is hospitalized for the second. The wealthy family keeps on the infant nurse for the care of the first and further children. In still other families a grandmother will take over the care of the household until the new baby and mother are firmly installed at home. Sometimes a toddler has to be "farmed out" to neighbors or friends while his mother spends her lying-in period away from home. In the larger cities homemaker services are increasing for just such assistance to families whose wife and mother is temporarily "out of service." One thing is sure, the American mother cannot take her family along with her when she goes to be delivered, as is possible in some other cultures.

When mother, father, and other family members are intimately involved in caring for the children, there tends to be more joint consultation about family size and more specific plans made for further children than in cultures where a man takes pride in sheer fertility and a woman's role is defined in terms of one pregnancy after another throughout her active reproductive life.

American couples want to have children. Men and women generally say they want to have two, three, or more children.[1] The figures from a study at Cornell University shown in Table 17 are fairly typical of college men and women.

[1] Ronald Freedman, David Goldberg, and Harry Sharp, " 'Ideals' about Family Size in the Detroit Metropolitan Area: 1954," *The Milbank Memorial Fund Quarterly*, Vol. 33, No. 3, April 1955, p. 195.

TABLE 17. *Distribution of University Students According to Number of Children Wanted* [1]

Number of Children Wanted	Men (N = 190)	Women (N = 174)	Both (N = 364)
None	0	0.6%	0.3%
One	1.1%	0.6%	0.8%
Two	34.2%	19.0%	26.9%
Three	40.0%	48.3%	44.0%
Four or more	20.0%	29.9%	24.7%
Question unanswered	4.7%	1.7%	3.3%

Studies of the spacing of children agree that up to the third birth the interval between births tend to increase.[2] These longer intervals can be roughly seen as "breathing spaces" in which the young family re-establishes itself and mobilizes its resources after the birth of one child before attempting the next.

Finding the time, privacy, and energy for tender, close relationships as a married couple may be difficult when children are young. Sharing bed or room with a child old enough to be aware of what is going on robs a husband and wife of much-needed privacy. Days and nights of nursing a sick youngster rob even the most loving husband and wife of their ardor for each other. Just getting through the day's work may bring the couple to bed too tired for anything but sleep. Knowing from experience the power of their fertility tends to make the woman wary of her husband's approaches unless she has great confidence in the family planning pro-cedures in operation. What once was entered into with joyous abandon, now may become a marital duty, unless they as a couple provide for their sex life together amid the welter of other demands.

CREATING AND MAINTAINING EFFECTIVE COMMUNICATION SYSTEMS WITHIN THE FAMILY

The tower of Babel had nothing on family life at the preschool stage. The baby babbles and gurgles and sputters and fusses and "practices" his

[1] Reprinted with permission from Lemo D. Rockwood and Mary E. N. Ford, *Youth, Marriage and Parenthood* (New York: John Wiley and Sons, 1945), p. 135.
[2] Gerald Leslie, Harold Christensen, and Glenn Pearman, "Studies in Child Spacing: IV. The Time-Interval Separating All Children in Completed Families of Purdue University Graduates," *Social Forces*, Vol. 34, No. I, October 1955, pp. 77–82.

vowels; the preschooler talks a blue streak, jumping from one topic to another and from the answer to one question to another miles removed; mother tries to get through to her preoccupied spouse and her energetic youngsters her suggestions, ideas, and feelings; and father grumbles out his frustrations oblivious to the goings-on around him.

With the coming of the new baby, the emotional constellations of the family shift as the firstborn accepts his displacement as well as he can and as the parents find a place in their home for the little newcomer at the same time that they safeguard the security of the older child. There may be a tendency for parents to be emotionally warmer with the second baby than they were with their first.[1] This probably is not so much that they love the second baby more, but rather that they have become more familiar with their roles, and so are able to relax and enjoy the new baby more fully than they could in their first experience as parents.

Understandable as the parents' feelings and emotional expressions are, it may be hard for the firstborn to accept their open display of affection for the little new rival. Therefore, the mother and father may need to create new modes of emotional communication with the older child that will give him the assurance that he is loved and needed and wanted for himself. Wise parents provide some special time with their firstborn when the new baby does not intrude. It sometimes helps to let the firstborn know that just because he is the older, he occupies a special place in their lives that no younger sibling can ever fill. Some increase in responsibility for the firstborn may be reassuring to him if it is not overdone. The older child sometimes has to let his parents know of his need for being babied too, in regressive acts: wetting himself when he has long since learned to be dry, wanting to take his milk from a bottle when he has already established more mature eating and drinking habits, wanting to be cuddled and fussed over as the baby is, even trying to put himself in the baby's place—literally in the buggy or the crib. These are signals a sensitive parent can read that indicate the older child's need for more close, demonstrable affection and attention than he has been getting. Ridiculing, belittling, ignoring, or denying a child's efforts to communicate his emotional needs cripple the communication systems and bottle up explosive feelings with unfortunate results to the youngster, the younger sibling, and the family-as-a-whole.

[1] J. K. Lasko, "Parent Behavior toward First and Second Children," *Genetic Psychology Monograph*, Vol. 49, No. 1, February 1954, pp. 99–137.

The child who is prepared for the coming of his new baby sister or brother, can take with less distress the jealousy and rivalry so usually generated by his displacement by the new rival. Before the baby comes, the older child needs from his parents an understanding of what is happening, an assurance that this is to be HIS baby as well as theirs and that they will love him after the baby comes, as they have before. In this a mother or father can get helpful books to read to the preschool youngster, as well as find sound guides on the early sex education of their children, of which the following are examples:

Ets, Marie Hall, *The Story of a Baby* (New York: Viking Press, 1948).

Faegre, Marion L., *Your Own Story* (Minneapolis: University of Minnesota Press, 1943).

Gruenberg, Sidonie M., *The Wonderful Story of How You Were Born* (Garden City, New York: Hanover House, 1952).

Hymes, James L., *How to Tell Your Child about Sex* (New York: Public Affairs Committee, 1949).

Levine, Milton, and Seligmann, J. H., *The Wonder of Life* (New York: Simon and Schuster, 1940).

Peller, Lili, and Mumford, Sophia, *Our New Baby* (New York: Vanguard Press, 1943).

Shane, Harold and Ruth, *The New Baby* (New York: Simon and Schuster, 1948).

Strain, Frances Bruce, *New Patterns in Sex Teaching* (New York: Appleton-Century-Crofts, 1951 edition).

Little children are so everpresent and so demanding of the time and attention of their parents, that husband and wife may need to inaugurate new times and ways for getting through to each other. The little children may be fed by one or both parents, and then put to rest while the parents have an occasional quiet meal together. Or, the preschooler can be given some special time of his own by either the father or the mother just before the family meal, so that he can relate the excitements of his day and get some of his more pressing questions out of the way before the family as a whole assembles for mealtime. One young family developed a "green light" system by which the "traffic" of conversation could flow in both directions across the table, each in its turn, thus assuring the parents of some access to each other between the gusts of chatter from their preschool youngsters.

This developmental task is being achieved in the family as each member of the family increasingly feels free to express his ideas, his feelings, and, his values with assurance of their acceptance by the others in the family. The expanding stage of the family life cycle is so explosive, and so full of new experiences, feelings, decisions, and needs to evaluate, that communication systems become extremely important at the very time that they are most difficult to keep open and in good working order. But few things are more important to happy family life.

CULTIVATING THE FULL POTENTIALS OF RELATIONSHIPS WITHIN THE EXTENDED FAMILY

At few stages in the family life cycle can relatives be as important as during the preschool period. Grandparents can do much to ease the pressures upon the parents while children are young. A loving relative who is on hand while the new baby is coming, and through the illnesses and accidents that occasionally hit the young family, cushions these crises in many a home. An aunt and uncle may get valuable experience at the same time that they relieve the young parents in child care. They may take over for a long evening or over a weekend or even for a week or two while father and mother slip off to regain their perspective as a couple on a brief vacation, on a business trip, or for a quick visit to old friends.

Problems come up, of course, when the substitute parents do not agree with the child guidance procedures or philosophy that the parents are trying to practice. A grandmother can "spoil" her young charges, in ways that take weeks to rehabilitate, if she is not aware of the parents' goals for their children. Or a too-rigid program of discipline suddenly imposed by some well-meaning aunt or uncle may boomerang in any number of ways. These things are being openly discussed in many families today in ways that allow the parents to brief explicitly any child-serving relative of what is the usual practice, and why; what the child is and is not customarily allowed to do, and why; and what routines are followed most conscientiously and which can be let slide when the situation warrants.

Children are remarkably resilient creatures and can take a great deal of inconsistency from the various adults that attend them, as long as they feel basically secure. Although there are some procedures and policies that are considered better than others according to sound child-development principles,[1] few children can be severely damaged by occasional

[1] James Walters, "Attitudes Concerning the Guidance of Children: A Study of the Differential Effects of an Introductory Course in Child Development on the Attitudes of College Women," Unpublished Ph.D. thesis (Tallahassee: Folrida State University, 1954).

lapses or changes of pace. Extremists who insist that grandparents are bad for children fail to see how much a child can learn from being differently handled by different persons or how much a youngster benefits from the sense of ongoing family relations he gets as he clamors for tales of when his mother or father was young. One nine-year-old puts both values neatly when he says solemnly, "I like to go to Grandma's house, because she scolds so soft, and she tells me all about the olden days when Daddy was a little boy just like me."

TAPPING RESOURCES, SERVING NEEDS, AND ENJOYING CONTACTS OUTSIDE THE FAMILY

One hazard of the family with little children is its preoccupation with itself. The young father is seen putting in a full day on his job, rushing to night school or union meeting to better his chances for advancement, and helping out at home in the many roles he feels are his in the family. The young mother is tied down with little children so much day after day that she may long for adult companionship, stimulation, and contact.

The little child will lead the family out into wider horizons if he is allowed to range further afield. He goes to nursery school and then to kindergarten, bringing home with him new problems and experiences and later taking his parents out to parents' meetings, neighborhood projects, and community affairs. The preschooler is big enough now to go to Sunday school, and often starts his family in church activities that carry through the years. Periodic trips to the pediatrician or family doctor for preventive shots and check-ups, as well as treatment for the various illnesses that befall him, bring both him and his parents into relationship with the health facilities of the community. His enjoyment of the park, the zoo, the playground, the fire department, and the bakery frequently gets his whole family out for jaunts into activities and facilities never before explored.

The young mother finds meanings in life as a person outside the family at intervals around her homemaking and childcare responsibilities. It may be in some parents' group, community service project, church circle, political campaign, course of study in the evening, or Saturday afternoon employment that she finds her identity as a woman and brings home, after a few hours of wider horizons, the perspective and point of view that enriches the family-as-a-whole. Here it is that the stereotyped reactions of the "Woman's place is in the home" or "Little children need a mother's care," if interpreted too rigidly, can be suffocating not only

Nursery school offers a little child an opportunity to play with other children and to explore a variety of materials, settings, and situations—good ways of growing up, for the pre-schooler and for his family too.

to the young woman but to her family as well. A major complaint of college educated mothers of young children is that they long for intervals of adult association, mature stimulation, and challenging activities with persons their own age. This is one of the prime motivators back of the young mother's desire for a job. Openly recognized by the family, many opportunities besides gainful employment may appear as satisfying, unless the financial needs of the family require it.[1]

The young father driven through his twenties and thirties by efforts to get himself established vocationally and to keep his little family afloat financially, may push himself so hard that he has little time for continuing his interests as a person or for enjoying his family on their new horizons. This is especially true in some middle-class families, where mobility drives keep a man lashed by hopes for advancement and chained to his job and its demands. Upper-class fathers find it easier to keep up their club memberships (for business and professional reasons, it's true), and to maintain regular programs of recreation with other men as well as in the young married couple set. Lower-class families make the poorest articulations with the wider community in the health, recreational, educational, vocational, and social aspects of life, as studies previously quoted (Chapter Four) so emphatically indicate.

FACING DILEMMAS AND REWORKING PHILOSOPHIES OF LIFE IN EVERCHANGING CHALLENGES

By the time the oldest child is four or five and the next baby already on the scene, the family is face to face with a number of dilemmas that challenge its ways of life. Kirkpatrick[2] mentions several that are particularly relevant at this stage of the family life cycle: (1) freedom versus order and efficiency, (2) free expression of personal potentialities versus stable goal expectations, (3) personal self-expression versus childrearing, (4) work achievement versus love-reproduction functions, (5) flexible training versus rigid childrearing, (6) high aspiration levels for children versus realistic expectations, (7) family loyalty versus community loyalty, and (8) extensive casual association versus restrictive intensive association. Each horn of each dilemma has its values and its price. Freedom

[1] Virginia Evans, "I Wanted to Go Back to Work," *McCall's*, March 1956, pp. 61–62.
[2] Clifford Kirkpatrick, *The Family As Process and Institution* (New York: The Ronald Press, 1955), Chap. 4, "Family Types and Dilemmas."

One of the dilemmas that challenge the preschool family is that of freedom (to clutter, to mess, to spill, and to play with a minimum of restraint) versus order and efficiency.

is greatly to be desired, but its price is conflict and confusion in the family. On the other hand, order and efficiency are values, but at the cost of personal frustration and submission to authority. And so it goes. Every family must work out in ways that make sense to its members and to itself as a unit, those answers to the eternal questions of life that make sense for them in their situations.

A simple "nonintellectual" family may deny its absorption in philosophical matters. Yet, every day is full of decisions and choices that depend upon how the family conceives of itself and what its operational definitions of life are. These conceptions of their common life are constantly undergoing change: (1) with the addition of each new member; (2) with the stimuli of other ways of life in the community and among their associates; (3) with the new ideas and insights any of the family members gets (in association with others, in reading, in educational, social, religious, and other contexts); (4) with the old and new tastes of joys and satisfactions that ought to be safeguarded; and (5) under the various stresses, strains, and challenges that back them to the wall and force them to take another look at life as they are living it.

SUMMARY

Families with preschool children are those whose first children are between 2½ and 5 years of age. There quite possibly is a second child, and sometimes a third, born into the family before the stage is completed, who will be preoccupied with the developmental tasks of infancy, while the preschool child is working on his developmental tasks, and the parents are attempting to accomplish those they face as parents, as married partners, and as persons. Family developmental tasks of this stage may be seen as (1) supplying adequate space, facilities, and equipment, (2) meeting predictable and unexpected costs of family life with small children, (3) sharing responsibilities within the expanding family, (4) maintaining mutually satisfying sexual relationships and planning for future children, (5) creating and maintaining effective communication systems within the family, (6) cultivating the full potentials of relationships within the extended family, (7) tapping resources, serving needs, and enjoying contacts outside the family, and (8) facing the dilemmas and reworking philosophies in everchanging challenges of family living.

SUGGESTED ACTIVITIES

1) Review Katharine Whiteside Taylor, *Parent Cooperative Nursery Schools* (New York: Bureau of Publications, Teachers College, Columbia University, 1954), looking especially for the ways in which cooperative nursery schools (1) help preschool children accomplish their developmental tasks, (2) assist parents of preschool children achieve their developmental tasks as parents and as persons, and (3) are of value to the family of the preschooler in its accomplishment of the developmental tasks of the preschool family. Document specifically task by task from explicit and implicit materials in the volume.

2) Outline a feasible program in preparation of the firstborn child for the coming of a new baby into the family, using references suggested in this chapter under the heading, "Preparing the Preschooler for the New Baby" and/or other sound materials. Discuss the relevance of each step in the program for the achievement of the goals for the child, and for the family.

3) Role-play several of the family situations presented in either Jackson's *Life Among the Savages* or McConnell's *Trampled Terraces* (full references in *Readings* for this chapter), portraying the child's as well as the parents' roles in each situation presented. Discuss the nature of the conflict between the developmental tasks of little children and the developmental tasks of parents of little children in each connection.

Indicate in what ways these are normal conflicts of developmental tasks between the generations or how they may be atypical of this stage. Document your opinions as far as you can from materials in your readings and in the chapter.

4) Copy on the blackboard one of Hank Ketcham's cartoons of *Dennis the Menace* showing a predicament in which the developmental tasks of the child are in opposition to those of his parents. Discuss.

5) Review the film *Preface to a Life* (29 minutes, sound, produced by Sun Dial Films, Inc., for National Institute of Mental Health, U. S. Public Health Service, 1950), looking especially into how a preschool child feels about the coming of the new baby into his family. What did the parents do that helped? What made the problem more difficult for the firstborn? What else might have been tried?

6) Invite a preschool teacher to tell you what she finds most usual in the behavior of her children. Discuss what the children seem to be after in these situations in terms of what you know about their developmental tasks.

7) Elaborate any one of Kirkpatrick's dilemmas of family life that particularly applies to the preschool stage, citing illustrations, and giving sources for both aspects of the dilemma you have chosen (see *Readings*).

8) Write a paper on the development of trust and of autonomy in early childhood, using as basic references, Erik Erikson, *Childhood and Society* (New York: W. W. Norton & Company, 1950), and Robert J. Havighurst, *Human Development and Education*, Part One (see *Readings*).

9) Discuss what is meant by the concept of a child's identifying with the parent of the same sex. Give illustrations, sources, and indicate the relationship between this tendency and the accomplishment of the developmental tasks of early childhood.

10) Write a paper on the role of the father in the preschool family, touching on the amount of responsibility he may assume in homemaking and childcare, and what effect he has upon the development of the child. (See English and Foster in your *Readings* as well as the discussion of division of responsibility in this chapter).

READINGS

Bacmeister, Rhoda W., *Growing Together* (New York: Appleton-Century-Crofts, 1947).

Barker, Roger; Kounin, Jacob; and Wright, Herbert, eds., *Child Behavior and Development* (New York: McGraw-Hill Book Company, 1943).

Baruch, Dorothy, *New Ways in Discipline* (New York: Appleton-Century-Crofts, 1949).

Bigelow, Howard F., *Family Finance* (Philadelphia: J. B. Lippincott Company, 1953), Chaps., 5, 6, and 7.

Breckenridge, Marian, and Vincent, E. Lee, *Child Development* (Philadelphia: W. B. Saunders and Company, 1949).

Chittenden, Gertrude, *Living with Children* (New York: Macmillan Company, 1944).

Duvall, Evelyn Millis, *Family Living* (New York: Macmillan Company, 1955 edition), Chaps. 16, 17, and 18.

English, O. Spurgeon, and Foster, Constance, *Fathers Are Parents, Too* (New York: G. P. Putnam's Sons, 1951).

Faegre, Marion; Hymes, James; Chandler, Caroline; and Work, Henry, "Section III, Pre-School Family Stage," for the Committee on the Dynamics of Family Interaction, Preliminary Report, Evelyn Duvall and Reuben Hill, co-chairmen, National Conference on Family Life, February 1948, unpublished materials.

Gruenberg, Sidonie, *Your Child and You* (New York: Fawcett Publications, Inc., 1950).

Havighurst, Robert J., *Human Development and Education* (New York: Longmans, Green and Co., 1953), Chaps. 2 and 3.

Jackson, Shirley, *Life Among the Savages* (New York: Farrar, Strauss and Young, 1953).

Ketcham, Hank, *Dennis the Menace* and *More Dennis the Menace* (New York: Henry Holt and Company, 1953).

Kirkpatrick, Clifford, *The Family: as Process and Institution* (New York: The Ronald Press, 1955), Chap. 4, "Family Types and Dilemmas."

Langdon, Grace and Stout, Irving, *These Well-Adjusted Children* (New York: John Day Company, 1951).

Levy, D. M., *Maternal Overprotection* (New York: Columbia University, 1943).

McConnell, Raymond, *Trampled Terraces* (Lincoln, Nebraska: University of Nebraska Press, 1950).

Parsons, Talcott, and Bales, Robert, *Family, Socialization and Interaction Process* (Glencoe, Illinois: The Free Press, 1955), Chapter 2, "Family Structure and the Socialization of the Child."

Podolsky, Edward, *The Jealous Child* (New York: Philosophical Library, 1954).

Rand, Winifred; Sweeny, Mary; and Vincent, E. Lee, *Growth and Development of the Young Child* (Philadelphia: W. B. Saunders, 1946).

Smart, Mollie and Russell, *Living and Learning with Children* (Boston: Houghton-Mifflin, 1949).

Smart, Mollie and Russell, *An Introduction to Family Relationships* (Philadelphia: W. B. Saunders and Company, 1953).

Spock, Benjamin, *The Pocketbook of Baby and Child Care* (New York: Pocket Books, Inc., 1946).

Strain, Frances Bruce, *Your Child . . . His Family and Friends* (New York: Appleton-Century-Crofts, 1943).

CHAPTER TEN

Families with school children

The stage of the family life cycle characterized by school-age children starts when the first child goes to school, at five to six years of age, and continues until he or she becomes a teenager at thirteen. Before the end of this period, it is likely that the family has seen the birth of younger siblings and that the family has reached its maximum size in number of members and of interrelationships. These are the big bulging years of family living, with the children running in and out of the home, with many projects begun and underway, with the adults busy keeping the household in good running order and following their growing youngsters out into wider and ever more meaningful contacts in the community.

Several stages of the family life cycle may overlap during this period. When the eldest child reaches school age, his next younger sibling is probably a preschool child, the third child is possibly either an infant or a preschooler and there may be still another child on the way. So, while the family explores the schoolager's world for the first time in the new developmental tasks of that period, those of the younger children are being simultaneously worked through with old-shoe familiarity of having been through this before, or with the difficulties and hazards that come as a different child tries to accomplish his developmental tasks in his own way. Concurrently, the family may be the scene of action in efforts to work out the developmental tasks of the school ager, the preschooler, and the infant. In addition the parents themselves have chang-

When the eldest child reaches school age, his next younger sibling is probably a preschool child and still a third may be on the way.

ing needs, tasks, and roles as adults both as a married couple and as persons. These are busy active days for most families.

What Is a Boy? [1]

BY ALAN BECK

Between the innocence of babyhood and the dignity of manhood we find a delightful creature called a boy. Boys come in assorted sizes, weights, and colors, but all boys have the same creed: To enjoy every second of every minute of every hour of every day and to protest with noise (their only weapon) when their last minute is finished and the adult males pack them off to bed at night.

Boys are found everywhere—on top of, underneath, inside of, climbing on, swinging from, running around, or jumping to. Mothers love them, little girls hate them, older sisters and brothers tolerate them, adults ignore them, and Heaven protects them. A boy is Truth with dirt on its face, Beauty with a cut

[1] Copyright New England Mutual Life Insurance Company, Boston, Mass., quoted with permission.

on its finger, Wisdom with bubble gum in its hair, and the Hope of the future with a frog in its pocket.

When you are busy, a boy is an inconsiderate, bothersome, intruding jangle of noise. When you want him to make a good impression, his brain turns to jelly or else he becomes a savage, sadistic, jungle creature bent on destroying the world and himself with it.

A boy is a composite—he has the appetite of a horse, the digestion of a sword swallower, the energy of a pocket-size atomic bomb, the curiosity of a cat, the lungs of a dictator, the imagination of a Paul Bunyan, the shyness of a violet, the audacity of a steel trap, the enthusiasm of a firecracker, and when he makes something he has five thumbs on each hand.

He likes ice cream, knives, saws, Christmas, comic books, the boy across the street, woods, water (in its natural habitat), large animals, Dad, trains, Saturday mornings, and fire engines. He is not much for Sunday School, company, schools, books without pictures, music lessons, neckties, barbers, girls, overcoats, adults, or bedtime.

Nobody else is so early to rise, or so late to supper. Nobody else gets so much fun out of trees, dogs, and breezes. Nobody else can cram into one pocket a rusty knife, a half-eaten apple, 3 feet of string, an empty Bull Durham sack, 2 gum drops, 6 cents, a sling shot, a chunk of unknown substance, and a genuine supersonic code ring with a secret compartment.

A boy is a magical creature—you can lock him out of your work shop, but you can't lock him out of your heart. You can get him out of your study, but you can't get him out of your mind. Might as well give up—he is your captor, your jailer, your boss, and your master—a freckled-face, pint-sized, cat-chasing, bundle of noise. But when you come home at night with only the shattered pieces of your hopes and dreams, he can mend them like new with the two magic words—"Hi Dad!"

What Is a Girl? [1]
BY ALAN BECK

Little girls are the nicest things that happen to people. They are born with a little bit of angelshine about them and though it wears thin sometimes, there is always enough left to lasso your heart—even when they are sitting in the mud, or crying temperamental tears, or parading up the street in mother's best clothes.

A little girl can be sweeter (and badder) oftener than anyone else in the world. She can jitter around, and stomp, and make funny noises that frazzle your nerves, yet just when you open your mouth, she stands there demure with that special look in her eyes. A girl is Innocence playing in the mud, Beauty standing on its head, and Motherhood dragging a doll by the foot.

Girls are available in five colors—black, white, red, yellow, or brown, yet

[1] Copyright New England Mutual Life Insurance Company, Boston, Mass., quoted by permission.

Mother Nature always manages to select your favorite color when you place your order. They disprove the law of supply and demand—there are millions of little girls, but each is as precious as rubies.

God borrows from many creatures to make a little girl. He uses the song of a bird, the squeal of a pig, the stubbornness of a mule, the antics of a monkey, the spryness of a grasshopper, the curiosity of a cat, the speed of a gazelle, the slyness of a fox, the softness of a kitten, and to top it all off He adds the mysterious mind of a woman.

A little girl likes new shoes, party dresses, small animals, first grade, noise makers, the girl next door, dolls, make-believe, dancing lessons, ice cream, kitchens, coloring books, make-up, cans of water, going visiting, tea parties, and one boy. She doesn't care so much for visitors, boys in general, large dogs, hand-me-downs, straight chairs, vegetables, snow suits, or staying in the front yard. She is loudest when you are thinking, the prettiest when she has provoked you, the busiest at bedtime, the quietest when you want to show her off, and the most flirtatious when she absolutely must not get the best of you again.

Who else can cause you more grief, joy, irritation, satisfaction, embarrassment, and genuine delight than this combination of Eve, Salome, and Florence Nightingale? She can muss up your home, your hair, and your dignity—spend your money, your time, and your temper—then just when your patience is ready to crack, her sunshine peeks through and you've lost again.

Yes, she is a nerve-racking nuisance, just a noisy bundle of mischief. But when your dreams tumble down and the world is a mess—when it seems you are pretty much of a fool after all—she can make you a king when she climbs on your knee and whispers, "I love you best of all!"

DEVELOPMENTAL TASKS OF SCHOOL-AGE BOYS AND GIRLS

Out at the growing edge of the family at the school-age stage is the firstborn at work with all that is involved in becoming a competent school-age boy or girl. Anyone who insists that "school days are happy-go-lucky, carefree days" has never focused his attention closely on the care an actual school-age youngster gives to the achievement of his developmental tasks. Watch him long enough, with awareness of what is happening just beneath the surface, and you realize how hard he works at these growth responsibilities of his and how complex and interwoven his many developmental tasks really are. The more insistent of the school-ager's developmental tasks may be introduced by the question: What is the child in our complex American society called upon to learn during this period? In many areas these learnings are in terms of "continuing," "extending," and "expanding" previous abilities. In others, whole new aspects of life open up.

1) *Learning the basic skills required of school children:*

Mastering the fundamentals of reading, writing, calculating, and the scientific rational approach to solving problems.

Extending understandings of cause and effect relationships.

Developing concepts essential for everyday living.

Continued development in ability to reason and to do reflective thinking.

2) *Mastering the physical skills appropriate to his development:*

Learning the games, the sports, and the various roles in activities pursued by children of his age and sex in his community (ride a bike, swim, skate, play ball, row a boat, climb a tree, etc.).

Developing abilities needed in personal and family living (bathe and dress himself, care for his clothing, make his bed, cook and serve food, clean up after activities, maintain and repair simple household equipment, etc.).

3) *Developing meaningful understandings of the use of money:*

Finding socially acceptable ways of getting money for what he wants to buy.

Learning how to buy wisely the things he most wants with what he has, and to stay within his available resources.

Finding the meanings of saving for postponed satisfactions.

Reconciling differences between his wants and his resources, and those of others both poorer and richer than he.

Getting basic orientation into the nature of money in everyday life in the family and in the larger community.

4) *Becoming an active, cooperative member of his family:*

Gaining skills in participating in family discussions and decision-making.

Assuming responsibilities within the household with satisfactions in accomplishment and belonging.

Becoming more mature in giving and receiving affection and gifts between himself and his parents, his siblings, and his relatives within the extended family.

Learning to enjoy the full resources and facilities available within the family, and to take initiative in enriching them as he becomes able.

5) *Extending his abilities to relate effectively to others, both peers and adults:*

    Making progress in his ability to adjust to others.

    Learning to stand up for his rights.

    Improving his abilities both to lead and to follow others.

    Mastering expectancies in simple conventions, rules, customs, courtesies, and standards of his family and groups.

    Learning genuinely cooperative roles with others in many situations.

    Making and keeping close friends.

6) *Continuing the learnings involved in handling his feelings and impulses:*

    Growing in his ability to work through simple frustrations.

    Exploring socially acceptable ways of releasing negative emotions effectively.

    Becoming more mature in channeling feelings into the ways and time and places appropriate within his culture.

    Gaining skill in sharing his feelings with those who can help (parents, teachers, close friends, scout leaders, etc.).

7) *Coming to terms with his or her own sex role both now and as it will become:*

    Learning what is expected as appropriate behavior for boys, for girls, for men, for women, for married people, for parents, and grandparents.

    Clarifying knowledges about the nature of sex and reproduction.

    Adjusting to a changing body in the pubertal growth spurt as teen years approach; (accepting the new size and form, function and potentials of pubertal growth).

    Thinking wholesomely ahead to what it will be like to be grown up as a man or woman.

8) *Continuing to find himself as a worthy person:*

    Identifying with his own age and sex in appropriate ways.

    Discovering many ways of becoming acceptable as a person; gaining status.

    Growing in self-confidence, self-respect, self-control, and self-realization.

    Extending the process of establishing his own individuality.

9) *Relating himself to loyalties beyond the moment and outside himself:*
Finding new meanings in religion, in the universe, in the nature of
things.
Discovering satisfactions in music, art, drama, nature, and the literature of his culture, appropriate to his age.
Devoting himself to group goals (scouts, boys' and girls' clubs, etc.).
Laying foundations for patriotism, for pride in men's achievements
through history, and for a sense of belongingness to the human
race.
Gaining experience in essential morality in action at home and with
others.
Learning and accepting the eternal realities of birth, death, and
infinity.

How well a given boy or girl accomplishes any of these many complex
developmental tasks before he or she enters the teens depends on many
things. It depends first of all on how good a start that particular child
had in development through the early years of childhood. The little child
who succeeded in achieving most of the developmental tasks of infancy,
early childhood, and the preschool years continues on in these achievements as his or her horizons expand through the school years. Success
depends upon how many opportunities there are for development in the
home, in the school, and in community life. It depends in large measure
on how skilled parents and teachers are in anticipating, recognizing, and
providing growth opportunities for the child's developmental tasks as
they come along. But children differ widely, as do parents. And, while
children are struggling through their growth stages, the parents too are
hard at work on their developmental tasks.

DEVELOPMENTAL TASKS OF PARENTS OF SCHOOL-AGE CHILDREN

Parents are expected to make most of the adjustments during the early
years of childhood, but they are just as human, with their own needs
and strivings, as they were before they married, or as they will be during
the empty-nest stage as parents who no longer have to reckon with the
imperious demands of offspring. The parents know full well that they
are needed through the bustling years of the school-age period. But by
this time, the household routines have become established and the children are growing at a less rapid rate than they did as infants or pre-

schoolers. Parents now can get their children in focus and understand them better because they are not changing so fast, and because parent-child intercommunication is better. The shouting and the tumult of infancy has ebbed and still the children have not yet reached adolescence, with its pickup in growth and its characteristic difficult-to-take repudiation of childhood patterns and parental guidance. No other stage has so much to offer in solidarity. The school-age family is probably the most pleasant stage of all from the standpoint of the compatibility of the developmental tasks of parents and children.

BEING SENSITIVE TO AND PROVIDING FOR CHILDREN'S GROWTH NEEDS

To know a given child's capacities, parents must study the growth needs and developmental readinesses of the particular youngster. To know how much responsibility a child may take at a given age is an achievement for the parent and an assurance of success for the child. It takes a sensitive ear, a watchful eye, and a sympathetic heart to be aware of children's needs and readinesses. Once a need is recognized, it often takes some doing to meet it well with the resources at hand, in the midst of the pressures both from within and outside the family.

A recurring challenge to modern parents is providing opportunities for the child to do things for himself that are within his abilities. It is helpful to the accomplishment of the child's developmental tasks if he can share in family decisions, responsibilities, and opportunities. Family discussion and joint planning offer openings for schoolagers to join with their parents and their brothers and sisters in establishing family policies and getting firsthand experience in democratic interaction and orderly ways of doing things.

A child meets new ideas and faces new standards of behavior as soon as he gets into school. His family can help him understand and reconcile these inevitable differences by helping the child see that although "our family does it this way," other ways are appropriate for other people. This requires an ongoing evaluation of new experiences and exposures in a continuity of guidance and interpretation within the family. Parents find that now they must know what is going on in the school and neighborhood, as well as keep in touch with their child's reactions to them, if situations are to be met effectively and the child's questions answered wisely.

A recurring challenge to modern parents is providing opportunities for children to do things within their abilities. A school-age child is able to do a great many things about the house and to carry real responsibilities with the joy of knowing that she or he is a participating member of the family.

Parents are under pressure from neighbors and other members of their social class to have their children measure up to the demands and expectancies of the culture. This tends to shape even the most developmental family into more traditional lines as soon as the children reach school age, as we saw in Chapter Three. "What will the neighbors think?" or "What will the teacher say?" are powerful pressures to conform in the school-age family. When traditional striving for good manners collides with developmental conceptions of parent-child rapport, the traditional patterns win out in most homes studied. Two examples:

Billy, age 10, hurries home to snatch his lunch and get back for an important school football game. As he gobbles, he tells his mother excitedly all about the team. As he pauses for breath, his mother breaks in severely, "Billy, take your elbows off the table. How many times must I tell you? And, stop eating so fast!"

Immediately Billy wilts. He obediently removes his elbows and hurries through the remainder of the meal in silence . . .

Mother has a point. Billy will have to learn good manners. But what is more important at the moment—good manners or good feelings shared between mother and son? How ready will Billy be next time to share his excitements with his mother?

. . . . .

Mary dashes home from school. She breaks in on her mother's club meeting with all the ladies sitting around. Mary is 12, happy, friendly, and outgoing. She is unself-conscious. She says cheerily, "Hello, Mrs. Brown," as she stumbles over Mrs. Smith's feet.

Mother rises to the situation. She must teach Mary some manners right now. She must save her own face by scolding Mary. So she speaks, sweetly but pointedly, "Mary, my dear! Do look where you are going!" Then she turns to her guests, saying, "Mary is just at the awkward age, so you'll have to excuse her."

Is Mary's face red? Does she approach the next roomful of guests with more or with less ease as a result of this experience? Has her feeling of friendliness increased or decreased? Is she closer to or farther from her mother now?

ENJOYING LIFE THROUGH CHILDREN'S EYES

Parents who can relax and enjoy their children, find life unfolding all around them as they see it through children's eyes. Long-forgotten joys and pleasures are renewed as they are shared with children who delight in them. New vistas and fresh perspectives from different vantage points open up with a child companion. What might have been an ordinary

Parents who can relax and enjoy their children find life unfolding all around them.

business trip turns out to be an adventure when a ten-year-old goes along, as we see in one father's experience:

I was at the meetings in Omaha for three days; took Janice along, and we had a great time. As you would guess, I did many things I would not have done had I gone alone: climbing on foot to the top floor of the hotel and looking out over the city from the fire escape; climbing to the very top seat in Omaha's immense auditorium; walking all the way across the Missouri river bridge to Council Bluffs and standing midway on the bridge with one foot on the Iowa side of the line and the other foot on the Nebraska side; going to the top of the Woodmen of the World Building . . .

There was much other fun too: being proud of how sweet she looked; enjoying her ways of packing and unpacking; watching her select items at Bishops Cafeteria and her enjoyment of her favorites; appreciating the fact that she surprised me the second afternoon and did the wash for us in the bathroom sink while I was down at the meeting (the clothes barely dried in time for us to pack and go home); observing the things she enjoyed most on the train; and then all the little joys that one forgets . . . People without children miss half the fun in the world! [1]

LETTING THE CHILD GO AND GROW

Encouraging a child's growth involves letting him go. As the school years progress, there are longer and longer absences from home. He is away from home through the school hours, which often include the lunch period as well as morning and afternoon sessions. If he or she is getting normally involved in sports, and clubs, and friendship groups, the after-school hours increasingly are given to these interests, with the youngster coming home tired and bedraggled just in time for the evening meal. There are frequent requests to spend the evening at someone else's home and occasions when spending the night with a close buddy is terribly important. Soon there are weekend trips with scouts or other youth groups, and then come the longer periods during summer vacation when children of school age are off to camp or visiting relatives for weeks at a time. All this is good for the child's development of independence, widening social experience, and general personality growth.

Parents adjust more easily to the child's absence from home if they keep close to his interests and share his experiences with him, both in the planning and the postmortem stages. It is easy to see in these first experiences away from home the evidence of the child's growing ability to handle himself when away from his parents. Studies indicate that these abilities develop earlier than many persons think. Letting a child widen his areas of life as his readiness and interest develop is important both for the child's development and for the parents' maturation as parents and as persons.

School-age boys and girls are beginning to see the differences between their parents and other adults. They may quote the all-wise teacher as authority for resisting some parental request; they may question some opinion or attitude at home. An insecure parent may find it hard to take the child's flat, "But, teacher says so," for what it is in the youngster's development—a growing out and away from home in some intellectual as well as physical respects, with new authorities, new attitudes, and new viewpoints being explored beyond the family circle. Parents who can loosen the apron strings at this point have much less difficulty unty-

[1] David Fulcomer, personal communication, July 12, 1956.

Among school-age children, the afternoon hours are increasingly devoted to friends and interests that friends enjoy together. This is good for children's development of independence and general personality growth.

ing them in another few years, when the youngsters become teenagers.

Fathers and mothers who continue their growth as persons beyond their roles as parents do better in letting their children go than do those men and women who try to live for their children. Parents whose lives are absorbed with their parenting functions often find that nothing else matters. Even the busiest mother occasionally needs to get away to feel that her life as an individual is worthwhile. Some continuing interests outside the family keep a woman spruced up, mentally alert, and spiritually alive to the wider world that will soon claim her offspring. Fathers are less often so closely tied to their growing children. Getting out of the house and off to work helps give a man the perspective a full-time homemaker misses. When the house teems with children and the pressures of the job are most strenuous—bills mounting up and demands at home never-ending—a man needs some corner of his life to call his own. By keeping alive some spark of his own individuality a man protects his sons and daughters from his oversolicitude and releases them as well as himself for mature living.

FAMILY DEVELOPMENTAL TASKS AT THE SCHOOL-AGE STAGE

By the time the oldest child is old enough to go to school the family has been established seven to eight years or more. Father and mother have been parents a half dozen years and are beginning to settle into familiar ways with each other and with their children. The second and possibly third child has arrived, and the family interrelationships grow even faster than does the family itself. The now familiar routes traversed by infants and preschoolers are gone over once again with the younger children each in his turn, and each in his own way. There are all the new problems and challenges inherent in individual differences between children, and the inevitable changes within the family itself from year to year, from child to child. In a very real way, no two children are ever born into the same family, anymore than does a man bathe in the same water, even though he comes frequently to the same stream. For life goes on and families change as they grow, never to turn back to former days and ways.

PROVIDING FOR PARENTS' NEEDS FOR PRIVACY, QUIET, AND ORDER DURING CHILDREN'S VIGOROUS YEARS

Now that families live mostly in cities, towns, and suburbs, homes are smaller and space is more limited, both indoors and out, than it once was (see Chapter Two). Thanks to better nutrition and preventive medical care, today's children are bigger, stronger, and more vigorous—age for age—than was true a generation or two ago. No comparable change has occurred in the desire of parents for privacy and a little peace and quiet in their lives. Todays' developmental family's house during the pre-school and school-age periods is cluttered, toy-strewn, noisy, and hazardous for unwary adults (see Chapter Three).

Providing outlets for the needed exploration and activity of vigorous growing children within the limits of cramped housing, small yards, remote playgrounds, traffic-filled streets, and cranky neighbors is not an easy task. Lower-class neighbors in some places settle the problem by letting the children roam the streets, play in the alleys, and run the risks of life and limb. Social clubs and settlements set up programs that help in some of these congested areas, but the needs are still unfulfilled. Upper-class families usually have more space and, except for those urban cliff-dwellers who live in crowded metropolitan apartment houses, have areas the children can call their own to play in, either on the home grounds or at their private schools. Many middle-class families feel the pinch in living so closely with their children in common living quarters; space requirements must be worked out in elaborate rituals and routines.

This is the time when many families move out of congested areas and into the suburbs, where children can have space for play, enjoy congenial companions, and attend good schools and community activities. The price that these families pay for such a move is real, both in monetary and psychic terms. The suburban father faces the commuter problem, as well as more hours away from home; the family reorganizes itself around a mother-head. Father comes home too tired and is there too infrequently to play the role he could if he lived nearer his work.

The irony is that just when a man is most needed around the house for all the repairs and refurbishing that are part of home-ownership, the man is not as readily available as he was when they lived in the city, where services around the place were provided without tapping the man of the house. The pressure is eased somewhat by the five-day week, which gives father to his family Saturdays and Sundays—unless the golf bug bites him first, that is!

KEEPING FINANCIALLY AFLOAT WHILE THE FAMILY NEARS THE FLOOD STAGE

The triple threat of keeping up payments, keeping up with the Joneses, and keeping out of debt is a real strain now. Costs will zoom even higher before there is any relief. But now, when the firstborn is in school and younger children are coming along, comes the bulging budget characteristic of expanding families. In low- and moderate-income families where food, clothing, and medical costs are always a big part of the household expenses, these items take a big bite out of what money there is. Childhood diseases run through the family at this period. Serious accidents to children of this age are an even greater threat;[1] less serious accidents are much more frequent.

Shoes wear out, dresses get too short, and pants too tight. Somebody is always hungry, and the variety of appetites has never been plumbed. All the while the house payments, car expenses, and maintenance costs of house and yard must be met, along with other essential costs such as utilities, insurance, and bus and lunch money, not to mention all the expected items like dues, allowances for the children, recreation, and all the rest. No wonder the family man may look a little frayed around the edges!

Before the end of the school-age period, Junior may have a paper route and be earning some of his own money and Mother may have found a part-time job that fits in with the demands of her growing brood.[2] Grandparents help out now and then in some families, especially with the use of a summer place for a family vacation, purchase of big items of equip-

---

[1] The leading causes of accidental death among children between the ages of 5 and 14 are (1) motor vehicle accidents (40%), (2) drownings (26%), and (3) burns and conflagrations (9%), as quoted by the Metropolitan Life Insurance Company, *Statistical Bulletin*, Vol. 36, No. 8, August 1955, page 2. Source: National Office of Vital Statistics, *Special Reports*, Vol. 40, No. 4.

[2] "After all the children have reached school age, nearly one-third of the wives are in the labor force. Aside from the first couple of years of marriage, this is the period when the wife is most likely to be supplementing the husband's earnings by working outside the home." Paul C. Glick, "The Life Cycle of the Family," *Marriage and Family Living*, Vol. XVII, No. 1, February 1955, p. 8.

ment,[1] sitter services, and nursing care through childhood sicknesses and childbirth of the little newcomer.[2] Income tax exemptions for the children and unemployed wife are a help, but are by no means adequate to cover the costs of childrearing at this stage of family living.[3] Many a middle-class father gets what overtime he can, or pieces out his earnings with a part-time job during his "leisure" hours.

The lower-class family frequently solves the problem by the mother's employment, leaving the children under the casual supervision of whomever happens to be home. The upper-class family's financial problems are less, for by definition the upper-class home is more affluent. But even so the strain of keeping up appearances, sending the youngsters to the proper private schools, maintaining memberships in exclusive clubs, and participating in the right charities adds up faster than the money rolls in, in many a supposedly well-to-do family. Here the problems are compounded by pride. What lower-status families can do without losing face become last resorts to the families "on the hill."

COOPERATING TO GET THINGS DONE

Each family has its own ways of getting things done. Mother does everything. Father pitches in as he can. Older children care for the younger ones. Grandmother may be close enough to help out. A maid works by the day or month. Some way or another food has to be purchased, prepared, and served. Clothes have to be washed, ironed, mended, and put away. Dishes have to be washed, the house cleaned, beds made, and belongings put where they belong. The too-young, the too-sick, and dependent members of the family must be cared for, and extended family relationships must be kept in good repair. Someone must answer the doorbell, the phone, the questions of the youngsters, and the demands of salesmen. Someone has to plan the meals, supervise the spending, and attend to the special and the everyday routines, in even the sketchiest family situation.

---

[1] Marvin B. Sussman, "The Help Pattern in the Middle Class Family," *American Sociological Review*, Vol. 18, No. 1., February 1953, pp. 22–28.

[2] Evelyn Millis Duvall, *In-Laws: Pro and Con* (New York: Association Press, 1954), pp. 89–99.

[3] Rueben Hill estimates that income tax exemptions meet about 1/20th of the cost of rearing his children in any given year; each child's exemption is worth from $50 to $75 cut in tax per child per year, while it costs on the average $1,000 a year per child to rear him or her to age 18 (Louis Dublin, and Alfred Lotka, *The Money Value of a Man* [New York: Ronald Press, 1946], Chapter 4, pp. 44–58).

Casual impressions of homemaking in this push-button age are that now the housekeeping day has been so shortened, thanks to these marvels of science, that there is really very little to do around the house. Actually quite the opposite is the case. A recent study of 52 Midwestern homemakers with two to four school-age children indicated that these women spent more time in laundering now than was spent by a similar group of homemakers twenty-five years ago, automatic washers to the contrary notwithstanding![1] Interpretations are two: (1) our miracle fibers take special care and no longer can the family wash all go through together and (2) our standards are higher; we have more clothing, and we expect to be cleaner now than we did a generation ago.

Increased standards of living put a heavier load of responsibility on the home than used to be expected. It is no longer enough to put food on the table. It must be a carefully balanced meal, supplying just the right number of calories for the individual family members; attractive in color; tasty as to the right combination of textures, flavors, and personal preferences; full of vitamins, body-building proteins, minerals, and even trace minerals. It isn't enough to keep a child neat, clean, and obedient; today we must be concerned for his growth as a personality (Chapter Three). It isn't enough to keep a man's shirt buttons on; now a wife must be concerned and interested with all that goes into mending a wounded ego, and keeping her husband a growing, happy person. It isn't enough to keep house for the family; now a woman is expected to do her share of community housekeeping in working for a school bond issue, getting out to parent-teacher meetings, and helping run the block meeting, or whatever is the pressing issue of the day. It is the plethora of new tasks and expectations that take the time and energy of families at this stage in the life cycle.

Cooperation is the answer, not only for getting things done, but for helping everyone grow in the process. What becomes "a chore" if one person gets stuck with it all the time, becomes "a project" when the whole family pitches in and works together to get a job done. Cooperative efforts in meal preparation-serving-cleaning up make for pleasant companionship as well as shared responsibilities. Daily routines, weekly cleaning, and seasonal gardening, housecleaning, leaf-raking, and holiday preparations are planned by the family; tasks are allocated on the basis of inter-

[1] Dorothy G. Van Bortel, "Conception of Woman's Role in the Home in Two Social Classes," reported at the Seventh Annual Symposium, the University of Chicago, Committee on Human Development, February 25, 1956.

est, ability, and preference and are accomplished with family members working side by side.

A child growing up in such an atmosphere of cooperation learns that he gains more through joint effort with parents and siblings than through his own puny strivings. He learns that it is fun to share tasks, to feel with the others the success in their work. He helps with the planning and so sees the reasons for the work to be done. He helps work out the rules and agreements and so sees the sense in abiding by them. He increasingly disciplines himself as he works *with* his parents rather than *for* them. Parents in this type of cooperative family life do not have to carry the full burdens, for they are shared as they come along with the rest of the family. Their satisfaction is in growing along with their children in deepening companionship as a family and personal fulfillment as individuals.

CONTINUING TO SATISFY EACH OTHER AS MARRIED PARTNERS

If the woman has received good postnatal care and has established a satisfactory sex response in the marriage, she now is at the peak of her sexual powers. Her main problem now is in getting over enough of her busyness to relax and give herself wholeheartedly to her husband. The man old enough to have school-age children is beyond the peak of his sexual capacities, but still a virile man with needs not only for sexual intercourse, but also for the renewal of faith in himself as a man that a truly loving wife can give him so well.

The couple successful in accomplishing this developmental task is usually one who keep their love for each other central in their family life. Children are loved, of course, but the husband-wife relationship remains paramount. Such a couple finds many a chance to slip away, for a Saturday afternoon or a week end together, for a little holiday, with perhaps the wife going along on a business trip and making it a "second honeymoon." They maintain the kind of companionship as a couple in which they can get through to each other fully—enriching, renewing, recreating, and creating together within the fullness of marriage.

EFFECTIVELY UTILIZING COMMUNICATION SYSTEMS WITHIN THE EXPANDING FAMILY

The school-age family is a network of communication ties. By now the family has theoretically expanded to two, three or more children with possible interpersonal relationships numbering up to ten in a three-child family. If the children are growing normally, they are full of experiences to relate, questions to ask, interpretations to be sought, and sheer exuberance to express. Unless they are twins, their ages differ so widely that their interests as children of school age, preschool age, and infancy are worlds apart. Yet they compete for the resources of the family (the TV set is a good example), for status and affection, and for all the other qualities that children need in intimate association.

The school-age youngster comes home from his rigorous day in classroom and playground full of the pent-up emotions that could not be fully expressed in front of teachers and classmates. He brings his frustrations, disappointments, and unexpressed hostilities home, where he very likely takes them out on the first available family member. This is not to be condemned. One of the chief functions of family life is to serve as an emotional reconditioning center for its members. But this does not make for peace and quiet. On the contrary, feelings explode all over the place, the children get into squabbles seemingly without provocation. Junior topples over the baby's blocks, baby scrawls in Mary's book, she teases Junior, and they are at it again.

A group of mothers exploring the children's squabbles in their own homes discovered that most of the quarreling took place in the late afternoon after the school-age youngsters had returned from school, and before the evening meal was served. Operating on one member's theory that children are irritable when blood sugar is low, this group of mothers set themselves into an experiment in which half of them awaited their school children's return home with a glass of fruit juice, an apple, or some other simple dietary supplement. The control group kept things as they were with no special attention given to the youngsters' homecoming. Quarreling in the "food pick-up" group of children dropped significantly over a period of a full month.

Discussion among the mothers was animated. The blood-sugar theory seemed to be substantiated until one mother observed that now she was there along with her food offering, tales of woe came tumbling out as soon as her youngster reached the kitchen door. Her hunch was that it was this immediate release from the tensions of the day that made her son more tractable, rather than the food in itself. Again, using themselves and their children as guinea pigs, these mothers set up a simple experimental situation in which the mothers who had paid no special attention to their youngsters homecoming now were on tap with a smile, a warm welcome, and an interested ear for the day's event before the child went out to play. The controls this time were the feeding group, who left the snack out on the table for their returning children, but who themselves were not available. Over the following month quarrels increased appreciably in the group that had the food but no interested attention, and squabbles decreased significantly in the homes where mother awaited her school children's return home with an interest in their feelings and affairs.

These results of a very simple experiment parallel those of the famous studies [1] of factory workers in which it was the *attention* paid the people that increased their work output and job satisfaction. They give a challenge to family members who must weather the emotional storms that generate outside to blow their full fury within the home. Not only the children, but father and mother too, bring home their tensions and unresolved conflicts from office, factory, or PTA meetings. The family that is satisfactorily providing effective means by which tensions can be drained off before they become either chronic or critical, is one that keeps communication free and full.

One mother who is aware of the importance of these functions, when her husband is in a particularly exacting and trying spot, has the makings of a picnic supper in her pantry for the occasional afternoon when her husband comes home looking as though he has had "one of those days." As soon as she takes a good look at her husband's face, she suggests a picnic for the whole family, or a quiet tete-a-tete for just the two of them, with the children having their picnic supper on the back porch or yard. This is a way of not only helping her husband work through a difficult job, but is also effective in maintaining the kind of sensitive communication needed in the hurly-burly of family life.

It works the other way too. An empathic husband returning home to find his wife at the end of her rope, with the youngsters irritable and the house a mess, may take her out for dinner, with a quickly imported sitter for the children more than paying for her charge in the release the husband and wife get when they need it most.

The wonders and delights of the school-age family need to be communicated too. At this stage, when children's horizons are expanding

[1] F. U. Roethlisberger and W. J. Dickson, *Management and the Worker* (Cambridge, Massachusetts: Harvard University Press, 1940).

When children's horizons are expanding and life is so full of so many wonderful things, the whole family can glow and grow with its younger members.

and life is so full of so many wonderful things, the whole family can glow and grow as it shares the questions and the interests of one of its younger members. Now is the time when music can mean so much in family life, with the whole family singing its familiar repertoire together around the piano or campfire or in the car en route to anywhere. Storytelling, reading aloud, acting out, impromptu shows, sports and family games and fun, even favorite television programs enjoyed together —these are ways of communicating that life is good and that old and young can share it together.

When communication systems are open within a family, love can flow through, removing the waste products of everyday living and renewing the spirit of every member. For love is a two-way flow, going and returning between each person and the next, taking away one's hates and angers and bringing back the warmth of belonging and the joy of living in a family. Like a river that purifies itself as long as it keeps running freely, so the stream of human emotions within a family renews and refreshes the human spirit so long as communication systems run free.

FEELING CLOSE TO RELATIVES IN THE LARGER FAMILY

Relatives come into their own during the school-age stage of family living. When a boy is old enough to handle himself with some independence, his uncles and cousins may take him along on a fishing trip, to ball games, and all the rest of the activities that delight the young man of the family. A school-age boy or girl is old enough to visit relatives for a week or more, even a whole summer vacation without becoming homesick or being too dependent upon a hospitable household. Going to grandparents' home for special holidays is a thrill now, when the children are old enough to appreciate such treats, and to take care of their own needs and interests in new settings with only casual supervision.

With family routines fairly well established and the children knowing the ropes of everyday family living, it is possible for them to take over for a few days at a time with a visiting relative keeping a general eye on things, while the parents leave for a brief holiday or business trip. "Sitting" now becomes a mutual process in which the youngsters share their interests and achievements with the aunt, uncle, or grandparent in charge, at the same time that they tap this rich source of family-lore and gain a sense of the continuity of family living from those who knew their parents when they were small.

Even more important than what the relatives *do* for the school-age boy or girl, is what they *are*. In even the most homogeneous family, there are so many differences in personality strengths and weaknesses, behavior patterns, and value systems represented in the members of the extended family group, that these variations are of great interest to all. The family is worried about one of its black sheep who has stepped out of line again, and hashes over his past history, the details of the current escapade, and their opinions as to why he has turned out so badly. The family is proud of some honor bestowed upon one of its relatives and proudly exhibits mementos of the glorious moment, the picture of the person with prestige, and regales even the most casual visitor with the wonderful qualities that have helped this special one turn out so well. One relative is ill, another is mentally unstable, a third is out of work, still another is leaving for an extended voyage, and so on and on through the multitude of permutations and combinations of experiences and predispositions represented in the members of any family.

All this is grist for the children's mill. As they get close to these differing relatives and hear them discussed in the family, they see value systems in action. They find themselves lining up on one side or the other in accordance with their own personality needs and tasks of the moment. The twelve-year-old girl may ardently defend some impulsive cousin who has run away to be married in defiance of her family, not because the girl actually believes that such actions are wise, but because this represents for her the emancipation she is mobilizing for and has not yet accomplished personally. The ten-year-old boy may idolize a young uncle who flexes his muscles and talks big about the manly art of self-defense, not because he is going to turn out to be a prize fighter, but because growing up to be a strong man is the boy's goal for himself.

Feeling close to the relatives of the family is accomplished through the years in the letter-writing, visiting, holiday observances, vacation sharing, gift giving, services rendered and received, and all the other ways in which the members of the family maintain contact with each other. The process is futhered by the family loyalties that bind the family together, regardless of what any member may or may not do. The task is delayed or incomplete in the little family in which such high standards of perfection are maintained that it ostracizes any relative who steps out of line. Sniping at in-laws is one way of venting hostilities against the mate. Or mutual dislike of any relative on either side of the family may be a common bond between a couple. Complete harmony in the larger family is rarely realized, but, to the extent to which it is achieved, it contributes much to the ongoing life of the family.

TYING IN WITH LIFE OUTSIDE THE FAMILY

The schoolager takes the family with him out into the larger community. Pressure is on the parents to become active in the parent-teacher association, to visit the school for special parents' functions, to participate in parents' study groups, and to become an active part of community life as soon as their children are enrolled in school.

Father now gets tied into father-son affairs with his boy through church and youth programs, as well as in the informal going and coming within the neighborhood. As soon as the youngster becomes a Little Leaguer, he becomes a part of the male set in town, with other men and boys recognizing him and his father and the rest of the family in ways that are new and exciting.

Mother is asked to bake a cake for a scout bake-sale or to help serve at a Campfire Girls' mothers' tea. She may take on the job of den-mother, or teach a Sunday School class, or help her youngsters canvass for Red Cross funds, as soon as her own children are drawn into community projects and group life.

Life in the larger community becomes of more personal interest when children are intimately involved. Raising interest in a new school building or getting pledges for the Community Fund, or a special neighborhood project now makes sense in a personal way, when the family's own children are directly benefited. Candidates for political office may have been only remote pictures in the newspaper before; now they are seen for the issues for which they stand, for the kind of family life they represent, and for what they promise to do for the welfare of the community. Corruption may once have seemed like something that is always with us; but when children get out into the streets, ridding the city of its harmful elements becomes urgent family business. The teacher shortage, once a general social problem, now becomes an imminent family concern. And so it goes. As the child grows up and goes forth into the world, he takes his family with him into larger and larger circles of interest and influence. Widening participation in community life helps mature the family as well as the individual, and this is one of the developmental tasks that must be tackled and worked through together.

TESTING AND RETESTING FAMILY PHILOSOPHIES OF LIFE

As soon as the yard child gets out into the street and begins to go to school, he comes face-to-face with ways of life that are different from those of his family. Some of these variations on the theme of life, look good to him and he brings them home in questions about and demands for a new order of things. The family then must test its way of life in terms of child-introduced, community pressures. Something has got to give. Either the family gives way to the child's pleas that "all the other kids are doing it," or the youngster faces up to the finality of "this is the way we do it in *our* family." Either outcome is the result of some testing and review of the merits and penalties of a certain stand or value.

By the time the boy or girl reaches the third or fourth grade in school, these culture conflicts may be in the form of episodes of open rebellion. The preadolescent finds adults generally trying. Both boys and girls are skeptical of the other sex and band together in tight little groups of children of the same age and sex. Boys now reject such adult imposed "sissy stuff" as cleanliness, obedience, and politeness, and often become antagonistic, rebellious, uncooperative, restless, and very noisy. Dr. Luton D. Ackerson studying 5,000 nondelinquent boys and girls at the Illinois Institute for Juvenile Research, found that behavior problems are more frequent among the nine- to thirteen-year-olds than among any other age group—more fighting, rudeness, and disobedience among preadolescent children than among either the younger or the older age groups.[1] These problems are so characteristic of the third- to sixth-grader, that Fritz Redl defines preadolescence as, "That phase when the nicest children begin to behave in the most awful way."[2]

Families need not make issues of these outbursts of rebellion; they accomplish their tasks best when they patiently accept the youngster casually and with love, at the same time holding to the truths by which they live. Religious practices on a whole-family basis may help a youngster stabilize at this stage. Close friends and buddies who share each others' most secret thoughts and plans play a large role in every child's efforts to work his way out of little childhood toward maturity. Some understanding adult, as teacher, scout leader, relative or close friend of the family may give the youngster a real boost in discovering and accepting his own way of life at the same time that he develops tolerance for differences.

When mother and father have successfully undertaken their developmental tasks of developing a workable philosophy of life in the earlier stages of their marriage and in their individual personality development, they can accept the querying and the challenging of the school-age boy or girl without being personally threatened or feeling personally attacked or repudiated. It is when one or the other of the parents feels basically insecure about the area under question that confusion reigns and the family fails to make progress in refining and developing its way of life to meet the test of real life situations. Actively interpreting why some things are wrong and others right, why some actions are good and others

[1] Quoted in *Junior Guidance Newsletter* (Chicago: Science Research Associates, December 1952).
[2] *Ibid.*, p. 1.

Religious practices on a whole-family basis may help a youngster feel secure.

bad, are aspects of this developmental task that families face all through the school-age stage. Such teaching is not easy, especially in this day and age when moral values are so cloudy. But nothing is more important to a family's basic integrity, or to a youngster's sense of what he and his family stand for, in a world where individuals have to stand for something, lest they fall for anything.

SUMMARY

The school-age stage of family life represents the crowded years that begin with the firstborn going off to school and flow into the teen years as he becomes a teenager. Younger children have already arrived, and are hard at work on their developmental tasks, while the schoolager works out his at the growing edges of the family where all is new both to it and to him. He faces a multitude of growth responsibilities as he makes a place for himself at school, with his peer group and with other adults, and becomes a participating member of his family and of the larger community. His parents meanwhile are occupied with their tasks as parents, as a married couple, and as individuals. Family developmental tasks of this stage may be summarized briefly: (1) providing for parents' needs for privacy, quiet, and order during the children's vigorous years; (2) keeping financially afloat while the family nears the flood stage of its needs; (3) cooperating to get things done; (4) continuing to satisfy each other as married partners; (5) elaborating communication systems within the expanding family; (6) feeling close to relatives in the larger family; (7) tying in with life outside the family; and (8) testing and re-testing family philosophies of life.

The school-age family has its challenges in dovetailing the many developmental tasks of all members of the family in harmonious satisfying ways. It has its rewards in the sense of accomplishment that comes from both individual and group achievements, as well as in the family solidarity that is peculiarly meaningful at this stage.

SUGGESTED ACTIVITIES

1) Review the School-Age Study Course in the *National Parent-Teacher*, for the current year, relating the materials covered to the developmental tasks of the school-age family.

2) Visit a session of a parents' study group, record what transpired, especially the questions the parents asked during and after the meeting. Interpret the parents' questions in terms of what you now know about what is happening to them and to their children at this stage of family life.

3) Make a bar graph of the frequencies of the causes of serious accidents of children between the ages of 5 and 14, using data given in *Statistical Bulletin* for August 1955 (or more recent figures). On the basis of these findings, work out a program of safety education for a) a family living in a crowded slum area, and b) a family living in a spacious suburban community.

4) Plan a budget for a school-age family with three children for a) a low-income family, b) a medium-income family, and c) a high-income family. Base your figures on current prices and standards of living in your community. Discuss in what ways the three budgets differ and interpret why.

5) Prepare a "Dos and Don'ts for Fathers" based upon what you know about fathers' role in the school-age family. Document your recommendations from references and other valid sources.

6) List the pros and cons of moving to the suburbs from the city as children reach school age. Interview at least one middle-class homemaker whose family has chosen to remain in the city, and at least one family member from a similar social status where the decision has been to move

out to a suburb, for flesh and blood experiences in terms of the rewards and regrets already experienced in the family choice of home neighborhood.

7) Summarize the recommendations of various authorities on the matter of allowances for school-age children, documenting your items with specific references from the professional and popular literature for parents.

8) Write your mother a letter telling her what you appreciate and what you regret about your home life as a school-age boy or girl. Tell her what you remember most warmly of the rituals and routines and practices in operation in your family then. Share as much as you can of your feelings of satisfaction and annoyance as you remember them as a schoolager. Tell her how you plan to raise your children differently and in what ways you will continue the policies that worked with your rearing and why.

9) Role play three ways of handling children's quarrels within the family where there are two or more children of school age or younger. Discuss your feelings and behaviors and relate to relevant materials in this chapter and its references.

10) Review Carleton Washburne's *The World's Good* (New York: John Day Company, 1954), for ways in which parents and teachers can help push out a child's horizons toward world-mindedness and interest in other peoples around the globe.

11) Interview a local principal of an elementary school on the ways he sets about improving home-school relationships in his situation. Review the literature, especially that available from the National Congress of Parents and Teachers, 700 North Rush Street, Chicago, Illinois, for still further action programs in parent-teacher-pupil cooperation.

12) Write a critique of the philosophies in child development at Yale University under Dr. Arnold Gesell and under Dr. Milton Senn, by reading carefully the references under these two names in your *Readings*.

READINGS

Bachmeister, Rhoda, *Growing Together* (New York: Appleton-Century-Crofts, 1947).

Bossard, James H. S., *Parent and Child* (Philadelphia: University of Pennsylvania Press, 1953).

Division on Child Development and Teacher Personnel, Staff, *Helping Teachers Understand Children* (Washington, D. C.: American Council on Education, 1945).

Duvall, Evelyn, and Hill, Reuben, co-chairmen, Committee on the Dynamics of Family Interaction, Part IV. The School Age Family, National Conference on Family Life, 1948, unpublished materials.

Duvall, Evelyn, and Hill, Reuben, *When You Marry* (Boston: D. C. Heath and Company, 1953 revision), Chapter 18, "What It Means to Be Parents."

English, O. Spurgeon, and Foster, Constance, *Fathers Are Parents, Too* (New York: G. P. Putnam's Sons, 1951), Chapter 6, "The Latency Period."

Frank, Mary and Lawrence K., *How to Help Your Child in School* (New York: The Viking Press, 1950).

Gesell, Arnold, and Ilg, Frances, *The Child from Five to Ten* (New York: Harper & Brothers, 1946).

Gruenberg, Sidonie, *Your Child and You* (New York: Fawcett Publications, 1950).

Gutheim, Frederick A., *Houses for Family Living* (New York: Woman's Foundation, 1948).

Havighurst, Robert J., *Human Development and Education* (New York: Longmans, Green and Company, 1953), Part Two: "Middle Childhood."

Jackson, Edgar N., "The Religious Development of the Preadolescent," *The Christian Home*, March 1953, pp. 30–32.

Jersild, Arthur T., and associates, *Child Development and the Curriculum* (New York: Teachers College, Columbia University, 1947).

Langdon, Grace, and Stout, Irving W., *These Well-Adjusted Children* (New York: John Day Company, 1951).

Mackenzie, Catherine, *Parent and Child* (New York: William Sloan Associates, 1949).

Ojemann, Ralph H., "The Effect on the Child's Development of Changes in Cultural Influences," *Journal of Educational Research*, Vol. 40, #4, pp. 258–270.

Osborne, Ernest G., *The Family Scrapbook* (New York: Association Press, 1951).

Overstreet, Harry and Bonaro, *Where Children Come First* (Chicago: National Congress of Parents and Teachers, 1949).

Parsons, Talcott, and Bales, Ralph F., *Family, Socialization and Interaction Process* (Glencoe, Illinois: The Free Press, 1955), Chapter 2, "Family Structure and the Socialization of the Child."

Prescott, Daniel A., *Emotion and the Educative Process* (Washington, D. C.: American Council on Education, 1938).

Ross, Helen, and Johnson, A. M., *Psychiatric Interpretation of the Growth Process* (New York: Family Service Association, 1949).

Senn, Milton J. E., "The Epoch Approach to Child Development," *Woman's Home Companion*, November 1955, pp. 40–42, 60–62.

Smart, Mollie and Russell, *An Introduction to Family Relationships* (Philadelphia: W. B. Saunders Company, 1953).

Spock, Benjamin, *The Pocketbook of Baby and Child Care* (New York: Pocket Books, Inc., 1946).

Stendler, Celia Burns, "Social Class Differences In Parental Attitude toward School at Grade I Level," *Child Development*, Vol. 22, No. 1, March 1951, pp. 37–46.

Stendler, Celia Burns, and Young, Norman, "The Impact of Beginning First

Grade Upon Socialization as Reported by Mothers," *Child Development,* Vol. 21, No. 4, December 1950, pp. 241–260.

Superintendent of Documents, *The Child's Bookshelf, A Book List for Parents* (Washington, D. C.: Government Printing Office, 1953).

Superintendent of Documents, *Your Child from Six to Twelve* (Washington, D. C.: Government Printing Office, 1949).

Symonds, Percival M., *The Psychology of Parent-Child Relationships* (New York: Appleton-Century-Crofts, 1939).

Washburne, Carleton, *The World's Good* (New York: John Day Company, 1954).

Witmer, Helen Leland, and Kotinsky, Ruth, *Personality in the Making* (New York: Harper & Brothers, 1952).

Old and young, even of the same breed, find themselves at different phases in the vital cycle, and cannot agree in mood, opinion, impulse or affection. Contact means restraint on both sides, and a hearty unison can seldom be established except amongst comrades of the same age.

GEORGE SANTAYANA

CHAPTER ELEVEN

Families with teenagers

The gulf between generations is wider in the teenage family than at any other stage. Young people are stretching their wings and getting ready to leave the nest. They are full of a get-up-and-go that makes their activities seem hectic to their more settled parents. In many respects they live in a different world than the one in which their parents grew up, and so quite rightly, if not politely, remind their parents, "But times have changed since you were our age."

Young people are always "going to the dogs" in a sense. Some differences between the parent generation and young people are only natural. These differences are recognized by members of each generation in the familiar way each justifies its position by discrediting the other. Hence, young people for many generations have referred to their elders as "old fogies," who "don't understand," are "old-fashioned," and "out-of-date." Similarly, the elder generation has continued through the years to express its concern over the follies of youth in such terms as "flaming youth," "the lost generation," "irresponsible," and "headed for trouble." [1]

Teenagers in America are so frequently attacked by a hostile press that popular opinion has it that they are a generation of troublemakers who will become juvenile delinquents unless parents or teachers or somebody gets tough with them. This negative attitude toward children in the second decade of life has roots in our larger insecurities and anxieties. Its bitter fruits are heightened fear of the teen years. Many a

[1] Evelyn Millis Duvall, *Keeping Up with Teenagers* (New York: Public Affairs Committee, 1947), p. 2.

This farm lad, in raising and showing beef cattle, is making a positive contribution to his family, his community, and to his world.

family who has survived the bulging years of childhood tenses up and prepares for the worst at the first signs of adolescence in their children. Study of the facts indicates that only a very small percentage of our young people get into trouble during these "turbulent teens," and that the many positive contributions young people are making to their families, their communities, and their world are largely unheralded. A review of research in adolescent development provides a fairly clear picture of just what does (and does not) normally happen through the teen years, and in teenage families. More important than anything else is the recognition of individual differences both among teenagers and among families with teenagers.

FAMILIES WITH TEENAGERS VARY ENORMOUSLY [1]

Families with teenage children vary in the composition, size, and age of their members. There is, for example, the man in his early thirties, with a wife still in her twenties. They married very young, and now their first child is in his early teens, entering pubescence. Five younger children, including a month-old baby, complete the family circle. The man of the house has an unskilled job at "the plant," and there is a constant struggle to make ends meet financially. The young teenage boy is scornful of the childishness of school and is already making thrusts out into the workaday world, where his income may soon supplement that of his father's.

In striking contrast is the college professor who at forty married a colleague somewhat younger. Now at ages fifty-eight and fifty respectively, they have a fourteen-year-old daughter who has grown up as an only child in a high-intellectual atmosphere. The home life of this teenager is characterized by a quiet respect of each family member for the others and by considerable freedom for her to use her leisure in the home as she pleases, to attend the college of her choice when the time comes, and generally to move smoothly from girlhood through the teen years into a poised and pleasant young womanhood.

Children of older parents do not have it so good in many homes, as Bossard illustrates with the following case:

Thomas Orcott was 55 when his youngest child, a daughter, was born. Now she is 17 and her father is 72. She is pretty, vivacious, and popular. She has many friends among both sexes. Some of them gang up together in a particularly active round of social life. Her active life, and that of her friends, is a great trial to her father, with his rigid living habits. As a result, father and daughter have been in continual conflict in recent years, despite the restraining intervention of the mother. The 72-year-old father rails against her teen-age activities, calls them silly; flays her friends as uncouth barbarians; and issues one ultimatum after another to her. The 17-year-old daughter fights back, says he is unreasonable, an unnatural father, a selfish old man, out of joint with his times. In her softer moments, she is content to say that

[1] Freely adapted from Leland H. Stott, chairman, Robert G. Foster, Robert J. Havighurst, and Fritz Redl, "Section V, The Family with Teenagers," for the Committee on the Dynamics of Family Interaction Preliminary Report, Evelyn Duvall and Reuben Hill, co-chairmen, National Conference on Family Life, Washington, D. C., February 1948, mimeographed materials.

he is in his dotage. In the past year, he has embarrassed her greatly by being rude to her guests, ordering them out of the house on several occasions. One cannot contemplate this case record without a profound conviction that the real difficulty here is that the daughter is at one stage of the life cycle that calls for action and expression, and the father is at the stage that wants peace and quiet and orderliness.[1]

Teenage family situations differ widely in where and how the family lives. The sharecropper's adolescent boy stays home and chops cotton with the other members of his family in the Deep South; the Iowa farm boy is active in 4-H programs and travels to Omaha and Chicago with his club. The small-town teenager grows up under the watchful eye of interested neighbors, friends, and extended family members; while the big city's youngsters are on their own five minutes from their front doors. Suburban teenagers follow in junior form the social patterns of their parents in the country club and social set; while other teenagers shift for themselves in the highly competitive social whirl around them.

The period of history in which a teenager emerges greatly influences his development and that of his family. In wartime, families are disrupted when men of military age leave for service. As the older youth of the family and community are taken, the adolescent is left without their models to follow. Parents are inclined to neglect their children in their preoccupation with war work, money-making, and their own anxieties. When business conditions are good, as they are in a military economy, anyone can get a job, and teenagers as well as their fathers and mothers make money and gain a sense of independence that is full of possibilities in the dynamics of family interaction. Periods of depression or recession usually come suddenly and with devastating results upon families with adolescent children. Unemployment becomes the mode. Investments and savings are lost. Levels of living shift downward. Family problems become multiplied. Parents lose their confidence. Children old enough to support themselves are often forced by circumstances to try to do so and with no jobs available they become discouraged and demoralized.

No matter where or when the family with teenagers is, or what problems it is wrestling with, it faces some developmental tasks evolving directly out of its stage in the family life cycle. While the man of the house is refining his roles as a person, a husband, a father, a provider,

[1] James H. S. Bossard, *Parent and Child* (Philadelphia: University of Pennsylvania Press, 1953), pp. 187–188.

Teenage family situations vary widely in where and how the family lives; but rural, small-town, suburban, and city families all face similar developmental tasks as their children become teenagers.

a homemaker, and as a father of a teenager (and possibly younger children), his wife is functioning as a woman, a wife, a homemaker and home manager, possibly a worker, and certainly as a mother of children with the oldest already in his or her teens. Concurrently, the teenager is discovering himself as a person with all that that means for him or her both now and in the future; he is working through new relationships with his age mates, with adults, and with the members of his family in a series of developmental tasks that take him from later childhood as he enters the teens through to young adulthood as he leaves the teens and his family in his twenties.

Few families are ideal for their teenage children. Each young person must come to terms with his or her own family situation as he grows up out of it. Whatever the family strengths and weaknesses, they eventually must be faced and accepted as "the givens" by any young man or woman. Learning to live with one's family, understanding why parents feel and behave as they do, and recognizing one's father and mother for the real persons they are, are important tasks for all young people in every kind of family. At those points where families do not meet the pressing needs of youth, other resources within the community may be tapped by the enterprising youth who does not demand that his family be everything and do everything for him. The developmental tasks of teenagers are outlined briefly below.

DEVELOPMENTAL TASKS OF TEENAGERS [1]

1) *Accepting one's changing body and learning to use it effectively:*
    Coming to terms with new size, shape, function, and potential of one's maturing body.
    Reconciling differences between one's own physique and that of agemates of the same and other sex, as normal and to be expected variations.
    Understanding what puberal changes mean and wholesomely anticipating maturity as a man or as a woman.
    Caring for one's body in healthful ways that assure its optimum development.
    Learning to handle oneself skillfully in the variety of recreational, social, and family situations that require learned physical skills.
2) *Achieving a satisfying and socially accepted masculine or feminine role:*
    Learning what it means to be a boy or girl in one's culture.
    Anticipating realistically what will be involved in becoming a man or a woman.
    Finding oneself within the leeway of sex-role expectations and practice allowed by one's family and community.
3) *Finding oneself as a member of one's own generation in more mature relations with one's agemates:*
    Becoming acceptable as a member of one or more groups of peers.
    Making and keeping friends of both sexes.
    Getting dates and becoming comfortable in dating situations.
    Getting experience in loving and being loved by one or more members of the opposite sex.

---

[1] Freely adapted from the schema used by Robert J. Havighurst, *Human Development and Education* (New York: Longmans, Green and Co., 1953), Chaps. 9, 10, 11.

Finding oneself as a member of one's own generation involves making and keeping friends of both sexes.

Learning how to get along with a wide variety of agemates in school, neighborhood, and community settings.

Developing skills in inviting and refusing, solving problems and resolving conflicts, making decisions, and evaluating experiences with one's peers.

4) *Achieving emotional independence of parents and other adults:*

Becoming free of childish dependencies upon one's parents.

Developing more mature affection for parents as persons.

Learning how to be an autonomous person who is capable of making decisions and running one's own life.

Growing through the dependence of childhood and the impulsive independence of adolescence to mature interdependence with others (parents, teachers, and all authority figures, especially). Learning to be an adult among adults.

5) *Selecting and preparing for an occupation and economic independence:*

Seeking counsel and getting specific knowledges about possible fields of work within the limits of real possibilities.

Choosing an occupation in line with interests, abilities, and opportunities.

Preparing oneself through schooling, specialized training, and personal responsibility to get and hold a position.

Getting try-out or apprenticeship experiences wherever possible in the lines of future vocational interests.

6) *Preparing for marriage and family life:*

Enjoying the responsibilities as well as the privileges of family membership.

Developing a responsible attitude toward getting married and having a family.

Acquiring knowledge about mate selection, marriage, homemaking, and childrearing.

Learning to distinguish between infatuation and more lasting forms of love.

Developing a mutually satisfying personal relationship with a potential mate through processes of dating, going steady, effective courtship, and becoming involved with a loved one.

Making decisions about the timing of engagement, marriage, completion of one's education, fulfillment of military service requirements, and the multiple demands upon young people of marriageable age.

Becoming ready to settle down into a home of one's own.

7) *Developing intellectual skills and social sensitivities necessary for civic competence:*

Developing concepts of law, government, economics, politics, geography, human nature, and social organization which fit the modern world.

Gaining awareness of human needs and becoming motivated to help others attain their goals.

Acquiring problem-solving methods for dealing effectively with modern problems.

Gaining abilities to communicate competently as a citizen in a democracy.

Becoming involved in causes and projects outside oneself and becoming a socially responsible person.

8) *Developing a workable philosophy of life that makes sense in today's world:*

Achieving a mature set of values and the ethical controls that characterize a good individual in one's culture.

Desiring and achieving socially responsible behavior.

Selecting worthy ideals and standards to live by and identify with.

Practicing and working through the meanings of religious experience that motivate and inspire.

Finding oneself in the universe and among one's fellowmen in meaningful ways.

> *Each youth sustains within his breast*
> *A vague and infinite unrest.*
> *He goes about in still alarm,*
> *With shrouded future at his arm,*
> *With longings that can find no tongue.*
> *I see him thus, for I am young.*
> By an Oklahoma High School Boy

Traditional tendencies in thinking, feeling and behaving often hinder and delay development of today's young people (Chapters Two and Three). Positive, flexible attitudes tend to help in the accomplishment of the developmental tasks of adolescents. Attitudes of shame, guilt, and embarrassment about sex and reproduction make difficult the young person's full acceptance of his or her maturing body, while adequate sex education in the knowledge, skills, attitudes, and values of maturing is beneficial. Achieving a mature sex role is delayed by dissatisfaction with or a feeling of being deprived because of one's sex; it is helped by full acceptance and encouragement in becoming a mature man or woman. Getting along with one's agemates is delayed by feelings of shyness, inferiority, anxiety, or suspicion; it is made easier by an attitude of being willing to learn the social skills required for moving comfortably among people in a variety of situations. Emancipating oneself from childish dependence upon parents is hindered by emotional bondage to one's parents; it is facilitated by the mutual freedom to grow beyond the parent-child relationship. Finding one's self occupationally is made difficult by traditional stereotypes and by tendencies to live in a world of dreams and fantasy; it is helped by the willingness to cope with reality and the courage to explore real possibilities. Preparing for marriage and family life is blocked by outmoded restrictions and limitations in education and greatly helped by forward-looking programs for equipping young men and women to become competent husbands and wives, fathers and mothers. Becoming a competent citizen is often side-tracked by outmoded biases and stereotyped ideas ("you can't buck the system"); it moves straight toward its goal with worthy adults to emulate in determining a sound, acceptable set of values. Finding oneself as a person means coming to terms with one's self, as one was, as one is, and as one might become. Acceptance, encouragement, and guidance are pivotal requisites for many a teenager in accomplishing these manifold tasks of growing up.

DEVELOPMENTAL TASKS OF THE ADULTS AS PARENTS, AS SPOUSES, AS WORKERS, AS HOMEMAKERS, AND AS PERSONS IN THE FAMILY WITH TEENAGERS

Just as traditional tendencies in thinking, feeling, and behaving often hamper an adolescent's developmental task accomplishment, so too there are hazards for both parents in their achievement of their growth responsibilities as persons, as spouses, as homemakers, and as parents that can be plotted step by step for each adult within the teenage family. We see this in the charts that follow.[1]

THE MAN OF THE FAMILY
AS FATHER

Developmental Tasks, Goals, and Responsibilities	Traditional Tendencies in Thinking, Feeling, and Behaving
Providing "good" patterns for the roles of the growing adult man, loving husband, and accepting father.	Inability to regard adolescent "cockiness" and impudence as growth manifestations but interpret them as attacks upon parental dignity.
Learning to understand each child as an individual, believe in and trust him, respect his personality and delight in seeing him grow into adoles-	Tendency to more or less unconsciously look upon adolescent child as his rival for the attention of others and in importance and prestige.

[1] Freely adapted from Stott et al., op. cit., pp. 5–15.

Developmental Tasks, Goals, and Responsibilities	*Traditional Tendencies in Thinking, Feeling, and Behaving*

cence and adulthood, and thus maintaining the confidential, affectionate and companionable relationship earlier established. Providing time to spend with adolescent on a companionable basis, and to get the youth's point of view.

Understanding that growth is not identical with "improvement," that what the adolescent *needs* is often *not* what he seems to "deserve." Also that what the youngster *needs* has no relationship to the kind of treatment the father received when young.

Fear of loss of control, hence the tendency to be more autocratic toward the adolescent. Tendency to deal with child in terms of his own adolescent experiences—either try to repeat or to avoid what happened to himself. (Repeat the strict handling he received from his own parents, or avoid all firmness, not in terms of the child's needs but because of what happened to him.)

Getting insight into, and a realistic evaluation of his own emotional reactions, not to stifle or hide them, but to avoid consciously or unconsciously over-reacting to them in dealing with the child.

Tendency to fear his own emotions (fear of "spoiling" child through the expression of affection and so become unduly cold and over-strict).

Arriving at a common understanding and cooperating with mother on matters of guidance and control of children.

Assumption of an authoritarian attitude, following perhaps the pattern of his own parental home, and attempting arbitrarily to order the lives and activities of his older children, without consultation with mother, or the young people.

Taking no particular interest, and assuming no part of the responsibility for the guidance and control of children.

THE WOMAN OF THE FAMILY
AS MOTHER

Developmental Tasks, Goals, and Responsibilities	*Traditional Tendencies in Thinking, Feeling, and Behaving*
Providing "good" patterns for the roles of the *growing* adult woman, wife, and mother. Being alert to matters of her personal and social behavior, dress, and appearance that the adolescent may or may not be proud of.	Tendency not to think of her own attitudes, behavior and appearance as being important for adolescent children.
Trying to understand each child as an individual, believing in and trusting him, respecting his personality and delighting in seeing him grow into adolescence and adulthood, and thus maintaining a confidental, affectionate and companionable relationship with the adolescent as well as with the younger children. Understanding also that what the child needs in the way of guidance has no relationship to the kind of treatment she herself received when young.	Tendency to be anxious upon seeing the child grow up. Tendency to deal with the adolescent in terms of her own adolescent experiences—either repeat, or try to avoid what happened to herself (repeat strict handling of own parents, or avoid firmness, not in terms of child's needs but because of what happened to her). Tendency more or less unconsciously to feel that the adolescent daughter is her rival—is replacing her in the attention of the father—is outdoing her in attractiveness.
Understanding that growth is not identical with "improvement," that what the adolescent *needs* is often not what he seems to "deserve."	Tendency to be over-concerned with "improvement" in the child's behavior in relation to certain stereotypes of socially acceptable conduct.
Getting insight into, and a realistic evaluation of her own emotional reactions, not to stifle or hide them, but to avoid consciously or unconsciously over-reacting to them in dealing with the adolescent.	Tendency to fear her own emotions (fear that her strong affection for child is "spoiling" and to try to compensate by becoming unduly cold and over-strict, or fear of her rejecting and aggressive wishes may result in a compensatory suppression of all control and firmness with an "overdose of overprotection.")

THE MAN OF THE FAMILY
AS HOMEMAKER AND PROVIDER

Developmental Tasks, Goals, and Responsibilities	*Traditional Tendencies in Thinking, Feeling, and Behaving*
Taking a renewed interest in the activities of the home and cooperating with and supporting wife in adapting the household routines to the changing and varied demands of the family members at this stage.	Tendency to resist changes and to be irritated at variations from routines he has become accustomed to.
Relieving his wife of some of the actual work and assuming a share of the responsibility of the family and household management—encouraging and facilitating participation of children in the daily work.	Tendency to hold to the point of view that housework is woman's work and beneath the dignity of men. Tendency to follow the pattern of home participation set in his own parental home and to take for granted that that pattern is normal and desirable.
Taking on more responsibility in the management of interpersonal relationships and problems, particularly in relation to adolescent children.	Feeling that the handling of the children is their mother's job and responsibility.
Regarding his responsibility for providing for the material requirements and the general economic security of his family as taking precedence over his own desires to speculate or to quit.	Irresponsibility in the matter of providing financially for the family— tendency to take chances and go into financial ventures that jeopardize the economic security of family, or to run away in one escape or another.
Acquainting the rest of the family with the realities of the family's financial situation and thus enlisting their intelligent sharing of responsibility.	Feeling that the money he makes is his own—that after all money matters are a man's business.
Enlisting the participation of the family in making decisions regarding important expenditures or financial ventures, and regarding the equitable sharing and apportioning of the family funds.	Feeling that he, as head of the family, should continue to maintain complete control of the family finances.

THE MAN OF THE FAMILY
AS HOMEMAKER AND PROVIDER (*Continued*)

Developmental Tasks, Goals, and Responsibilities	*Traditional Tendencies in Thinking, Feeling, and Behaving*
Accepting and encouraging the wife's sharing of the economic burden of earning the family living if she is so talented and so minded.	Feeling that to provide the income to support the family is the task of man alone.

THE WOMAN OF THE FAMILY
AS HOMEMAKER AND FAMILY MANAGER

Developmental Tasks, Goals, and Responsibilities	*Traditional Tendencies in Thinking, Feeling, and Behaving*
Checking on her health needs and habits and taking steps to insure strength and energy for the job of making a home for a family with adolescents.	Tendency to neglect her own health at a time of life when it is especially important.
Reviewing her work habits and routines with the purpose of adapting them to the real needs and demands of all members of the family, including herself.	Tendency to overstress the housekeeping aspects—orderliness, cleanliness, things always in their places. Tendency either to follow slavishly or to repudiate the homemaking patterns of her parental home.
Reviewing homemaking schedules and routines with the view of obtaining optimum family participation and satisfaction.	Tendency to perfectionism—husband or children not able to participate in homemaking activities because they cannot do them to suit her.
Managing the family budget efficiently—buying economically, and with an understanding of the nutritional requirements and other material needs of the family. Devising means of keeping family, including the father, informed as to costs, available goods and relative values and enlisting their intelligent cooperation in the use of the family's resources.	Tendency to be extravagant, or unwise in buying. Failing to cooperate fully with the "provider" or to enlist his sympathy and his understanding of the problems of managing efficiently the household budget. *Struggling* with the children rather than helping them to understand the problems of "making ends meet."

Developmental Tasks, Goals, and Responsibilities	*Traditional Tendencies in Thinking, Feeling, and Behaving*
Acquiring the attitudes, knowledge and skills necessary to create a "home atmosphere" which is comfortable, wholesome, easy, friendly, happy, and *to take joy and professional pride in that accomplishment.*	Tendency to feel that the status of the homemaker is low in comparison with business or professional work. Assuming an attitude of one betrayed —an attitude of self-pity. Failing to see the challenge or the possibilities for satisfaction and development in homemaking.

THE MAN OF THE FAMILY AS HUSBAND

Developmental Tasks, Goals, and Responsibilities	*Traditional Tendencies in Thinking, Feeling, and Behaving*
Maintaining or reinforcing habits of personal care and grooming.	Tendency to "let down" with the approach of middle age, to be careless in care of clothes and in personal care and grooming.
Strengthening his attitudes of acceptance with respect to his wife—to be able more than ever to recognize the necessity for, and her right to be different—to be as she is, and to be able really to accept her thus.	Tendency to hold to a preconceived notion as to personality, talents and behavior of a wife. Tendency to follow or to repudiate compulsively the husband-wife relationships of own parents.
Maintaining or re-establishing habits of outward courtesy and attentiveness toward wife and a genuine concern for her comfort and welfare.	Tendency to take wife for granted, to forget to be courteous or to show appreciation of her, or concern for her welfare and comfort.
Understanding the needs and tendencies of his wife at this particular stage and be increasingly alert to ways of facilitating her personal growth and satisfactions.	Tendency to assume a self-centered individualistic attitude in his relationships with wife, to be concerned with his own satisfactions,—to be self-centered and exploitive in marital relations.

THE MAN OF THE FAMILY
AS HUSBAND (*Continued*)

Developmental Tasks, Goals, and Responsibilities	*Traditional Tendencies in Thinking, Feeling, and Behaving*
Cultivating a closer confidential and sharing relationship with his wife; to share with her his experiences—his triumphs and worries, etc. Being really interested in her activities, domestic and social. Regarding her as a partner and sharer in all aspects of their life together.	Tendency to regard men's and women's spheres of action as separate, to feel that he must maintain his authority, that a "woman's place is in the home," "has no business working outside the home," "has no sense about money," "it's her job to take care of the kids."
Cooperating in the development of new joint interests, activities, hobbies, etc.	Tendency to want to "take it easy" —to follow old established habits in the use of leisure resisting something new.

THE WOMAN OF THE FAMILY
AS WIFE

Developmental Tasks, Goals, and Responsibilities	*Traditional Tendencies in Thinking, Feeling, and Behaving*
Maintaining and enhancing her personal attractiveness and charm.	Tendency to "let down" with the passage of years—to forget the importance of being personally attractive, particularly to her husband.
Showing tender concern about husband's health and welfare. Being sympathetic with his need for quiet, for understanding and occasional "ego inflation."	Tendency to take husband for granted; to be nagging and critical when he needs sympathy and understanding; to be thoughtless and inconsiderate toward him.
Being understanding of her husband's needs for affection and response and to be able to respond to them adequately.	Inability to respond maritally with warmth and affection, or to be self-centered, responding or not responding according to her present whim.

Developmental Tasks, Goals, and Responsibilities	*Traditional Tendencies in Thinking, Feeling, and Behaving*
Being able to accept her husband's differences and peculiarities with sympathy and with interest.	Tendency to continue to try to make her husband over after her own preconceived notions, which may represent a compulsive adherence to, or a repudiation of the husband-wife relationships of her own parents.
Maintaining or acquiring a genuine interest in husband's business or profession and thus being able to function as an understanding and sympathetic listener, confidant and sharer in his triumphs and worries.	Boredom in relation to husband's work; tendency to be disparaging of his job, lack of appreciation of its importance, nagging with respect to the prestige value or income from the job.
Encouraging the development of additional joint activities and interests with husband.	Lack of inclination to participate in the type of activities in which husband is interested.

THE MAN OF THE FAMILY
AS A PERSON

Developmental Tasks, Goals, and Responsibilities	*Traditional Tendencies in Thinking, Feeling, and Behaving*
Adjusting to the realities of constantly growing older—accepting realistically his present age and stage of development with its limitations as well as its potentialities for satisfactory functioning and enjoyment.	Tendency to continue to base feelings of personal prestige on the exploits and accomplishments of youth, maintaining image of self, established in youth. Tendency to feel that life is "passing him by." Feeling that the supreme pleasures and satisfactions of life are limited to youth and young manhood.
Keeping "up-to-date" on current thinking, social attitudes and changing folkways and mores.	Tendency to continue to think in terms of the norms and social standards of his youth, failing to move along with the times.

THE MAN OF THE FAMILY
AS A PERSON (*Continued*)

Developmental Tasks, Goals, and Responsibilities	*Traditional Tendencies in Thinking, Feeling, and Behaving*
Broadening interests and knowledge and thus growing in terms of civic and social responsibility.	Tendency to become so engrossed in making a living or achieving business or professional success as to have no time or energy for growth in other areas. Tendency to attitude that "politics is rotten business" and that government is the business of incompetent, irresponsible, and corrupt individuals.
Bolstering feelings of adequacy and self-confidence and personal worth by constantly developing new personal skills, hobbies, etc.	Tendency to foster basic feelings of inadequacy through lack of growth in skills and personal proficiency (sometimes compensated for in rigid, unyielding, domineering behavior toward wife, children and associates).
Continuing to work toward his personal ideals and goals of achievement, always in terms of the realities of his own resources and limitations.	Tendency to seek to become, and to attain *through his child* the ideals and goals of achievement which he failed to achieve in his own life.

THE WOMAN OF THE FAMILY
AS A PERSON

Developmental Tasks, Goals, and Responsibilities	*Traditional Tendencies in Thinking, Feeling, and Behaving*
Adjusting to the realities of constantly growing older—to approaching middle age. To accept realistically and with equanimity her present age and stage of development with its limitations and its potentialities for satisfactory functioning and enjoyment.	Tendency to feel that she is "missing out," that life is passing her by. Becoming anxious, irritable, complaining or discouraged. Trying to "have her fling" while she can, or to recapture the appearance and the pleasures of youth.

Developmental Tasks, Goals, and Responsibilities	*Traditional Tendencies in Thinking, Feeling, and Behaving*
Keeping up-to-date on current thinking, social attitudes, and changing folkways and mores.	Tendency to fall "behind the times" because of her preoccupation with home duties, tendency to neglect, or sacrifice and submerge self for family.
Developing new interests and broadening scope of activities outside the home and thus maintaining or re-establishing herself as an independently growing, yet interacting member of the family group.	Tendency to limit activities and interests more and more exclusively to home and family and thus to have no time or energy for growth in other areas. Tendency to feel that civic and political problems are not the concern of women.
Bolstering feelings of personal adequacy and worth by developing new skills, hobbies, interests, and commitments.	Tendency to compensate for inadequacy feelings by controlling or domineering over others by means of various devices or to "outdo" others in appearance, clothes, or show of wealth, etc.
Continuing to get satisfaction from her own efforts toward the achievement of personal ideals and goals.	Tendency to live and to experience the realization of her own dreams and ideals through, and in the life and the triumphs of her daughter.

If each of the adult members has been able realistically to accept himself as he is—his physique, with its weaknesses and strengths, its defects and superiorities, his sex and the sex role he must play, his age and stage of maturity, all without inner conflict and undue sensitivity— he thus has set the pattern for a similar sort of self-acceptance on the part of the children. The adolescent girl then has the pattern for accepting with satisfaction her role as a girl and woman; and the boy, even though he may be small in stature or a bit behind schedule in his physical development, has before him a healthy pattern to follow and an understanding attitude in his parents to help him to live happily with himself and his family. This in turn gives him the necessary fortitude to establish himself with his peers which is so important to every adolescent boy. "Experience has shown that during adolescence the individual becomes increasingly aware of 'self' and strives not only for the development of self ideals but for the acceptance of himself in harmony with those ideals. He is concerned with himself in the world of his peers; to be accepted by them, to feel he has a place among them."[1]

Inseparable from the attitude of self-acceptance in family life is the tendency for each to accept the other as a matter of course, and this acceptance again is based upon understanding. Children, as they live and grow together, grow also in understanding the differences between boys and girls, and progressively gain a realistic appreciation of differences in function between the sexes and how people live together in harmony.

FAMILY DEVELOPMENTAL TASKS AT THE TEENAGE STAGE

While mother and father, teenager, and younger siblings are working out their developmental tasks within the traditional tendencies and social pressures that oftentimes thwart and hinder them, let us put the entire family in focus and outline briefly some of the developmental tasks that confront the family-as-a-whole as it goes through the teen years with its firstborn.

PROVIDING PHYSICAL FACILITIES FOR SIMULTANEOUS AND OFTEN CONFLICTING NEEDS OF DIFFERENT FAMILY MEMBERS

At no time in the family life cycle do family members feel as intensely about the house and its facilities as they do during the teenage family stage. Now the teenager's need for acceptance in larger social circles makes him (even oftener when she is a girl) push for nicer, better, bigger, more modern furnishings and equipment. The house that some years ago was child-proofed and stripped of all breakable elegance, now must bloom in the styles of the period as teenagers see the house as a reflection of themselves and their family.

The dating adolescent girl wants an attractive setting in which she can entertain her boy and girl friends. She needs some privacy in these facilities at least part of the time away from the everwatchful eyes and

---

[1] H. R. Stolz, and L. M. Stolz, "Adolescent Problems Related to Somatic Variations," Nelson B. Henry (ed.), *The Forty-Third Yearbook, Part I, Adolescence,* of the National Society for the Study of Education (Chicago: University of Chicago Press, 1944), p. 73.

ears of younger siblings, parents, and other family members. The rest of the family needs to be somewhat protected from the noisy activities of teenagers, with their radios turned up full-blast, the record player grinding out the same popular tune over and over again, the giggles, the chatter, the shrieks, and the endless telephone conversations that mean so much to teenagers and yet so often fray the nerves of adults. Now, when so much emphasis is put upon popularity and social life, most families want to encourage their teenagers in their social growth and so do what they can to provide the facilities for it.

The teenage boy starts dating a little later, and he dates less frequently than the girl of the same age.[1] He does less of his dating and entertaining at home than does the girl, and so tends to demand less in refurbishing and "style." The pressures he puts on the home as a teenager are more apt to be in space for his hobbies and for his gang of buddies. As the fellows gather in the basement to fix a model plane, or in the yard to "soup up" the jalopy, or over the short wave set in his room, there is bound to be some invasion of the house and its supplies for food and drink and rags and string and all the other necessities that go into the completion of a project—and a man!

Teenagers tend to crowd their parents in the use of household equipment as they begin to adopt adult ways. They monopolize the bathroom; take over the kitchen and its foodstuffs; and intrude on their parents' quiet hours in front of the TV set in the evening.

We have two teen-age children who stay up until 10:30 or 11 o'clock every evening. Much as we love the children, this keeps my husband and me from having any private evenings together. When the children were younger, they went to bed early and this was no problem. I miss the former evenings of talking freely and choosing the radio or television programs ourselves. What do families do in this case?[2]

The extent of teenagers' use of the home for leisure activities is seen in a survey made by the Social Welfare Council of the Oranges and Maplewood, N. J., the results of which are shown in Table 18.

The top-ranking activity, "doing homework," suggests still another need

[1] Samuel Lowrie, "Factors Involved in the Frequency of Dating," *Marriage and Family Living*, Vol. XVIII, No. 1, February 1956, pp. 46–51.
[2] From letter quoted by Katy P. Collins, "Kids and TV 'Divorce' Their Parents," *Chicago Daily News*, January 18, 1956.

TABLE 18. *How Teenagers Spend Their Leisure Time* [1]

Percentage of Teenagers	Leisure-time Activity	Number of Hours a Week Reported
83.8	Doing homework	9.2 hours
81.0	Watching television	11.3 hours
77.6	Listening to radio	9.7 hours
61.0	Talking on the telephone	4.4 hours
47.5	Having dates	8.2 hours
46.3	Doing nothing at all	8.0 hours

for the teenage family's facilities—a place suitable for study. Where an atmosphere conducive to study is provided and teenagers are expected to finish their assignments before relaxing with their parents in front of the television set or around a snack on the kitchen table, the early evening pressures are off whole-family equipment. A portable radio in the youngster's room gives him or her "company" for study but does not intrude on concentration as does television. Examples of adult interest in intellectual and cultural things, as well as patterns of work habits and family expectations, facilitate the teenager's effective use of study times and places. It isn't as easy for the lower-class youngster whose home offers few if any of these models and resources.

While the teenager is crowding the house with his or her dating, recreational, and work interests, younger siblings are growing up with their interests and needs to be taken into account. Younger brothers and sisters often resent teenage interests and activities and the break in customary patterns of former years of play together. At the same time, father and mother continue to be persons with rights and needs for a little peace and quiet in their lives. The home that fulfills this multidimensional demand for adequate facilities during the teenage stage has some tall stepping to do, with adaptations and elaborations that more than likely cost money—plenty of it, as we see in the next section.

WORKING OUT MONEY MATTERS IN THE FAMILY WITH TEENAGERS

The teenage family feels pressures for physical expansion and renewal of its facilities. Junior campaigns for a new car. Sally needs a party dress.

[1] Reported in *Time*, September 29, 1952.

The refrigerator is no longer large enough to meet the demand for snacks and meals of the many appetites represented in the family. It would be nice to have another bathroom, or a second TV set, or a deep freeze, or a rumpus room, or a den where mother and father could find some place to call their own when the teenagers are entertaining, or some new furnishings to replace "this old stuff" that is suddenly so hideous in adolescent eyes. All the while, father sees costs of college, social life, and weddings ballooning up ahead of him.

Adolescents are very much concerned with the problems of money. Many of our junior and senior high school young people have difficulty keeping up with school expenses and feel embarrassed because of lack of funds.[1] Dates cost money—clothes and grooming for the girl, and, for the boy, actual financial layout for entertainment and food on the date. There is a wide range of the costs of a date, all the way from less than a dollar for something simple to a great deal of money for elaborate special affairs. One study of freshmen and sophomore college students reports that they spend $2 to $3 for routine dates, $5 to $6 for special dates, and $20 to $35 for big affairs like homecoming, in a range of dating costs running from less than $1 to $300 (reported by a former member of the armed services).[2]

This is the time when a teenager gets a part-time job that will not interfere too greatly with his school work and yet will bring him some regular money of his own. When employment is good, a teenage boy can find work in his neighborhood shop or store, golf links, or garage. The adolescent girl is in demand as baby-sitter, household helper, and in many places as saleswoman or clerk in local store or office. These may be valuable experiences if they do not cut short the young person's educational program and if the income from self-employment may be jointly recognized in the family as of special interest to the adolescent.

Families differ greatly in money practices. Some appropriate the children's earnings as part of the family income as once was traditional. Others consider the child's earnings as his to do with as he or she pleases. Still others keep a supervisory eye on teenagers' earnings, and while they

[1] Martin Bloom, "The Money Problems of Adolescents in the Secondary Schools of Springfield, Massachusetts," *Doctor of Education thesis,* New York University, 1955.

[2] Ruth Connor and Edith Flinn Hall, "The Dating Behavior of College Freshmen and Sophomores," *Journal of Home Economics,* Vol. 44, No. 4, April 1952, pp. 278–281.

The teenage girl is in demand as a baby-sitter—a valuable experience as well as one way of earning money of her own.

respect the young person's wishes, try to counsel for wisdom in planning for future needs. There are still some traditional homes in which either the father or the mother holds the purse strings and the young people have no voice in the family finances. In growing numbers are the more democratically oriented families in which family income and expenditures are discussed and money planning is done jointly with all members of the family participating. In these homes, young people gain experience in handling money and in dealing with financial problems, at the same time feeling that their wishes and rights are being considered in the family as they grow up.

There was a time when women had little say about the family monies. Linnie Day had to wheedle her way into her husband's closely held moneybags, according to Clarence Day's vivid descriptions of his family at the turn of the century.[1] Since World War II, there has been a rapid increase in women workers, especially among the over-45 wives.[2] As a wife gets and holds a job, she brings her earnings home to swell the family coffers and she becomes more of an economic partner in the getting and spending of the family income. This makes sense, especially in the family where the children are old enough so that they do not require the full-time attention of the mother. In fact, some evidence indicates that the adjustment between adolescents and their parents is better when the mother is employed part-time than when she is a full-time homemaker.[3] One interpretation is that as children become adolescent and need to untie the apron strings, the task is less difficult if the mother is not entirely dependent upon her children for her sense of being needed. If she has a part-time job, she not only helps out financially, but very likely she widens her horizons and enriches her role in her family as she becomes a self-sufficient person as well as wife and mother. Individual women and families differ widely, and many wives find it impossible or impractical to work outside the home. With the removal of traditional taboos about women working, a family has a choice about the matter today. That so many families in the teenage stage find that economic and emotional pressures are eased when the mother has some gainful employment is a trend worthy of note.

SHARING THE TASKS AND RESPONSIBILITIES OF FAMILY LIVING

As children grow up into the teens, they are able to assume more and more responsibility for themselves and for the household. Authority that once rested entirely in the parents now can be shared with the adoles-

[1] Clarence Day, *Life with Father* (New York: Alfred A. Knopf, 1935).
[2] According to the Bureau of the Census, 10% of the wives 45–65 years of age had jobs in 1940; in 1955 the percentage was nearly 30%.
[3] Ivan Nye, "Adolescent-Parent Adjustment: Age, Sex, Sibling Number, Broken Homes, and Employed Mothers as Variables," *Marriage and Family Living*, Vol. XIV, No. 4, November 1952, p. 331; also research in progress under Margaret S. Jessen of the Woodland Public Schools, Woodland, California on "Factors in Parents' Understanding of Adolescent Attitudes," reports that working mothers tend to show more understanding than mothers at home.

cents in the family as they become ready. The traditional family, with its father-head, is on the wane in twentieth-century America, with democratic patterns more frequent in families with teenagers.[1] Teenagers are still accountable to their parents, but progressively assume more and more responsibility for their behavior and for the well-being of the family as a whole.

Middle-class family rituals are evidenced in cooperative activities of adults and teenagers working together at jointly assumed responsibilities. Father and son wash and wax the family car on Saturday afternoon. Mother and daughter together do the weekend cleaning and straightening up in the house. The children assume responsibility for getting the Sunday evening meal. Father and children occasionally prepare and serve mother's breakfast as a special treat on a Sunday morning. The whole family pitches in to do some major project like painting or remodeling or gardening or preserving foods in season, as we see in the following episode drawn from real life.

The Jones family is canning tomatoes. Two bushels must be done while they are still fresh. The whole family likes tomatoes and will enjoy them next winter. They all approve of getting them canned. But only Mother knows just how to can tomatoes. If she does not look out she will be bossing the activities of the others so much they will not get much fun or sense of accomplishment out of the project. If the others are not careful they will be making uncomfortable and bothersome mistakes in their efforts to help. The only way around these hazards is to plan just what has to be done, just how each specific function goes, where each person will sit or stand, what he or she will do, and agree, on the basis of interest and skill, on just which tasks are allocated to which family member.

Now the Joneses are settled in the project with Junior and Johnnie bringing in tomatoes from the porch, sorting them for size and washing them in a tub of cold water by the door. Dad is in charge of scalding the washed tomatoes and putting them on the table for Betsy and himself to peel. Mother packs the jars and puts them in the canner. All moves along smoothly. The radio is on to a favorite program. Mother pushes back a wisp of her moist hair and smiles at the family. Betsy grins up at her

[1] Vivian Briggs and Lois R. Schulz, "Parental Response to Concepts of Parent-Adolescent Relationships," *Child Development*, Vol. 26, No. 4, December 1955, pp. 279–284.

and says, "Ain't we got fun?" while Dad nudges her with his free elbow and whispers, "Lucky people, aren't we?"

Yet what a mess canning can be! How a woman usually hates to get into it by herself. And how men and children avoid it like the plague! The difference lies in making the job interesting, sharing the responsibility, and then letting each do his own job without interference. Mother does not enjoy getting stuck with the drudgery jobs all alone. Dad and the youngsters get no fun out of the project when Mother's suggestions and criticisms fall around them thick and fast. With joint planning, and mutually assumed responsibility, everyone pitches in, has fun in working together, and feels the satisfaction of achievement in the completion of the task.

FINDING ZEST IN MARRIAGE AND SERVING AS GOOD EXAMPLES IN MARRIED LIVING

Give an adolescent a family in which "Mama loves Papa" and he sees the sense of retraining some of his insistent impulses for the long-term values of marriage and family life. Let the marriage relationship sag through boredom or neglect or friction, and the teenager is deprived of an emotional climate good to grow in at the moment. And also he is deprived of the models of happy fulfilled adults worthy of his emulation and living out the way of life that the sex-social code calls for in our society.

Yet what a task it is for many husbands and wives to find the zest in their life together that inspires them or impresses their offspring! The husband at marriage continued with little interruption the work in which he was engaged before marriage. As success progressively came to him he became more and more interested in his work. His contacts with people broadened and his satisfactions in life came more and more from outside the family. His wife, on the other hand, has become "bogged down" through the years with what can be deadening routines of housekeeping and child care. She has seemed to have little time for outside activities. She has not been able to carry on in the work or profession for which she was trained. She feels "boxed in," removed from the interests that satisfy her husband. Husband and wife now find less and less in common. Dissatisfaction with life on her part, and with home life on the part of the husband, increases. Resentment for each other is fostered. The wife tends to become frigid and the husband indifferent in a gradual decline of interest in each other that represents not so much physiological decrease in "sex output" as a neglect of their primary relationship as man and wife.

These are the years when a man's interest may turn to a young woman with whom he works, not so much because she is attractive in herself, but because he is bored with himself and his marriage. At the same time his wife may feel so taken for granted that she rushes off in a frenzy of home decoration or club activities, or she sulks at home day after day and thus expresses her discontent. For years both man and woman have been so wrapped up with their roles as parents and breadwinners or housekeepers that they may have lost each other as emotionally and sexually satisfying mates.

Renewing the spirit of play in marriage is the answer for many a couple. Getting away for an occasional weekend together sweetens all but the sourest of relationships. Letting the teenagers perk up their parents and their family as they want to is often fun for the parents as well as the youngsters. As mother gets a smart new hat, she gets the feelings that go with it and once more attracts her husband's interest in her as a woman. When father gets into the tweed jacket his son insists is right for him, he assumes the gay blade air that seems appropriate, he throws back his shoulders, pulls in his tummy, and woos his own wife as only he can charm her. Keeping a marriage vigorously alive consists of much more than so-called marriage hygiene: it rests upon the eagerness of the husband and wife to attract and be attractive to the other—with the life and the lilt that is to be found in a radiantly alive marriage.

KEEPING COMMUNICATION SYSTEMS OPEN IN THE TEENAGE FAMILY

Youngsters long for sympathetic understanding from their parents during their teen years. They frequently complain, "If only my parents would listen to me and respect what I have to say!" "I can't seem to talk with my folks without someone getting mad." "Some parents don't seem to care what happens to you; others breathe down your neck in eternal 'snoopervision.'" More than anything else teenagers appreciate parents that they can talk to man to man; parents who do not get shocked or excited, but can take teenagers' problems as they are, and discuss them calmly and sensibly with their youngsters. This is not an easy task for parents whose children have grown away from them through the years. It can be accomplished best by those parents who have grown up as their children have and can see things from an up-to-date point of view, rather than in terms of "when I was your age . . ."

Children approaching adulthood sometimes begin to regard the adult both as a parent and as a symbolic representative of the adult world. Much adolescent rebellion is a defiant "emancipation proclamation" against any and all adult authority as such. In response to this, adults are apt to mobilize against youth as youth. The little incident of freshness by a son, suddenly isn't Johnny being confused at all; it becomes "one of those things modern youth wants to do and we better show them where to get off." Child and adult then view each other not as familiar persons, but as symbolic representatives of a hostile outgroup.

As children become teenagers, parents often fear what the neighbors may say, and so they are unable to allow the youngster to behave in ways that might be quite temporary and very normal for him at that particular time. This fear is perhaps strongest in small communities where everyone knows everyone else. Studies have shown that small-town adolescent girls, on the average, experience more conflict with their parents than any other adolescent group, a fact that is associated with the tendencies of their fathers to be more strict with them.[1] At times and in places where the misdeeds of teenagers are magnified out of all proportion as they are in the scares of juvenile delinquency that sweep across many a community, even the most innocent mistake of a teenager may be exaggerated into a portent of ominous significance that seriously blocks communication between the generations.

Teenagers feel differently about their parents than they did as children, or than they will as they become adults. A child's love for his or her parents is a dependent, appreciative, even enthusiastic kind of devotion. Adolescent feeling for parents is normally less vocally affectionate, and more openly critical than it has been before or will be again. Mark Twain observed that when he was sixteen he could not understand how his father could be so stupid; by the time he reached twenty-one, he was amazed at how much the old-man had learned in the past five years!

---

[1] Leland H. Stott, "Some Family Life Patterns and Their Relation to Personality Development in Children," *Journal of Experimental Education*, Vol. 8, 1939, pp. 148–160; and also, L. H. Stott, "Morale in the Home," Nebraska College of Agricultural Extension, Circular No. 5–105, p. 13.

Family projects and whole-family interests help keep communication systems open within the teenage family.

Little children can be openly dependent. Teenagers frequently find irritating, evidences of their continuing need for their parents. Watch a central school letting out in the afternoon. As the children come to find parents waiting to take them to a picnic or music lesson, the younger child not unusually welcomes his mother with enthusiastic warmth. Not so the junior or senior high school student, who more typically resents his parents' presence near the school building and has been known to greet his mother with the critical query, "What do you think you are doing here?"

Parents, who have been considered perfect by little children, come in for criticism and fault-finding as these same children reach adolescence. The schoolboy brags about his father's prowess and boasts of his mother's beauty. The same young fellow as a teenager groans over his father's old-fashioned behavior and begs his mother not to appear at a parent-teacher meeting in "that old hat." Adolescent criticism of parents is evidence of the young person's struggle to free himself from his close emotional attachment to his parents and to mature in his relationship to them.

The teenager who achieves emancipation from his parents emerges as a young adult capable of mature affection for his mother and father as persons. He becomes an autonomous person, capable of reciprocal inter-dependence with his father and mother, and of mature feelings of genuine affection and appreciation for them. But in the meantime, through ado-lescence, relationships between the generations are frequently strained.

There is some normal slackening off of telling parents everything as children get into their teens. Then it is normal for intimate confidences to be shared first with close friends within the peer group, and only secondarily with the parents and other significant adults. Adults who recognize how normal it is for young people to identify now with their own generation, as they must if they are to emerge as full-fledged adults, restrain from the prying pressures that only serve to alienate them fur-ther from their teenagers.

Wise parents guide their adolescents with a loose rein, letting them have their heads, knowing that they will not stray too far from the fold if they are not driven from it. Being available for companionable chats now and then is better than letting loose a barrage of questions as soon as the teenager sets foot inside the door. Adolescents need parents and go to them willingly in families where communication systems are kept in good working order.

Some families experience more alienation between generations than do others. Ethnic groups in which the parents hold to the old ways, while the young people reach out to the new, find it hard to bridge the growing chasms between the generations. In general, middle-class and upper-class families maintain more democratic patterns of interaction and have fewer problems with their adolescent youth than do lower-class families.[1]

Youth is ever more explorative, daring, and "up to the minute" than are parents. Young people enjoy that contrast. They want to be out ahead. But it is also exceedingly important to the adolescent for Dad and Mom

---

[1] Leonard G. Benson, "Family Social Status and Parental Authority Evaluations among Adolescents," *Southwest Social Science Quarterly*, Vol. 36, No. 1, June 1955, pp. 46–54; also Ivan Nye, "Adolescent-Parent Adjustment—Socio-Economic Level as a Variable," *American Sociological Review*, Vol. 16, No. 3, June 1951, pp. 341–349; and Henry S. Maas, "Some Social Class Differences in the Family Systems and Group Relations of Pre- and Early Adolescents," *Child Development*, Vol. 22, No. 2, June 1951, pp. 145–152.

not to get *too* far behind. They take pride in their parents' progressive point of view and in their social and civic activities and interests. They are concerned about the way their parents look and behave in public. For parents to possess some social grace and an interest in cultural activities and events apparently gives the young person the needed sense of pride in them that makes communication free and full.

MAINTAINING CONTACT WITH MEMBERS OF THE EXTENDED FAMILY

The teenage stage of the family life cycle is the testing time for the immediate relatives. If they pass youth's rigorous standards of acceptability they can contribute much to and gain much from association with the young relatives. If they remain rigidly rooted in "old-fashioned" ways and ideas, young people eschew them heartily and will avoid them except under duress. An understanding grandparent can bridge the gap not only between the first and third generations but also between grandchild and parent. A sympathetic uncle, aunt, or cousin has a real role to play as a home away from home—a parent once removed, a guide without the heavy hand of authority, or the wise counselor who is not too close to the teenage boy or girl. The narrow-minded "old maid," male or female, married or unmarried, is rarely a welcome guest in the teenage family, for he or she brings too much implied criticism and personifies too clearly the frustrations that burden youth.

Broad-gauged or narrow, generous or stingy, wise or foolish, relatives have to be taken in their stride in most families.

You dare not offend Aunt Amy no matter what you think of her. You can not go live with your sophisticated cousin however much you would love it. You need not imitate drifting Uncle Mike regardless of how much you envy his freedom. You go to family gatherings and size them all up, maintaining the courtesies that are expected, and learning a great deal about your roots and your forebears as you see these kinfolk in action.

When graduation day arrives, and your relatives sit there beaming up at you, you can afford to be proud of your family, and glad to be a part of them. You want to be worthy of them, and to measure up to their expectations of you. You recognize yourself as a member of the larger family group, and feel sorry for the boy and girl in your class who have no family to call their own.

Younger cousins and other relatives may idolize the teenager and play significant parts in his or her development. Relatives have a real place in the family, less perhaps in the teenage family than before or after, but

Telephoning becomes especially important as teenagers begin to reach out for associations with persons of their own generation.

a place, nevertheless, that is real and a part of family living that is important.

GROWING INTO THE WORLD AS A FAMILY AND AS PERSONS

The teenage family ranges farther afield than it ever has before. The children are now old enough to enjoy a whole family vacation to more distant points of interest than before was feasible. Trips to historic shrines and cultural areas now take on real meaning for the family. Individually, horizons expand too. The teenager goes off with his friends for a weekend or a summer. Father is away on business trips from time to time. Mother is sent as a delegate to the state or national convention of her favorite organization. The family is beginning to scatter in a preview of the individualization characteristic of the empty nest stage just ahead.

Teenagers normally reach out for associations with people outside the family. The adolescent boy or girl must identify with the younger generation. Social growth is dependent upon friendships with members of

both sexes and on the activities that go with dating, courtship, and becoming involved emotionally with one or more members of the other sex.
During the entire second decade of life, members of the peer group are
especially important to the young person. It is in the face-to-face contacts with friends of one's own age that decisions are made, skills are
developed, and values are weighed in everyday interaction. Guidance,
confidences, and counsel from beloved older friends (teacher, minister,
youth leaders, etc.) may be more important to the teenager than one
suspects. Such close ties outside the family may threaten the parent who
is not prepared to release the teenage child. Accepting the teenager's intimate friends and the confidences that young people normally share, parents can take adolescence in their stride. Otherwise this task of growing
out to others may be frightening for the parents who stand by and resist
or retreat.

A frequent example is found in the teenager's early love experiences.
For him or her the crushes and infatuations of early adolescence are
important and especially precious. If one or both of the parents ridicule
these early involvements as "puppy love" or ignore them as "kid stuff,"
they alienate their own youngster and only rarely weaken the outside
ties. When the family can make this special friend welcome at home,
treat him or her and the relationship with respect, and take it for what
it is and nothing more, both the family and the adolescent are free to
grow through the experience to new levels of maturity.

Group life is a magnet for the adolescent. Many a teenager wants to
belong to more organizations and get into more activities than can comfortably be carried. He or she wants to belong to the band or the glee
club, to the drama group or the ball team, to social clubs and hobby
groups. Life is opening up and everything must be tried and tested.
Political organizations and social action groups quite distant from the
family's orientation may be explored, as much to see what they are like
as to stretch away from the family's affiliations into those peculiarly one's
own.

Parents who can take these adventures of their youngsters as a normal
part of growing up, without feeling unnecessarily afraid or personally
threatened, can argue the merits of this cause or that with their budding
citizen without going off the deep end in repression or repudiation. Families who can go along with their young people in the various explorations

into new ways of looking at things can grow up with the flexibility that the modern age requires.

REWORKING AND MAINTAINING A PHILOSOPHY OF LIFE THAT FITS THE NEW LEVELS OF DEVELOPMENT AS A FAMILY AND AS MEMBERS OF A CHANGING WORLD

A family cannot be buffeted about by every social wind that blows and feel steady and strong within itself. Conversely, a family that does not bend with the pressures of the times will break under their stress. With no convictions and values, the family is a tumbleweed, without roots or stability. With a philosophy of life that is too rigid and narrow, a family risks alienation of its teenagers and grown children and its own integrity as a unit.

The stresses of adolescence that so often shake families to their roots often grow out of conflicting value systems of the old and the new generation. Parents were brought up in one way of life, where definite standards of right and wrong prevailed. Circumstances have changed; teenage young people see life situations differently. The developmental tasks for the family involve holding fast to those verities that have continuing meaning, while venturing forth into wider, broader orientations that new levels of development and experience require. Successful in this concurrent maintenance and testing of values and truths by which life is lived, families weather the storms that beset them without losing their integrity as units or as individual members.

POSITIVE VALUES IN TEENAGE FAMILY LIFE

Family life, with its potentials for promoting human growth, becomes complicated and often threatened by the struggle and clash of diverse strivings, emotional difficulties, misconceptions, and rationalized behavior of individual family members. It is, nevertheless, the area of life from which come some of the deepest satisfactions in human experience. Fulfillment comes from adequate functioning. Those forms of functioning involved in human interaction can be the most satisfying of all.

Adults and youth in the family group are constantly striving toward their goals as persons and as family members. Many of the growth tasks and needs in terms of which the teenager strives to function are consistent and harmonious with the desires and felt responsibilities of the parents. But usually some yielding and a lot of "accepting" may be necessary on the part of youth as well as by the parents. It is in the very process thus of arriving at an integration of purposes (dynamic interaction) that both grow and experience deep satisfaction.

The adolescent, for example, needs to function more and more as a free agent in his own right. He is striving toward an independent adult status. The parent normally delights in the young person's attainments in the direction of adult-like functioning, and from them derives the satisfaction of the fulfillment of his own purposes and responsibilities. In adolescent strivings toward independence, however, there are likely to be some fumblings, errors in judgment, and behavior that looks like arrogance, impudence, and lack of respect for his elders. Parents are inclined to feel these concomitants of growth as threats to their status—assaults upon their dignity as parents. But parents can, through experience and some effort, come to take them for what they are, and become yielding and understanding.

The young person, on the other hand, senses any resistance the parent may feel to his strivings and awkward attempts at independence. He is inclined to resent that resistance. But if he also senses in his parent's behavior a genuine interest in his problems and some evidence of an understanding acceptance of him, he is able to yield a bit, eventually to accept the advice and counsel of his parent. Each grows through understanding the other. They both grow in their ability to accept others as they are. The relationship between them then grows closer, more affectionate and companionable.

In our culture the smallness of the family group limits the personal sources from which the child can draw for security and a sense of belonging. The kind of persons his parents happen to be, therefore, is for him an exceedingly important matter. If they are secure and growing individuals, happy in their relationships with each other, they are the greatest source of inner security a youngster can have. They not only provide a home atmosphere in which he can feel secure, but they also set the pattern of attitudes and interpersonal relationships which is conducive to human adjustment and growth.

When mutual respect for each other's point of view and a real concern for each other's well-being and peace of mind is the prevailing pattern of interaction, the child is inclined to follow that pattern. As he increasingly does so the adult's confidence in him grows. He is allowed to assume more and more responsibility for his own activities and conduct. In such matters, for example, as being in at night he will not need to be *told* when he must be home. He clears his plans with his parents and gradually takes on the full responsibility himself. Because of his regard for his parents and his desire not to cause them worry or inconvenience, and especially because he knows they trust him, he meets family standards on his own responsibility. He thus achieves self-control and personal integration.

Parents need the love, confidence, and the respect of their teenage children. They need it for the sense of success and accomplishment it gives them, for they have invested a great deal of themselves in the rearing of those sons and daughters. But they gain and maintain that love and respect only as they meet dependably, day by day, the developmental needs of their children. During adolescence those needs are just as vital as at any other period of the child's development, and the understanding parent is just as necessary in the adequate meeting of those needs. Adolescents do want parents. Not only this, they really need parents.

The basic security that gives one courage to use one's powers and test one's vision depends most of all upon the unwavering love of one's parents. To be happily secure, every child must feel that somewhere he is wanted for himself, that to someone he is of supreme importance.[1]

Thus, through family interaction, life's motive—to function—may be supremely satisfied. The giver is richer for the giving because he grows in the process as he stimulates the others to growth.

SUMMARY AND IMPLICATIONS FOR NEEDED SERVICES

If the hazards and obstacles to constructive family interaction are to be lessened and if individual functioning in the various family roles is to become mutually more satisfying, the vicious circles of faulty thinking, of negative attitudes and hostile feelings about roles and relationships in family life which are perpetuated and passed from parents to children must somehow be broken effectively. The adolescent years, when young people are ready to question the authority of their elders and to realize that their parents are fallible, is an opportune time to effect this break.

[1] Katharine W. Taylor, *Do Adolescents Need Parents?* (New York: D. Appleton Century Company, 1938), p. 15.

It is at this level also when the whole area of relationships between the sexes and in marriage is of vital interest.

Educational programs in the principles of human development and interaction as they apply to boy-girl relationships and to marriage and family life, combined with opportunity for the development of social skills, and facilities for individual counseling, are being widely developed and promoted (Chapter Fifteen). Teachers are being trained not only for competent group guidance but also for effective individual counseling. The very nature of the subject matter taught and the general problems discussed tend to open the avenues of communication between the individual students and the teacher and so pave the way for effective group and individual counseling.

Another need that is felt and frequently expressed by young people is for better community facilities for recreation designed specifically for teenagers. They want places where they can talk and play and dance, places that are supervised and have the support of the parents. It is very important that these facilities be planned and that the activities be conducted by the boys and girls themselves.

As children approach adolescence parents express a need for greater understanding and often for individual help with their children. This calls for an expansion of present parent education programs more adequately to meet this need. Provision for individual counseling in connection with group instruction is important. Simply to make parents feel guilty for what they have done or failed to do in the rearing of their children helps not at all. What parents do need is knowledge about what to expect of adolescents and positive help with their problems.

An example is seen in the overprotective parents who keep their teenager from some of the normal high school experiences, so that he comes to college with impulses that arise out of his "unfinished business." Irrational behavior appropriate of an earlier stage interferes with his study and living in college and gives rise to undesirable or forbidden activities. The college student often gets into trouble because he has not yet completed the earlier tasks of adolescence within the too restrictive atmosphere of his home and high school. Helping parents and teachers to learn what to expect of their adolescents and what teenage experiences are to be encouraged as growth-promoting does much to prevent later escapades, as well as to contribute to the security of the teen years.

Mutual interpretation of each generation to the other has been found

Many a teenager wants to belong to young people's organizations and to get into youth activities, now when life opens up beyond his family.

to be especially valuable during the teenage family stage. Parents and their teenage young people meet together to discuss common community problems, plan social activities, and work through desirable standards of conduct for specific situations. A competent professional leader is of value in helping each age-group see and accept the values the other is trying to preserve, and to come to terms that are mutually acceptable and agreements that are generally satisfying. No family lives to itself alone, especially at the teenage stage. Its developmental tasks now are jointly faced and mutually accomplished between the generations, as well as between any one family and the others within the community.

SUGGESTED ACTIVITIES

1) For any one of the developmental tasks of teenagers listed early in this chapter, write a paper on the hazards and problems adolescents face in our society and its various subcultures in achieving the task, and the programs in home, school and community that assist the young person

Young people need wholesome recreation that they can plan and carry out themselves, with adult support and supervision.

    successfully accomplish the task. Document with readings, references, and research findings.

2) Pull together into focus the developmental tasks of the man of the teenage household, as father, husband, provider, homemaker, and individual, with especial reference to the ways in which these various roles may possibly conflict with one another. Write a paper on contradictory roles of the father of teenagers as you hypothesize them from this analysis.

3) Popular opinion once had it that a married woman with children should not work outside the home. Using data from this chapter and from related readings and research, refute the traditional stereotype in a paper on "When an Outside Job for Mother May Benefit a Teenage Family."

4) Interview a personnel manager of a local business or industry employing married women with teenage children. Ask him about his experience with mothers as workers considering such factors as: reliability, permanence, loyalty, days off in sickness, accident rate, manual skills, abilities to work with people, and other relevant points. Find out what opportunities this business concern provides for older workers to learn while they work through special courses, incentives for continuing education, etc.

5) Conduct an informal discussion among teenagers whose mothers work outside the house on a part-time or a full-time basis. Focus the discussion on how the adolescents feel about having their mothers work. Encourage full freedom of expression of both positive and negative attitudes as well as of the detailed anecdotal material that breathes life into the responses. Keep notes sufficient to write up the group interview as an exploratory report of how adolescents feel about having their mothers work.

6) Explore what some communities are doing in the development of parent-youth codes in which both parents and teenagers discuss together their various conflicts over social standards and come to mutually acceptable agreements on a number of specific issues. Representative codes are published in the following sources:

> Evelyn Millis Duvall, *Family Living* (New York: Macmillan Company, 1950 and 1955 editions), pp. 134–136 and 134–137 respectively.
>
> Evelyn Millis Duvall, "Community Codes by Common Consent," *The National Parent-Teacher*, December 1954, pp. 8–10.
>
> Evelyn Millis Duvall, "Toward a Parent-Youth Code for a Midwestern City," *Journal of Home Economics*, Vol. 46, No. 1, January 1954, pp. 36–37.

See if you can find others being developed in neighborhoods near you. Visit one or more sessions, talk with some of the parents and teenagers, and write up your findings, impressions, and evaluations of such endeavors as helping teenage families meet one or more of their developmental tasks.

7) Arrange a simple production of *High Pressure Area*, a short skit available from the National Association for Mental Health, 1790 Broadway, New York 19, N. Y., depicting a provocative situation between an adolescent girl and her family. Discuss your reactions to the skit by identifying one by one with each of the principal characters: analyzing how the person felt and why, what he or she did and why, how he or she might have responded differently, and how these different responses might have altered the others reactions and the course of the story.

8) Write a letter to your Superintendent of Schools, to your State Department of Education at your state capital, to the National Association of Secondary School Principals, 1201 Sixteenth Street, N.W., Washington 6, D. C., and to the United States Department of Health, Education

and Welfare, Social Security Administration, Washington 25, D. C. In each case, inquire about what is being done in educating teenagers for friendship, love, marriage, and family living in the schools known to them. Collect and analyse your findings in the light of what you believe the need to be for education of a young person for mature living with the significant others of his life now and in the foreseeable future.

9) Discuss the following situations from case excerpts developed by Dr. Hazel Ingersoll, Department of Home Life, Oklahoma A&M College, Stillwater, Oklahoma:

a) Judy's mother loves to see Judy have a good time. She would, by her own admission, "work her fingers to the bone" for Judy. She wants Judy to have the most clothes and the most dates! She is overcome with joy when she is selected May Queen. She even suggests that she has a stage career all lined up for Judy. "And I'll go with her to see that she gets along all right. She will need me, then, more than now. And maybe she will meet and marry some rich nice young man." Meantime Judy's mother neglects her own appearance and has no life of her own apart from her child. She was widowed young after an early marriage and a frugal upbringing. What do you think are the mother's developmental tasks? How do they affect Judy? What suggestions do you have for Judy's mother? for Judy?

b) Father grumbles constantly at Junior (a teenager) about his using the car, his carelessness of dress and his language. Junior appears to be gone with the gang most of the time these days and often doesn't get his chores done. Father, when he can catch him, deluges his ears with tales of "when I was young, young man, I had to take my girl friends by bus to the movies. No sense in this *always* having to use the car!" or "My father always insisted that I clean up my room and mow the lawn before I went to play baseball. You are just spoiled! Now is the time you learned to do a little work. Why at your age I was earning my own spending money. I don't see what has got into this younger generation." What are the developmental tasks of father and son? In what ways might they be accomplished? What may happen if the present situation persists? Why?

READINGS

Baruch, Dorothy W., *How to Live with Your Teen-Ager* (New York: McGraw-Hill Book Company, 1953).

Bossard, James H. S., *Parent and Child* (Philadelphia: University of Pennsylvania Press, 1953).

Duvall, Evelyn Millis, *Facts of Life and Love for Teen-Agers* (New York: Association Press, Revised Edition, 1956).

———, *Family Living* (New York: Macmillan Company, Revised Edition, 1955).

Elkin, Frederick, and Weslley, William A., "The Myth of Adolescent Culture," *American Sociological Review*, Vol. 20, No. 6, December 1955, pp. 680–684.

English, O. Spurgeon, and Foster, Constance J., *Fathers Are Parents Too* (New York: G. P. Putnam's Sons, 1951), Chapters 9 & 10.

Frank, Mary and Lawrence K., *Your Adolescent at Home and in School* (New York: The Viking Press Inc., 1956).

Havighurst, Robert J., *Human Development and Education* (New York: Longmans, Green and Co., 1953), Chapters 9, 10, 11.

Havighurst, Robert J., and Taba, Hilda, *Adolescent Character and Personality* (New York: John Wiley and Sons, Inc., 1949).

Henry, Nelson B. (ed.), *The Forty-Third Yearbook, Part I, Adolescence*, of the National Society for the Study of Education (Chicago: University of Chicago Press, 1944).

Hollingshead, August B., *Elmtown's Youth* (New York: John Wiley and Sons, Inc., 1949).

Kirkpatrick, Clifford, *The Family as Process and Institution* (New York: The Ronald Press, 1955), Chapter 11, "Adolescence in the Family Situation."

Landis, Paul H., *Adolescence and Youth* (New York: McGraw-Hill Book Company, Revised Edition, 1952).

Polier, Justine Wise, *Back to What Woodshed?* (New York: Public Affairs Committee, 1956).

Rea, Lois, "What Can Parents Teach Adolescents?" *The Christian Home*, July 1953, pp. 23–27.

Seidman, Jerome M. (ed.), *The Adolescent: a Book of Readings* (New York: The Dryden Press, 1953).

Smith, Ira M., *Looking Ahead: to Go or Not to Go to College* (LesStrang Associates, Wolverine Building, Ann Arbor, Michigan, 1956).

Superintendent of Documents, *The Adolescent in Your Family* (Washington, D. C.: Government Printing Office, 1955).

———, *Job Guide for Young Workers* (Washington, D. C.: Government Printing Office, 1954 and 1955 supplement).

———, *Marilyn Wants to Know—After High School What?* (Washington, D. C.: Government Printing Office, 1954).

Taylor, Katharine Whiteside, *Do Adolescents Need Parents?* (New York: Appleton-Century Company, 1938).

Zimmerman, Gereon (producer), "U.S. Teen-Agers," *Look*, Volume 20, No. 2, January 24, 1956, pp. 21–32.

PART 3

Contracting families

*There is a time for holding
close and a time for letting
go. What happens as families
launch their young adults into
lives of their own? With what
do middleaged parents fill their
years in the empty nest? Why
are problems of aging families
of special interest now? And,
what makes the dynamics of
family interaction so potentially
explosive at every stage of the
life cycle?*

This time, like all times, is a very good one if we but know what to do with it.

EMERSON

CHAPTER TWELVE

Families as launching centers

There comes a time when the young of the family are ready to be launched from the home base and to sail off into a life for themselves. In twentieth-century American families this stage usually begins late in the teen years. It is sharply marked by the young person's departure from home to marry, to take a full-time job, or to begin military service or college—each of which removes the person from the parental home, never again to return as a child.

The launching stage is a process of departure marked by some periods of disillusionment and some of real happiness as parents and young adults learn to accept each other in ways new to both generations. Reuben Hill suggests some of this in his report of college students' launching days:

The families of college students are characteristic launching-center families, and their experiences offer us valid data. College students report some disillusionment on returning home for the holidays for the first few times. They come home to find their rooms in use or their possessions appropriated by other members of the family. Or they may find, after eagerly anticipating the holidays, that things are not as they used to be, that the peer ties have been broken; and so, after a few days with the family, they are ready to leave home again for college with a different view of their place in the home setting. Idealization has played them tricks, and their idealized home turns out to be a disillusion. In some homes there is awkwardness when the college adult returns, an unexpected uncertainty as to the in-between-stage roles the parents and he expect to play. Sudden awkward silences occur—for the good reason that parents and their young adult did not visit with each other much before he left for college. Some homecomers report resentment that the community considers them now "visitors in the home." At the other extreme are the students who return for vacation to be caught up in a whirl of activities with the old crowd, leaving little time for their hungry parents. More usually, the holidays are a source of satisfaction to parents and young people alike, filled with family activities and family-centered fun.[1]

This stage begins with the first child leaving home as a young adult; it ends with the emptying nest as the last child leaves home for a life of his or her own. This stage may be an extremely short one, as is the case in the family with one child, a daughter who marries the year she graduates from high school. The stage may extend over a considerable period of time, even for the duration of the family, as happens in an occasional family in which an unmarried son or daughter stays dependent in the home through the years. In mid-century United States the stage typically lasts six to seven years (Chapter One).

The processes of launching start during the earlier life cycle stages of the family, as the child and young person prepares for the decisions that will shape his future. His or her vocational future is planned or is left to chance long before the young person is out of school. Educational plans are formed or they go by default early in the high school years. Timing for his military service depends in part upon his educational decisions. His or her marriage readiness is determined by previous successes or failures in making heterosexual adjustments. The process of cutting apron strings characterizes the teen years and sets the stage for the son's or daughter's emergence as an emancipated young adult. No matter how abrupt this may seem to be, the departure of the young person from his home is a process that goes on through the years.

FACTORS AFFECTING THE YOUNG ADULT'S LIFE PLANS

Some young people plan farther ahead than do others. In general, as social class rises, the interest in life planning, and the ability to predictably plan one's life increases. A study of 2,700 public, private, and trade high school students, and 349 Yale undergraduates, explored the question, "How far ahead have you planned your life?" The percentage of high school students planning five or more years ahead doubled from the lowest to the highest social class (from approximately 20 to 40 per cent).

[1] Reuben Hill, revision of Willard Waller's, *The Family* (New York: Copyright 1951 by The Dryden Press, Inc., reprinted by special permission), pp. 432–433.

The researchers conclude that "length of life planning had a reliable positive correlation with both the occupational and educational status of the young respondents' fathers." [1]

A further factor related to the young adult's plans for his life is the mobility of his family. Upward mobile parents tend either to carry their children along with them or to encourage their young people to climb; young people from nonmobile families tend to remain static in the great majority of cases (85 per cent in one recent study). [2]

Significantly more boys than girls tend to make extended life plans, [3] probably because a girl knows her future will be greatly influenced by her marriage and the plans of her husband. In both sexes there is more upward mobility drive among those whose family and interpersonal relations have been difficult than among those whose early interpersonal relations have been satisfying. [4] One relevant study shows that high levels of aspiration of 350 university students are related to (1) feelings of not being wanted by parents, (2) favoritism shown by parents, and (3) little attachment to parents (Table 19).

These findings support current psychoanalytic assumptions and gen-

TABLE 19. *Interpersonal Relationships in the Family and Aspirational Level of 350 University Students* [5]

Feelings of Not Being Wanted by Parents	Levels of Aspiration		Favoritism Shown by Parents	Levels of Aspiration		Degree of Attachment to Parents	Levels of Aspiration	
	HIGH	LOW		HIGH	LOW		HIGH	LOW
Father	(N = 117)	(N = 223)	Father	(N = 95)	(N = 188)	Father	(N = 110)	(N = 222)
Some	41.9	24.7	Yes	45.3	30.9	Much	33.6	50.9
None	58.1	75.3	No	54.7	69.1	Little	66.4	49.1
Mother	(N = 122)	(N = 223)	Mother	(N = 95)	(N = 188)	Mother	(N = 123)	(N = 223)
Some	34.4	20.2	Yes	41.1	25.0	Much	52.8	66.8
None	65.6	79.8	No	58.9	75.0	Little	47.2	33.2

[1] Orville G. Brim, and Raymond Forer, "A Note on the Relation of Values and Social Structure to Life Planning," *Sociometry*, Vol. 19, No. I, March 1956, pp. 54–60.

[2] Carson McGuire, "Conforming, Mobile and Divergent Families," *Marriage and Family Living*, Vol. XIV, No. 2, May 1952, p. 113.

[3] Orville G. Brim and Raymond Forer, *op. cit.*, p. 58.

[4] Evelyn Ellis, "Social Psychological Correlates of Upward Social Mobility among Unmarried Career Women," *American Sociological Review*, Vol. 17, No. 5, October 1952, pp. 558–563; and Karen Horney, *The Neurotic Personality of Our Time* (New York: Norton and Company, 1938) pp. 162–187.

[5] Data from Russell R. Dynes, Alfred C. Clarke, and Simon Dinitz, "Levels of Occupational Aspiration: Some Aspects of Family Experience as a Variable," *American Sociological Review*, Vol. 21, No. 2, April 1956, Tables 1, 2, and 3, pp. 212–215.

eral social theory that unsatisfactory interpersonal relationships in the family of orientation are significantly related to high aspirational levels and that satisfactory relationships are related to low aspirational levels. Thus we see that some young people, whose family life has been unhappy, struggle to better themselves as soon as they can cut loose from family ties. In some cases the high levels of aspiration are fantasies not related too closely to what is realizable. In others actual social mobility results from realistic efforts to improve.

The final factor influencing the young person's vision of who he may become, is the factor of identification with some older person who serves as a model for the emerging young adult. The girl identifies with her teacher and wants to be just like her when she grows up. The boy greatly admires his coach or his leader at the YMCA and goes off like his hero for specialized training, possibly at the same college and professional school. In such cases, the young adult patterns himself after the much admired adult and so makes the decisions and follows the course that bring him closer to his ideal.

To summarize, factors influencing the young adult's life planning and specific decisions upon leaving his family of orientation, tend to operate in the following directions:

1) The higher the social class of the parents, the farther ahead the young person plans his life
2) Young people from upward mobile families tend to continue climbing
3) Young men tend to plan further ahead than do young women
4) Young people from unhappy homes tend to have higher levels of aspiration than do young adults from satisfactory family backgrounds
5) Young people who identify closely with an admired adult tend to pattern themselves after that older person in their own life plans.

DEVELOPMENTAL TASKS OF YOUNG ADULTS

The developmental tasks of young adults in the United States are intertwined with the decisions that must be made concurrently along several related lines. Throughout his life as a child and teenager, the individual has lived within the expectancies of his age and grade. Now, upon his emergence from the norms of the age-grade system, he steps out into a life of his own, with his success or failure largely dependent upon the choices he makes as an individual. This very freedom is confusing, as Robert Havighurst so vividly points out:

Early adulthood seems . . . to be a period of storm and stress in America, and especially in the middle-class part of American society. The basic reason for this, when expressed in sociological terms, is that this is a relatively unorganized period in life which marks a transition from an age-graded to a social status-graded society. During childhood and adolescence one climbs the age ladder, getting new privileges and taking on new responsibilities with each step up the ladder. The ten-year-old has such and such privileges and such and such responsibilities, which enable him to look down on the eight-year-old, but also cause him to look up to the twelve-year-old. He climbs the age ladder, rung by rung, year by year, knowing that each step up gives him more prestige, along with new tasks and pleasures.

This simple age-grading stops in our culture somewhere around sixteen to twenty. It is like reaching the end of the ladder and stepping off onto a new, strange cloud-land with giants and witches to be circumvented and the goose that lays the golden eggs to be captured if only one can discover the know-how.

In the adult society prestige and power depend not so much on age as on skill and strength and wisdom, and family connections. Achieving the goals of life is not nearly so much a matter of waiting until one grows up to them as it was in the earlier years. There must be a strategy, based on an understanding of the new terrain, which can only be got by scouting around and getting the lay of the land for a few years. This is what young people do, and it often takes several years to learn how to get about efficiently and to go where one wants to go in the adult society in America.[1]

CHOOSING A VOCATION

In some cultures a young man is expected to follow in his father's footsteps and carry on the family business. In the United States this pattern tends to hold largely in the upper-class families, where wealth and holdings necessitate grooming the sons of the family to carry on the family traditions. Young people today face many more vocational possibilities than were formerly available. In 1870 there were but 338 vocations, in contrast to many thousands by the middle of the twentieth century (20,000 by 1940,[2] and 50,000 estimated more recently with rapid development since World War II in electronics, atomic fission, radar, television, plastics, medical and chemical advances etc.).[3]

Historically, a young woman groomed herself for marriage; all other interests were secondary. Today, a girl may be marriage-minded but

[1] Robert J. Havighurst, *Human Development and Education* (New York: Longmans, Green and Company, 1953), pp. 258–259.
[2] *Occupational Dictionary* (Washington, D. C.: U. S. Department of Labor, 1940).
[3] *Job Guide for Young Workers*, 1956–57 Edition (Washington, D. C.: Superintendent of Documents, 1956).

As more fields open up for women, girls face vocational choices that will serve them through the years both before marriage and after.

she believes in women seeking public offices,[1] and she may look forward to carrying some vocational interests both as an unmarried woman, and as a wife and mother. During the first year of marriage some 40 per cent of American wives work outside the home. In 1952, one-third of all families had two earners—the husband and the wife.[2] Marriage still holds first place in the future plans of the great majority of American girls, but many of them think realistically also in terms of developing vocational skills that will serve them well through the years both before marriage and after. As more and more fields open up for women workers, girls as well as boys face inevitable vocational choices.

[1] Harold Christensen and Marilyn M. Swihart, "Postgraduation Role Preferences of Senior Women in College," *Marriage and Family Living*, Vol. XVIII, No. 1, February 1956, pp. 54–55.

[2] Paul C. Glick, "The Life Cycle of the Family," *Marriage and Family Living*, Vol. XVII, No. 1, February 1955, p. 8.

Occupational decisions do not have to be made from among the many thousands of potential vocations. For any one young adult, the factors influencing his life plan tend to limit his fields of interest, and to influence the direction his life work will take. Yet within a given direction, there still is much that must be learned about specific vocations, and about one's individual aptitudes, interests, and preferences. Try-out experiences in part-time jobs, summer employment, and apprentice-like opportunities are helpful to many young people. Vocational guidance is available in many schools. Testing and counseling programs are designed to help young people find themselves in an occupational field suited to their personal abilities and social availability.

Parents who encourage their sons and daughters to explore various possibilities and to get the training needed for the chosen field greatly assist their young people to accomplish this developmental task. Attempting to force a young person into a field in which he or she is not personally interested often results in parental disappointment and failure of the young adult in an area in which he has little or no interest or ability.[1]

GETTING AN EDUCATION

The choice of a vocation determines in large measure the amount and the kind of education the young person must pursue. Conversely, the education the young person has obtained greatly influences his vocational opportunities. Tony, who drops out of high school to get "quick money" that will allow him to buy a car and entertain his girl, thereby limits his future possibilities for vocational choice and advancement. The economic advantage of an education is strikingly apparent in the relationship between the amount of education and the lifetime earnings of an American, as of 1956 (Table 20).

In dropping out of school, Tony, in the case above, is depriving himself and his family of the more than $100,000 that he might have earned if he had gone on through college. Of course, as we saw in Chapter Four, lower-class young people have less chance of finishing school and still less likelihood of graduating from college than do young people from

---

[1] Dr. Dean J. Plazak of Bethesda, Maryland reported to the 1956 meeting of the American Psychiatric Association in Chicago, that "A study of midshipmen discharged from the U. S. Naval Academy shows few wanted to go there in the first place, but came as a means of raising family prestige or because their father desired it." Reported in *Chicago Daily News*, May 1, 1956, p. 15.

TABLE 20. *Estimated "Life-Time" Income for Men by Amount of Education* [1]

Education	Life-Time Earnings
4th grade or less	$ 72,000
8th grade	116,000
12th grade	165,000
1–3 years of college	190,000
College graduate	268,000

SOURCE: Derived from 1950 Census of Population, Vol. IV, Special Reports, PE, No. 5B, Education, Table 12.

the higher-class levels. So, economic and vocational advantages and disadvantages tend to be "socially inherited," in the sense that they tend to pass from generation to generation. The mobile young person from a lower-class home may push on through school even though no one in his family ever graduated from high school before. In doing so, he greatly increases his vocational and economic future. Using the census figures of Table 20, we find his life earnings as a high school graduate come to $49,000 more than might have been expected had he dropped out of school at the eighth grade. This means that each year of high school is equivalent to $12,250 in cash earnings in the years ahead.

Getting an education is especially important today when there are relatively few nonskilled jobs, in comparison with the large number of highly skilled occupations requiring specialized training. A good general educational background is important not only for earning a living, but especially for living a life. The educated person who knows his way around in the physical and biological sciences, the humanities, and the social sciences, is at home in much more of the world than the relatively illiterate. Every citizen today should have enough orientation to know how to tackle a problem and how to think through a point.

The question of how much education a girl should have has been often discussed. The general consensus today is that education is important for a woman, as a worker, as a wife and mother, as a citizen, and as a person. The girl with an education has something to offer that assures her of a better job at more money than is generally available to the less well-educated woman. The statement "when you educate a

[1] From Paul C. Glick and Herman P. Miller, "Educational Level and Potential Income," *American Sociological Review,* Vol. 21, No. 3, June 1956, page 310.

woman, you educate a family" recognizes that the woman's cultural background becomes the foundation of her family. Whatever she has learned of music, the arts, literature, medicine, history, philosophy, and religion can become part of the children's day-to-day education in the home. As a citizen and as a person, education is quite as important for a woman as it is for a man. This is recognized by members of both generations today. A study of 1,100 college girls and 752 of their mothers found between 80 and 95 per cent of both groups feeling that a woman should have an education equal to her husband's.[1] Now, when so many men of college age leave school for military service, it is not unusual to find the woman the better educated of the two, both among courting couples and young married people.

Both schools and families face real challenges for helping boys and girls get an adequate education. Schools that gear their educational offerings to the needs and readiness of their students, that provide effective counseling services and social opportunities, that use testing programs that are not flagrantly class-biased, help the young person who might otherwise become discouraged and drop out to remain in school for as long as is feasible. Lyle M. Spencer lists four things that schools can do to help children from the lower classes continue their education, when he says,

Research studies and the experiences of school staffs who have tackled this problem suggest some of the most promising approaches:

1) *Help teachers understand class differences.*
   While 6 out of 10 pupils are from lower socio-economic groups, 90 per cent of their teachers have a middle-class orientation and tend to stress middle-class views about manners, ambition, and aggressiveness. . . .
2) *Recognize that IQ tests may be biased in favor of pupils from upper socio-economic groups.*
   No valid evidence has been produced to show that native intelligence varies according to social status, yet the average IQ of adolescents in the lowest socio-economic group is from 20 to 23 points below that of higher groups. . . .
3) *Eliminate stumbling blocks for lower-class pupils that exist in the school.*
   . . . Eliminate 'hidden tuition costs' and expensive school customs . . . broaden participation (of the students), and . . . modify factors in the cliques that are cruel to other pupils.

[1] Arlene Sheeley, Paul H. Landis, and Vernon Davies, *Marital and Family Adjustment in Rural and Urban Families of Two Generations* (Pullman, Washington: The State College of Washington, May 1949), Bulletin No. 506, pp. 6–7.

4) *Help pupils to understand our social status system.*

. . . Help all pupils by giving them a realistic idea of their opportunities in life, the statuses that go with them, and the "rules of the game" through which young people can preserve their socio-economic position or move to a higher status." [1]

Families encourage their sons and daughters to get an education when they express real interest in the student's school progress. Other family helps include (1) providing opportunities for the pupil's participation in both academic and extracurricular activities, (2) maintaining intellectual interests within the family, and (3) refraining from pressing the young person to premature work to support the family before his or her educational program has been completed. These things are easier for some families than for others (Chapter Four), but as education becomes generally more highly valued, more families want to make the effort.

SATISFYING MILITARY SERVICE REQUIREMENTS

Before a young fellow is out of his teens, he faces the possibility of military service. He may volunteer for service in order to "get it over with." He may wait until he is drafted, deferring it as long as the law allows. Official estimates in 1956 are that about 80 per cent of young men in the United States see military service before they are 26 years old. [2] It is possible that the percentage may decrease in the future.

A young man over 18 years of age may be deferred as 4-F (unqualified by some physical or mental defect). He may be deferred if he is in some essential industry. If he becomes a father before the draft gets to him, he has greatly increased his chances of avoiding service. As long as he remains in school, he is not as likely to be drafted. But if he is qualified, available, and not deferred as a student, father, or essential worker, the chances are that he will serve his hitch in service sometime early in his twenties.

Military service is a responsibility that thrusts itself upon a young

---

[1] Lyle M. Spencer, *Guidance Newsletter* (Chicago, Illinois: Science Research Associates, April 1953), pp. 1–2.

[2] "Our experience indicates that about four out of five of our young men who are not fathers, and who are otherwise physically and mentally qualified and available, can expect to enter military service before they reach age 26." (Admiral Arthur W. Radford, Chairman of the Joint Chiefs of Staff, in a recent speech, quoted in *U. S. News & World Report*, April 20, 1956, p. 55.)

Military service comes at a time when a young man is fitting himself for a vocation, completing his education, choosing a wife, and getting married.

man at the time when he is leaving home to establish a life of his own.[1] It comes at the time when he is working on the universal developmental tasks of fitting himself for his vocation, completing his education, becoming socially acceptable, choosing a wife, getting married, and settling down in a home of his own. Questions of the timing of military service, education, work, and marriage are difficult. Should the young man volunteer for service directly from high school and count on his veterans' benefits to help him complete his education when he has finished his

[1] Disruption of plans "ranks as concern number one affecting attitudes toward military service held by university students in the study": Edward Suchman, Robin Williams, Jr., and Rose Goldsen, "Student Reaction to Impending Military Service," *American Sociological Review*, Vol. 18, No. 3, June 1953, p. 302.

military service? Or should he get just as much education as he can before Uncle Sam catches up with him? Should he attempt to get a job and at least start his vocation before he goes into service, with the hope of establishing seniority on the job? Or, is it better to get his service behind him before becoming vocationally established? Will he be wise to get things settled with his girl and get married before he is pulled off into service? Or will it be more advisable to postpone marriage until he can really settle down in a home of his own? If he does marry before military service, will his wife try to follow him as far as she can? Or should she try to maintain a home base for them both until he is out and can join her in homemaking?

These are but a few of the many questions that come tumbling in upon both the young man and the girl who loves him as he reaches draft age. There is no single answer to any of these questions. One way that may be wise for one fellow, or couple, may not work out well for another. Each young man, each young woman, each young couple today must work out the solution that makes the most sense in their particular situation. That so many young adults accomplish this task so well is a credit to the generation of young adults today. At the same time, it is understandable that many fellows and girls are anxious, baffled, and be-wildered by the multitude of major decisions that must be made during this period. The impulsive, the impetuous, the hysterical fringe of the young adult population who rush into some premature "solution" (only to find themselves in one of the traps for the unwary) are the problematic minority.

There are many community, church, school, and family aids to young men and women facing the likelihood of military service. Today, more than ever before, young people need opportunities to think through, under qualified leadership, the many paths that stretch ahead for them, of which military service is but one. Boys need some preparation for what to expect in service, what the alternatives are, and how to choose the time that will be best for each of the demands and responsibilities they face as young adult males. Girls in their teens and early twenties are ready for discussion of what it means to be a woman, whom to marry, and when and what their role is in the many months and miles of separation from lover or husband that military service imposes. To-gether the sexes face the developmental tasks of dating, courtship, marriage and family establishment, in the midst of a military economy, as they enter the launching years. The decisions about military service are made with vocational, educational, social, marital, familial and personal values all crowding in for multifocused attention.

BECOMING MARRIAGEABLE

Today's young people have full responsibility for finding a place for themselves among their peers, making friends, getting dates, and becoming the kind of marriageable young men or women who can win and hold a mate. This is not an easy task. Many young women who are of good marriage potential miss out because of shyness, social ineptness, and inability to get along comfortably with eligible young men. Some of our most able young men lose themselves so completely in their vocational interests that they miss out on normal social contacts with members of the other sex. A man may be a good engineer or an outstanding physician, but if he has not learned to get along pleasantly with women and to find deep satisfaction in warm friendships with one or more especially compatible women, he may be easy prey for some unscrupulous female when the time comes for him to marry. There are many instances of a young man of outstanding ability hurriedly plunging into marriage with some relatively inferior woman largely because he has not developed the social, emotional, domestic sides of his personality.

Leonard S. is a case in point. He is a brilliant scientist. But in social affairs he feels lost. He is embarrassed at meeting new people. He is shy and uncomfortable with women generally. His conversational abilities are limited to the field of his specialty and superficial comments about the weather. He is now nearly twenty-seven, has never gone seriously with a girl, doesn't know how to dance, and has no contacts with mixed groups of young adults his own age. Several weeks ago, a girl behind the salad counter at the corner cafeteria began to flirt with him. At first he blushed and stammered some nonsensical reply. She told him she thought he was "real sweet," and on her day off brought her dinner out to eat with him. Things moved fast from then on, and they are to be married next Saturday. Leonard's family is shocked at his marrying a lower-class girl who never went beyond sixth grade. Leonard has questions himself about what he is getting into. The girl's family is happy about the financial security she will acquire by the marriage, but openly ridicules Leonard as a "brain." But, at the moment, Leonard is powerless to stop the affair.

Surely there are many factors contributing to such a situation as Leonard faces. The obvious ones are social inexperience and lack of competency with others in personal and social relationships. Failures in accomplishing these developmental tasks become problems for many teenagers and young adults. Such continuing failures seriously block or distort the processes that lead to marriage.

Getting the feeling of belonging to one's own generation is a major developmental task of the second decade of life. The young person who feels that he or she is personally attractive and socially acceptable is able to make the decisions about occupation, education, military service and the other elements of life-planning without insistent dreams of friendship and popularity distorting his vision. The young man or woman who has attained some measure of success in social situations is able to move among members of both sexes, to make and keep friends, to date and go steady, to choose a mate wisely and become engaged through the process of association that leads to marriage. Failures in this developmental sequence of social acceptance appear prominently in nationwide surveys of youth problems (Table 21).

TABLE 21. *Problems with People Reported by Youth from a Nationwide Sample* [1]

60% want to make new friends
54% want people to like them better
42% wish they were more popular
36% want to develop more self-confidence
33% wish they could carry on a pleasant conversation
32% want to learn to dance
25% say they feel ill at ease at social affairs
24% feel they need to learn to be good listeners
23% don't know how to act toward people they dislike
23% say they can't live up to the ideals that are set for them
21% want to feel important to society or their own group

One of the more thoughtful of the young people reporting in the above quoted survey observes,

Perhaps one of the greatest problems to the majority of teenagers is that feeling of not belonging. How that feeling gets started is hard to tell, but once imbedded in one's mind, it is hard to erase.[2]

[1] H. H. Remmers and C. G. Hackett, *What Are Your Problems?* (Chicago: Science Research Associates, 1951), pp. 29–30.

[2] H. H. Remmers and Lyle M. Spencer, "*All Young People Have Problems,*" *National Education Association Journal,* March, 1950, p. 182.

There is some evidence in this and other studies that social poise and acceptance tend to increase with age, but this is not the case for all young people, nor in all areas. One analysis of 25,000 questions asked by both high school and college men and women, found two questions occurring more frequently than any others: (1) How do you get a date? and (2) What do you do with a date when you get it? [1] Such expressed concerns of young people bring us to the old question of what do boys and girls, men and women, expect of one another in their associations with each other on dates.

A study of 8,000 teenage students living throughout the United States revealed two different patterns, assigned separately to the two sexes, and accepted by each sex as problems.

Males tended to be more self critical than females on such items as being vulgar in speech and action, wanting too much necking and petting, withholding compliments, being careless in dress and manners, shunning date's friends and folks, being overmoney-minded, and being disrespectful of the other sex. . . .

In contrast, females tended to be more self-critical than males on such items as being easily angered and hurt, being shy and self-conscious, being too possessive, being too serious, being emotionally cold, being flighty and unsettled, and acting childish or silly. . . .

With few exceptions, the traits on which each sex exceeded the other in self-criticism are the very traits which characterize the patterns of the respective sexes . . .[2]

These same high school students generally agreed in rating items they considered important in making or accepting a date. The seven items rated highest, in order of rank were: (1) Is physically and mentally fit, (2) Is dependable, can be trusted, (3) Takes pride in personal appearance and manners, (4) Is clean in speech and action, (5) Has pleasant disposition and sense of humor, (6) Is considerate of me and others, (7) Acts own age, is not childish.[3]

A study on the University of Michigan campus in 1953 indicates that college men and women look primarily for the kind of mature, socially acceptable person who is a good companion (Table 22).

[1] Evelyn Millis Duvall, *Facts of Life and Love for Teenagers* (New York: Association Press, Revised edition, 1956), p. v.

[2] Harold T. Christensen, "Dating Behavior as Evaluated by High School Students," *The American Journal of Sociology*, Vol. LVII, No. 6, May 1952, p. 583, copyright 1952, University of Chicago.

[3] *Ibid.* p. 580.

TABLE 22. *Significant Differences Between Percentage of Students Preferring Specified Characteristics in Casual and Serious Dating Partners for All Students, for Men Students and for Women Students* [1]

Items	Per cent of Respondents Choosing Item Personal Preferences	
	CASUAL DATES	SERIOUS DATES
A. *Discriminations Made by Both Sexes*		
1. Is emotionally mature	84.2	100.0
2. Is dependable	87.8	99.3
3. Is a well-rounded person	84.6	98.5
4. Is affectionate	69.6	97.6
5. Is a good listener	88.3	97.4
6. Gets along with friends of own sex	80.6	96.4
7. Is ambitious and energetic	65.3	84.7
8. Person has my family's approval	24.5	72.1
9. Knows how to dance well	52.6	31.9
B. *Discriminations Made by Men Students*		
10. Has good sense, is intelligent	88.4	100.0
11. Is an intelligent conversationalist	85.3	100.0
12. Is honest, straightforward	80.0	96.8
13. Is willing to join a group	82.1	93.7
14. Has polished manners	66.3	81.1
15. Doesn't have a reputation for petting	38.9	74.7
16. Doesn't have a reputation for necking	34.7	67.4
17. Dates popular students only	9.5	3.2
C. *Discriminations Made by Women Students*		
18. Is willing to neck on occasion	34.3	67.7
19. Is willing to pet on occasion	8.2	32.1
20. Is good looking, attractive	61.2	45.5
21. Goes to popular places	38.8	22.6

The researcher observes from these data,

The over-all impression given . . . is one of increasing rapprochement between the sexes as they begin to get serious with one another. Moreover, this rapprochement centers about themes of emotional maturity, intelligence, and affectionateness which appear conducive to marital adjustment.[2]

[1] Robert O. Blood, Jr., "Uniformities and Diversities in Campus Dating Preferences," *Marriage and Family Living*, Vol. XVIII, No. 1, February 1956, p. 43.
[2] *Ibid.*, p. 44.

Success in dating and in becoming marriageable seem to be dependent upon a number of factors. There is evidence that such success is closely related to personal and family background. One study finds that:

The seniors not dating presented a more negative, less wholesome picture in family relationships, feeling of self-regard, and social relations than did the other seniors. . . .

. . . A relatively large number of young people had worried during childhood about their physical characteristics, development and appearance. These students had had and were still having difficulty in their relations with others because of shyness and sensitivity . . .

The most significant finding with respect to their *social relationships* was the relatively large number of young people who, by their senior year in high school, were having few social contacts, especially with the other sex.[1]

Opportunities for gaining social experience as well as for dating, appear to be related to the social class of the young person's family (Chapter Four). In general, a larger percentage of young people in the higher social classes date and they date more frequently and with more persons than do boys and girls from the lower socio-economic groups.[2]

Success in dating and in gaining social experience tends to be cumulative. The more dating is done, the smoother it becomes. Studies of the frequency of dating, among both high school and college students, indicate that from the ages of sixteen to twenty-one years, the frequency of dating increases with age; furthermore, the earlier university students had begun to date in their teens, the more frequently they dated in college.[3]

Frequency of dating is significantly related to one's dating status. Those who are playing the field have fewer dates than do those who are going steady or are engaged. Among college students the findings of one study are:

Among the men those going steady in each age classification date around twice as frequently as those playing the field. Among the women . . . those going steady or engaged date much more frequently than those playing the

[1] Opal Powell Wolford, "How Early Background Affects Dating Behavior," *Journal of Home Economics,* Vol. 40, No. 9, November 1948, pp. 505, 506.

[2] A. B. Hollingshead, *Elmtown's Youth* (New York: John Wiley and Sons, Inc., 1949), pp. 229–230.

[3] Samuel H. Lowrie, "Factors Involved in the Frequency of Dating," *Marriage and Family Living,* Vol. XVIII, No. 1, February 1956, pp. 49–51.

field. These differences are statistically highly significant for each sex and for all age levels, except eighteen among the women.[1]

Table 23 shows data on dating frequency for both sexes, ages 18 through 21, by dating status among university students.

TABLE 23. *Mean Number of Dates Per Week by Sex, Age, and Dating Status of University Students Dating the Previous Month* [2]

| Age | MEN | | | | | WOMEN | | | | |
| | Playing Field | | Going Steady | | | Playing Field | | Going Steady | | |
	Mean	No. of Students	Mean	No. of Students	Critical Ratio *	Mean	No. of Students	Mean	No. of Students	Critical Ratio *
18	1.2	110	2.5	39	4.6	2.0	119	2.5	68	1.9
19	1.5	165	2.8	90	8.3	2.2	129	2.9	100	3.5
20	1.7	112	3.5	77	8.3	2.2	105	3.6	69	6.0
21	1.8	91	3.2	55	5.5	1.9	62	3.6	66	6.8
Total	1.5	478	3.0	261	—	2.1	415	3.1	303	—

° A critical ratio of 3.5 or over is considered statistically significant, that is, the relationship between the two variables is such that it can not be attributed to chance.

Going steady is usually defined as dating exclusively one person with whom there are generally recognized expectations, loyalties, and some mutual identification.[3] It has arisen in recent years, with the coming of large, heterogeneous high school populations and complex urban communities, for what seem to be several interrelated reasons, in the words of young people themselves:

1) "If you go steady, you are more sure of a date when you want one." (*Date insurance.*) [4] Table 23 shows clearly that those university students who go steady have significantly more dates than those who play the field. Among high school students a frequent observation is, "If you go at all, you have to go steady."

2) "You aren't anybody in our school if you don't go steady." (*Group acceptance.*) High school students report that going steady is important for status reasons, and that "going steady was the thing to do in my high school." [5]

[1] *Ibid.* pp. 48–49.
[2] *Ibid.*, p. 49.
[3] Robert D. Herman, "The 'Going Steady' Complex: A Re-Examination," *Marriage and Family Living*, Vol. XVII, No. 1, February 1955, pp. 36–37.
[4] Ruth Connor and Edith Flinn Hall, "The Dating Behavior of College Freshmen and Sophomores," *Journal of Home Economics*, Vol. 44, No. 4, April 1952, p. 280.
[5] Robert D. Herman, *op. cit.*, p. 39.

3) "Be seen twice with the same person, and you are going steady—the crowd sees to that." (*Social pressure.*) If John dates Mary a couple of times over the weekend, by Monday they are going steady whether they have decided to or not, for by then their friends line up behind them as a pair and expect them to go steady from then on.[1] Such social pressure is found in many high school, community and campus situations.

4) "Going steady is a lot easier and safer than dating unknowns." (*Personal security.*) A girl knows what her steady boy friend will expect of her on a date, she is secure with him as she can not be with a strange boy whom she may or may not be able to manage. A boy is secure knowing his steady girl expects him, and finds it easier and cheaper to go steady than to play the field. There is probably less exploitation in going steady than in random dating, as Herman observes.[2]

5) "We would rather go steady than to date anyone else available." (*Mutual preference.*) The two persons prefer each other to any other possibilities on the scene. They may be fond of each other, and so prefer associating with one another than with other more casual dating partners.

6) "When you go steady, you learn to adjust to one person, and to become more mature in your understanding of each other." (*Mature association.*) In this sense, going steady is good preparation for marriage based upon companionship and mutual understanding.

Adults and many young people themselves see some of the problems related to going steady. In general, these tend to be: (1) going steady limits social contacts, (2) going steady interferes with work responsibilities and takes up too much time, (3) going steady often brings more emotional and sexual involvement than the two people are ready for, and (4) it is hard to get out of going steady after both names have been coupled together for a long time. Young people tend to agree that it is not wise to go steady too soon before the two people have had some general experience with members of the other sex. They recognize generally that going steady is not wise if the two people are to be separated for a considerable period of time. Then their social life will be severely curtailed if they try "to be true to each other" and yet they are not close enough to participate socially as a couple. College men and women are particularly aware of the importance of breaking off going steady when the two people have outgrown each other. The solu-

[1] Evelyn Millis Duvall, *Facts of Life and Love for Teenagers* (New York: Association Press, revised 1956), p. 347.
[2] Robert D. Herman, *op. cit.*, p. 40.

tion of the dilemna of becoming seriously involved with a steady who will not be a suitable mate is difficult to work through comfortably, posing a serious problem in present-day patterns in going steady.

The most favorable situations for those who want to become more marriageable are found in the families, in the schools and colleges, in the community programs that foster wholesome contact between the sexes in a wide variety of interests and activities. The responsibility is upon the young man or woman, to develop the social skills, and to introduce oneself into the situations where mingling with congenial persons is increasingly comfortable and competent. For those young adults who have reached marriage age without accomplishing this developmental task, there are at least two types of supportive services that might be helpful. The first is the introduction service that offers help, for a small charge, to those desiring friendship or marriage.[1] The second is the group counseling or educational programs designed to help socially inept young men and women develop the specific skills, social graces, and personal adequacies needed to become more marriageable. Many churches, YMCA's, YWCA's, and other community agencies sponsor "Charm Schools," classes in "Personality Development," and other programs designed particularly to assist the slow-developing young adult to become more socially adequate. The American Institute of Family Relations in Los Angeles has a well established service called a *Human Relations Program* that is widely publicized as a "How to Be Marriageable" course.[2] The program is two-fold: individual testing and counseling on the personality potentials and problems; and group discussion under the leadership of a staff member. Health, grooming, speech, posture, leisure-time pursuits, job-satisfaction, living conditions, and marriage ideals and dreams all come into the program. The time may come when such programs of remedial socialization are widespread, just as programs in remedial reading, remedial speech, and the like are now generally available.

In summarizing this section, we recognize the relevancy of the concept of the "teachable moment" (Chapter Five) in the process of becoming marriageable. If the person as a young teenager learns to dance and to

---

[1] Ernest W. Burgess and Harvey J. Locke, *The Family: From Institution to Companionship* (New York: American Book Company, 1953), pp. 354–362.

[2] Norma Lee Browning, "Want to Find a Husband?" *Chicago Tribune Magazine,* October 9, 1955, p. 51; and the series of articles on "How to Be Marriageable" that appeared in the *Ladies Home Journal,* through the Spring of 1954.

date and to associate with his peer group acceptably, while the others are working on these same tasks, he gets group support in his efforts. When he is awkward the others are too, so the learning process is tolerable. But if, for some reason, he or she has been delayed in this particular task, it will be more difficult later on when it must be done in relative solitude, carrying the added burden of feelings of personal inadequacy and social isolation (Chapter Eleven). Social success in the past facilitates success in present efforts. The process of becoming marriageable is one that typically goes on through the entire second decade, and some of the third decade of life for many, many persons.

LEARNING TO APPRAISE AND TO EXPRESS LOVE FEELINGS APPROPRIATELY

Learning to love is a lifetime achievement. It begins in infancy, it flowers in the teens and twenties, bears fruit in the rich full years of childbearing and rearing, and colors and warms life throughout the rest of life. At no stage of life is it more difficult to assay and to express responsibly than in the teen and young adult years when it is confused and intertwined with maturing sex drives.

In a culture that allows freedom of access between the sexes from an early age, and establishes marriage on the basis of being in love, it is not surprising to find young people repeatedly asking three questions about love and its expression: (1) What is love? (2) How can you tell when you are really in love (enough to build a marriage on)? and (3) How far is it wise to go in physical expression of love and sex interests before marriage? Each of these questions is complex. There are no completely satisfying or well-substantiated answers to any of these questions. Yet, when so many young men and women want to base their behavior upon some understanding of what is involved, it behooves us to rally resources that are available for their use.

What is love? Love is the most powerful force known to man. It is indeed "the greatest thing in the world." It is also the most mysterious, and the hardest to describe. In the outline below we see some outstanding attempts at definition or description made by men and women of various orientations through the years:

The Apostle Paul   Love is patient and kind; love is not jealous or boastful; it is not arrogant or rude. Love does not insist on its own way; it is not irritable or resentful; it does not rejoice at wrong, but rejoices in the right. Love bears all things, believes all things, hopes all things, endures all things.

I CORINTHIANS, 13:4–7

The poetess Elizabeth Barrett Browning

How do I love thee? Let me count the ways.
I love thee to the depth and breadth and height
My soul can reach, when feeling out of sight
For the ends of Being and ideal Grace.
I love thee to the level of every day's
Most quiet need, by sun and candlelight.
I love thee freely, as men strive for Right;
I love thee purely, as they turn from praise.
I love thee with the passion put to use
In my old griefs, and with my childhood's faith.
I love thee with a love I seemed to lose
With my lost saints,—I love thee with the breath,
Smiles, tears, of all my life!—and, if God choose,
I shall but love thee better after death.[1]

The anthropologist Ashley Montagu

To love and to be loved is as necessary to the organism as the breathing of air. Insofar as the organism fails in loving, it fails in living, for to live and love is, for a human being, the equivalent of healthy living. To live as if to live and love were one is not simply an ideal to be achieved, but a potentiality to be realized, a destiny to be fulfilled.[2]

The human relations professor F. Alexander Magoun

Love is the passionate and abiding desire on the part of two or more people to produce together the conditions under which each can be and spontaneously express his real self; to produce together the intellectual soil and an emotional climate in which each can flourish, far superior to what either could achieve alone. . . .

Love is concerned with the realities of life; not with ideas about romantic idealism which cannot be embodied in life. Love sees faults as well as virtues. Love knows and unhesitatingly accepts the fact that no one is perfect. . . .

Love is self-discovery and self-fulfillment through healthy growth with and for the other person.[3]

The biologist and philosopher Julian Huxley

As a biologist, but also as a human being, I want to affirm the unique importance of love in life—an affirmation badly needed in a tormented age like ours, where vio-

[1] "How Do I Love Thee?" from the Standard Book of British and American Verse (Garden City, New York: The Garden City Publishing Co., 1932), pp. 431–432.

[2] Ashley Montagu, ed., The Meaning of Love (New York: The Julian Press, Inc., 1953), p. 19.

[3] F. Alexander Magoun, Love and Marriage (New York: Harper & Brothers, 1948), pp. 4, 16, 17.

lence and disillusion have joined forces with undigested technological advance to produce an atmosphere of cynicism and crude materialism. . . .

Personal love is indispensable both for the continuation of the species, and for the full development of the individual. Love is part of personal education; through love, the self learns to grow. . . . Love is a positive emotion, an enlargement of life; it leads on toward greater fulfillment and counteracts human hate and destructive impulses.[1]

The human development educator Daniel A. Prescott

Love involves more or less empathy with the loved one. . . . One who loves is deeply concerned for the welfare, happiness, and development of the loved one. . . . One who loves finds pleasure in making his resources available to the loved one . . . the loving person seeks a maximum of participation in the activities that contribute to the welfare, happiness, and development of the loved one. . . . Love is most readily and usually achieved within the family circle but can be extended to include many other individuals. . . . The good effects of love are not limited to the loved one but promote the happiness and further development of the loving one as well. . . . Love is not rooted primarily in sexual dynamics or hormonal drives, although it may well have large erotic components.[2]

The psychologist and philosopher Harry A. Overstreet

The love of a person implies, not the possession of that person, but the affirmation of that person. It means granting him, gladly, the full right to his unique humanhood. One does not truly love a person and yet seek to enslave him—by law or by bonds of dependence and possessiveness.

Whenever we experience a genuine love, we are moved by this transforming experience toward a capacity for good will.[3]

The psychiatrist Smiley Blanton, M.D.

. . . It is in the joyful union of a man with a woman that the jangled forces of life fall at last into harmony. Here, in the eternal longing of one to join with the other, we may discern an infinite wisdom distilled from billions of years of patient evolution. Here lies the primordial pattern of all our striving and all our bliss. It is the secret spring that

[1] Julian Huxley, "All about Love," *Look*, Vol. 19, No. 14, July 12, 1955, p. 29.
[2] Daniel A. Prescott, "Role of Love in Human Development," *Journal of Home Economics*, Vol. 44, No. 3, March 1952, pp. 174–175.
[3] Harry A. Overstreet, *The Mature Mind* (New York, W. W. Norton and Co., 1949), p. 103.

animates our deepest desires and shapes our loftiest dreams. It generates the restless tension, the driving energy, that ever moves us to aspire and to achieve. From its profound yearning comes all creation, whether of the body or spirit. Man and woman, united in loving endeavor, truly encompass the sum and substance of human life.[1]

The sociologist Clifford Kirkpatrick

Every human is born into a culture which provides certain viewpoints and expectations in regard to love. There may be emphasis upon free sex expression, property values, kinship ties, love security, love adventure, aggression and tenderness. The present-day American culture is sex-repressive but does place a high value upon romance and defines "falling in love" as the basis for marriage. The romantic complex nurtured in the medieval courts of love has been powerfully strengthened by movies, romance magazines, popular music and the example of others. Young persons of dating age fully expect that sooner or later they will be caught in the magic spell of love and experience the pangs and delights which seem inevitable. . . .[2]

By the time a young person reaches the late teens and twenties he or she is experienced in loving. One of the most important things he or she has learned within the family through the years of childhood and adolescence is to learn to love.

Love does not simply spring forth some moonlight night without warning. We do not *fall* in love. We *learn* to love through a lifetime of experience in loving. By the time boy meets girl, a great deal has happened to both of them to make them ready for their interest in each other. In fact, by that time they both are old hands at loving, in many ways. Each has grown up through the phases of emotional maturity to the place where he and she are capable of loving and being loved. In a real sense we *grow* into love, both individually and as couples.[3]

If, through the years of growing up within the family, the young adult has learned how to love and be loved, he or she is ready for the urgent developmental tasks of appraising love feelings in terms of readiness for marriage. If there has been deprivation or distortion of love

[1] Smiley Blanton, M.D., "Love or Perish," *Woman's Home Companion,* Jan. 1956, p. 70, copyright, 1956, The Crowell-Collier Publishing Co.
[2] Clifford Kirpatrick, *The Family as Process and Institution* (New York: The Ronald Press Co., 1955), pp. 272–273.
[3] Evelyn Millis Duvall, *Facts of Life and Love for Teenagers* (New York: Association Press, Revised Edition, 1956), p. 257.

through the years of growing up, it may be exceedingly difficult to achieve and gauge the level of mature love that is needed as a foundation for a successful marriage.

The young person often needs a functional answer to the urgent question, "Is this *it?*" If the marriage is to be based upon love, it becomes imperative to know whether the feeling one has toward a particular person is "the real thing," especially when love comes and goes, as apparently is quite usual. One study of 896 love affairs of college men and women, found that 644 of them (71.8 per cent) had been broken off.[1]

Another study of 500 college girls found half the students reporting that they had had five to seven or more infatuations between the ages of 12 and 18.[2] Such multiple experiences are confusing and give rise to the question of the differences between infatuation and "real love." One convenient device used by college women themselves is to call past loves "infatuations," and to reserve the designation "love" for any present involvement.[3] More helpful may be the distinctions between infatuation and love that may be made from the findings of contemporary studies, a few of which are summarized in Table 24.

Opportunities for discussion, individual and group counseling, education for marriage, premarital conferences, and confidential relationships with trusted adults in the family, the community, the church, and in schools and colleges, prove helpful to many young adults who are at the point of making personal decisions on the basis of the mutuality and potential permanence of their love feelings. High school and college teachers report that it is not unusual for some young people to break off unpromising affairs during and after completion of a course in Preparation for Marriage.[4] This may be a measure of the effectiveness of the educational program in being of real and practical help. The students otherwise might have found themselves trapped in too impulsive, immature, or unsuitable marriages. Parents who have maintained effective two-

---

[1] Clifford Kirkpatrick and Theodore Caplow, "Emotional Trends in the Courtship Experience of College Students as Expressed by Graphs with Some Observations on Methodological Implications," *American Sociological Review*, Vol. X, No. 5, October 1945, pp. 619–629.

[2] Albert Ellis, " A Study of Human Love Relationships," *The Journal of Genetic Psychology*, Vol. 75, 1949, p. 64.

[3] *Ibid.*, p. 69.

[4] Personal communications.

TABLE 24. *Differences between Love and Infatuation as Revealed in Contemporary Research Studies* [1]

Love	Infatuation
1. Tends to occur first in late teens and in the twenties *	1. Tends to be more frequent among young adolescents and children under teen age *
2. Attachment simultaneously to two or more tends not to be frequent *	2. Simultaneous attachments to two or more tends to be frequent *
3. Most cases last over a long period of time *	3. Tends to last but a short time (only a few weeks in most cases) *
4. More slowly develops again after a love affair has ended *	4. More quickly reoccurs soon after a given involvement has ended *
5. Often used to refer to present affair *	5. Is often the term applied to past attachments *
6. Object of affection is more likely a suitable person †	6. Tends to focus more frequently on unsuitable person †
7. Parents tend to approve †	7. Parents more often disapprove †
8. Broadly involves entire personality †	8. Narrowly focused on a few traits; mostly physical thrill †
9. Brings new energy and ambition, and more interest in life ‡	9. Less frequently accompanied by ambition and wide interests ‡
10. Associated with feelings of self-confidence, trust and security ‡	10. Feelings of guilt, insecurity, and frustration are frequent §
11. Accompanied by kindlier feelings toward other people generally ‡	11. Tends to be self-centered and restricted §
12. Joy in many common interests and an ongoing sense of being alive when together precludes boredom §	12. Boredom is frequent when there is no sexual excitement or social amusement §
13. Relationship changes and grows with ongoing association, developing interests, and deepening feelings §	13. Little change in the relationship with the passing of time §
14. Accompanied by willingness to face reality and to tackle problems realistically ¶	14. Problems and barriers are often disregarded; idealization may have little regard for reality ¶

* Albert Ellis, "A Study of Human Love Relationships," *Journal Genetic Psychology* (1949), No. 75, pp. 61–71.
† Paul Popenoe, "Infatuation and Its Treatment," *Family Life* (March 1949), IX, No. 3, pp. 1–2.
‡ Albert Ellis, "A Study of the Love Emotions of American College Girls," *International Journal of Sexology* (August, 1949), pp. 1–6.
§ Joe McCarthy, "How Do You Know You're in Love?" *McCall's Magazine*, Reprint, pp. 26–27, 88–90.
¶ Stephen Laycock, Director of Mental Hygiene, Canada (informal communication).

way, open, non-judgmental communication with their growing children may be of special help as the young people work through their entangling alliances as best they can.

[1] Evelyn Millis Duvall and Reuben Hill, *When You Marry* (Boston: D. C. Heath Company, Revised Edition, 1953), pp. 40–41, quoted with permission.

Whether a love affair goes on into marriage or breaks off after a few dates, there still remains the question of the degree of expression of affection between the two lovers. How much intimacy is appropriate to various situations and relationships? How far is it wise to go before marriage? These are two questions especially pertinent today. It is generally agreed that two lovers need to express their affection for each other, not only for their emotional well-being and development, but as good preparation for marriage. There is general recognition too that there is a progression of intimacy through the process of dating, going steady, being engaged, and getting married. Holding hands, kissing goodnight, and the lighter forms of contact are typical early in the relationship. As the involvement increases there is commensurate development of intimacy patterns through what young people themselves generally recognize as "necking," "light petting," "heavy petting," and "going all the way." At what point an unmarried couple stops depends upon a number of factors.

According to one research study of two university populations, "there is a striking tendency for females to be less tolerant than males with respect to petting to climax, premarital sex intercourse, intercourse with prostitutes, and extramarital sex intercourse." [1] The influence of social class is seen in a study within another state university student group:

> The marked tendency of males to descend the social ladder for dating companions seems to be motivated primarily by a desire to find willing sexual partners. [2]

Similar findings are reported from other studies, indicating that girls from the lower classes are more willing and available sexual partners than those from higher educational and social levels. [3] Boys, too, show striking differences in premarital sex experience by social class as indicated by level of education achieved. Studying the percentage of total sex outlet in intercourse with companions among 16–20 year old boys,

[1] Clifford Kirkpatrick, Sheldon Stryker, and Philip Buell, "Attitudes towards Male Sex Behavior," *American Sociological Review*, Vol. 17, No. 5, October 1952, p. 586.
[2] Winston H. Ehrmann, "Influence of Comparative Social Class of Companion upon Premarital Heterosexual Behavior," *Marriage and Family Living*, Vol. XVII, No. 1, February, 1955, p. 52.
[3] August B. Hollingshead, *Elmtown's Youth* (New York: John Wiley and Sons, 1949), pp. 232, 240; and Alfred C. Kinsey *et al.*, *Sexual Behavior in the Human Female* (Philadelphia: W. B. Saunders Company, 1953), p. 78.

Kinsey found the highest percentage of sex intercourse among the least well-educated: 50.62 per cent among males with less than eighth grade education, 39.49 per cent among males with high school education, and 9.13 per cent among males with some education beyond high school.[1]

Other factors related to premarital sex experience are gleaned from a study of premarital pregnancies in which higher frequencies were found, (1) during the depression years when marriage was more difficult, (2) among people who married young, (3) among couples who were married in a civil or secular ceremony, and (4) for those who were classified occupationally as laborers.[2]

The moral, as well as the emotional and psychological aspects of premarital sex behavior have been widely discussed.[3] A sociological exploration of the factors that distinguished happily married from divorced couples found, "A significantly larger per cent of divorced than happily married men reported premarital intercourse." [4] Another student of the question suggests that the romantic ideal and permissiveness in sexual practice before marriage may be incompatible, when he says,

When a couple chooses to "go all the way," it should be prepared for the possibility that the romantic bubble may collapse in the process.[5]

He cites loss of the sense of mystery, and of the image of perfection, as well as the waning of interest in the other when the two have "gone the limit," as factors that may start one or both members of the pair to wondering if they were really meant for each other after all, with the possible outcome of a broken love affair and a search for a new partner.

The individual young man or woman faces the question of premarital sexual behavior not so much in terms of the findings of studies as in terms of conceptions of self. The young person who sees himself or

[1] Alfred C. Kinsey et al., Sexual Behavior in the Human Male (Philadelphia: W. B. Saunders Company, 1948), p. 378.

[2] Harold T. Christensen, "Studies in Child Spacing: I—Premarital Pregnancy as Measured by the Spacing of the First Birth from Marriage," American Sociological Review, Vol. 18, No. 1, February 1953, p. 52.

[3] Sylvanus M. Duvall, Men, Women, and Morals (New York: Association Press, 1952), Chapter 9, "The Morality of Fornication;" and Bibliography, pp. 319–330.

[4] Harvey J. Locke, Predicting Adjustment in Marriage (New York: Henry Holt and Company, 1951), p. 133.

[5] Robert O. Blood, "Romance and Premarital Intercourse—Incompatibles?" Marriage and Family Living, Vol. XIV, No. 2, May 1952, p. 108.

herself as a person with a future, who has long-term professional and personal goals has a basis for conforming to traditional codes of premarital chastity; while the individual whose past has been bleak, whose future seems to offer little, and who tends to see himself as a creature of impulse feels there is nothing much worth waiting for. Success in the developmental tasks of building an adequate self-concept and meaningful philosophy of life through the years of childhood and adolescence in the family contributes to success in this task of learning to express responsibly the love and sex feelings of young adulthood.

CHOOSING A MARRIAGE PARTNER

Three factors are found to play a part in choosing a life partner: propinquity, homogamy, and complementarity. Persons of both sexes tend to marry those who live and work near them. Residential propinquity is significantly related to mate selection in both urban and rural populations, in various regions and among the several racial groups. Studies of marriages in Philadelphia, Pennsylvania, and in New Haven, Connecticut, in the thirties, both found more than half of the couples living within twenty blocks of each other at the time of their marriage.[1] In a later study in New Haven, one of the original researchers discovered an even higher percentage (an increase of 18.4 per cent) of marriages among persons residing within an area of twenty blocks.[2] Studies in rural counties in Michigan and Minnesota turned up 58 per cent and from 58 to 70 per cent of the couples living in the same county respectively.[3]

A recent study of both Negro and white marriages in Nashville, Tennessee, finds that residential propinquity operates significantly more frequently among the colored than among the white populations (79.6 per cent of the Negroes, as compared with 46.6 per cent of the white

[1] James H. S. Bossard, "Residential Propinquity as a Factor in Marriage Selection," *American Journal of Sociology*, Vol. 38, 1932–33, pp. 219–224; and Maurice R. Davie and Ruby Jo Reeves, "Propinquity of Residence Before Marriage," *American Journal of Sociology*, Vol. 44, 1938–1939, pp. 510–517.

[2] Ruby Jo Reeves Kennedy, "Premarital Residential Propinquity and Ethnic Endogamy," *American Journal of Sociology*, Vol. 48, 1942–1943, pp. 580–584.

[3] Howard Y. McClusky and Alvin Zander, "Residential Propinquity and Marriage in Branch County Michigan," *Social Forces*, Vol. 19, 1940, pp. 79–81; and Donald Mitchell, "Residential Propinquity and Marriage in Carver and Scott Counties, Minnesota," *Social Forces*, Vol. 20, 1941, pp. 256–259.

couples living within a twenty block radius).[1] Several factors possibly related to the high propinquity tendencies are suggested: (1) segregation, (2) neighborhood organization, and (3) neighborhood self-sufficiency (schools, churches, shopping centers, etc.).[2]

Homogamy, the tendency of marriage partners to have similar characteristics, has been shown in scores of studies of many characteristics, in thousands of couples, by hundreds of social scientists through recent decades.[3] Homogamy is especially evident in tendencies to marry within the same group, as Hollingshead has pointed out in his study of all marriages in New Haven during 1948:

> The data presented demonstrate that American culture, as it is reflected in the behavior of newly married couples in New Haven, places very definite restrictions on whom an individual may or may not marry. The racial mores were found to be the most explicit on this point. They divided the community into two pools of marriage mates and an individual fished for a mate only in his own racial pool. Religion divided the white race into three smaller pools. Persons in the Jewish pool in 97.1 per cent of the cases married within their own group; the percentage was 93.8 for Catholics and 74.4 for Protestants . . . The ethnic origin of a person's family placed further restrictions on his marital choice. In addition, class position and education stratified the three religious pools into areas where an individual was most likely to find a mate. . . . In a highly significant number of cases the person who marries is very similar culturally to one's self.[4]

Neither propinquity nor homogamy tell us how mates are chosen within a pool of eligibles. To explore the theory of complementary needs as a factor in the dynamics of individual choice, Winch and others have conducted a series of studies that indicate that individuals tend to marry those persons who are purposefully *unlike* in significant personality characteristics.[5] The senior author concludes,

[1] Alan C. Kerckhoff, "Notes and Comments on the Meaning of Residential Propinquity as a Factor in Mate Selection," *Social Forces*, Vol. 34, No. 3, March 1956, pp. 207–213.

[2] *Ibid.*, p. 212.

[3] A carefully selected bibliography of studies on homogamy is found in the footnotes of August B. Hollingshead, "Cultural Factors in the Selection of Marriage Mates," *American Sociological Review*, Vol. 15, No. 5, October 1950, pp. 619–627.

[4] *Ibid.*, p. 627.

[5] Robert F. Winch, Thomas and Virginia Ktsanes, "The Theory of Complementary Needs in Mate Selection: An Analytic and Descriptive Study," *American Sociological Review*, Vol. 19, No. 3, June 1954; and Robert F. Winch, "The Theory of Complementary Needs in Mate-Selection: A Test of One Kind of Complementariness," *American Sociological Review*, Vol. 20, No. 1, February 1955, pp. 52–56.

The bulk of the evidence, therefore, supports the hypothesis that mates tend to select each other on the basis of complementary needs.[1]

The element of personal choice is strongly influenced by powerful unconscious needs that apparently strive to be met through a mate whose personality complements rather than replicates one's own. In such interplay of mutually complementary need patterns may be the answer to the question of "What can he see in HER?" That marriage partners may tend to choose those whose life style, and personality patterns mutually strengthen and encourage their development as persons, is a theory that may yield still further insight in further research.

Granted that persons generally tend to marry those individuals who live and work nearby, and to choose mates from within their own social, religious, and racial groups, an increasingly large number of mixed marriages are taking place today. How successful marriage is that crosses religious, racial, nationality, or socio-economic group lines depends upon a number of interrelated factors: (1) the motivation for the selection of the marriage partner, (2) responsibility of the sweethearts and mates for bridging the gulfs between them, and their families, (3) ability of the two people to live with their differences. Since there are usually more problems in building a marriage that spans two different cultures, the two people face a greater task, and more is expected of them both in maturity and in responsibility than might be necessary in a homogamous union.

Choosing a suitable partner for marriage can be and often is a confusing task. Families help by standing by with assurance, encouragement, and opportunities for free exploration and development of available possibilities. Premarital counseling and education has proven of invaluable aid to many young men and women who want to be sure before they plunge into anything as serious as marriage.

GETTING ENGAGED

Getting engaged may seem like a pleasant "task" to set up for young adults, but it is a many-faceted responsibility that is not easy for many a couple. Some of the more frequent questions young people ask about the engagement period are:

[1] Robert F. Winch, "The Theory of Complementary Needs in Mate Selection: Final Results on the Test of the General Hypothesis," *American Sociological Review*, Vol. 20, No. 5, October 1955, p. 555.

How soon should a couple get engaged?
How long should an engagement be?
Is it necessary for the man to ask the girl's father for her hand in marriage?
Why does an engagement ring mean so much to a girl?
How much freedom should be allowed the engaged couple?
Does engagement mean "no stepping out?"
Is it necessary to reveal your past to your fiance (é)?
Is it natural to have doubts about your engagement? about yourself?
What are justifiable reasons for breaking an engagement?
How can an unsatisfactory engagement be terminated without being painful?
What is the engagement period for?
What should be discussed during the engagement period?
Is it wise for two people to visit each other's families before they marry?
How can you know when you are really ready for marriage? [1]

No two persons will ever answer such questions in the same way. The answers to most engagement questions depend upon the two people, the nature of their relationship, the motivating forces within them both, their dreams, disappointments and readiness. The way they conduct their engagement is predictive of their marriage success, as we see from how closely the engagement success scores parallel the marriage success scores of both men and women in the longitudinal study of 666 couples through engagement into marriage by Burgess and Wallin, reported in Table 25.

TABLE 25. *Relation between Engagement Success and Marital Success for Men and Women* [2] (Percentage Distribution for 666 Couples)

Engagement Success Scores	MEN Marriage Success Score			WOMEN Marriage Success Score		
	Low	Inter-mediate	High	Low	Inter-mediate	High
High (180 and over)	0.0	16.0	84.0	0.0	9.1	90.9
Median (150–159)	6.7	38.7	54.7	6.7	32.2	61.1
Low (100–109)	40.0	40.0	20.0	28.6	57.1	14.3

[1] Taken from questions discussed in Evelyn Millis Duvall and Reuben Hill, *When You Marry* (Boston: D. C. Heath and Company, Revised Edition, 1953), Chapter 5, "The Meaning of an Engagement," pp. 87–106; and in Evelyn Millis Duvall, *Facts of Life and Love for Teenagers* (New York: Association Press, Revised Edition, 1956), Chapter 16, "Getting Engaged," pp. 361–383.

[2] Ernest W. Burgess and Paul Wallin, *Engagement and Marriage* (Chicago: J. B. Lippincott Company, 1953), excerpts from Table 81, page 547.

Engagement rituals contribute to the success of the engagement period. Many an engaged pair share the rituals of their respective families as a way of giving a sense of belonging to both families, and also as a way of selecting those common rituals that both may enjoy and want to continue in their own family-to-be. Having Sunday dinner with his or her family, participating in family celebrations, going on family picnics, and attending church and community functions with one or the other family are illustrations of the way rituals in the engagement weave the couple into the larger family life.

Some engagement rituals are oriented toward the future in anticipating and preparing for their marriage and family life. Ritualized house-hunting, Saturday afternoon window shopping, contributing to the piggy bank for special funds, calling on recently married friends, having a series of premarital conferences, and attending courses for engaged couples, all are practices that tend to emerge in engagement as future-oriented rituals.

By the time the couple is ready for marriage, it will have accomplished several important purposes of the engagement period: (1) to place themselves as a pair in their own eyes, and in the eyes of both families and their mutual friends, (2) to work through intimate systems of communication that allow for exchange of confidences, and an increasing degree of empathy and the ability to predict each other's responses, (3) to plan specifically for the marriage that lies ahead, in terms of both the practical decisions of where and on what, as well as the value consensus of how the common life will be lived.

BEING MARRIED

Being married is a multiple developmental task for both partners. If the marriage is to get off to a good start in its establishment phase (Chapter Six), several important jobs must be satisfactorily accomplished when the two people marry. The two people face several urgent questions as they become one in marriage: (1) Are our parents with us or against us in our marriage? (2) Where will we live, and on what? (3) Are we both really ready to settle down in marriage? (4) How well prepared for marriage are we? (5) What kind of ceremony will we have?

A marriage that starts off with the blessing of both sets of parents has much smoother going than if one or both families oppose the match. Modern young people growing up in an era of extreme individualism may operate under the illusion that they are not marrying into each other's families, and that what anyone else, including their parents, thinks about their marriage is none of their business. Actually the opinions of both families are very important, and influence the marriage either positively or negatively in many crucial ways through the years. The task of coming to terms with real attitudes about the proposed marriage within both sets of families is urgently relevant.

ONE IN THREE COUPLES WED ON "SHOESTRING" headlines a release in early 1956.[1] The report goes on to say that 35 per cent of all newlyweds are married on an income of less than $60 a week (about $3,000 a year). How young couples manage on so little is a story in itself. About 10 per cent of young married couples live with their families. Others are receiving regular assistance from their families in the form of money, food or gifts. Many of the young marriages take place when they do because of the willingness and the ability of the girl to work.

The too-young couple may be getting themselves caught in the tender trap of love and marriage, as a woman professor of education warns:

Funny . . . how ideas about love and marriage change with something so unromantic as the national economy. In the depression years of the 1930's the average young woman was willing or at least reconciled to waiting before mating. Now she knows that her parents can and probably will help. And she knows she can get a job that will enable her husband to manage. It may well be an uninteresting (if fairly well-paid) job with no chance for advancement, but she can thereby Help Her Husband with His Education—or make it possible for *him* to take, if necessary, a thirty-six-dollar-a-week-job with a whale of a future. Perhaps she has always wanted to work her way up in a New York publishing house—or with the Department of State in Washington. She drops her plans like a hot cake to follow her husband to the spot on the globe where he can do what he wants to do—and she can't. It doesn't occur to her until later that she has walked wide-eyed into a trap.

She does not stop to think that, while the early sacrifices of the ardent young bride can be made with happy generosity, they will lead to later resentment when she discovers that she is an uninteresting person, unqualified for either self-respect or respect of others in a world that has moved ahead without her, where her own growth has been slowed and stunted. The husband will forget, in time, that it was she who helped him win success and grow beyond her very reach, that it was she who took upon herself the limiting routines and denied her own personal goals.

An early marriage . . . can trap the husband as well as the wife. He is

---

[1] "One in Three Couples Wed on 'Shoestring,'" *The Family Economist* (New York: Institute of Life Insurance, December, 1955), release January 6, 1956, page 1.

Many young marriages take place when they do today because of the willingness and ability of the girl to work.

not allowed the time and leisure for intellectual growth. His perceptions and judgments are sharpened only in his own professional directions. Weighed down by his desperate pressures in earning power, he has too many responsibilities too early—financing his wife, the two, three or four babies, the mortgage. He does not have the leisure to write, experiment, explore, create. He too is cramped and harassed.[1]

Readiness for marriage is measured most easily by chronological age. Data on age at marriage by success in marriage indicate that teenage marriages are the riskiest of all. However, the number of birthdays an individual has had is not as good an indication of his or her readiness for marriage as is emotional age, or maturity as a person. Discriminating questions like these are pertinent: Am I really ready to stop playing around and settle down with one person in marriage? Am I grown up

[1] Kate Hevner Mueller, "The Marriage Trap," *Mademoiselle*, Spring 1955, taken from release from *Mademoiselle*, pp. 1 and 2.

enough to be responsible for my own behavior without blaming someone else, or "running home to mother" when I get in a jam? Am I emotionally weaned from my parents? Are my motives for marriage to this person at this time sound and mature? Are we both prepared for what lies ahead for us?

Such questions as these, and many others, are usually freely discussed in functional courses in marriage and family living. Studies have shown that college students are generally appreciative of such course work, their attitudes ranging from "favorable," to "strongly favorable." [1] Of the married graduates who had taken the course in "Marriage and the Family" at Florida State University between 1930 and 1946, 34.8 per cent responded to a poll by saying they believed the college course had helped them "a great deal," 52.8 per cent, "helped somewhat," and 12.4 per cent "made no difference." [2] An evaluation of the effectiveness of the course at Syracuse University summarizes findings in part as follows:

. . . Students enrolled in a functional course in Family Relationships do make significant gains in their understanding; they do gain insights which they, themselves, consider to be of personal value; they do apply these understandings and insights in their efforts to solve personal problems they are currently experiencing on campus . . . individuals who formerly have had the course and who are now married are applying learnings and insights derived from the course. These people feel the application of learnings derived from the course has contributed much to the quality of their marriages.[3]

Courses in preparation for marriage are offered by many public and private schools, YMCAs, YWCAs, and other youth-serving agencies in many communities. Churches of all three faiths increasingly assume responsibility for preparing their teenage and young adult constituents for marriage and family life. The Pre-Cana and Cana Conferences under Roman Catholic auspices, the excellent materials (course outlines, books, pamphlets, film-strips, recordings, leader's guides, etc.) published by many Protestant denominations for their work in Christian Family Life

[1] Lawrence S. Bee, "Student Attitudes toward a Course in Courtship and Marriage: Educational Implications," *Marriage and Family Living*, Volume XIII, No. 4, Fall, 1951, pp. 157–160.

[2] George H. Finck, "A Comparative Analysis of the Marriages and Families of Participants and Non-Participants in Marriage Education," *Marriage and Family Living*, Vol. XVIII, No. 1, February 1956, p. 63.

[3] Virginia Musick Moses, "A Study of Learnings Derived from a Functional College Course in Marriage and Family Relationships by Students as Undergraduates and as Married Alumni," unpublished dissertation, Syracuse University Library, 1955.

programs, as well as the outstanding work being done in many Jewish temples and synagogues are all resources that may be tapped by any interested group or individual. For those situations in which such organized resources are not yet available, there are readily available readings. The books most frequently reported as texts for marriage and family courses in the 1948–1949 survey were:

Baber, Ray, *Marriage and the Family* (New York: McGraw-Hill, 1939).
Becker, Howard, and Hill, Reuben, *Family Marriage and Parenthood* (Boston: D. C. Heath, 1948).
Bowman, Henry, *Marriage for Moderns* (New York: McGraw-Hill, 1948).
Burgess, Ernest, and Locke, Harvey, *The Family* (New York: American Book Company, 1945).
Duvall, Evelyn, and Hill, Reuben, *When You Marry* (Boston: D. C. Heath, 1945).
Nimkoff, Meyer, *Marriage and the Family* (Boston: Houghton-Mifflin, 1947).[1]

Specific plans for the wedding may be for anything from a simple home ceremony, with just members of the family present, to elaborate society affairs running into thousands of dollars and months of preparation. Whatever the type of ceremony, the most important factors are the *persons,* rather than the things. A wedding that is planned to meet the needs of the situation, in accordance with the wishes of the families, and the values of the couple is a many-faceted responsibility involving a number of specific decisions.[2] These tasks are usually jointly assumed by the couple and their parents, with the bride and her parents taking the major responsibility for the social aspects of the affair.

The successful accomplishment of the many urgent developmental tasks of young adulthood is the best foundation for the establishing of a sound marriage in the stages of the new family that lie ahead, (Chapters Six to Eleven). In the launching stage of the family life cycle, members of the younger generation stretch out from the family of orientation toward the establishment of the family of procreation. Concurrently, the family serving as launching center has a two-way look, with one important focus pointing to the establishment of the young

[1] Henry A. Bowman, *Marriage Education in the Colleges,* American Social Hygiene Association, New York City, 1949. A current survey being conducted by Judson T. Landis (University of California), will doubtless include many of the newer books that have appeared since the earlier study.
[2] Evelyn Millis Duvall and Reuben Hill, *When You Marry* (Boston: D. C. Heath and Company, Revised Edition, 1953), Chapter 9, "Wedding Plans," pp. 170–193.

adult as an independent unit, and the other focus of attention on the business of maintaining the integrity of the parents' family.

DEVELOPMENTAL TASKS OF FAMILIES AS LAUNCHING CENTERS

There is a commonly held opinion that families play only a passive role as their children depart for an independent life of their own. Like the young hero of Horatio Alger novels the youth is seen, stalwartly striding from the door darkened by the figure of his weeping mother, to go out into the world and make his fortune. Occasionally one knows of a boy who runs away from home at sixteen or seventeen, not to return until years later when he returns with his wife and children to seek his family's belated blessing. Once in a while a news story comes out of a girl who has suddenly eloped, or a boy who has joined the Marines, or a youngster who walks barefoot across the mountains to work his way through college all on his own. But these are the exceptions that keep alive the Cinderella and Horatio Alger fictions. In reality, most families today, as they always have, play active roles over a considerable period of time in getting their young people successfully launched into the world.

While the first child is at work getting established as an autonomous young adult there probably are one or more younger children still in the family, each with his or her own developmental tasks to accomplish. So, the family's tasks are not only in assisting the young adult to become successfully autonomous, but also in maintaining a home base in which the other members of the family can thrive.

ARRANGING PHYSICAL FACILITIES FOR A VARIETY OF FUNCTIONS AS LAUNCHING FAMILIES

These are the accordion years of family life. The young adult's room lies empty through the college year, or while he is away for service, only to suddenly become swollen over a holiday or through a leave, with the young person and his or her friends swooping in for a few days and nights. The family goes along on an even keel for some weeks, and then must mobilize itself and all of its resources for a wedding, or a graduation, or both, that keeps the household humming and house bulging at the seams.

The physical plant is sorely taxed at this stage. The family car that Dad uses to get to work and that is needed for the weekly shopping, is in constant demand by the young man or woman of the family with engagements far and wide looming large in importance during the launching stage. Teenage siblings clamor for their share of the use of the car, the telephone, the TV set, and the living room, until, as one harassed father described it, "This is the stage of life when a man is dispossessed in his own home." A mother comments somewhat ruefully that she doesn't mind the noise and the expense of young people in the home, but she will be glad to regain the use of her own living room when the courting couples have finally found homes of their own. Few families complain when facilities are sorely taxed at this stage of family living, but the fact remains that for many, the flexible rearrangement of available resources to meet the variety of functions within families at the launching center stage, is a task indeed.

MEETING THE COSTS AS LAUNCHING CENTER FAMILIES

With some exceptions, families at this stage are at the peak load of family expenses. These are the years when the young adult needs financial help to carry him or her through college or other educational plans, to get specialized training and experience, to get established in the "starvation period" of any of the professions, to pay union initiation fees and dues as workers, to finance the wedding, and the new home-in-the-making. Such costs are over and above the already established expenditures budgeted for the family. Many young people today help earn what they can as young adults always have, but few are in a position to contribute heavily to the family budget at the very time that they are establishing themselves independently.

Chart 14 clearly indicates that family expenditures are highest when the oldest child is about nineteen, in families of one, two or three children. Costs mount until this period and rapidly decline as the children are launched. Only the family with no children escapes this peak load that comes typically twenty to twenty-five years after the parents' marriage.

These are the years when a man is glad he is near the peak of his earnings (Chapter Eight, Chart 13); but even so, some supplementation may be necessary to carry the additional expenditures that go with launching center functions. The husband may do overtime as a laboring man, or get a summer job as a teacher, or a part-time job around the edges of his regular position whatever he does. His wife now is possibly

CHART 14. Relative Annual Cost of Supporting Four Families for Forty Years [1]

"Family A consists of a husband and wife who bring up three children, a boy born at the end of the second year, a girl born at the end of the fourth year, and a boy born at the end of the sixth year of their married life.

"Family B consists of a husband and wife who bring up two children, a boy born at the end of the second year, and a girl born at the end of the fourth year of their married life.

"Family C consists of a husband and wife who bring up one child, a boy born at the end of the second year of their married life.

"Family D has no children."

"It is assumed in each case that the husband and wife were married when he was 25 and she was 23, and that each family supports each of its children for 19 years, providing them with a high school education. On the 19th birthday, each child leaves home and becomes self-supporting."

in the labor force, as 30 per cent of wives 45–65 years of age were in 1955.[2] The young adult and other children in the family possibly have jobs of some kind, on a part-time basis while in school, and full-time after education is completed. These sources of income may not be suf-

---

[1] Howard F. Bigelow, *Family Finance* (Chicago: J. B. Lippincott Company, 1953), p. 333.

[2] United States Bureau of the Census (see details in Chapter Eleven).

Tasks and responsibilities are allocated among the members of the family on the basis of interest, ability, and availability.

ficient to meet such special costs as are involved in an expensive wedding, or college tuition and fees. The family may float a loan or borrow on life insurance or increase the mortgage on the house or tighten its belt wherever it can to meet the current emergencies. Providing for a family at the launching center stage is a task, as few will deny.

REALLOCATING RESPONSIBILITIES AMONG GROWN AND GROWING CHILDREN IN THE FAMILY

Young adults and older teenagers thrive with real responsibilities of their own. Now is the time when father and mother can sit back and let the children run their own affairs in many a situation. These are the years when the "smothering Mom" is a liability, and a Dad who is too prone to "snoopervise" is a threat to the autonomy of the young adult. The happy family at the launching center stage is one in which tasks and responsibilities are allocated among the members of the family on the basis of interest, ability and availability.

The successful accomplishment of this task depends upon the flexibility of roles of the two parents as well as the growing abilities of the young adult(s) and younger siblings to assume and carry through effectively the tasks of the household. As young adults begin to take on more real responsibility for their own and for the family's welfare, the parents play the complementary roles of letting go, and standing by with encouragement, reassurance and appreciation.

COMING TO TERMS WITH THEMSELVES AND EACH OTHER AS HUSBAND AND WIFE AMID THE THREATS OF THE LAUNCHING PERIOD [1]

Being a parent is not easy at any stage in the child's growth. In many ways being a parent of older youth today is the hardest of all. For parents often vicariously live through all the terrors and threats of emancipation that beset their youth, at the same time that they as people in their late thirties, forties, and fifties are living through the "crisis of the middle years."

Being middleaged today is a far more powerful business than it used to be in the day of Whistler's mother. Then, a woman in her forties was physically and psychologically ready to retire to her knitting. Today's middleaged woman, thanks to better nutrition, medical services, lightened burdens at home, and shifting feminine roles, still has a "head of steam up" both physiologically and emotionally. She is apt to be vigorous, often feeling better than she has in her whole life. Even menopause, the dread of women in earlier eras, now can be taken in stride (Chapter Thirteen). The woman with nearly grown children has found her strengths and her weaknesses. She has tasted the sweetness of affection and learned to enjoy creative companionship with her husband and children.

Now, suddenly, before she has quite prepared herself for it, her children are no longer children; they are taking their confidences and their loves outside. Her husband is engrossed in the peak of his business or career. Her house is in order. And she—where does she go from here? What loves can take the place of those so suddenly torn away? What tasks will absorb the energies and the skills that cry for channeling? If she clings to her children she is a "Mom." If her interests in her husband's career become too absorbing she is a "meddler." If she spends her time in a dizzy round of matinees, bridge parties, and beauty parlors, she is a "parasite." If she devotes herself to a quest for her soul through

[1] Excerpts from Evelyn Millis Duvall, "Editorial Introduction," Part VI, *The Family as a Launching Center, Committee on Dynamics of Family Interaction,* National Conference on Family Life, Washington, D. C., February 1948, unpublished materials, pp. 2–5.

devious cults and sundry religions, she is suspect. Her salable skills are at least two decades old where she left them when she married to make her place in her home. These are but a few of the questions the wife must face in her middle years (Chapter Thirteen).

And the man, the middleaged father—what of him? Are the middle years any easier on him than on his wife? Can he more comfortably help his children launch themselves into the shadowy adulthood in which he is to be but a small part? Does he too face tasks as a person that shake him to his very roots, and cry urgently for attention just when his youngsters scare him with their first efforts at "trying their wings?"

There is evidence to indicate that men too face a crisis in the middle years, for the basic problem is the same for men and women alike. Briefly it is this. Throughout their lusty twenties and pushy thirties most American men, driving to "get ahead," fasten their eyes on distant goals and dream hopefully of success. But few reach the top. Even those who do, struggle to maintain and improve their position in the competitive scheme of things where others are always jockeying for more favorable positions. The glamour dies in the struggle, and "success" for too many American men in their forties and fifties is but ashes in the mouth.

The multitude of hard-working fathers who never reach the top must face the realities of their limitations, and accept their lot for what it is, mediocre and bitter though it may be. "I am just a minor guy in a minor rut, living life in a minor key," says one man.

Men are further troubled by signs of diminished masculinity, so ever dear to American males. The slowing up characteristic of the middle-aged father, seen in contrast with the youthful vigor of his growing sons and daughters, is personally threatening to many men. Lessened potency and sexual excitation is too frequently attributed to monogamous monotony. The "dangerous period" for men comes when a man must prove his virility to himself, even with more youthful partners if need be. With the burden of guilt that this carries, is it any wonder that he is too easily upset by his son's girl-troubles or his daughter's involvements? The timing of launching, both for parents and for young adults, today is unfortunate. Two types of crises piled one on top of the other means trouble in many homes.

The question of "how well have we done by our children?" is pertinent. In the dark hours of the night, parents toss with the haunting fear that some how, some way, they might have done a better job with those children who are now beyond their parental ministrations. Parents recognize that the family at the launching stage is being evaluated on its success through its products, the children. Yet the problems of their achieving full adulthood maritally, vocationally, and intellectually are so many and the solutions so few!

Someday we will know more about these things. We will be prepared for the head-on collisions of children and their parents bent on urgent, not-to-be-denied tasks. Today we stumble along doing amazingly well considering all the threats with which we live in these launching center stages.

MAINTAINING OPEN SYSTEMS OF COMMUNICATION WITHIN THE FAMILY AND BETWEEN THE FAMILY AND OTHERS

Being able to get through to each other in the family is especially important during the launching stage. This is the time when the young adult is emerging from his family, and is working through some of the most important and the most complex tasks of his life. The young person who can freely bring his questions and his alternative solutions to his parents as sounding boards can get invaluable help through their perspective, at the same time that the family avoids the hazards of feeling "left behind" or "discarded."

Only an understanding non-judgmental family can hope to keep the confidence of its young adults, busy with the gaining of true autonomy. Families who "make a scene" or create an issue over some youthful blunder lose, at least for the moment, contact with the young person at the very time when the generations may need each other most. This is especially true in the relationships the young adult is establishing outside the family. If the parents are unduly critical of visiting boy friends, a girl often has to make a choice between complying with her parents' wishes or being true to her "heart" and loyal to her friend(s). This is a lot to ask of a young person. Yet, the evidence is that parental disapproval of boys dated has increased appreciably in the last three generations.

Table 26 summarizes data from a study made of young college-trained, married women, their mothers, and their maternal grandmothers, in which a pattern emerges of increasing frequency of disapproval of boys dated, with the youngest generation reporting more disapproval than either the mothers or the grandmothers had known in their time.

TABLE 26. *Parental Approval of Boys Dated in the Early Courtships of Respondents from Three Married Female Generations* [1]

| Parental Approval | Generations | | |
	First (Grandmothers)	Second (Mothers)	Third (Young Wives)
Did not approve	62	91	109
Did approve	104	89	69
Uncertain	25	20	22
Unknown	9	0	0
Total	200	200	200

The reasons for such a significant increase of parental disapproval of the boys a girl dates are a matter of conjecture. One may result from rapid social change in which each generation departs farther from its predecessor than the former had from its parents. A second may be that the increase in social contacts in the larger community brings girls into contact with more boys and young men of whom parents disapprove than was possible in more limited situations characteristic of an earlier day. Still a third possible explanation is that parents had more control over courting couples and dating choices in former times and were therefore more likely to approve the dating partners than today when friends are selected by the young person with little assistance from the family.

Families at the launching center stage walk the tightrope between the pressures from outside the family and the forces of cohesion that integrate the family as a unit. This developmental task is one of the most difficult to achieve satisfactorily. It is competently accomplished if a solid foundation of good parent-child relationships has been established, and if now at the "proving time" the young adults feel that whatever happens, their family is back of them, with faith in their ability to work things through, and willingness to look at any situation, with loving concern.

WIDENING THE FAMILY CIRCLE

With the first marriage of one of the children of the family comes the first experience of sudden expansion of the extended family to include both the new family unit being established, and also with more or less

[1] Marvin R. Koller, "Some Changes in Courtship Behavior in Three Generations of Ohio Women," *American Sociological Review*, Vol. 16, No. 3, June 1951, p. 367.

interaction, the family of the son- or daughter-in-law. The family in its earlier expanding stages took upon itself one child at a time (except in multiple births), and that as a tiny infant. The widening of the family circle at the launching center stage is dramatically different in two major respects: (1) the addition is multiple, consisting of the entire family of in-laws and (2) the additional persons are at varying levels of maturity with a preponderance of adults.

The situation is complicated by the fact that while the young adult of the one family is intimately known within his or her own family, he or she, for awhile, remains an outsider to the young mate's family of orientation. If there is too close a bond between one young adult and his or her parents, it is difficult to establish the new unit with equilibrium, as we see in the following analysis:

Every married couple belongs to three families. They belong first of all to themselves. They are the WE of the new family they are founding together. But, at the same time they belong also to *his* family, and to *hers*. If they are to establish a strong family unit of their own, they must inevitably realign their loyalties to the place where *our* family comes before either *yours* or *mine*.

"This is the elemental triangle of married living. Unless the cohesive force in the new family unit is stronger than that which ties either of the couple to the parental home, the founding family is threatened, as we see in the figures.

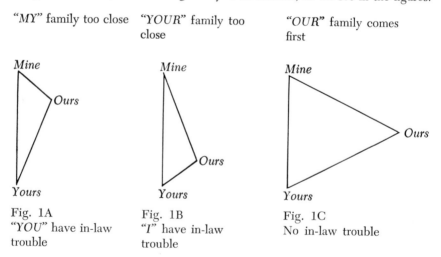

"MY" family too close   "YOUR" family too close   "OUR" family comes first

Fig. 1A
"YOU" have in-law trouble

Fig. 1B
"I" have in-law trouble

Fig. 1C
No in-law trouble

In Figure 1A, "YOU" have in-law trouble because "MY" family is too close. It may be because I am still immature and not ready to emancipate myself from my parental home. It may be that one or more members of my family is possessive and finds it difficult to let me go. It may be that circumstances within my family require from me more loyalty and attention than I can comfortably give at the time that I am involved in building my own home and marriage. Whatever the reason, if the forces pulling me/us toward loyalties to "MY" home are too strong, the development of "OUR" common sense of identity is delayed or weakened.

In Figure 1B, "YOUR" family is too close, and so "I" have in-law trouble. Because "YOU" are bound so tightly to "YOUR" family, I am pulled away from mine, and "WE" make little progress in establishing "OURS."

In Figure 1C, "OUR" family unit comes first in our joint loyalties. We are threatened neither by the ties that bind us to "YOUR" family, nor by the bonds that unite us to "MINE." We are able to make progress as a new family because the force of our common identification pulls us out and away together into a home of our own. Now we can share in the common heritage of both your family and mine because we are not threatened by the pull from either. Only thus are WE free to enjoy being members of the entire extended family, without the stress of in-law strains.[1]

RECONCILING CONFLICTING LOYALTIES AND PHILOSOPHIES OF LIFE

In establishing his autonomy as a young adult, the son or daughter of the family has to question at least some of the premises by which life in his family has been lived. These are the days when many a young person tries out conflicting ways of life in an effort to test his background and catch a glimpse of his potential future. When a young adult is being launched from his home base into a life of his own, it is the one time within his life span when he will be free to pull loose from old allegiances without basic threats and instabilities.

The young man or woman critically reviews his life within his family of orientation and makes comments from time to time that may severely challenge his parents and their ways with him. Ruth Ann startled her parents one night with her observation that she would never make last year's hat do, and look as shabby as her mother in order to let any child of hers go to college. The fact that the family's sacrifice had been for *her* college education was not irrelevant! Junior soberly reflects one night when his father is working late at the office that life is too short to spend couped up on any job; he promises himself that when he gets out into life of his own, he will never knuckle under to any position the way he

[1] Evelyn Millis Duvall, *In-Laws: Pro and Con* (New York: Association Press, 1954), pp. 278 and 279.

has seen his father do through the years. Young Sam, son of a prominent Republican leader, is active in a leftist organization in college. Mary, brought up in a pious home, refuses to continue in church as soon as she gets a job in the mill. Illustrations are nearly as numerous as young people themselves. In one or more ways many young people repudiate their parents and strike out for ways of their own. This is especially true for the mobile youngster whose drive thrusts him upward in social climbing, or whose resistance pushes him downward in the social scale.

Many young adults from conforming homes rather unquestioningly follow through the life style established by their parents. But even the most stable are in some ways different from their parents, if only that they are emerging as young adults into a different world than that in which their parents established themselves. In times of social change there are inevitable shifts in ways of life from one generation to the next, so that the task of reconciling differences between the generations becomes almost universal.

Some young people get into trouble as they push out into strange new ways. Queenie in Noel Coward's *This Happy Breed,* runs off with a married man, is deserted, tries to make a go of running a teashop in Southern France, and finally is brought back home to a reconciliation by a loyal lover who grew up next door. Not all youthful mistakes are as critical. Not all turn out so well in the end. But in some way or other most young people blunder as they try their wings and attempt to fly off into life on their own. Parents who are patient while these efforts are being made are of far more help than those who stand by clucking their fears as the fledgling leaves the nest. Families who stand by with assurance and encouragement, giving help as needed, especially in any of life's firsts (first formal party, first job, first trip away from home, and the rest), give their young people the stable home base that is needed for a successful launching.

While the young adults are gaining strength to live independently, and showing by their words and actions that their lives are not going to be complete carbon copies of their parents, the younger children in the family may be torn by the obvious conflicts between their parents and their older siblings. It is normal for younger children in the family to value highly the attitudes and judgments of their older brothers and sisters. During World War II when large numbers of young men left for military service, there was a sudden upsurge of juvenile delinquency among the next younger teenage boys. Two explanations were given, one that they felt unneeded in the sense that their older brothers were needed, and secondly, that their models of behavior in showing what a young man is and does were no longer at home to keep them in line. Very possibly there were other factors operating too. But the influence of older young people on the lives of their younger brothers and sisters is not to be denied.

Families that keep a secure home base for the younger members of the family during the launching center stage are those that attempt to accept comfortably the way of life the young adult has chosen. They do not feel too threatened by it. They help the younger siblings see that there are many good ways to live a life, and that when his time comes, he too will find his way for himself.

In a democratic society, in a democratic home, such a course is not hard to follow. Difficulties come in the autocratic, rigid ways in which little latitude is allowed, and where all must follow the one path already established by the dictator of the family.

SUMMARY

Families enter the launching center stage as the first child leaves home as a young adult. The stage ends as the last child departs leaving the parents in their empty nest. The stage may be short or long; typically it lasts from six to seven years. Developmental tasks of young adults in the United States include the following: choosing a vocation, getting an education, satisfying military service requirements, becoming marriageable, learning to appraise and to express love feelings appropriately, choosing a marriage partner, getting engaged, and being married. The developmental tasks of families as launching centers include: meeting costs as launching center families, reallocating responsibilities among grown and growing children in the family, coming to terms with themselves and with each other as husband and wife amid the threats of the launching period, maintaining open systems of communication within the family and between the family and others, widening the family circle to include the new relatives by marriage within the extended family, and reconciling conflicting loyalties and philosophies of life.

This is a period full of teachable moments for the young adult and for all those who live with and love him. New possibilities, new problems, and new ways bring new tasks for the young person to accomplish. He is helped to achieve his developmental tasks as a young adult by family members who have confidence in him and who encourage him to become an autonomous person in his own right. He may find especially meaningful the courses, counseling, and guidance offered in many communities to assist the young adult in one or more of his growth responsibilities.

Parents at this stage are breaking the patterns and habits of two decades, as they let their children go. Never again will the relationship between themselves and their offspring be quite the same. Fathers and mothers who successfully launch their children into the world are usually those whose emotional lives do not depend upon the continuing dependence of their children. This is the time when their ways of life are being challenged by their own flesh and blood. This is either a threat or a challenge depending upon their basic security in a democratic acceptance of difference.

SUGGESTED ACTIVITIES

1) Review Jan de Hartog, *The Fourposter* (New York: Random House, 1952), Act Three, Scene 1, pp. 89–104. Then, chart the indicated developmental tasks of both Agnes and Michael, as they meet the crisis of the marriage of their daughter, by listing the revealing phrases (quotes) in the left hand column, and the developmental task implied on the right hand column of your paper. Interpret and summarize.

2) Compare the launching of a conforming son as revealed in the character of young Apley in John P. Marquand's *The Late George Apley* (Boston: Little, Brown and Company, 1937), with the mobile climber depicted in the character of Sammy in Budd Schulberg's *What Makes Sammy Run?* (New York: Bantam Books, 1945). Indicate in what significant ways the two patterns differ, and how the various developmental tasks of young adulthood are accomplished by the young men.

3) Review Edward Strecker, *Their Mother's Sons* (Philadelphia: Lippincott, 1946) and Phillip Wylie, *Generation of Vipers* (New York: Rinehart, 1942) with special reference to the theory of "momism." Write a paper on possible explanations for the phenomenon of "momism" in contemporary American culture.

4) Review Edward Streeter, *Father of the Bride* (New York: Simon and Schuster, Inc., 1948), looking especially for the hazards a father faces in letting his daughter go in marriage. Write a paper outlining ways of minimizing these hazards in making wedding plans.

Parental Subsidies

Pro

Parents better
established, can
lessen burden on young
family financially

Satisfies parents need
to be helpful to
children

Prevents young husband
from stopping education
that he will need
but won't be able to
get later on.

Con

① Encourages
dependence in
adult young family

② Possibility of
interference of
parents in decisions
children should
make

③ Indebtness for
financial help
"above & beyond call of
duty" – feeling that
this can never be
paid on children's
part

5) Poll the class on the question, "Is it wise to get as much education as is possible before going into service or getting married?" Tabulate replies and document with verbatim statements of the various positions taken. Discuss in terms of what you know about the multiple developmental tasks young adults face today.

6) Write an autobiography outlining specifically the factors in your life history that played some direct or indirect part in your choice of a vocation. Consider such factors as the social class placement of your family, your mobility drives, your sex, your identification with some significant adult, vocational guidance and tests you have had, as well as other factors that are relevant.

7) Visit a class in personality development in your local YMCA, YWCA, church or other community group, and observe what is being done to help young adults become more marriageable in your area. Write a report of your findings.

8) Write a paper on how much parents should try to influence the choice of a life mate. Give illustrations of parents who have tried to exert too much influence and those who have seemed not to care enough about the choice of their child's life partner. Show possible consequences of each extreme.

9) Chart the pros and cons of parental subsidy in the marriage of their young adult children. Summarize with a documented paper showing why you have placed the items mentioned where you did.

10) Debate the proposition that there are more intrafamily conflicts at the launching center stage of the family life cycle than at any other period.

11) Discuss one or more of the following situations adapted from case excerpts developed as class discussion stimuli by Dr. Hazel Ingersoll, Department of Home Life, Oklahoma A&M College, Stillwater, Oklahoma:

a) Jack and Martha came from different home backgrounds and from different parts of the country. Martha's parents had hoped she would marry a western boy. Jack wants Martha's parents to accept him and his New England ways; Martha wants to please his parents as well. During the engagement period they plan to spend their vacations in each others' homes. How will they go about really getting to know and understand the early childhood experiences of each other? How can they use this interest in each other's background to further their relationships with their prospective in-laws? How can they come to understand and appreciate the differences in their upbringing? In what ways will these explorations facilitate their marriage adjustment?

b) Judy and her widowed mother have always been very close. Now Judy's mother thinks John is taking Judy away from her. Her whole life has been wrapped up in Judy. She is encouraging Judy to delay marriage and to go on with her career. She says, "We've worked and sacrificed so much for your education. Now you are giving up everything to marry this stranger!" John feels he is unwanted, so he has avoided Judy's mother as much as possible. Judy's mother cries and becomes ill when Judy talks about marriage, and because Judy can't bear to hurt her mother, she is considering asking her to live with John and her. John objects. What is the real problem here? What might Judy do? John? Judy's mother? Judy and John as a couple? What developmental tasks does each individual face in this situation?

c) Al's parents had his life all planned. He was to devote his life to medicine as his grandfather had done. After completing medical training they envisaged him married to one of his own set and settled nearby. But Al, aware that he must soon enter military service, married Louise, a classmate, a girl his parents had never met. Louise had planned to finish school (one year more) and then work. But she became pregnant. Al, wanting her to have good care, asked his parents to take her in until his return. Louise objects because she feels the parents-in-law will treat her like a child and try to run her life. What developmental tasks are inherent in this situation for Louise, for Al, and for his parents? What difficulties may arise in the young couple's efforts to launch themselves as a separate family unit? What possible outcomes are there to the problem situation? Which course will best assure the various members and the two family units of achieving their developmental tasks?

d) Mary Ann's father "dotes" on her and thinks no man could ever be good enough for his daughter. Mary Ann, an only child, is very devoted to her father, so much so that she has chosen a man who is very much like him. Bill, her fiancé, resents the affection and attention Mary Ann gives her father; and the father wastes no words in his criticism of Bill. The father is accustomed to taking Mary Ann with him to games, etc. Now Mary Ann wants to go with Bill, or wants her Dad to include Bill. But the tension between the men makes her uncomfortable. What is the source of Mary Ann's difficulty? What developmental task(s) is she struggling with? What can be done to better the relationship, by each of the three persons?

e) Beverly is a city girl who is engaged to Tom, a student in the College of Agriculture, who is going back to the ranch in partnership with his father. Beverly does not know anything about being the wife of a rancher. How best can she learn her new roles on the ranch? What may be involved in her relationship with her prospective mother-in-law who is an experienced rancher's wife? What hazards and challenges, what resources and advantages do both of the young people face in the accomplishment of their developmental tasks in the months ahead?

READINGS

Becker, Howard, and Hill, Reuben; *Family, Marriage and Parenthood* (Boston: D. C. Heath and Company, 1955).

Black, Algernon D., *If I Marry Outside My Religion* (New York: The Public Affairs Committee, Inc., 1954).

Blood, Robert O., Jr., *Anticipating Your Marriage* (Glencoe, Illinois: The Free Press, 1955).

Bowman, Henry A., *Marriage for Moderns* (New York: McGraw-Hill Book Company, Inc., 1953 Revision).

Burgess, Ernest W.; Wallin, Paul; and Shultz, Gladys Denny, *Courtship, Engagement and Marriage* (Philadelphia: J. B. Lippincott Company, 1954).

Cavan, Ruth Shonle, *The American Family* (New York: Thomas Y. Crowell Company, 1953), Chapters 12–15.

Duvall, Evelyn Millis, *In-Laws: Pro and Con* (New York: Association Press, 1954).

Duvall, Evelyn Millis, and Hill, Reuben, *When You Marry* (Boston: D. C. Heath and Company, 1953 Revision).

Duvall, Sylvanus M., *Before You Marry* (New York: Association Press, 1949).

Dreese, Mitchell, *How to Get the Job* (Chicago: Science Research Associates, Inc., 1949).

Ellzey, W. Clark, *How to Keep Romance in Your Marriage* (New York: Association Press, 1954).

Fisher, Lowell B., chairman *et al.* Prepared under the direction of the Defense Committee of the North Central Association of College and Secondary Schools, *Your Life Plans and the Armed Forces* (Washington, D. C.: American Council on Education, 1955).

Havighurst, Robert J., *Human Development and Education* (New York: Longmans, Green and Company, 1953), Chapter 16.

Hill, Reuben, revision of Waller, Willard, *The Family* (New York: The Dryden Press, Revised Edition 1951), Chapter 20.

Humphreys, J. Anthony, *Choosing Your Career* (Chicago: Science Research Associates, 1949).

Humphreys, J. Anthony, *Helping Youth Choose Careers* (Chicago: Science Research Associates, 1950).

Ivy, A. C., and Ross, Irwin; *Religion and Race: Barriers to College?* (New York: Public Affairs Committee, Inc., 1949).

Kirkendall, Lester A., *Understanding Sex* (Chicago: Science Research Associates, 1948).

Koos, Earl Lomon, *Marriage* (New York: Henry Holt and Company, 1953).

Kuder, G. Frederic, and Paulson, Blanche B., *Discovering Your Real Interests* (Chicago: Science Research Associates, 1949).

Landis, Judson T. and Mary G., *Building a Successful Marriage* (New York: Prentice-Hall, Inc., 1953 revision).

Locke, Harvey J., *Predicting Adjustment in Marriage: A Comparison of a Divorced and a Happily Married Group* (New York: Henry Holt and Company, 1951).

Mueller, Kate Hevner, *Educating Women for a Changing World* (Minneapolis: University of Minnesota Press, 1954).

Pike, James A., *If You Marry Outside Your Faith* (New York: Harper & Brothers, 1954).

Schloerb, Lester J., *School Subjects and Jobs* (Chicago: Science Research Associates, 1950).

Taylor, Florence, *Why Stay in School?* (Chicago: Science Research Associates, 1948).

Vincent, William S., and Russell, James E., *You and the Draft* (Chicago: Science Research Associates, 1952).

Warner, W. Lloyd, and Havighurst, Robert J., *Should You Go to College?* (Chicago: Science Research Associates, 1948).

Sing a song of seasons!
Something bright in all!
Flowers in the summer,
Fires in the fall.
ROBERT LOUIS STEVENSON

CHAPTER THIRTEEN

Families in the middle years[1]

Throughout the life of the family certain events serve as milestones to mark the transition from one stage to another. Such a milestone is the departure of grown children from home to establish their independence. Although the process of achieving independence may be gradual, as when children are in college part of the year or are in service with only occasional leaves at home, the decisive event usually is the marriage of the children. In American life, parents are expected to observe a "hands off" policy toward married children. The daily stream of thought, activities, tenderness, and love that has flowed from parents to children must now be checked in its outward expression and diverted into other channels in order to allow the young married couple an opportunity to develop their own new family life. This change from the child-centered family to the family whose children have left comes during the middle-age of the parents.

To some people it seems that with the marriage of their children the essence of living is lost, that only the dull tag-end of life remains. At one time, this attitude was more or less justified. Large families prolonged the period of childrearing to the sixties, and the interval between the

[1] Introductory paragraphs freely adapted from Ruth Shonle Cavan, chairman, Ernest W. Burgess, and Robert J. Havighurst, Section VII, "The Family in the Later Years," for the Committee on the Dynamics of Family Interaction, Preliminary Report, Evelyn Millis Duvall and Reuben Hill, co-chairmen, National Conference on Family Life, Washington, D. C., February 1948, mimeographed materials.

Median Age of Wife

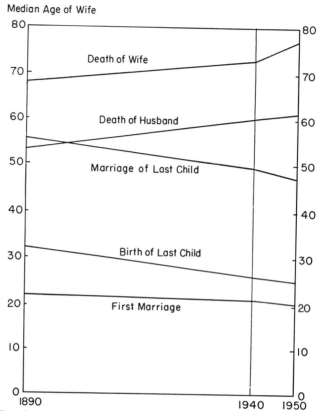

CHART 15. Stages of the Life Cycle of the Family in the United States: 1890, 1940, and 1950.[1]

marriage of the last child and the advent of widow- or widowerhood was very brief. But this interval is constantly increasing. Fewer children give an earlier release from childrearing; medical advances postpone the time when death of husband or wife will break the marital bond. After the marriage of the last child, husband and wife have a period in the middle years, less common in the past, when they, rather than their children, are the center of family life. As Chart 15 indicates, in 1950, the couple typically had between thirteen and fourteen years together after the marriage of the last child. This contrasts with the situation in

[1] Paul C. Glick, "The Life Cycle of the Family," *Marriage and Family Living*, Vol. XVII, No. 1, February 1955, p. 4, Figure 1.

1890, when the likelihood was that a woman was already widowed before her last child left home for marriage.

Stage Seven of the family life cycle, as defined in Chapter One, starts with the departure of the last child from the home and continues to the retirement of the husband or the death of one of the spouses. This may be a period of only a few months or years as in the case of a late launching of a son or daughter, or an early retirement of the man of the house. The stage may abruptly stop with the premature death of either husband or wife. It may be delayed indefinitely by a dependent child who stays on in the home through the years. Typically, in 1950, the period of the middle years lasted longer than any stage in the family cycle that a couple had had since its marriage. The stage comes as a "breathing spell" for a man and wife between the busy years of childrearing and the aging years when important changes (retirement from employment, curtailed social life, decreased physical vitality, and finally the death of husband or wife) must be anticipated.

Ever since MacIver dubbed this "the stage of the empty nest" twenty years ago,[1] it frequently has been discussed in terms of the bleakness that awaits the man and woman in the middle years. Reuben Hill summarizes some of the usual American difficulties as follows:

. . . Both husband and wife face similar problems in the middle years because ours is a youth-oriented society. As a young country, America has rewarded youth and deprecated middle age and later maturity. Our schools and families have failed to prepare us systematically for the roles that may be played in middle age, and consequently we approach the period with great hesitancy and conflicting emotions. This is true whether we are burdened with the task of launching our own children into jobs and marriage or are facing the complications of a childless old age. For it is in the middle years . . . that men must face their diminishing bargaining power in the market place, their decreasing virility and powers of attraction for women, and their limited stature as persons in a society geared to poor-boy-makes-good stories. It is in the middle years that the wife-and-mother discovers that raising one or two children and caring for a husband turns out not to be a permanently full-time job.[2]

---

[1] R. M. MacIver, *Society, A Textbook of Sociology* (New York: Rinehart, 1937), pp. 199 *ff*.

[2] Reuben Hill, revision of Willard Waller, *The Family: A Dynamic Interpretation* (copyright, 1951, by The Dryden Press, Inc. Reprinted by special permission), p. 430.

These are the years when a couple can tour the countryside, take a trip to faraway places, and enjoy their freedom for a weekend or a season.

In recent years a variety of patterns has emerged as characteristic of the middle years in the family. With well-nigh universal military service has come the common practice of a married daughter returning home with her baby until her husband is discharged. One grandfather in his early fifties comments, "What's all this about the empty nest? The old nest here is bursting at the seams with five wonderful grandchildren and two sons-in-law extra—all besides the two daughters who used to roost with us!"

Another not infrequent pattern is for the husband and wife in their middle years to take off in a grand scale of couple living. Not since their honeymoon have they been as free as they now are with all their children grown and accounted for. These are the years when one meets middleaged couples touring the countryside, taking trips to faraway places, enjoying their new-found freedom for a weekend or a season as they have not been able to do since their children came.

Other middleaged men and women go in for a variety of self-enriching pursuits that range all the way from Spanish lessons to campaigning for membership on the board of education. The empty nest is not as empty as it looks at first sight, when it fills up with committee meetings, old friends on new footings, and the bright sparkle of fresh paint, new faces, and novel ideas. As one energetic woman states her position,

Empty nest my eye! This is going to be a time of personal fulfillment. For the first twenty years I did what my parents wanted me to do. The next twenty-five years I did what my children wanted to do. This next twenty-five years, my husband and I are going to be free as air to do what we want to do.[1]

DEVELOPMENTAL TASKS OF MIDDLEAGED ADULTS

The difference between the "dull tag-end of life" experience and the years that are full to over-flowing lies not in the circumstance of middle-age as much as in the success the two people have, as individuals and as a couple, in accomplishing the developmental tasks of the period. For this is a developmental phase. Just as the young woman can be miserably lonely as an adolescent if she does not achieve the tasks of actively participating with her peers, so too she can feel abandoned as a middleaged woman if she does not work effectively toward the meeting of the developmental tasks of her middle years. The problem lies not so much in the period, as in the person.

It is true that many men and women fail to find success and happiness in their life tasks during the middle years. Our society has but poorly defined what is expected of persons at this stage of life. Little is done to prepare individuals for it. Few guides are available, and many tangled paths criss-cross the wilderness of human maturity.

At this writing the first intensive study of performance in developmental tasks in adulthood is underway as part of the Kansas City Study of Adult Life. In this research, carried on by members of the University of Chicago Committee on Human Development in cooperation with Community Studies, Inc., of Kansas City, Missouri; the developmental tasks of middle adulthood (45 to about 60 years) are listed as follows:

1. Setting adolescent children free and helping them to become happy and responsible adults.

[1] Ralph G. Eckert, *Sex Attitudes in the Home* (New York: Association Press, 1956), p. 234.

*1a. As aunt or uncle, serving as model and, on occasion, as parent-substitute for nephews and nieces.
   2. Discovering new satisfactions in relations with one's spouse.
*2a. Working out an intimate relationship with brothers and sisters.
   3. Working out an affectionate but independent relationship with aging parents.
   4. Creating a beautiful and comfortable home.
   5. Reaching a peak in one's work career.
   6. Achieving mature social and civic responsibility.
   7. Accepting and adjusting to physiological changes of middleage.
   8. Making an art of friendship.
   9. Making a satisfying and creative use of leisure time.
  10. Becoming or maintaining oneself as an active club or organization member.
  11. Becoming or maintaining oneself as an active church member.

> * Roles which unmarried people may perform more fully than the average person, as a partial substitute for the roles of parent and spouse.[1]

Success in any of these tasks results from effective expenditure of time and energy. None of them comes automatically as an inevitable part of life after forty. Failures are possible in any of them, with the unhappiness now and the delays in future growth that go with failure in any of the developmental tasks of life (Chapter Five).

Developmental tasks of adults arise from (1) the biological maturing and aging of the physical body, and (2) the social expectations or cultural demands upon the person (Chapter Five). As at all other stages in the life history, the individual's aspirations constitute a powerful secondary source of his or her developmental tasks. Personal aspirations are by nature idiosyncratic and highly individual, and therefore difficult to name or measure. Social expectations, on the other hand, tend to be general within a culture and as such can be listed and scored. It is possible to appraise an individual's success in his social roles as one measure of his achievement of his developmental tasks as an adult.

A man or woman in modern society is expected to fill such social roles as (1) parent, (2) spouse, (3) child of aging parent, (4) homemaker (male or female), (5) worker, (6) user of leisure time, (7) church member, (8) club or association member, (9) citizen, and (10) friend. The

[1] Robert J. Havighurst and Betty Orr, *Adult Education and Adult Needs, A Report,* Center for the Study of Liberal Education for Adults, 940 East 58th Street, Chicago 37, Illinois, 1956, p. 9.

quality of a person's life is judged generally by the way he or she fills these roles. When performance approaches the ideal expectations of American society generally, it is rated "high"; when performance is average (4 to 5 on a 0–9 scale) it is rated "medium"; while failure is rated "low." Actual scores on performance in each of ten social roles for men and women in four social classes in the Kansas City study, gives the multi-celled picture seen in Table 27.

TABLE 27. *Performance Scores of Kansas City Adults on the Developmental Tasks of Middleage* [1]

	MEN (Age 40–70) Social Class *				WOMEN (Age 40–70) Social Class *			
Area	I	II	III	IV	I	II	III	IV
Parent	6.00	5.50	5.21	3.90	6.44	5.48	5.88	4.84
Spouse	6.00	5.57	4.87	4.13	6.17	5.94	5.46	3.62
Child of Aging Parent	5.89	6.06	5.89	5.00	5.75	5.90	5.94	5.75
Homemaker	5.64	5.70	5.55	4.38	5.93	4.86	5.40	3.68
Worker	7.31	5.67	5.36	3.54	6.25	5.97	4.50	3.61
Leisure	5.97	5.64	4.21	3.50	6.32	5.05	4.33	2.66
Church Member	4.19	3.39	3.19	3.06	4.70	3.57	4.23	4.18
Club and Ass'n	5.55	3.03	2.47	1.89	5.13	2.34	1.91	0.84
Citizen	5.21	4.11	3.64	3.44	4.57	4.01	3.06	3.91
Friend	5.27	4.38	4.02	3.75	6.32	4.59	3.85	2.52

* I—Upper-middle; II—Lower-middle; III—Upper-lower; IV—Lower-lower (as defined by Warner and other writers on social class in America).

Several observations are of interest in comparing the performance scores on the developmental tasks of middleage (Table 27) by social class, sex, and social role. In general we note that:

a) The higher the social class, the higher the performance score on developmental tasks for both men and women in all social roles.
b) Women tend to get higher scores than do men in such roles as parent and church member; but men do better than women as club and association members and as citizens, generally for all social class levels.
c) Scores range from .84 (lower-class women as club and association members) to 7.31 (upper middle-class men as workers) with more than half (47 out of 80) getting "medium" scores between 4 and 6; 24 out of 80 scoring less than 4 ("low"); and 9 of the 80 scoring over 6 or "high medium."

[1] *Ibid.* p. 32.

COMPLEMENTARY ROLES OF HUSBAND AND WIFE IN THE MIDDLE YEARS

Husband and wife roles through the middle years are largely complementary. Each role exists because of the other. The husband is husband because of his wife, and vice versa. Traditionally the husband-wife complementarity was based upon a sexual division of labor. Certain things were man's work, others were typically woman's work in the farm family of earlier days (Chapter Two). With the changing form and function of families has come new freedom in the roles of men and women, especially after they have reared their families. How they work out their roles in relationship to each other is an interesting area for study.

One student of the roles played by middleaged husbands and wives has found six different patterns of complementarity in the Kansas City middle-class sample being studied in research in progress: [1]

1) *Reciprocal bolstering,* through appreciation, consideration and standing by with encouragement through crisis.

2) *Mutual activities,* in increased recreational pursuits that both enjoy together.

3) *Relaxing together,* as "joint idlers in a restful paradise of peace and quiet."

4) *Joint participation in husband's occupation,* in which the wife becomes absorbed in helping her husband in his work.

5) *Constructive projects,* in which both members of the couple join forces to fix things up, in one project after another.

6) *Separate interests,* as husband remains absorbed in his work and the wife goes on with what interests she has or can find.

Parsons anticipates the modern-day tendency for the complementarity of husband-wife roles to be disrupted by the husband's preoccupation with his career, when he says,

The effect of the specialization of occupational role is to narrow the range in which the sharing of common human interests can play a large part. In relation to his wife the tendency of this narrowness would seem to be to encourage on her part either the domestic or the glamorous role or community participation somewhat unrelated to the marriage relationship.[2]

[1] Irwin Deutscher, "Husband-Wife Relations in Middle-Age: An Analysis of Sequential Roles Among the Urban Middle Classes," Unpublished manuscript, Department of Sociology, University of Missouri, July 1954, pp. 122–130.

[2] Talcott Parsons, "Age and Sex in the Social Structure of the United States," in *Essays in Sociological Theory, Pure and Applied* (Glencoe, Illinois: The Free Press, 1949), p. 228.

The healthy middleaged man and woman would like to keep on growing together if they can. Too often they do not know what to do to achieve continued development as a couple. Their lessons in life have failed to show them where they go or what they do when their children are launched and they are on their own. Give them a glimpse of what is necessary to do, give them a hand in their efforts to work out their developmental responsibilities, provide them opportunities to work with others who are facing the same tasks—given these things they too may continue their growth potentialities now, as they have before.

Ask any woman in her forties or fifties, "What would you rather have—a dull, dreary, gone-to-seed life from now on while your husband is busy on his job? Or a bright, alive, creative period that gives you both a chance to contribute all you are capable of to each other, your youngsters, your community, and your world?" Only the most apathetic woman will choose the chaise longue to rest her weary spirit. The woman in the middle years today is tired not from the work she has done, but from the failure she has met that has crushed her will to work.

DEVELOPMENTAL TASKS OF THE WIFE AND MOTHER IN THE MIDDLE YEARS

1) *Helping grown and growing children to become happy and responsible adults:*

  Setting young adult children free as autonomous persons.

  Freeing herself from her emotional dependence upon her children.

  Relinquishing her central position in the affection of her grown and growing children, and sharing them freely with their husbands, wives and friends.

  Standing by with assistance as needed, without hovering and smothering.

  Withdrawing from active motherhood roles and diffusing nurturance drives into wider areas of mothering (through community service, interest in children and young people generally).

  Accepting her young adult sons and daughters and their husbands, wives, and children as dear friends whose independence is respected and promoted.

  Enjoying her grandchildren without intruding and meddling.

2) *Discovering and developing new satisfactions as a wife with her husband:*

Giving her husband the encouragement, reassurance, support and appreciation he needs as a middleaged man.

Enjoying her part in joint activities as a couple again.

Exploring new hobbies, vacation possibilities, friendship groups and community projects they both may enjoy as a pair.

Becoming a desirable and desiring companion.

Plumbing the possibilities of deep and abiding intimacy, in mutual understanding, empathy, and the sense of unity as a couple.

3) *Working out an affectionate and independent relationship with aging parents:*

Helping her own and her husband's parents find wholesome happy ways of living out their sunset years.

Assisting both sets of aging parents find satisfactory supports for their failing powers as needed.

Giving the expressions of interest, affection, and care that aging parents need from their grown children.

Serving as a buffer as need be between the demands of aging parents and the needs of the young adults, emerging in the family.

Weathering the inevitable illnesses, accidents, and eventual death of aging parents in wholesome, supportive ways.

4) *Creating a pleasant, comfortable home for her husband and herself:*

Refurbishing the home for couple-living after the children have grown.

Reworking household facilities and routines for ease and comfort of upkeep.

Investing time, energy and resources in making home a place of enjoyment and comfort according to the interests and values of husband and wife.

Getting satisfactions from achieving proficiency in one or more of her chosen roles.

Sharing the family home at intervals with grown children, grandchildren and friends with satisfaction in hospitality.

Giving, receiving and exchanging hospitality with grown children with mutual interdependence and freedom.

5) *Finding satisfactions in her work if she is an employed woman:*

Becoming more relaxed about the quantity of her work.

Making progress in line with her powers, wisdom, and proficiencies as a woman on the job.

Getting real satisfactions from being of service, being creative, being recognized as competent, and being a pleasant colleague and a growing person.

Balancing the values of her work with those of her homemaking and other roles to avoid strain and grossly unequal devotion to any one.

6) *Achieving mature social and civic responsibility:*

Becoming alert and intelligently informed about civic affairs and her role in them.

Taking an active part in one or more organizations at work on civic and political problems in the neighborhood, community, nation, or world.

Giving time, energy, and resources to causes beyond herself and her home.

Working cooperatively with others in the mutual responsibilities of citizenship.

Committing herself to the democratic ideal in any of its many manifestations.

7) *Accepting and adjusting to the physical changes of middle age in healthful ways:*

Taking menopause in her stride with whatever medical and psychological supports may be needed.

Accepting changes in skin, hair color, body tone, energy output, and physical rhythms without distress.

Eating a well-balanced diet high in proteins, fresh fruits and vegetables.

Keeping her weight within normal limits.

Getting a healthful balance of sleep and exercise.

Going periodically for medical and dental check-ups and following prescribed routines.

Dressing comfortably and attractively to please both herself and others.

Relishing the bloom and pace of maturity as a woman.

8) *Making an art of friendship:*

Cherishing old friends for themselves and the mutual experiences and values that have been built together through the years.

Choosing new friends from among the many interesting new contacts with "our kind of people" as well as novel, refreshing personalities.

Enjoying active social life with friends of both sexes and a variety of ages.

Giving and receiving freely in social interaction with her friends.

Accepting at least a few friends into close sharing of real feelings with intimacy and mutual security.

Becoming an increasingly friendly person who values her friends and her friendships highly.

9) *Using her leisure time creatively and with satisfaction:*

Choosing the interests and activities that she finds most personally rewarding without yielding too much to social pressures and "styles."

Learning to do some things well enough to become known for them among her family, friends and associates.

Losing herself sufficiently in one or more areas of interest so that she gets creative satisfactions from her leisure hours.

Balancing her program of leisure activities with active and passive, collective and solitary, service-motivated and self-indulgent pursuits.

Keeping alive and interested in the world around her and her part in it.

10) *Becoming or maintaining herself as an active club or association member:*

Choosing her affiliations with discrimination.

Assuming real responsibilities in those she considers important.

Refusing conflicting, contradictory or too burdensome invitations with poise.

Getting a sense of pleasure and satisfaction from her affiliations.

Enjoying a sense of belonging with kindred minds and spirits.

Working through her own ways of dealing with intraclub tensions, power systems and personality problems within the membership, comfortably and effectively.

11) *Becoming or maintaining herself as an active church member, as may be socially expected and personally meaningful:*

Finding a soul-satisfying place for herself in a religious affiliation in which she has an abiding faith.

Holding one or more responsible positions within the church.

Gaining personal satisfaction from worship and the rituals, ceremonies, and celebrations of her church.

Contributing her services and her resources to the upkeep of her church.

Serving in ways that help her contribute her best talents to the causes and purposes in which she believes.

Discovering new depths and meanings in the brotherhood of man and the Fatherhood of God that go beyond the fellowship of her particular church.

Any woman who accomplishes all this is quite a woman! No one is expected to score high on every task, now or at any other time of life. Certain social roles that are expected in some communities are not important in others; *i.e.*, church membership. Some tasks will proceed smoothly and well. Others will labor or go by default. In those areas where she builds upon past successes, the middleaged woman will be likely to find happiness and relative success in the tasks of the middle years. In the tasks in which she has had past difficulties, failures or little experience, her accomplishments in the middle years may reflect her inexperience or incompetence.

Some of the developmental tasks of the middle years are particularly difficult for the middleaged woman, partly because she does not relish them. It is an unusual woman who really enjoys relinquishing her active role as mother, to see her children, whom she has loved and cared for for twenty years, pack their suitcases and leave home. A woman's children represent for her, more than they do for her husband, not only an emotional investment of her adulthood until now, but also the main reason for her existence. Throughout her life as wife and mother, her children have been her job. Now, when they leave, she feels that they take with them her very reason for being. Unless she has prepared herself through the years for a life beyond her children, helping them become independent adults is apt to be a highly unpleasant and difficult job for her.

Difficult too, may be the re-establishment of a close companionship with her husband now that the children have grown. If she has been a "devoted mother" she may have put the children first, and her husband in second place in her thoughts and actions through the years. Now it may come as a shock to realize that she hardly knows this man of hers in terms of his deepest hurts and disillusionments, his dreams and aspirations, or even how he really feels about her. She may feel that they have grown apart through the years of childrearing while he had to keep his

Re-establishment of a close relationship with her husband is especially important now that the children have grown and gone.

nose to the grindstone to make ends meet, and she was so everlastingly busy with the thousand and one details of homemaking. She may find life dull and drab in the same old routines with him day after day, and long for a fling that will help her get a taste of LIFE before it is too late, as Fran Dodsworth attempted (Sinclair Lewis, *Dodsworth*, New York: Harcourt Brace and Company, 1929). She may find initial efforts to get close to her husband now peculiarly embarrassing, self-conscious, and hardly worth the effort. But, if she has maintained a real fellowship with her mate as their children were growing up, she does not have as far to go now in re-establishing a meaningful companionship. Husband and wife have learned what to expect of each other. They have already established some personally delightful little whimsicalities as well as a deeply meaningful unity so that further fellowship is a constant discovery and delight.

A third developmental task that tends to be shunned by the middle-aged woman in American culture is that of coming to terms with her age and the processes of aging. There is such a high valuation on youth in society at large, that she fears for her status, her acceptance, her desirability, her very security in the gradual loss of her youth. Now, more than ever, she wants to feel that she is attractive. The appearance of gray hair, wrinkles in her skin, flabbiness in upper arm and abdomen may be frightening reminders that she is no longer the appealing young thing she once was. She may lie about her age and prop up her sagging tissues, with society approving. She may paint on an artificial complexion, with the disapproval of some of her friends and associates. Or she may cultivate the charm of maturity that will see her through for several decades. Marlene Dietrich, Claudette Colbert, Helen Hayes, and countless other women have proven that the years need not rob a woman of the charm of true femininity.

Some developmental tasks of the middleaged wife and mother are highly motivated and relatively pleasantly undertaken. Now, as at other times in the life cycle, there are certain teachable moments that are full of eagerness to learn and grow and achieve. The woman may get a special pleasure in helping her husband rearrange their lives, to "live it up" a little now, when their responsibilities are not as great as they have been and their income is still near its peak. It may be fun to expand their recreational budget to take a trip or build a summer place, or join a club they haven't been able to afford before. Redoing their home as a place they are proud to call their own may become a joyful task, highly motivated, and richly rewarding in ways for all to see.

Becoming a satisfied and satisfying grandmother may be another easy, happy developmental task. In wanting to become worthy of these exciting new roles with these wonderful little people who are indeed her "own flesh and blood," she may take a refresher course in child care, and learn more now than she ever knew about children and child development, her nature as a person, and of life itself.

Difficult or easy, late or soon, every wife and mother faces her new developmental tasks in her own way with the coming of her middle years. She is successful if she finds happiness and satisfaction in this stage of living. As she meets life's challenges now she prepares herself for the aging years that lie ahead. She is all of a piece, building on what has gone before, and laying the foundation now for what still lies ahead.

DEVELOPMENTAL TASKS OF THE HUSBAND AND FATHER IN THE MIDDLE YEARS

1) *Setting young adult children free and helping them become happy, responsible adults:*

Getting along with grown children as friendly equals in most areas of life.

Encouraging grown children to make their own choices of clothes, college, military service, friends, marriage partner, job, etc.

Supporting grown children where necessary, unobtrusively and without any strings attached.

Being an advisor as requested, and an impartial "listener" for young people who are trying to work out their problems.

Expecting grown children to want and need autonomy, privacy and freedom.

Giving and receiving affection and attention from grown children and their families.

Becoming a pleasant, beloved grandfather who finds joy in his grandchildren.

2) *Discovering and developing new satisfactions with his wife:*

Giving his wife the reassurance, the recognition (both in private and in public), the appreciation and the affection she needs as a middleaged woman.

Enjoying being with his wife and participating with her in a variety of shared activities.

Feeling close to his wife with mutual understanding and empathy.

Sharing his work, his thoughts, his feelings and his hopes and disappointments with his wife, and encouraging her to tell him of hers.

Developing mutually satisfying ways of attracting and holding her interest in him as a man, a male, and as a husband.

3) *Working out an affectionate and independent relationship with aging parents:*

Being friendly without too much dominance or dependence in relations with his own and his wife's parents.

Taking responsibility for failing parents as needed in ways that help them maintain their self-respect.

Keeping in touch with the needs, interests, and plans of his parents.

Working through, with the others involved, the best possible living arrangements when parents no longer are able to live by themselves.

Interpreting aging parents and young adult family members to each other as needed.

Giving personal support as illnesses, accidents, and eventual death of one or both parents bring their crises to the bereaved one(s).

4) *Creating a pleasant, comfortable home:*

Taking a real interest in the physical upkeep of the home.

Assuming responsibility for the care of the heavier chores around the house, basement, and yard.

Helping plan for and taking a real interest in decorating the home and keeping it nice.

Enjoying full partnership in planning for the home, its remodeling, redecorating, and ongoing routines.

Taking pride in his and in his wife's accomplishments in making the home a good place to live in as a couple.

Finding pleasure in having grown children home at intervals for celebrations, vacations, and in times of need.

Assuming his share of responsibility for entertaining friends, associates, and members of the extended family.

5) *Working productively and efficiently in his job:*

Liking his work and doing well in it.

Being able to lead and to follow, to give and to take orders comfortably on the job.

Coming to terms with the degree of success that is his without regret or recriminations.

Getting satisfactions on his job from: friendships with associates, feeling of being needed and of service, self-respect and prestige, and feeling of creative productivity.

Taking his work at a more leisurely pace as time goes on, letting established routines and wisdom on the job take the place of earlier over-zealous drive.

Letting younger men take over without threat of lost status, and planning for his eventual retirement constructively.

6) *Achieving mature social and civic responsibility:*

Keeping informed and enjoying discussing civic affairs and national and international problems.

Understanding where he fits into the pressure groups and politics of the society.

Taking active part in some one or more movements for community improvement, civic reform, or national and world conditions.

Encouraging his wife and family to be good citizens.

Standing for democratic practices and the good of the whole in issues where vested interests may be at stake.

7) *Accepting and adjusting to the physical changes of middleage in healthful ways:*

Getting regular medical and dental check-ups and keeping physically fit.

Using the glasses, hearing aid, or other helps prescribed for him as needed.

Eating what is good for him, in healthful quantities, avoiding excesses in rich, caloric foods, and keeping tobacco use and alcohol consumption within reasonable limits.

Getting some physical exercise appropriate to his age, strength, and endurance.

Dressing comfortably and attractively with attention to good grooming and the self-respect of cleanliness, neatness and appropriateness.

Wearing his mature years with poise, without undue concern over such inevitables as balding, graying hair, and lessening vitality.

8) *Making an art of friendship:*

Choosing friends of various ages with mutual interests and ongoing satisfactions.

Enjoying old and new friends of both sexes in a variety of settings, rituals, and functions.

Reciprocating hospitality and finding satisfactions in both roles of host and guest.

Being gracious to his wife's friends and associates, for themselves as well as for his wife's sake.

Sharing feelings intimately with close friends in whose fellowship he feels basically secure.

Considering himself a warm friendly person with others generally.

9) *Making satisfying and creative use of leisure time:*

Welcoming the increased leisure of the middle years as a chance to do all the things he has never had time for before.

Choosing some activities that have personal meaning for him as well as doing some things for fellowship primarily.

Mastering some arts and skills sufficiently to gain recognition and a heightened sense of self-respect and pride from his workmanship.

Losing himself in some of his pursuits so that he is never at a loss for things to do.

Sharing an increasing number of his leisure time activities with his wife.

Keeping alert and alive to the world around him.

10) *Becoming or maintaining himself as an active club or association member:*

Dropping the unrewarding affiliations that may have interested him early in his career but that may be burdensome or boring now.

Attending meetings and assuming responsibility in the associations he considers important.

Finding satisfactions in using his talents and abilities in group activities.

Enjoying fellowship with like-minded people.

Becoming a mature "elder statesman" in diplomatic roles within the relationships of his clubs.

11) *Becoming or maintaining himself as an active church member, as may be socially expected or personally rewarding:*

Coming to terms with what religion and his church mean to him.

Holding responsible positions in his church.

Finding personal satisfactions through the various rituals, activities and programs of the church.

Enjoying the opportunities for service available through the church and its related activities.

Being increasingly willing to lose himself in causes that are bigger than he is, and in movements that go beyond the present.

The husband and father in the middle years finds some of his developmental tasks easier than the parallel tasks his wife is facing. It probably is easier for him, than it is for her, to encourage the autonomy of their children, largely because the children have been her main responsibility, her Number One job through the years of their growing up. It usually is easier for a middleaged man to find ongoing satisfactions in his work than it is for his wife whose employment has probably been secondary to her homemaking responsibilities through the years.

In some areas of life the man in the middle years of the family life cycle may find difficulties greater than those his wife is facing. He may

Grandfatherhood can be a challenging task for a man who does not know what to do with little children.

refuse to recognize his decline in vitality, and brag that he can work and play as vigorously as he did twenty years ago. He may have been so preoccupied with his work through the years of getting established that he has built little foundation for more relaxed living with his wife and family. He may be dismayed in the face of so much leisure now available, and postpone much-needed vacations, or hurry back from those he takes, largely because he has never learned to play. Some men even feel guilty if they "play" since recreation used to be considered wasteful of time rather than re-creative.

After years of tight financing, and trying to make ends meet within the pressures of his growing family, he may find that he has built habits of scrimping and "making do" that now are inappropriate. It may be a struggle for him to cooperate with his wife in making their home pleasant and comfortable. He may seem to be "tight" with their money now when they might be enjoying it in ways that are rightfully theirs. He is likely to be uncertain about how much should be saved for the future and how much could be spent for today's pleasure.

Even grandfatherhood can be a challenging task. During the years when his own children were growing up he may have been so involved outside the home that he never seemed to have the time for close companionship with them that now is possible with his grandchildren. He may not know what to do with little children, and so miss out on some of the joys and satisfactions that otherwise would be his. He can find peculiar pleasure in his grandchildren, and contribute richly to them and to the entire family from the wisdom and richness of his years.

A man is sometimes a better father to his grandchildren than he was able to be to his own children. He is getting older now and the years have passed so swiftly that he is suddenly aware of all that he has missed. He wants to make up for lost time and one way to do it is to enjoy his grandchildren and savor their youth, though he had little inclination for this sort of thing when his own children were small . . .

. . . . .

. . . Grandfather, who has read many men and women in his lifetime, often catches the tremble in the lip or the hangdog look of shame that a busy parent misses beneath the overt defiance. Being a wise man he has relinquished the intense competition of his earlier days, the ceaseless striving to keep up with the Joneses, get ahead of a business rival, or acquire a new-model car every year. He has learned to be content with his lot whatever it may be. He is relaxed enough to have fun with his grandchildren and that is the master recipe for being good friends with children.

A thoughtful, well-seasoned, leisured man in a home where there are young children can be of great service in their well-rounded development. Grandfather has time to mend a broken toy or coax a stubborn one to work. He can read or tell stories. He is not too busy to admire the shape of a pebble a young one discovers on the beach and wonder with him about it—why it is different from all the others, from what far shores the ocean waves washed it, where it got its opalescent gleam.

. . . . .

Children need grandparents who have come to terms with life and accept it philosophically as parents seldom have yet learned or had time to do. When those who are at the beginning of the journey hold hands with those who have travelled a long way and know all the turns in the road, each gains the strength needed by both. They are like the pair who were seen wandering together in the summer over the winding paths of a Maine island in Casco Bay.

"My grandfather takes me everywhere," the small boy told a summer visitor happily.

"He doesn't know it," the white-haired man smiled, "but he's the one who takes *me*. I'm blind, you see." [1]

A man may flee from the new expectations and possibilities of middle-age. He may bury himself blindly in his accustomed work and refuse to anticipate his impending retirement. He may neglect his wife, his grown children, his grandchildren, and his friends. He can deny his own failing strength, and refuse to accept his feelings of regret, frustration, disappointment and panic. He may fail in any or all the developmental tasks of this stage of life, and be miserable in the process, nursing his neurotic symptoms and his grudges until he chucks it all in an early grave soon after retirement. Such failures to meet the challenge of the middle years do happen, but they are not necessary.

A husband and father who is willing to keep on growing can, during his middle years, reap the harvest of good living, that he has sown in earlier years. He can relax and enjoy the fruits of his labors, in the sense of "You Can't Take It with You," or in the spirit of this being "the last of life for which the first was made." He can rediscover the richness of marriage, the satisfactions of fellowship with grown children, the warmth of friendship, the excitement of adventure and novel experience, the rewards of creative productivity. But not one of these automatically "comes due" at this time, without effort on his part. They all are satisfactions that accrue from success in achieving the developmental tasks of this stage of life. When he does a good job in them, he finds the happiness that goes with their successful accomplishment. As long as there is life, there can be growth, and the middle years are no exception.

THE CRISIS OF THE MIDDLE YEARS

The crisis of the middle years arises out of the human necessity to come to terms with the realities of life. This is the time of life when a person's self-concept must tally with what he or she actually is. All through childhood and adolescence the boy feels that he is in the process of becoming, and that someday he will be as he wants to be. Through the twenties and thirties a man pushes ahead, looks for "a break" and believes that if he works hard enough he will achieve his dream of "success." By the time he gets to be middleaged, he probably is still

[1] O. Spurgeon English and Constance J. Foster, *Fathers Are Parents, Too* (New York: G. P. Putnam's Sons, 1951), pp. 260–261, 268–269 and 271.

short of realizing these personal aspirations. But now he knows he has less chance of achieving all his goals, and must settle for what he is, however disappointing and disillusioning this may be.

Through the first two decades of life a girl dreams of growing up, getting married, and having a family. Her twenties and thirties are filled with the realization of that goal in the busy round of childbearing and childrearing activities. Then in her forties and fifties, she finds herself jobless, at the end of her goal, with still half her adulthood ahead of her. Who she thinks she is and what she does about the latter half of her marriage, depends in large measure on how well the woman meets the crisis of finding herself once more as a creating, developing, purposeful person.

There is evidence that many men and women fail to find happiness in the middle years. A recent study of the marital happiness and un-happiness of married persons (as rated by their brothers and sisters) reveals the forties and early fifties as a crisis period for married women, and the fifties as critical for men.[1] For women, this study finds that the crises revolve around the mothers' joblessness when their children no longer need their mothering, the inadequacy of their middleaged hus-bands as sexual partners, and the problems of the menopause.[2] For men, the unhappiness tends to center around occupational rather than sexual problems.

. . . Two groups of men are identified by our informants. One consists of men who have attained some degree of prominence and success in their chosen field, only to find that their wives have not kept pace with them in their up-ward climb. Such men often make a determined effort to remain loyal to their mates. Some of them are reported as succeeding; others fail and are aware of it; and still others appear to their siblings as failing in spite of outward evidences of success.

A second group of men, identified by their siblings, are in their fifties and have failed, absolutely or relatively, in their occupational efforts. Such failures lead them to rationalizations: they never had a chance to succeed, they say. Their wives were no help to them. If it were not for the handicaps which

[1] James H. S. Bossard and Eleanor S. Boll, "Marital Unhappiness in the Life Cy-cle," *Marriage and Family Living*, Vol. XVII, No. 1, February 1955, pp. 10–14.

[2] Dr. Ruth Albrecht feels that menopause is given as "a popular excuse for person-ality and adjustment inadequacies, since our findings indicate that this is a problem for only about 20% of the women, lasts only a short time (or a few years at the most) and may be reduced greatly by modern medical care," personal communication, July 2, 1956.

their wives imposed, they would have succeeded, as did other men. Such wives become scapegoats for the failure of their husbands. The husbands find comfort in the development of feelings of self-pity and animosity toward their wives. [1]

The findings of a study of 8,300 American business leaders and their wives, seem to show that business success depends not so much on whom a man marries, or on what his wife does, as on his talents, energies, and his singleness of purpose.[2] If these findings apply to vocational success generally, then it must be that a great many men unfairly blame their wives for their failures, to the impairment of the marriage relationship. If, at the same time, middleaged women complain about the inadequacies of their husbands as sexual mates, as Bossard and Boll find many of them do, then the probabilities are that the marriage itself is threatened in the middle years.

Somewhat more than one in every ten marriages breaks up after the twentieth year of marriage (10.4 per cent).[3] It is possible that some of these divorces represent the previous effort of the unhappy husband and wife to stay together "for the sake of the children," until the departure of the last child makes the effort no longer meaningful. In other cases, the divorce represents the couple's failure to work out a satisfying marriage after its childrearing phase is past.

In the insecurity of the middle years, it is understandable that the unhappy wife blames her husband for his inadequacies and her children for their lack of gratitude, while the unsuccessful middleaged man blames his wife for his failures. These attitudes are negative and ineffectual but not unusual as face-saving mechanisms in the crisis of the middle years. But, if the marriage is to continue, if the family is to survive intact and in harmony, if the relationships are to grow and develop through the years that lie ahead, more positive efforts must be made to achieve the developmental tasks of the family in its middle years. Only then will the family unit be assured of success, and its members of fulfillment.

---

[1] Bossard and Boll, op. cit., p. 14.

[2] W. Lloyd Warner and James C. Abegglen, "Successful Wives of Successful Executives," Harvard Business Review, March–April issue, 1956; also by the same authors, Business Leaders in America (New York: Harper & Brothers, 1956).

[3] Computed from data in "Divorces and Annulments, Detailed Statistics for Reporting Areas, 1953," Vital Statistics Reports, Vol. 42, No. 2, May 17, 1955, National Office of Vital Statistics, Table 5, pp. 34, 35.

FAMILY DEVELOPMENTAL TASKS IN THE MIDDLE YEARS

The middle years in the family are a challenge to more than the individual husband and wife as middleaged adults. This stage has its full complement of family developmental tasks that are necessary for family survival, continuity, and growth. These family developmental tasks can be briefly outlined as follows:

1) Maintaining a pleasant and comfortable home.
2) Enjoying financial peace of mind now while assuring security for the later years.
3) Carrying household responsibilities lightly and together.
4) Drawing closer together as a couple.
5) Maintaining warm, mutually supportive relationships with grown children's families.
6) Keeping in touch with brothers' and sisters' families and with aging parents.
7) Participating in community life beyond the family.
8) Reaffirming the values of life that have real meaning.

MAINTAINING A PLEASANT AND COMFORTABLE HOME

Chances are the middleaged couple stay on in the family home after their children leave. Some pick up and move to more favorable climates, or into more congenial neighborhoods, or closer to the husband's work or near one or more of their married children, or into a smaller place, but percentage-wise these instances are fewer than those who stay put. According to the United States Bureau of the Census data for 1952, only 10.3 per cent of all husbands between the ages of 45 and 64 years moved during the preceeding year.[1]

Reasons for remaining in the family home are several. The most powerful is probably the sense that this *is* home to husband and wife. Here their habits are built into the place. Here are their friends, neighbors, and the familiar ways of life that perhaps mean much to both of the couple. The husband still is on the job and he is accustomed to going and coming from this place. The children come home for special celebra-

[1] Paul C. Glick, "The Life Cycle of the Family," *Marriage and Family Living*, Vol. XVII, No. 1, February 1955, Table 2, page 7. (The 10.3 per cent of husbands moving in the middle years compares with 55.8 per cent of husbands under 25 years of age, 32.9 per cent of husbands 25–34 years of age, and 18.2 per cent of husbands 35–44 years old who change their place of residence.)

tions now and then, and seem to enjoy having a place to call their own within the home-base. If the family has been a happy one there are few unpleasant memories to escape, and many reasons for building themselves into the home for the enjoyment of the middle years as a couple.

Remodeling the home after the children leave is a pleasant project for the middleaged couple. Now that the place is theirs alone, it can be refurbished around their particular interests rather than in terms of what the children need. One of the upstairs bedrooms may become a cozy den or hobby center. The back porch may be closed in for intimate dining. They may decide to make a bedroom and bath on the first floor, which saves steps while they are alone and which comes in handy when sickness strikes or when aged relatives have to be given a home. The second floor may be rented out, or closed off except for times when the grown children are home with their families. There is time and money now to remodel the kitchen for good management and efficient operation as well as for its functions as living center of the home with telephone at hand, a comfortable chair or two, and a pleasant place to eat. They may redecorate with an eye to entertaining freely, or to using home as a pleasant comfortable haven from the world and its people. Whatever is done, it can express the needs, values, and interests of the husband and wife now in their middle years, and in the foreseeable future when their own failing powers will call for convenient, safe housing facilities.

Safety is particularly a factor to consider in remodeling the home for the middle and later years. A hand rail on the cellar stairs, a hand grip at the bath tub may prevent a nasty fall. Conveniently located electric outlets are important. Good lights at work centers are more essential now than ever. A quick glance at the incidence of home accidents by age groups shows a sharp increase for both men and women after fifty in accidents that disable for one week or more, Chart 16. Sensible middle-aged people plan for the gradual failing of their powers by making home as safe, convenient and comfortable as they can while they are rethinking their homemaking functions for the latter decades of life together as a couple.

After twenty or twenty-five years of marriage a man and his wife should have learned what is important to them in a home. If they enjoy their yard with its garden, it should be part of their plans for the future; but if it has been primarily for the children and of little or no interest to either of the married pair, then this may be the time to move into an

Annual frequency
per 1,000 persons

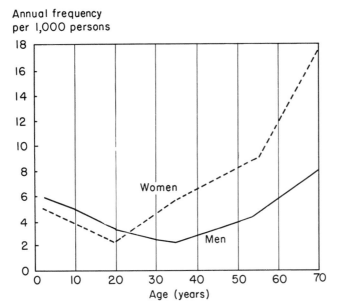

CHART 16. Home Accidents Disabling for One Week or More by Ages in Years for Men and Women by Annual Frequency per 1,000 persons.[1]

apartment or a less burdensome house. If they do move, they will need to look not only for present comfort and convenience, but also for the years ahead. Their task is in arranging for a home that expresses their interests so that it becomes for them both a satisfying place in which to live.

ENJOYING FINANCIAL PEACE OF MIND NOW WHILE ASSURING SECURITY FOR THE LATER YEARS

In the middle years, the husband's income is still at or close to its peak (Chart 13), while costs have dropped sharply as the children have left home (Chart 14). Thus, financially speaking, this is "Summertime, and the living is easy." The scrimping days of trying to make ends meet are over for most couples. The house is furnished, the car and the last baby are paid for, and the couple can relax and enjoy their earnings in the breathing spell that is theirs now before retirement and the costs of the later years are upon them. Two facets of this task call for special at-

[1] Adapted from Frederick Gutheim, *Houses for Family Living,* The Woman's Foundation, 10 East 40th Street, New York City, p. 39.

A man may wish he had saved enough during the peak years of childrearing to feel secure in the middle and later years of life.

tention: (1) learning to spend money for personal gratification after years of self-sacrifice and thinking first of the children and their needs, and (2) planning for a secure old age.

Planning financially for the later years is highly motivated during middleage. Few parents want to be beholden to their grown children for support during their own old age. They realize that neither Social Security nor Old Age Assistance will keep them on anything more than a subsistence level. They may not have accumulated enough during the peak years of childrearing to make them feel as adequately prepared for the uncertainties of their later years as they would like. And so they continue the pattern of putting their money away for a rainy day that has been established through their earlier years in the family. National analyses of saving by age groups indicate that middleage families tend to be the biggest savers, and to place more emphasis on building up a reserve than any other age group.[1]

Planning for old age should include recognition of the fact that the average age at which men die is lower than the average age at which women die. In the older age groups, there are many more widows than widowers. In fact, after age 70 there are more widows than women living with husbands. Men need to provide not only for their own support in old age, but for the support of their widows. This is more than a matter of stocks and bonds and life insurance. It means helping prepare the wife to fend for herself if and when she is left alone.

Few happily married women want to think of widowhood as a personal possibility. Yet, when one or more of their husband's friends or associates drop off in the prime of life, they begin to realize the importance of preparing for what may become inevitable for them too one day. Several steps in preparing for widowhood are indicated: (1) Find one or more close confidants besides the husband. A good woman friend will do. An understanding lawyer-friend, a sensitive pastor, or an old-friend-of-the-family may be tapped to serve as counsel and confidential ear when widowhood comes. (2) Make sure that both husband and wife know the full state of their financial affairs. The older pattern of the husband carrying the full responsibility for the money matters in the marriage meant that many mature women were as babes in the woods when their husbands died. They were easy prey for charlatans and sundry "widows' rackets." Today's couples more often share responsibility for financial planning through the years and so leave the widow better prepared to carry on when she is left in charge. (3) Encourage one or more absorbing interests in life that keep pulling toward the future. A crocheted afghan is a start, but it is not enough for most women. Active work in the community gives her something to grow on and into. A job outside the home may do it. Whatever it is, a woman in the middle years must have something to live *for* as well as to live *on*. If it can be both, she is doubly protected.

If the middleaged wife works, as do nearly a third of the married women 45–54 years of age,[2] the increased family income may be welcome

---

[1] Dorothy A. Brady and Marsha Froeder, "Influence of Age on Saving and Spending Patterns," *Monthly Labor Review*, Vol. 78, No. 11, November 1955, pp. 1240–1244.

[2] Paul C. Glick, *op. cit.*, p. 7.

A woman for whom widowhood is a personal possibility must have something to live *for* as well as on. Hobbies and interests such as gardening can continue to bring a sense of being creatively worthwhile.

for future security planning as well as for luxuries and pleasures. A combined income now may make it possible for the couple to buy a nice home, or fix up the old one, or take a long-dreamed-of trip abroad, spend a winter holiday in a southern clime, or budget more lavishly for their clothes and personal grooming than was possible before now. Some husbands are secure enough as males not to be threatened by their wives' earning power, enjoying the economic partnership involved in team earning, shared planning, and joint spending.

Learning to "live it up" may be more difficult a task in the middle years than is planning for the future. When two people have been future-oriented throughout their whole life together as a pair, it is not easy to suddenly shift into spending for present pleasures. Getting away for an occasional holiday while the children were growing up has prepared some couples for their freedom in the middle years. Spending something for immediate fun and pleasure through the years, even when the going has been rough, gives some basis for relaxing and just enjoying life now. Even finding pleasure in freedom and in enjoying life has to be learned, as many a lonely middleaged or older person discovers. This is the nature of developmental tasks, built on the past, pointed toward the future at every stage of the life cycle.

CARRYING HOUSEHOLD RESPONSIBILITIES LIGHTLY AND TOGETHER

Typically, the middleaged couple has no one but themselves to worry about in the daily routines of living. The grown children are in homes of their own; aging parents are being cared for independently; and the husband and wife are alone in the home, free to plan their daily routines as they will, without others' schedules to burden them.

Occasionally a married son or daughter will return home for a few weeks or months through a stint in military service, or for special training, or during an illness. Then the old place is crowded as two families try to live as one, getting into each other's way, and having to work out new ways of doing old chores.

There may be times when the only way to care adequately for aging parents is to bring the dependent one into the home. Then husband and wife divide the care of the aging or invalid one as best they can, so that no one gets completely unnecessarily tied down. If the old person is bedridden, the burden may be heavy indeed, perhaps for a long period of time. If the elderly one is able to care for herself (or for himself as is less likely), she may take over some of the household routine and free the middleaged wife for a life of her own outside the home in gainful employment, volunteer or community work.

When husband and wife are home alone, their household responsibilities may be kept at the level that they personally most enjoy. They may keep house quite casually, deciding at the last minute to go out for dinner, or invite neighbors over for potluck, or take a piece of beef out of the freezer and have a steak fry in the backyard. By the time a woman has reached her middle years, her skills in homemaking are at their peak, and she can care for her home with a minimum of effort and a maximum of enjoyment. By this time too, her husband has learned how to share the work load and the companionship in getting things done in ways that satisfy them both. Homemaking now can be fun, "just like playing house," as one fiftyish woman describes it.

DRAWING CLOSER TOGETHER AS A COUPLE

The most important task of the middle years is that of finding each other as husband and wife again. Not since their honeymoon days have the two been thrown as closely together, with no children or responsibilities of childrearing to divert them from each other. From a distance it looks as though this is a state of affairs that both the man and the woman he chose to be his own would welcome. Yet, for many a couple it is a real task to be worked on and achieved to the point where life together has meaning and purpose and richness once more.

Getting busy at fixing up the home, working out their financial affairs, and settling into mutually pleasant household routines—all can help the two develop a close companionship. But basically, now as before in the marriage, the fundamental feeling each has for the other sets the tone of the relationship. The big difference is that now a woman can not escape from the dissatisfactions of her marriage into the satisfactions of motherhood, and likewise it is not as easy for a man to excuse himself from his wife, evening after evening, for work when both of them know that it is no longer necessary for him to carry his job responsibilities so conscientiously.

The biological basis of this developmental task lies in the processes of aging for both the middleaged man and woman. Stereotyped conceptions of menopause, with its unpleasant physical symptoms, depressed mental state and the reproductive finality it represents, make it seem like a difficult phase to go through at the very time that a woman is being shorn of her main job of childrearing. The evidences of aging in skin and hair, body tone and contour, are difficult to accept by the woman for whom youth and beauty have been important features in her concept of herself as a woman. The woman's personal insecurity in her desirability may be heightened by the discrepancies in sexual activity in the middle-aged male and female.

The Kinsey studies indicate that the mean frequencies of intercourse among married men decline at an astonishingly constant rate from the youngest to the oldest ages, with men at 60 having an average frequency of about once a week.[1] Middleaged married women have as high or higher incidence of orgasm in their forties and fifties as they experience in their early twenties. Active incidences of married women reaching orgasm ages 21–25 years is 88 per cent, during ages 41–45 it is 93 per cent, and ages 51–55 it is 89 per cent.[2] Clinical evidence seems to indicate that by middleage many women have overcome the repressions that limited their sex lives early in marriage, and with the coming of menopause with its removal of the fear of pregnancy, enjoy sex experience more in their middle years than ever before in the marriage.[3]

With mature appreciation of sex, and of each other, a middleaged couple may become capable of a more prolonged mutual orgasm that is far more deeply satisfying to both partners than anything that they were able to achieve in their earlier years together. Meeting each other's needs emotionally as well as sexually draws the mates together as a couple. At this time the middleaged man and woman each need the reassurance, the appreciation, the encouragement to be what they each are that comes from feeling fully accepted and truly close to each other in marriage. Failure in this task brings the aching loneliness so frequent in later years. Success in intimate interaction brings contentment now, and paves the way for smooth going through the rest of life together.

[1] Alfred C. Kinsey, Wardell B. Pomeroy, and Clyde E. Martin, *Sexual Behavior in the Human Male* (Philadelphia: W. B. Saunders and Company, 1948), p. 253.

[2] Alfred C. Kinsey, Wardell B. Pomeroy, Clyde E. Martin, and Paul H. Gebhard, *Sexual Behavior in the Human Female* (Philadelphia: W. B. Saunders Company, 1953), p. 549, Table 154.

[3] LeMon Clark, M.D. "Sex Life of the Middle-Aged," *Marriage and Family Living*, Vol. 11, No. 2, Spring 1949, pp. 58–60.

MAINTAINING WARM, MUTUALLY SUPPORTIVE RELATIONSHIPS WITH GROWN CHILDREN'S FAMILIES

Becoming accepting and acceptable in-laws, welcomed and welcoming grandparents, in mutually satisfying intergenerational relationships is a highly rewarding developmental task to accomplish during the years immediately following the marriage of the grown children of the family. Fail in this task and the family is fragmented, with loneliness and heartache accruing to members of all three generations (parents, grown children, and their children). Succeed in this task, and the middleaged pair keeps a warm sense of being a family, the grown children feel secure in their roots, and the grandchildren inherit happy traditions and the values of ongoing family continuity.

An exploratory study of several thousand in-law relationships recently attempted to discover what causes difficulties and what is conducive to harmony between in-laws. More than 75 per cent of the factors making for in-law harmony had to do with mutual acceptance and mutual respect.[1] Problems arise when a middleaged parent has difficulty letting a grown child go, or accepting the grown son's or daughter's choice of a mate. Mothers more than fathers have and become in-law problems, probably because their childrearing responsibilities have been primary in their life interests through the years. The boy's parents more than the girl's are apt to find acceptance of the marriage and the marriage partner difficult, possibly because the girl's parents have had more of a hand in the mate choice as Komarovsky suggests.[2] Acceptance of the mates chosen by grown children seems to be easier for developmentally oriented parents than for those who have clung possessively to their children all along.[3]

The chances are that the mother-in-law who can whole-heartedly and enthusiastically welcome her children-in-law has been a good mother in the developmental sense all along, while the selfish, possessive mother finds it hard to be a good mother-in-law.

. . . . .

You (mother-in-law) have been "in training" for the full acceptance of your children-in-law for many years. As you accepted your children's friends and

[1] Evelyn Millis Duvall, *In-Laws: Pro and Con* (New York: Association Press, 1954), p. 336.

[2] Mirra Komarovsky, "Functional Analysis of Sex Roles," *American Sociolgical Review*, Vol. 15, No. 4, August 1950, p. 516.

[3] Marvin Sussman, "Family Continuity: Selective Factors Which Affect Relationships between Families at Generational Levels," *Marriage and Family Living*, Vol. XVI, No. 2, May 1954, pp. 112–120.

pals and playmates through the years of their childhood, you learned how to love others just because they were those your children loved. Adolescent crushes and love affairs you could take in your stride as further practice in letting children go and in accepting those they found lovable. So now, when the children marry, you can accept their mates, because you have learned to let your love for them swell to include their loved ones.[1]

Folklore has it that when grown children marry they become completely independent, neither asking for nor receiving assistance from their parents. Actually, there is a great deal of mutual support and help between the generations when grown children marry. Sussman's study of intergenerational help in middle-class families concludes that there are well-established patterns of giving and receiving between middleaged parents and their children's families that are related to the continuity and success of intergenerational family relationships.

Parents . . . wished to help their newly married children to become established on their own class level or even a higher one, and, in turn, wanted affectional response from them. They believed children to be more appreciative of their financial and service help after marriage. This was because they now faced the problems of establishing a new household and family. Many children realize, perhaps for the first time, the efforts their own parents had exerted in providing for them. However, most parents have no intention of subsidizing their children's families permanently, and many learned that help given in moderation was more prudent than unrestrained giving. When given in moderate amounts, it did not create conflict with the new family head. Parents also indicated that by mutual aid with married children in nursing care, house, repairing, vacation planning, and similar activities, they enriched one another's lives, took pride in their achievements, and felt that each had some part in the other's success.[2]

Becoming a satisfying grandparent involves a great many roles new to the middleaged man or woman. Standing by and seeing their grown children bring up their children in ways that differ from former methods of childrearing is not an easy task. Yet because styles in child training are changing (Chapter Three) there usually are some areas in which today's young parents repudiate older ways in the rearing of their children. It is likely that middleaged grandparents will be stricter and less permissive

[1] Evelyn Millis Duvall, *op. cit.*, pp. 347–348.
[2] Marvin B. Sussman, "The Help Pattern in the Middle Class Family," *American Sociological Review*, Vol. 18, No. 1, February 1953, pp. 27–28.

and developmental than their own grown children are. Or, on the other hand, some grandparents tend to be more indulgent with their grandchildren than they ever were with their own children. This often is resented by the young parents, not only because it undermines their authority and "spoils the children," but also because they remember how much more severely these same parents were with them as children. Helping without interfering, loving without smothering, being available without being intrusive: these are complex tasks for grandparents generally.

Grandparents can be a blessing when they are available to help out in a family crisis: a critical or chronic illness, an accident, the birth of a new baby, a period of military service or other necessary separation of the young husband and wife, temporary unemployment, or other situation that mobilizes all family resources for meeting the new problem. In occasional baby-sitting and inviting grandchildren to visit them, grandparents can do a great deal to relieve young parents of the confining burdens of childcare. Furthermore, they as grandparents can greatly enrich the lives of their grandchildren with the perspective, the memories of the former days when the parents were themselves children, the continuity of the family, and the mellow wisdom of maturity.

Much has been said about the relief from their children that grandparents provide for parents. Little usually is said of the need children may have for some relief from their parents. It is quite possible that grandparents serve a real purpose in providing for children a different touch, another approach, a new setting and emotional climate that is not possible in the day-in-day-out contact with parents alone.[1]

The satisfactions of being a successful grandparent are worth striving for. To feel needed and wanted at least occasionally by ones own flesh and blood is pleasant. To enjoy the fellowship of growing children, to be accepted by them as pleasant companions, to hear their confidences and to share the mysteries of life with them are deep-down satisfactions. To feel the satisfaction of a job well done as grown children establish themselves in their families and carry on some of the family traditions and values are rewards indeed. Grandparents who early learn to master the arts of intergenerational relationships build not only for the moment but also for the years that lie ahead as their grandchildren grow up and

[1] Evelyn Duvall, op. cit., p. 147.

become adolescents, are launched and go on into their homes. Today's middleaged men and women can anticipate many more years of the family life cycle, and often live to see childrearing go around a second, third or even fourth time (Chart 5, Chapter One).

KEEPING IN TOUCH WITH BROTHERS' AND SISTERS' FAMILIES AND WITH AGING PARENTS

With the coming of the middle years in the family there is time, money, and interest in cementing relationships in the family generally. During the peak years when children were growing, life was too busy to go visiting very much, or even to write the letters, send the gifts, and keep in touch with brothers' and sisters' growing families. In the middle years when one's own children are grown and gone, there often is a desire to become reacquainted with nephews and nieces and to come closer to the other relatives in the larger family circle.

There are certain hazards to be avoided in relationships with brothers' and sisters' families. In an exploratory study of in-law relationships, the one more difficult than any other, except for the mother-in-law, was that of sister-in-law. The findings indicate that some sisters-in-law are possessive, meddling, and intrusive in much the same way that mothers-in-law offend. In addition, there seems to be a considerable amount of sibling rivalry (competitiveness, jealousy, envy, comparing, bickering, and belittling) continuing on into adulthood. Sisters-in-law are especially susceptible to this problem in the larger family interrelationships.[1]

Problems with brothers' and sisters' families sometimes arise out of efforts to plan for the care of aging parents. When one's parents need financial support, or when one or both of them need a home in their later years, the problem may precipitate a crisis among the grown children in terms of whose responsibility it is, and which one should do what to help carry the load. Old grudges may be dredged up, and old resentments aired until feelings run so high that the whole family is unpleasantly involved. Bitterness in the family is of little comfort through the middle and later years. Better by far is the effort to work things through harmoniously with the others in the larger family.

Aging parents who are financially quite independent and whose health does not yet require special care, still need the attention and loving in-

---

[1] Evelyn Duvall, *op. cit.*, Chapter 11, pp. 221–243.

terest of their grown children. There are strong social pressures for "being nice to" one's aging parents, with everything from neighborhood gossip to newspaper headlines pouring criticism down upon the heads of the men and women who woefully neglect their parents in their later years. Respect for elders is not as strong in the Western world as it is in the East, but even so, some filial devotion is expected in terms of occasional visits, letters, telephone calls, and gifts on special days. Many of the little rituals help aging parents to feel that they are loved and appreciated.

For many mature men and women giving affection and attention to aging parents is an easy task. For others whose earlier relationships with their parents have been full of conflict or uncongenial, there may be real problems.[1] It is likely that keeping close to aging relatives is more difficult for the upward mobile man or woman than it is for the married couple whose ways of life are still quite similar to those of their parents. Being ashamed of the old-fashioned, old-world ways of parents of an ethnic group is a frequent hazard to the comfortable accomplishment of this task.

Whatever the hazards and problems, the middleaged couple must face and work through in some way the developmental tasks involved in maintaining close relationships with their kin. As they succeed they fill their social roles as adults, and they reap the rewards of intrafamily harmony that rounds out the family circle through the middle years.

PARTICIPATING IN COMMUNITY LIFE BEYOND THE FAMILY

There are times for staying in and times for getting out of oneself. During the childbearing stage of the family life cycle, little families keep much to themselves (Chapter Eight). But when children have grown and gone, and the middleaged husband and wife are alone with fully half of their adult lives together stretching ahead of them, is a time for getting out and building a broad base for life together. One middleaged woman who keeps active in many projects outside her home says that she feels that these are the years when she is storing up sweetness for the rest of life. Much as the honey bee fills up the many cells of the honeycomb for the winter months that lie ahead, so a middleaged human stores up

---

[1] See Robert M. Dinkel, "Parent-Child Conflict in Minnesota Families," *American Sociological Review*, August 1943, pp. 412–419; and also sections of Chapter Fourteen on these problems.

memories of activities enjoyed, projects completed, and friendships made as safeguards against loneliness in the later years when activities, of necessity, must be curtailed.

Participation in life beyond the confines of the home is of many types and forms through the middle years. The man has his work, and many satisfied active women have theirs too. Dr. Rose's study of life satisfaction among middleaged middle-class men and women turns up a larger proportion of satisfied than dissatisfied women among those gainfully employed outside the home.[1] Recreational interests too are related to life satisfaction in the middle years, as the study finds,

> Desire for having more amusement is associated with life satisfaction among both women and men. A significantly larger proportion of the relatively dissatisfied wives and husbands (44 and 39 per cent, respectively) than of the satisfied ones (22 and 13 per cent, respectively) would like to go out more often in the evenings for entertainment than they do now. The same relationship holds when this diversion is specified to take place with the spouse (52 and 64 per cent of the relatively dissatisfied women and men, as compared with 33 and 40 per cent of the very satisfied).[2]

Sussman's investigation of what middleaged parents do when their grown children leave, found that most couples increase their mutual undertakings both within and outside the home. Such joint interaction patterns as listening to the radio, viewing television, playing games, conversing, entertaining friends, doing housework and home repairs, dining out, attending clubs, movies and concerts, taking long vacation trips, and acquiring a summer place all increased with the leavetaking of the children. These new activities were associated with increased leisure and affluence that come as children no longer have to be reared.[3] That many parents find pleasure in their new-found freedom to do what they like is reflected in an excerpt from an interview with Mrs. Baxter who said,

> "Now we are living for the first time! We are in a much better position to do things now that they (children) are not our responsibility. We redecorated

[1] Arnold M. Rose, "Factors Associated with the Life Satisfaction of Middle-Class, Middle-Aged Persons," *Marriage and Family Living*, Vol. 17, No. 1, February 1955, pp. 15–19.

[2] *Ibid.*, p. 18.

[3] Marvin B. Sussman, "Activity Patterns of Post-Parental Couples and Their Relationship to Family Continuity," *Marriage and Family Living*, Vol. XVII, No. 4, November 1955, pp. 338–341.

A middleaged couple can enjoy much more social life and joint participation outside the home than has been possible before.

our house last year, and Mr. Baxter changed his position the first of the year. I don't feel it would have been possible if the children were still living at home." [1]

More than ever before the couple in the middle years of the family life cycle can contribute to community life and general welfare. These

[1] *Ibid.*, p. 340.

are the years when a woman is free to take an active part in some community project in which she has become concerned. While her children were small she did well to get to the parent-teacher meetings in their school. Now she may attend state and national meetings, she may hold a responsible office, she may go to the state capital to plea for a worthy piece of legislation. At the same time the middleaged man is taking on more responsible positions in his club, organization, or union. Together they can enjoy much more social life and joint participation outside the home than has been possible before. Community leadership is more generally frequent among members of middle-class families (Chapter Four), but the increase in the participation within labor unions, block organizations in urban redevelopment projects, and political activities all tend toward drawing more lower-class men and women into community life.

Success in participation within the community in the middle years is dependent on the foundations laid for it in the earlier years of marriage. As the family has tied into projects and purposes beyond its own immediate interests through the years, it has laid the track upon which may run the trains of accomplishment in the middle and later years. Some novel new activities are possible for the middleaged couple. But the likelihood is that the man and woman in their middle years continue on with extensions of their previous interests and activities. So too, the things they do now ready them for better or for worse in their sunset years that lie ahead.

REAFFIRMING THE VALUES OF LIFE THAT HAVE REAL MEANING— A SUMMATION

The couple's philosophy of life is being reaffirmed in everything they do toward the accomplishment of all the other developmental tasks of the middle years. They express their value systems as they create and maintain a pleasant and comfortable home; as they enjoy their financial peace of mind and plan for old age securities; as they carry out their household responsibilities together; as they draw closer together as a couple; as they work out warm mutually satisfying relationships with the families of their grown children; as they keep in touch with their brothers' and sisters' families, as well as with their aging parents; as they participate within the larger community and find themselves as persons, as a couple, as family members, as workers, as citizens; and in all the other roles that

By the time a husband and wife reach their middle years together, they have worked through a way of life that makes sense to them.

society expects of them, and that their personal aspirations define for them.

Few there are who have to talk long and loud about what life means to them, or what values they are living for. Most men and women speak most eloquently about what matters to them in the stand they take in current issues, in the way they are willing to be counted in a controversy, in what they do about what they believe to be right and just and good and true. By the time a husband and wife reach their middle years together they have worked through the life style that makes sense to them as a couple, so that it brings them a sense of peace and satisfaction (success), or so that it rankles as a conflict point between them (failure).

It's never too late to learn. Even in the reaffirmation of life's values, a couple can still make progress toward developing unity and integrity in the leisure of their middle years. Nothing can bring greater satisfaction than finding that life all adds up, and that together the two know who they are and where they are headed in the business of living.

In summary of the middle years, we may say that the family typically consists of husband and wife; the children are grown, married and in homes of their own. Although the parents miss the companionship and youthful gaiety of their children, they also feel a sense of relief that the responsibility of child-rearing is ended; a sense of achievement that their children are safely launched in the adult world; and a sense of relaxation in the peace of the quiet household. Husband and wife are finding new satisfactions together and are renewing, in a mellow tone, the romance of mutual companionship of the early married period. They are reaching out into the community for new satisfactions and services, and are planning for the last period of their lives.[1]

SUGGESTED ACTIVITIES

1) Chart the complementary nature of the developmental tasks of the middle-aged man and his wife, by indicating how the tasks of the two tend to draw them together and to operate in the same direction through the middle years. Star and discuss the exceptions that seem to be conflicting rather than mutually supportive.

2) Prepare a lecture on the menopause for an organization of middleaged women. Use such materials as Lena Levine and Beka Doherty, *The Menopause* (New York: Random House, 1952); E. C. Hamblen, *Facts about the Change of Life* (Springfield, Illinois: Charles C. Thomas, 1949); Therese Benedek, "Climacterium: a Developmental Phase," *Psychoanalytic Quarterly*, Vol. 19, 1950, pp. 1–27; or other valid source and/or consultation with a practicing gynecologist or psychiatrist. Prepare a list of questions you will anticipate from middleaged women on the subject of menopause and their adjustment to it.

3) Write a paper on what is meant by "the crisis of the middle years," in the man's life. Use research materials referred to in this chapter, or such books as Ira S. Wile, *The Man Takes a Wife* (New York: Greenberg, 1937), to document your material.

4) Conduct a panel of women whose children have recently married on "How It Feels to Become a Mother-in-Law." Encourage the women to speak freely of the problems, confusions, and satisfactions they are finding in these new roles. Ask them what they have had to learn about taking in a new son- or daughter-in-law as a member of the family. Plumb the problems they have faced in reorganizing their relationships with their own children as they marry. Summarize their experiences briefly both for the pros and cons of mother-in-lawhood.

5) Make a call upon some family in the middle years that is known to you, and through direct questioning and informal observation, discover what developmental tasks the middleaged couple is working on most actively at the moment, what problems they seem to be facing, and what satisfactions and successes are apparent.

[1] Ruth Shonle Cavan, Ernest W. Burgess, and Robert J. Havighurst, *op. cit.*, p. 13.

6) List all the helps you can think of that growing and grown children could give their own parents that would be of some assistance in their achievement of the developmental tasks of the middle years. Include intangibles as well as specific practical suggestions.

7) Write a letter to yourself outlining what you recommend as an ideal program for the middle years of your own life. How will it differ from the middleage of your own parents? of other middleaged people known to you? Why? What will you have to do to pave the way for these ideal circumstances in life in the middle years?

8) Debate the proposition that middleaged parents should help their grown children's families financially. Use all the data you can find that gives statistical support to your arguments, at the same time that you give adequate weight to the social, emotional and psychological aspects of parental subsidy and young adult dependence. Use actual case excerpts to document points on both sides of the question, where possible.

9) Discuss one or more of the following situations adapted from case excerpts developed as class discussion stimuli by Dr. Hazel Ingersoll, Department of Home Life, Oklahoma A&M College, Stillwater, Oklahoma:

a) Mrs. Flint is in her forties and still a vigorous woman. Her only child has gone away to school and now she finds herself without an interest in life. She writes to Joan daily, and urges her to come home every weekend. She complains about young people today being so "heartless." Dr. Flint, a physician is a very busy man. He married Mrs. Flint when she was a nurse in the hospital where he interned. He dislikes seeing his wife so disinterested in life and wonders what he can suggest that will help her. What developmental tasks confront Mrs. Flint? What can she do? How can Dr. Flint be of real help?

b) Mr. Douglas is a fine man and a respectable citizen. He has been hard working and honest all his life. When he was first married he had great dreams of success in his career. But the children came along pretty rapidly, and Betsy, his wife, was often ill. He found himself, instead of following his desire to be a great musician, a music teacher in a small town high school. At middleage he realized that success had passed him by. He looked about him to see the compensations—a small home, a busy wife, and four growing children. "Well one never knows which way fate will lead! Maybe I'm luckier than I think. But I can't help regretting what might have been." How can his family members help this father overcome his sense of failure?

c) Mr. Allison has always been a sportsman and, in his own words, "as healthy as a baby." When he goes camping with "the boys" he attempts to show them how young he still is by performing strenuous athletic feats. At parties he sometimes embarrasses his daughter by his attention to her girl friends. He prefers dancing with them to dancing with his own age group. Mrs. Allison laughs and says, "Oh, Daddy is just an overgrown boy, you know, we have to humor him."

What developmental tasks does he need to accomplish? Any suggestions for making aging more attractive?

d) Alice's mother and dad have been "jogging along" in marriage for twenty-five years. They take each other pretty much for granted. Daddy jokes about his increased girth and his bald head. Mom says, "Well, I'm no spring chicken either." Alice is a bit irked with her parents for "letting themselves go." As she puts it, "they appear to enjoy middle age! I wish they would try to stay young like other parents!" Discuss the attitudes of both parents and of Alice, evaluating the predominant attitudes and suggesting what developmental tasks they satisfy. How may Alice's attitude toward her parents be affecting their tasks of middleage? What does one do when young adults are ashamed of parents who do not look young and fashionable?

READINGS

Benedek, Therese, "Climacterium: a Developmental Phase," *Psychoanalytic Quarterly*, 19, 1950, pp. 1–27.

Bossard, James H. S. and Boll, Eleanor Stoker, "Marital Unhappiness in the Life Cycle," *Marriage and Family Living*, Vol. XVII, No. 1, February 1955, pp. 10–14.

Burkhart, Roy A., *The Freedom to Become Yourself* (Englewood Cliffs, N. J., Prentice-Hall, Inc., 1956).

Clague, Ewan, "After 45—How About a Job?" *The Survey*, April, 1950, pp. 173–176.

Clark, Le Mon (M.D.), "Sex Life of the Middle Aged," *Marriage and Family Living*, Vol. XI, No. 2, Spring 1949, pp. 58–60.

Deutscher, Irwin, *Husband-Wife Relations in Middle-Age: An Analysis of Sequential Roles Among the Urban Middle-Classes*, unpublished manuscript, Department of Sociology, The University of Missouri, July 1954.

Dinkel, Robert, "Attitudes of Children Toward Supporting Aged Parents," *American Sociological Review*, 1944, pp. 370–379.

Duvall, Evelyn Millis, *In-Laws: Pro and Con* (New York: Association Press, 1954).

Duvall, Evelyn Millis, *New Family Roles in Middle Life* (Ann Arbor, Michigan: University of Michigan, 1956).

Elliott, Grace Loucks, *Women After Forty* (New York: Henry Holt and Company, 1936).

English, O. Spurgeon (M.D.) and Foster, Constance J., *Fathers Are Parents Too: A Constructive Guide to Successful Fatherhood* (New York: G. P. Putnam's Sons, 1951), Chapter 16, "Father as Grandfather," pp. 260–284.

Frank, Lawrence K. and Mary, *How to be a Woman* (New York: Maco Magazine Corp., 1954), Section 5, "The Middle Years, 40–55," pp. 121–133.

Grinker, Roy R. (M.D.), "So Now You're Middle-Aged," *Survey Graphic*, December 1947, pp. 678–681.

Gross, Irma, ed., *Potentialities of Women in the Middle Years* (East Lansing: Michigan State University Press, 1956).

Gruenberg, Sidonie Matsner, "The Turbulent Middle Years," *The Survey,* March, 1950, pp. 121–125.

Gutheim, Frederick, *Houses for Family Living* (New York: The Woman's Foundation, Inc., 1948).

Hartog, Jan de, *The Fourposter* (New York: Random House, 1952), Act III.

Havighurst, Robert J. and Orr, Betty, *Adult Education and Adult Needs* (Chicago: Center for the Study of Liberal Education for Adults, 1956).

Havighurst, Robert J., *Human Development and Education* (New York: Longmans, Green and Company, 1953), Chapter 17, "Developmental Tasks of Middle Age," pp. 268–276.

Hoyt, Elizabeth, *et al., American Income and Its Use* (New York: Harper & Bros., 1954).

Komarovsky, Mirra, *Women in the Modern World* (Boston: Little, Brown and Co., 1953).

Kyrk, Hazel, *The Family in the American Economy* (Chicago: University of Chicago Press, 1953).

Levine, Lena and Doherty, Beka, *The Menopause* (New York: Random House, 1952).

Lewis, Sinclair, *Dodsworth* (New York: Harcourt, Brace, and Company, 1929).

Lynes, Russell, "Be Glad You're Middle-Aged," *Look,* Vol. 20, No. 4, February 21, 1956.

Overstreet, H. A., *The Mature Mind* (New York: W. W. Norton & Company, Inc., 1949).

Rose, Arnold M., "Factors Associated with the Life Satisfaction of Middle-Class, Middle-Aged Persons," *Marriage and Family Living,* Vol. XVII, No. 1, February, 1955, pp. 15–19.

Riesman, David, *The Lonely Crowd* (New Haven: Yale University Press, 1950).

Stern, E. M., and Ross, M., *You and Your Aging Parents* (New York: A. A. Wyn, 1952).

Sussman, Marvin B., "Activity Patterns of Post-Parental Couples and Their Relationship to Family Continuity," *Marriage and Family Living,* Vol. XVII, No. 4, November 1955, pp. 338–341.

Sussman, Marvin B., "Family Continuity: Selective Factors Which Affect Relationships between Families at Generational Levels," *Marriage and Family Living,* Volume XVI, No. 2, May 1954, pp. 112–120.

Sussman, Marvin B., "The Help Pattern in the Middle Class Family," *American Sociological Review,* Vol. 18, No. 1, February 1953, pp. 22–28.

Wile, Ira S., *The Man Takes A Wife* (New York: Greenberg Publisher, Inc., 1937).

Wolfe, W. Beran, (M.D.), *A Woman's Best Years* (Garden City, New York: Garden City Publishing Company, Inc., 1935).

Wylie, Philip, "What's Happened to 'Mom'?" *This Week Magazine,* Chicago Daily News, May 12, 1956, pp. 7, 36 & 37.

Grow old along with me!
The best is yet to be,
The last of life for which the first
*   was made . . .*
                    ROBERT BROWNING

CHAPTER FOURTEEN

Aging families

Three things have happened since the turn of the century to increase the number and proportion of the aging in our population. Millions of the young immigrants of pre-World War I are now old people. Our birth rates over the past century have declined rapidly, and in spite of resurgence since World War II, may possibly continue to decrease in the population as a whole. In the third place, vastly improved survival has radically changed our age distribution in the past five or six decades from a relatively young population to one that is aging rapidly.[1] At the present writing, practically a thousand men and women become sixty-five years old every day of the year.

The dramatic change in the number of persons over sixty-five years of age is summarized in Chart 17. In 1860, persons over 65 years of age constituted less than three per cent of the total population of the United States; at the turn of the century, the percentage of over 65 persons in the population was 4.1 per cent; by 1950, the proportion had doubled to 8.2 per cent; and by 1960 the estimate is 8.8 per cent. The trend toward higher percentages of the population among the over 65 age group will continue; by 1970, the United States Bureau of the Census estimates from 9.2 to 9.6 per cent of the total population will be 65 or over.[2]

[1] Louis I. Dublin, "Our Aging Population," *Annual Forum, New York Chapter of the Chartered Life Underwriters,* Metropolitan Life Insurance Company, April 7, 1949.

[2] Bureau of the Census, Ilustrative Projections of the Population of the United States by Age and Sex, 1955 to 1975, Series P-25, No. 78, Washington, D. C., August 21, 1953.

Year	Per cent of Total Population
1860	2.6 ☐ 833,000
1900	4.1 3,099,500
1950	8.2 12,365,000
1960	8.8 15,800,000

CHART 17.   Number and Percentage of Persons over 65 Years of Age in the Population of the United States [1]

None of us is getting any younger. Every man and woman grows old in time. With so many older people in our population, the questions of what aging means and what it involves both for the individual and for society become general concerns.

Some older men and women become petulant, demanding, and difficult to please. Life becomes a burden for them, and for those who care for them. They resent the "insults of aging" as they gradually lose their physical attractiveness and powers, their jobs and status, their loved ones, and their former sources of satisfaction and fulfillment.[2]

Other aging men and women find the "golden years" of life the most fruitful of all, as they gather the harvest of a lifetime, and keep on vigorously growing to the very last. Oliver Wendell Holmes observed in his later years that being seventy years young is far better than being forty years old. Helen Keller, deaf-blind since early childhood, at 77 was traveling all over the world, writing and lecturing in humanitarian service,

[1] The United States Bureau of the Census, Current Population Reports, Series P–25, No. 123; *Population Bulletin*, "Problems of an Aging Population," Vol. XI, No. 3, page 37.
[2] See Robert J. Havighurst and Ruth Albrecht, *Older People* (New York: Longmans, Green and Company, 1953), Chapter 2.

when she said, "Joy in adventure, travel and love of service to my fellow men were stronger than physical handicaps." [1]

Out of a group of typical older people studied, half of those between the ages of 65 and 69 answered the question "How old do you feel?" by replying "middleaged" or even "young." Not until the group past 80 years was polled did everyone say that they felt "old," or "aged." [2]

Why do some people age so gracefully and continue to find life good in the later years, while others get old before their time and fail to find their latter decades as "the best is yet to be?" The simplest answer is that old age is not a disease, it is a time of life. And, just as other stages of life, it has its challenges and rewards, its tasks and responsibilities.

Three patterns of aging in the United States are seen by David Riesman: [3] (1) the autonomous—persons like Toscanini, whose essential aliveness of spirit kept the body alive too; (2) the adjusted—typified by the American executive or professional man who is not supposed to allow himself to age, but must keep himself "well-preserved"; and (3) the anomic—the fate of some men forced to retire, or suddenly widowed who die shortly thereafter in a metaphorical suttee; "such people live like cards, propped up by other cards."

All older people must learn the new roles appropriate to their stage of life, in which some do well and others fail.

The movement through adulthood and old age involves changes in role activity. As one's children grow up and move away, as one's aging parents grow old and feeble, as physical energy and attractiveness decrease, as death takes away husbands, wives, and friends, as retirement takes away work, as the fires of ambition die down—as those things happen, people must learn to get new satisfactions in place of old ones out of new activities in place of old ones. They must withdraw emotional capital from one role and invest it in another one. [5]

Aging men and women find that some of their former roles are now greatly reduced, while other roles are intensified as the years roll by. Less

[1] Helen Keller, "My Luminous Universe," *Guideposts,* June 1956, p. 2.
[2] Robert J. Havighurst and Ruth Albrecht, *op. cit.,* p. 9.
[3] David Riesman, "Some Clinical and Cultural Aspects of Aging," *The American Journal of Sociology,* Vol. LIX, No. 4, January 1954, pp. 379–383.
[4] *Ibid.,* p. 383.
[5] Robert J. Havighurst, "Flexibility and the Social Roles of the Retired," *The American Journal of Sociology,* Vol. LIX, No. 4, January, 1954, p. 311, copyright 1954 by The University of Chicago.

time may be given in the later decades to active working for money, and more to enjoying the fruits of former labors. Less emphasis is now on the responsibility for young children, and more to the companionship of grandchildren, perhaps great-grandchildren. Fewer strenuous physical activities and more time for reflective thought and emotional interaction are possible now. Less time in being tied down to one place and more freedom to travel, to pull up stakes and settle in a new location, and to go where one will, and when, and with whom, in a new freedom of choice are open to many a man and woman. The possibilities are many, the chances for growth and development continue on for the human personality as long as there is a will to assume responsibility for them, within the life span.

DEVELOPMENTAL TASKS OF THE AGING HUSBAND

The man of the house faces two crucial developmental tasks through the later years: (a) finding life meaningful after he retires, and (b) adjusting to decreasing physical health and strength. All other developmental tasks tend to stem from this primary pair, as is seen in reviewing the outlined tasks of the aging husband below.

1) *Finding life meaningful after retirement:*
   Continuing on some central interests and purposes.
   Gaining status and recognition from some ongoing activities.
   Feeling needed and creative for what he is and does.
2) *Adjusting to his income level as a retired worker:*
   Tapping resources built up in his peak years of earning power.
   Supplementing income with remunerative activities.
   Adjusting living standards to the realities of current income.
3) *Making satisfactory living arrangements with his wife:*
   Deciding where and how they will live out their later years.
   Fitting physical arrangements to health and economic situation.
   Carrying out household routines without undue burden.
4) *Keeping well and taking care of himself physically:*
   Getting regular health examinations and care.
   Eating adequate diet of well-chosen and prepared foods.
   Keeping neat, clean, and pleasantly groomed.
5) *Maintaining social contacts and responsibilities:*
   Enjoying old friends and making new ones.

Carrying some responsibilities for life outside himself.

Maintaining adequate roles as a citizen.

6) *Finding emotional satisfactions in intimate contact with his loved ones:*

Re-establishing close warm relationships with his wife.

Keeping in touch with his children and grandchildren.

Feeling he belongs to his kinfolk in warm meaningful ways.

7) *Facing the possibility of death in constructive ways:*

Working out a meaningful philosophy of life and death.

Preparing for the inevitability of a last illness and death of his wife and himself.

Adjusting to widowerhood if his wife dies before he does.

DEVELOPMENTAL TASKS OF THE AGING WIFE

The married woman faces certain developmental tasks in common with her aging husband, and others that are more peculiarly hers as wife. She has already adjusted to being stripped of her main life-work in her middle years as she released her grown children. She personally is affected by her husband's retirement, and she vicariously carries her husband's struggles to work out his retirement problems. But the task remains primarily his. She, too, faces the challenges of adjusting to decreasing physical attractiveness, strength, and health. She, too, must continue to find life meaningful, and to feel that she belongs to others in satisfying ways. She faces the task of meeting the loss of her spouse more often than does her husband, because statistically wives tend to outlive their husbands by several years (Chapter One). Some of the more universal developmental tasks of the aging married woman are:

1) *Helping her husband find life meaningful after retirement:*

Encouraging him in the pursuit of new interests and the continuation of the central purposes to which he has formerly devoted himself.

Assisting him to find recognition for his accomplishments.

Making him feel important as a person, for what he is as well as what he does.

2) *Adjusting to the retirement level of income:*

Adjusting living standards to the realities of their economic situation.

Supplementing her husband's income as is appropriate.

3) *Making a pleasant comfortable home in whatever circumstances they choose:*

Adjusting happily to the situation in which they are to live out their years.

Keeping home safe and pleasant for their lives as older people.

4) *Taking care of herself physically:*

Adjusting comfortably to aging processes without undue rebellion or regret at her lost youth.

Maintaining good health practices in diet, exercise, prescribed routines and regular health check-ups and care.

Keeping fit and attractive through good grooming and healthy pride in her appearance.

5) *Keeping socially alive and active:*

Cherishing old friendships and finding joy in new friends and acquaintances.

Carrying some responsibilities for clubs and group life.

Keeping posted and active in civic life.

6) *Growing emotionally through satisfying contact with her family:*

Growing close to her husband in new intimacy patterns appropriate to the later years.

Maintaining close meaningful contacts with her children and grandchildren.

Feeling needed in some significant ways, for what she is and does.

7) *Living through the death of her husband wholesomely:*

Meeting bereavement courageously.

Going on alone in life after being a member of a wedded pair for most of her adult years.

Working out meaningful ways of living as a widow.

8) *Facing death as inevitable and as a part of life:*

Finding comfort in religion or a philosophy of life and death.

Accepting and adjusting to the realities of life and death constructively.

DEVELOPMENTAL TASKS OF AGING FAMILIES

The developmental tasks of both the aging husband and wife are intertwined with the aging family's developmental tasks. Aging families (herein described as at Stage 8 in the family life cycle) begin with retirement and continue to the death of the original spouses. Aging families typically consist of husband and wife, in the later years of life, whose children have grown and are living in homes of their own, bearing and bringing up their children. The aging couple usually continues to be "family" to grown children, grandchildren, and great-grandchildren. Even though they may not share a common domicile or keep intimately in touch with one another, the older husband and wife usually consider their descendants as their family, and maintain contact through reunions, holidays, visiting, mutual helpfulness, and eventually by sharing their economic burdens or wealth with their heirs. Therefore, we define this stage as one of aging families, rather than solely aging couples. Just as other stages in the family life cycle are made up of family members each working out their developmental tasks as persons within the family, and as families-as-a-whole, so now too we see aging families at work on their developmental tasks.

FINDING A SATISFYING HOME FOR THE LATER YEARS

Research studies indicate that aging families want a number of things in their homes for their remaining years: (1) quiet, (2) privacy, (3) independence of action, (4) nearness to relatives and friends, (5) residence among their own kind of people, (6) inexpensiveness, and (7) closeness to transportation lines and community activities to be found in libraries, shops, churches, etc.[1]

Most often the aging man and his wife continue on as long as they can at the place they have been calling home. There things are familiar; they are known among the neighbors and are close to family and friends. Aging families in the middle-income brackets can remain on as usual, while the poorer third of older people are forced into shabby quarters that are cheap. The upper third of older people tend to get better housing as they grow older.[2]

Migration to warmer climates is a well-known phenomenon in the United States. In the decade between 1940 and 1950, California gained 16 to 23 per cent through migrations of persons over 65 years of age,

[1] Robert J. Havighurst and Ruth Albrecht, *Older People* (New York: Longmans, Green and Company, 1953), p. 162.
[2] *Ibid.*, pp. 162–163; and Charles R. Manley, Jr., "The Migration of Older People," *The American Journal of Sociology*, Vol. LIX, No. 4, January 1954, pp. 324–331. Both studies indicate the greater migration among the higher income levels of older persons.

and Florida gained over 40 per cent in migrations of the same old age group, according to Professor Lynn T. Smith, University of Florida.

Streams of older persons into the South, Southeast, and Southwest represent but a small percentage of men and women over 65 from any one community. In the one year between 1949 and 1950 the United States Census reports that only .5 per cent of persons over 65 moved to a state that did not adjoin them. The Prairie City study in the Middlewest found that only 2 per cent of the over-65 age group went South or Southwest during the six-year period from 1942 to 1948.[1]

Older couples who migrate south to make their homes near other retired persons report that the chief advantages are sociability, social activities and association with others of fairly equal status.[2]

About one in five older people lives in the home of a relative, about 1 in 29 boards and rooms with a nonrelative, and approximately 1 in 23 lives in an institution, hotel, nursing home, or a large rooming house.[3] More women than men live with their relatives, and when they do it is most often with their married daughters.

A much more accurate and considerably more challenging breakdown of figures on the living arrangements of the aging is found in the sample census of April, 1952, obtained by the United States Bureau of the Census for the University of California at Berkeley through personal interviews with persons 65 and over in about 15,000 households in 68 sample areas located in 42 states and in the District of Columbia.[4]

This survey found that one-half (50.5 per cent) of the respondents 65 and over were married and living with the spouse. Of the older men, two-thirds (67.6 per cent) and of the women only one-third (35.1 per cent) were married and living with wife or husband. This study for the first time revealed the proportion of older persons residing in the same home with their children, distinguishing between those where the aging parent was head and those where an adult child was head of the family. Of the households in which older persons lived, just over one-third (35.2 per cent) were three-generation families. These were unevenly divided be-

[1] Robert J. Havighurst and Ruth Albrecht, *op. cit.*, p. 165.
[2] G. C. Hoyt, "The Life of the Retired in a Trailer Park," *The American Journal of Sociology*, Vol. LIX, No. 4, January 1954, pp. 361–370.
[3] Fact-Sheets on the Living Arrangements of Older Persons, Section VI, "Family Life, Living Arrangements and Housing," *National Conference on Aging*, Washington, D. C., August 1950, unpublished materials, pp. 3–4.
[4] United States Bureau of the Census, sample census April 1952.

tween those in which the aging parent is head and those in which an adult offspring is head. Data from this study are presented in Table 28.

TABLE 28. *Living Arrangements of Older People, 1952,*
Percentage Distribution [1]

Living or not living with children	Couples	Widowed, Single, Divorced, and Separated	
		Males	Females
Not living with children	74.1%	69.3%	54.7%
Living with children	25.9	30.7	45.3
Older person head	(22.6)	(11.0)	(15.9)
Adult child head	(3.3)	(19.7)	(29.4)
Total	100.0%	100.0%	100.0%

The first striking fact evident from these data is that very few older couples (only 3.3 per cent) are living in homes where an adult offspring is head. On the other hand, seven times as many couples (22.6 per cent) are living in a home where an aging parent is head.

The second outstanding fact revealed by Table 28 is the much higher proportion of females than of males, widowed, single, divorced, or separated who are living with their children (45.3 per cent and 30.7 per cent).

The third significant fact disclosed by these data is that nearly double the proportion of older persons who are widowed, single, divorced, or separated are living in homes where the adult child is head as where the aged parent is the head (19.7 per cent versus 11.0 per cent for men and 29.4 per cent versus 15.9 per cent for women).

Out of her wide experience in research on problems of the aging, Dr. Ruth Shonle Cavan suggests that separation of the generations, while having recognizable sociological roots in causes that even now are declining, is not the best solution for the aging, their middleaged offspring, their grandchildren, or the stability of the family as a whole:

. . . Alienation of children from parents is transitional in nature, the concomitant of temporary social changes. Some at least of the changes are already disappearing. The passage from rural to urban will undoubtedly continue as long as the rural birthrate exceeds rural needs for labor and city industries expand. However, the cultural rift in this movement is now being

[1] Quoted from Ernest W. Burgess, "The Older Generation and the Family," A paper prepared for the 8th Annual Conference on Aging, University of Michigan, 1955, and distributed by permission of the author, pp. 4 and 5.

nullified by the urbanization of rural life. Ethnic conflicts may remain acute for foreign-born groups but due to reduction in immigration they will affect a much smaller proportion of the population. Upward social mobility will be made less painful with the decline of the other two types of culture conflict, and with the continued spread of education into the lower class levels. . . .

. . . . .

The chief solution offered at present for generational conflicts is separate living quarters, with the institutional nursing home supplanting the independent dwelling as old age decline advances. Old people are urged not to identify themselves closely with their children but to seek friends of their own age. These suggestions are directed at reduction of conflict on a superficial basis by keeping the antagonists apart. *They overlook the need of the old for affection and primary group contacts; and they do not explore the benefits that would accrue to old and young alike from closer contacts maintained over the years.*[1] (Italics ours.)

Living with married children can be a hardship to members of all three generations. One study highlights some of the bases for the general belief that "no roof is big enough for two families," especially when one is the aging mother-in-law:

The three-generation household was recognized by most of the informants as a hazardous type of family living in which the combined virtues of diplomat, statesman, and saint are needed. The elders have had considerable authority in the past and they do not find it easy to relinquish power to their own children. The husband and wife have just begun to live their lives independently and somewhat resent the intrusion of a threat to this newly found authority. The youngest generation, in turn, are baffled by the splitting of authority among their elders and their own desires to be "grown up."[2]

Hundreds of cases of husbands and wives who have found ways of making a home for their aging parents that worked out happily for all concerned, volunteer their recommendations for harmonious three-generational living along the following lines.

WHEN YOU LIVE WITH YOUR IN-LAWS

1. Develop together a clear understanding of financial, household, and other responsibilities so that each one may know just what is expected of him or her.
2. Be reasonable in your expectations of one another. No one is perfect.

[1] Ruth Shonle Cavan, "The Old and the Middle-aged," unpublished manuscript, pp. 6–7.

[2] Marvin R. Koller, "Studies in Three-Generation Households," *Marriage and Family Living*, Vol. XVI, No. 3, August 1954, p. 206.

Many husbands and wives make a home for their aging parents in ways that work out well for everyone in the family.

Everyone makes mistakes from time to time. Perfectionists are hard to live with in any family.

3. Make some provision for protecting the personal property of each member of the family. It may be little more than a closet or a bureau of his or her own, but everyone welcomes some place for his things that will be respected as his alone.

4. Respect each person's need for privacy. It is not only the great who need their "islands of solitude," as Adlai Stevenson suggests. The elderly, the adolescent, and all the rest of us from time to time desire undisturbed privacy. We have the right to open our own mail, answer

Lighting the bathroom upon entering and wearing glasses when opening the medicine cabinet are recommended safety practices for older persons.

our own phone calls, and make our own friends with some sense of privacy.

5. Encourage each member of the household to develop his own talents and to pursue his own interests in his own way. This means you, too.

6. Jointly plan for whole-family activities so that each may have a share in deciding what is to be done and what part he or she will play in the affair.

7. As disagreements arise, and they will from time to time, take the time to hear the other(s) out. Listen well enough to get what the situation means to those who differ from you. Respond to their feelings as well as to the "sense" of the situation.

8. Unify the larger family unit sharing the household by celebrations and rituals that bring the family closer together in its own most meaningful ways.
9. Take a positive attitude toward your joint living arrangement by being appreciative of the benefits derived from sharing the household, rather than merely bemoaning the sacrifices involved.
10. Gain some perspective by realizing that through the ages, families have lived more often together than in the little separate family units more popular today.[1]

Wherever home is, there are certain desirables in good housing that make home pleasant at any time, but are particularly important for the later years. Henry Churchill, architect, includes features such as these:

One floor layout. This is desirable for any age—for the creeper, the housewife, the sick, and cardiac.
If not a one-floor home, the stairs should be easy and the hand-rails solid; the stairs should be well lighted. . . .
Floors should be warm and resilient. . . .
The possibility of reasonable privacy. . . .
Convenient arrangement of space, such as easy access to the bathroom, kitchen, entrances, and minimum laundry facility. That is to say, good planning.
Sunlight, of course.
Good lighting, no dark halls, closets or corners; plenty of switches.
Safe cooking equipment. . . .
Non-slip bathtubs, strong grab-bars. . . .
No drafts—sensible and easy-opening windows, perhaps louvred sub-sill ventilation.
Reduction of transmitted noise wherever possible. . . .
Outside sitting space, sunny and sheltered from the wind. . . .
Well-planned and accessible closet and storage space.
Doors wide enough for wheel-chairs. . . .[2]

Within the framework of good housing, there are specific practices suggested as sensible for aging persons' homes by the National Safety Council: putting a light near the bed, tacking down or removing throw rugs, lighting the bathroom upon entering, wearing glasses when opening the medicine cabinet, taking it easy on hot days, wearing a hat when working in the sun, carrying loads that are not too heavy, and holding the

[1] Evelyn Millis Duvall, *In-Laws: Pro and Con* (New York: Association Press, 1954), pp. 323–324.
[2] Julietta K. Arthur, *How to Help Older People* (Philadelphia: J. B. Lippincott Company, 1954), pp. 118–119.

handrail in going downstairs. Since accidents increase greatly through the latter decades of life (Chart 16, Chapter Thirteen), such precautions are important preventives for aging family members who want to remain active and independent as long as they can.

There comes a time in the life of some older men and women when it may be no longer possible to stay on at home. The very old, the critically or chronically ill, the infirm and the socially isolated older person frequently needs care that cannot be given within his or her home. These are the people who need some kind of institutional or foster home care, for which adequate provisions must yet be made in many communities.[1] Fortunately, the percentage of older persons who are completely disabled is relatively small, as we see from the health survey in Prairie City, summarized in Table 29.

TABLE 29. *Percentage of Persons over 65 Years of Age in Prairie City in Four Categories of Physical Well-Being or Disability* [2]

Physical State	Percentage of Men and Women Reporting
No obvious disability (Able to be out and around the city	79
Up and about but ill (Limited activity because of obvious defect or illness)	13
Homebound Not confined to bed, but cannot leave their homes)	6
Bedridden (Permanently bedfast and ill a long time)	2
Total	100

In this representative sample of older people eight out of ten are fairly well and vigorous, and not more than two out of ten are so ill or feeble as to need nursing care. One specialist in problems of the aging points out that the extension into the home of hospital, home management, housekeeping services, social case work, food, and visiting nurse services is enabling many infirm and ill to remain at home where they seem best satisfied.[3]

[1] Specific, practical helps are found in detail in Julietta Arthur, *ibid.,* Chapters 8–14, and in their related appendices.

[2] Data from Robert J. Havighurst and Ruth Albrecht, *op. cit.,* p. 65.

[3] Clark Tibbitts, "Retirement Problems in American Society," *The American Journal of Sociology,* Vol. LIX, No. 4, January 1954, pp. 301–308.

Whatever the situation, whatever the decisions that have to be made, the developmental tasks of the aging man and his wife must be accomplished as a team. Together they make their home where it suits them best, for as long as it meets their needs. As they accomplish this task successfully, they are content in their surroundings, and happy in their physical setting. As they fail to work out the fundamental responsibilities of finding a satisfactory and satisfying home for their later years, they face the unhappiness that so often accompanies failure in any of the developmental tasks at any stage of the life cycle.

ADJUSTING TO RETIREMENT INCOME

In the United States, it is generally assumed that a man retires at or about age 65. This is true particularly of men employed in industry and in some professions such as teaching, where policies for retirement are fixed. In general, fewer men are employed now after age 65 than was true in earlier decades as we see in Table 30.

TABLE 30. *Labor Force Participation Rates of Men over 65, 1900–1950, and Projections, 1955–1975* [1]

Year	Percentage Men Over 65 Employed
1900	63.2
1920	57.1
1930	55.5
1940	43.3
1950	45.0
1955	42.9
1960	41.2
1965	39.6
1970	38.0
1975	36.5

More than half of all men over 65 retire, as we see in Table 30. In 1955, of all husbands over 65 living with their wives, 35.9 per cent of the

[1] Philip M. Hauser, "Changes in Labor-Force Participation of the Older Worker," *American Journal of Sociology*, Vol. LIX, No. 4, January 1954, p. 315, Copyright 1954 by The University of Chicago; data drawn from Bureau of the Census, "A Projected Growth of the Labor Force in the United States under conditions of High Employment: 1950 to 1975." *Current Population Reports, Labor Force* (Series P–50, No. 42, Washington D. C., December 1952), and from John Durand, *The Labor Force in the United States, 1890–1960* (New York: Social Science Research Council, 1948), p. 208 ff.

"husbands only" were working, 8.3 of the families had both husband and wife in the labor force, 5.6 had the wife only working, and 50.2 of the couples had neither husband or wife at work.[1] These percentages of husbands working after age 65 contrast sharply with the 95 per cent of all married men under age 65 who are in the labor force.

There is nothing mandatory about retirement for many men. A good many self-employed men continue to work on through their later years for a variety of satisfactions: (1) a basis for self-respect and a sense of worth, (2) a source of prestige and recognition by others, (3) an avenue of social participation, (4) a source of intrinsic enjoyment and of creative satisfaction and self-expression, (5) a way of being of service to others, and (6) a continuation of pleasant routines and habits.[2] The doctor, the lawyer, the writer, the farmer, the artist, the carpenter, and the businessman who is not retired under company policy often continue to work long after retirement age, thus postponing the problems of retirement for themselves and their families.

One of the most immediate retirement adjustments is the sharp curtailment of family income. In general, the period after retirement is characterized by a lower income than for any other period in the family, as is seen in Table 31.

TABLE 31. *Family Income by Age of Husband, for the United States, 1952* [3]

Age of Husband	Median Total Money Income per Family
All ages	$3,890
Under 25 years	$3,069
25 to 34 years	$4,030
35 to 44 years	$4,339
45 to 54 years	$4,355
55 to 64 years	$3,805
65 years and over	$2,276

Nearly three quarters of all Americans over 65 either have no income of their own, or earn less than $1,000 a year. Another 11 per cent have

---

[1] "The American Husband," *Statistical Bulletin*, Metropolitan Life Insurance Company, Vol. 37, April 1956, p. 5.

[2] Robert J. Havighurst and Ruth Albrecht, *op. cit.*, p. 109.

[3] From Paul C. Glick, "The Life Cycle of the Family," *Marriage and Family Living*, Vol. XVII, No. 1, February 1955, p. 7.

an annual income between $1,000 and $2,000. Only 15 per cent of persons over 65 receive more than $2,000. These incomes in many cases must support the husband or wife and other members of the family.[1]

Therefore, nearly 40 per cent of all persons 65 years of age and older get some private or public financial assistance, according to the latest available data. As of December 1952, about 30 per cent (4.1 million) of the 13.3 million persons over 65 received income from employemnt, while the remaining 70 per cent (approximately 9.2 million) of those over 65 had no earnings from employment. Of these latter persons, about two-fifths (3.5 million) received Old Age and Survivors' benefits; another 300,000 beneficiaries under Old Age Insurance continued to work; more than one-fourth (2.6 million) were on public assistance rolls; and the remaining 2.8 million were self-supporting or received aid from children, relatives, and others.[2]

Postponement of retirement as long as possible makes sense, for the worker, the family, and for industry itself, as Robert K. Burns points out,

In the absence of widespread and prolonged unemployment, economic forces are likely to discourage earlier retirement and to encourage later retirement. The cost per dollar of benefit is 40–50 per cent greater to retire an employee at age 60 than at age 65. It is unlikely that Social Security or industry can bear such a substantial cost. By postponing retirement from age 65 to 68 or 70, pension costs could be reduced by one-third, assuming no less in the level of productive efficiency. Moreover, each year of continued employment after 65 makes possible a substantial increase in the amount of the retirement benefit. Using a straight life annuity basis, without death benefit, a pension of $100 per month at age 65 is the actuarial equivalent of $108 at age 66 or $130 at age 68. Economic forces may be expected to exert a powerful influence, together with other factors—medical, psychological, and social—to raise normal retirement age and to modify its compulsory character.[3]

Several studies indicate that while older workers tend to slow up, their steadiness on the job, their efficiency, and their regular attendance are

[1] John J. Corson and John W. McConnell, *Economic Needs of Older People* (Twentieth Century Fund, 330 West 42nd St., New York 36, N. Y., 1956).

[2] United States Bureau of Labor Statistics, *Employment and Economic Status of Older Men and Women* (*Supplement to Bulletin 1092*, Washington D. C., 1953).

[3] Robert K. Burns, "Economic Aspects of Aging and Retirement," *American Journal of Sociology*, Vol. LIX, No. 4, January 1954, p. 390, copyright 1954 by The University of Chicago.

quite as good as among workers at younger age levels.[1] The thinking of students on the problem leans toward a general recommendation of more flexible retirement ages, with more opportunities for creative activity for the man or woman who wants to continue active production than are now available.

Retirement means not only sharply reduced family income, but losses of a psychological and social nature as well. Work means an emotional investment for many middle-class persons who generally assume that the more experience one has the more valuable one is on the job. Such basic feelings of security are derived from one's job that one study indicates the retirement for many people "is like walking over a cliff, not only depriving the person of emotional security of work and work colleagues, but also because it is a complete undermining of the seniority system on which they have counted." [2]

Age for age, retired persons think of themselves as older than do men and women who are still actively at work. Data from the series of studies in social gerontology being conducted by the Department of Sociology and Anthropology at Cornell University disclose significantly larger percentages of retired as compared with employed persons at all age levels under 70, and at 70 and over, who think of themselves as "old." As one of the retirants in these studies says,

> When did I start to feel old? Why when I stopped working. I was always real proud that I'd come to Chicago and got a job and supported myself. Then when I couldn't work anymore, why I wasn't good for anything.[3]

Adjusting to retirement is a complex task, involving as it does not only getting along on a sharply reduced income for many aging families, but also finding life meaningful after active participation as worker has stopped. Personal and social supports are being encouraged to ease the economic burden of the aging. Age at retirement, now relatively rigid for many millions, could be much more personally adapted to the abilities and interests of the individual to the benefit of all concerned. Until more flexible practices in retirement are general, millions of aging families must

[1] Sidney L. Pressey, "Employment Potentialities in Age, and Means for Their Possible Increase," New York State Joint Legislative Committee on Problems of the Aging, *Growing with the Years*, Albany, Legislative Document No. 32, 1954, pp. 92–94.

[2] Martin B. Loeb, "The Social Factors in the Study of Aging" Part II, unpublished research paper, September 1955, pp. 5–6.

[3] Zena Smith Blau, "Changes in Status and Age Identification," *American Sociological Review*, Vol. 21, No. 2, April 1956, p. 200.

tighten their belts, rely on relatives, accept private or public assistance, or do what they can to make ends meet during the later years of life.

ESTABLISHING COMFORTABLE HOUSEHOLD ROUTINES

One of the most baffling tasks facing the aging couple involves getting used to having both husband and wife home together all day. Always before, except for brief periods of illness or lay-offs, the husband has been away at work through the working day, leaving the home and its care in the hands of the wife. Now that both of the pair are at home all day, every day, the man may "rattle around like a pebble in a pail" as one older man puts it, with nothing to do except get in his wife's way and feel that he is a nuisance around the place.[1]

The problem is quite different for the wife. She, in a sense, "retired" some years ago when the last child was launched and by now has made her adjustment to life. In another sense she never really "retires" as long as there are meals to prepare, beds to make, and household routines to see to. In her later years, she will taper off in the amount of heavy physical work she undertakes. She may get some additional equipment to carry some of the load that now is too burdensome for her failing strength. She may hire some of the heavy work done on a regular or a seasonal basis. But fundamentally her job continues as housekeeper and homemaker.

In many a family today, patterns of working jointly as homemakers have been established through the years, so that now, in the post-retirement period, the two continue on in the double harness to which they have become accustomed. Responsibilities are assumed on the basis of interest, ability, and strength, with the husband routinely assuming some chores, the wife others, and both tackling together the jobs that they enjoy doing as a team. As illness strikes, or one of the partners is out of the home for a time, the other then can take over, because he or she is already familiar with the processes involved. Decisions are jointly made, authority is assumed by the couple as a unit, and each is accountable to the other, and to the realities of the situation, in the family that has already laid a foundation for joint homemaking responsibilities through the various stages of the family.

[1] Florence Vickery, Director, Senior Recreation Center, San Francisco, California, reports that as she visits centers for older people across the country, she is impressed with the number of retired men who leave home early in the morning, taking their sandwich with them, and after spending the day at the center, return home in the late afternoon, much as they always did when they were at work.

MUTUAL NURTURANCE OF EACH OTHER AS OLDER HUSBAND AND WIFE

With the processes of aging comes a variety of human needs that husband and wife mutually can meet for each other and for themselves as a couple. Their active sexual life gradually diminishes as the years go by. Physical vitality declines. Eyes, ears, and perhaps teeth need mechanical assistance in the form of glasses, hearing aids, and dentures. In time they find they do not get around as much or as far or as easily as they did. All these things are normal and to be expected in the later years. Even more disconcerting is the accident or the illness that incapacitates one or the other and throws the burden of the household and the personal nursing on the able member of the pair.

Many illnesses of old age tend to be chronic. Heart disease, high blood pressure, hardening of the arteries, cancer, or a broken hip may seriously handicap the person over many months or even years. Since women live longer than men, on the average, it is usually the woman who nurses her husband through the illnesses that beset him in the later years. At first she may consider his condition as temporary. In time comes the realization that the husband cannot recover and that the disease causes death, and only after a long period of disability. The wife's acceptance of the chronic nature of her husband's illness is made easier by the fact that many of the illnesses of the aging begin with mild disabilities and progress very slowly toward complete helplessness; so she adjusts slowly, taking each change as it comes. One by one she takes over responsibilities new to her. She may have to make decisions in which she has had little practice or previous experience, such as taking charge of the finances of the household. She may have to give physical care and at times even protect her husband from the results of his mental wanderings. This kind of care of a chronically ill husband is one of the most difficult tasks that the older wife must meet.

The husband faced with the illness of his wife may have an even greater task, in that much of what is now expected of him is unfamiliar to him as the man of the house. His wife who has always provided for his needs, now helplessly awaits him to serve her. He must know how to cook an edible meal, care for a disabled patient, keep the house reasonably neat and clean, and function in what traditionally is the woman's sphere of the home.

Traditionally-oriented men who have never learned to be at home in

There is nothing mandatory about retirement for many men who continue to work on through their later years.

the house are apt to be uncomfortably awkward when the burden of home-making falls upon them. Men who define their roles as males more flexibly, who have always been at home within the intimate everyday routines of family living, find these tasks much easier and far more comfortable.

Husbands and wives who have maintained healthful routines through the years fare better in their mutual nurturance of each other as an aging pair than those who have neglected their common health in the earlier stages of life together as a married couple. A good example is found in nutrition, so closely related to the well-being of the older person. The family that has existed for thirty or forty or more years on a meat-and-potato-and-gravy diet may find it difficult to switch to the high protein, fresh fruit, and vegetable regimes recommended as adequate for the aging.

Chart 18 outlines the dietary needs of the man at 60 as contrasted with

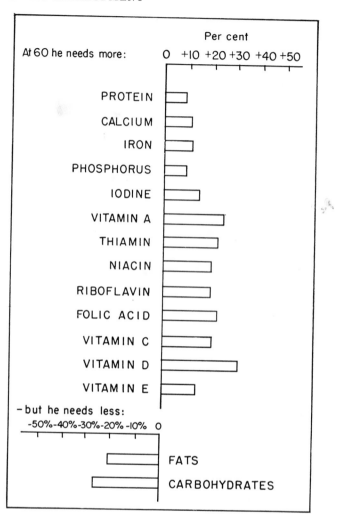

CHART 18.   Dietary Needs of Normal Man of 60 Compared to Standard Diet at Age 30 [1]

the standard diet at 30. We note that after age 60 the man or woman needs considerably less fat and carbohydrate, and more of the protective foods: vitamins, minerals, and proteins. Reasons for nutritional differences between age 30 and 60 are (1) the decrease in physical ac-

[1] C. Ward Crampton, *Live Long and Like It* (New York: Public Affairs Committee, 1948), p. 19.

Mutual encouragement and appreciation expressed in their relationship through the years give an aging husband and wife emotional support.

tivity between the active thirties and the slowing down of the post-60 period, and (2) the body building-blocks needed more by the aging to keep physically fit than was necessary at the peak of adulthood.

Further preventive regimens such as healthful balance of rest and activity; regular medical, dental and ocular checkups; wholesome acceptance of whatever aids and supplements may be prescribed, a variety of absorbing interests; and good mental hygiene go a long way toward assuring both husband and wife of maximum well-being during their later years together.

Less tangible, but quite as important is the emotional building up that each gives the other through their everyday life together. Too frequent is the soured embittered couple bent on belittling and tearing each other down in the myriad assaults upon ego and self that only the intimate can inflict. More successful is the support of one another by husbands and wives who have built up patterns of mutual encouragement and appreciation upon which they both can lean as other faculties fail. The wife who can bolster up her husband's sagging ego as he adjusts himself to retirement and a sense of diminished usefulness is often a key factor in his eagerness to start fresh in some other line, or find a place for himself in some single facet of older pursuits that now can pay off in fulfillment and satisfaction. The husband who can make his wife feel his devotion and appreciation for all she has done and all she is, helps her feel desired and desirable, more important than ever now in the sunset years. One explicit example of this is given in a report of a man who on his 55th wedding anniversary, inserted the following advertisement in his local paper:

To my sweetheart, Sophie Hensel, I wish to thank you publicly for your love and devotion and for 55 years of wedded happiness made possible by your unmatched qualities as wife, mother, mother-in-law, grandmother and great grandmother. We all revere you. Your husband, Henry Hensel.[1]

FACING BEREAVEMENT AND WIDOWHOOD

Facing the loss of loved ones is a sad task at any time. In the aging family, as dear friends drop off one by one, the sorrow is compounded by the realization, "It might have been I." Then, when inevitably the family undergoes its final break with the death of one of the original partners, the task of facing bereavement may be difficult indeed. Since women characteristically marry men older than they, and tend to live longer by several years, there are more widows than widowers. One out of four women between 55 and 64 years of age is a widow; after 65 more than half of all women (55 per cent) are widows.[2]

Bereavement is a compound crisis. It is a painful emotional shock, a sharp change in social status, often an economic catastrophe, and usually a philosophical challenge. It calls for reorganizing the habits and routines and ways of a lifetime of married living. It means the breaking of the identification that has made the marriage a good one through the years. If there have been some problems in the relationship, feelings of guilt and shame over what-I-might-have-done are often as painful as is the acute sense of loss of the familiar beloved companion.

Thomas D. Eliot has plotted the immediate effects and the secondary reactions to bereavement and outlines the various patterns found in his studies from total failure to readjust to conspicuous success in the task of facing bereavement, as follows:

[1] Associated Press release, February 28, 1953.
[2] "Marital Status and Household Characteristics: March 1950," *Current Population Reports, Population Characteristics,* Series P–20, No. 33, February 12, 1951, p. 10.

INDIVIDUAL EFFECTS OF BEREAVEMENT

A. *Total failure to readjust*
   (1) Suicide
   (2) Early death
   (3) Insanity
   (4) Moral disintegration
   (5) Obsession
B. *Partial failure*
   (1) Eccentricities
   (2) Physical illness or prostration
   (3) Aboulia, purposelessness
   (4) Isolation
   (5) Embitterment, misanthropy, cynicism
   (6) Reversion to or recurrence of griefs
   (7) Self-blame or personal hates
   (8) Fears
   (9) Loneliness
C. *Partial success*
   (1) Resignation, "God's will," etc.
   (2) Stoicism
   (3) Stereotyped formulae of immortality, misery escaped, etc.
   (4) Sentimental memorials
   (5) Effective repression of memories
   (6) Intensification of affections
   (7) Extension of affections
   (8) Deliberate absorption in distractions or duties
   (9) New or fantasied love objects
D. *Conspicuous success*
   (1) New love object
   (2) Thoroughgoing religious rationalization
   (3) Spontaneous forgetting, relaxation of tensions
   (4) Devotion to life work
   (5) Identification with role of deceased
   (6) Creation of constructive memorials
   (7) Transmutation of the experience into a productive reintegration of the personality.[1]

Even before the first shock has been fully felt, there are the funeral arrangements to see to, with all that is involved in balancing the love for the lost one with the economic considerations of the costs to be borne. The funeral usually comes on top of the expenses incurred for the last

[1] Thomas D. Eliot, "The Bereaved Family," *The Annals of the American Academy of Political and Social Science,* March 1932, p. 4.

illness. If that illness has been long, savings have possibly already been spent for doctors and nurses, hospital, and medication costs. If a sudden accident has eventuated in death, then the unexpected bills for ambulance service, hospital, doctors, mortician, and all the other costs come tumbling in simultaneously.

Even if there still is money enough for all these final services rendered the deceased spouse, the choice must be made as to the kind of funeral it shall be, and how much should justifiably be spent for it. Taboos on the discussion of death in our society keep many a husband and wife from discussing these things while they both live, and so the bereaved one is often unprepared for decisions revolving around the choice of a mortician, a casket, the burial place, and funeral service. The softly whispered, "Of course you want the best for your loved one," is too often answered with a numb nod that results in extravagant funeral costs far beyond the family resources or the standard of living represented. Even when a socially sensitive mortician attempts to help the family avoid ostentation, some "adviser" who comes to the aid of the bereaved too often runs the budget into the red in his or her efforts to be helpful.[1]

Remarriage is a likelihood for widowers more often than for widows in the United States.[2] Twice as many widowed men as widows remarry.[3] Actually the probability of remarriage for the widow over 65 is very small, only 2 for every 1,000 in the early 1950's.[4] One reason may be the smaller number of men of her age group, and the tendency for men to marry women younger than themselves that holds even for the older age groups. Another reason may be the greater self-sufficiency of the woman to maintain a household alone than is general among men.

Even though the widow may be relatively capable of living alone after her husband's death, she very probably will be lonely. Almost two-thirds of widowed persons report their single life unsatisfactory in the lonesomeness of living without a mate, even ten years after widowhood.[5] The widow may find herself socially marooned in a community

[1] Ernest Havemann, "Are Funerals Barbaric?" McCall's, May, 1956, pp. 33, 96–99.
[2] Jessie Bernard, Remarriage, A Study of Marriage (New York: The Dryden Press, 1956), p. 58.
[3] Paul C. Glick, "First Marriages and Remarriages," American Sociological Review, Vol. 14, No. 6, December 1949, pp. 726–734.
[4] Current Population Survey as of March 1950, April 1951 and 1952.
[5] E. G. Fried and K. Stern, "The Situation of the Aged within the Family," American Journal of Orthopsychiatry, Vol. 18, No. 1, January 1948, pp. 31–54.

Even though a widow may be relatively capable of living alone after her husband's death, she very probably will be lonely.

organized on a couple basis, so much that even entertaining in her own home may now become awkward. She may have to make drastic economic adjustments and change her residence to fit her financial situation. Philosophically, she has to come to terms with death, not only of her loved one(s), but within the foreseeable future for herself.

Most of these readjustments hold for the widower as well as for the widow. The tasks of facing death as a personal reality are real and urgent whenever they come. At the aging family stage, after years of couple and family living, they require rapid, flexible role changes on the part of both men and women.

The older family member left alone after the death of the spouse seems to accomplish this task best when he or she has already built some autonomy of personality, some ongoing personal interests, some backlog of economic security, a comforting philosophy of life, and a real investment in friendships. Maintaining active work and avocational interests prolongs interest in life, even after the original family has been irrevocably broken by death. Reintegration of life around remaining values is a real task involving courage, and imagination. The task is frequently made easier, especially by women, by success in relationships with grown children and grandchildren.

MAINTAINING MEANINGFUL CONTACT WITH CHILDREN AND GRANDCHILDREN

Some years ago, Dinkel pointed out some of the conflicts between the grandparent generation and those of grown children and grandchildren that arise out of contrasts and conflicts in the cultures of the three generations in a rapidly changing social scene. The grandparents in the fifty families that were studied in this research had grown up in and still held to rural ways of a pioneer culture, which to the members of the younger generations were irritatingly old-fashioned, dictatorial, and authoritarian.[1] Out of this sample's experience, Dr. Dinkel recommends the practice of mutual avoidance for those families in which there is intergenerational conflict,

> When parents and children do not get along, I would not try to promote family harmony, but would rather try to decrease the dependence of one generation on the other and to lessen the number of their contacts. By all means, I would not try to force children to give economic support to their parents. In such cases there are too many potential conflicts that would be brought into being by a common residence, and I assume that support by children most often involves the parent's going to live with a child.[2]

A decade later, another study of older people in a Midwestern town of about 7,000 population, yielded more hopeful results. In this research only 15 per cent of the parents over 65 years of age were characterized by dependence and neglect, while 85 per cent were seen as relatively in-

[1] Robert M. Dinkel, "Parent-Child Conflict in Minnesota Families," *American Sociological Review*, August 1943, pp. 412–419.

[2] Robert M. Dinkel, "Social and Economic Adjustments of the Aged," *Public Welfare in Indiana*, January 1942, p. 6.

dependent, as we see in Table 32 in which the items are ranked from most independent to most dependent and neglectful.

TABLE 32. *Relative Independence of Parents over 65 Years of Age* [1]

Independence	Per Cent	Dependence and Neglect	Per Cent
Parents and children are mutually independent but maintain a close social and affectional relationship	27	Parents share child's home but are somewhat burdensome	1
Parents and children are considered as independent adults but may share home or advice with each other	44	Parents live alone but children come in regularly to give care	5
Parents are responsible for children full or part time	1	Children are distant and seldom see parents	8
Parents have some responsibility for children	5	Parents have no interest in the children	1
Parents share home of children and are a help to them	8	Parents are completely neglected by children	0
	85		15

Albrecht's study finds that independent parents have certain characteristics in common: they are proud of their children, they brag about their children to strangers, they are realistic about them and treat them as adults, they can accept and give favors and suggestions without feeling threatened. Furthermore,

A basic security in loving and feeling loved removes any threat of authority or dominance of either generation. In fact, they enjoy working and playing with members of the second generation, actually like them as people, and maintain interests and a mode of life that keep some common bonds. But they also have interests outside of the family that help maintain their own self-hood. In addition, they accept the in-laws as members of the family and are not threatened by sharing or by extending parental warmth to include the spouse of the son or daughter.[2]

These qualities are those of developmental parents (Chapter Three) who have through the years encouraged their children's autonomy and

---

[1] Taken from, Ruth Albrecht, "Relationships of Older Parents with Their Children," *Marriage and Family Living*, Vol. XVI, No. 1, February 1954, excerpts from Table 1, p. 33.
[2] *Ibid.*, p. 33.

growth at the same time that they as members of the older generation found satisfaction in their own continued development. These are the older persons who find in-law relationships harmonious, with few complaints of meddlesomeness and intrusion, and a large measure of the mutual acceptance and respect.[1]

Grandparents rarely take full responsibility for the care of grandchildren except when the parents are unable to care for them. However, grandparents generally expect to help out in a crisis, with grandmother's active assistance in the home, and grandfather's financial help as necessary. Older couples occasionally have their grandchildren visit them for a while, and often enjoy their grandchildren's companionship even in pursuits that have little interest for them personally, such as going to Western movies.[2]

Finding joy in grandparenthood seems to be something that is learned through the years in incorporating the knowledges, skills, and attitudes that make one an older person who is loving and lovable, interested and interesting. Many older men and women report that they find more satisfaction in their grandchildren and great-grandchildren than they ever did with their own children when the pressures of young parenthood weighed too heavily upon them. Maintaining close and meaningful contact with married children and grandchildren can be a most reward·· ing task of the later years. It can warm the sunset years with the steady glow of two-way affection and belonging that is well-worth achieving.

AS AGING FAMILIES, CARING FOR ELDERLY RELATIVES

As more individuals live out their full life span, with greater vigor than in earlier times, it occasionally falls to aging family members to care for elderly relatives. Ruth Albrecht's study of parent-child relationships of people over 65 years of age shows that care of aged parents was a responsibility of about 11 per cent of those whose parents were in this country, with the task falling to single and widowed women more often than to married ones, and only occasionally to men.

Memories of pleasant and unpleasant experiences with parents that took place in adolescence 50 to 70 years before color the relationships

---

[1] Evelyn Millis Duvall, *In-Laws: Pro and Con* (New York: Association Press, 1954), Chapter 16.

[2] Ruth Albrecht, "The Parental Responsibilities of Grandparents," *Marriage and Family Living*, Vol. XVI, No. 3, August 1954, pp. 201–204.

between aging adults and their own parents. While most men and women remember strong attachment to their fathers, and even more to their mothers, somewhat more than one in eight report disliking their parents in adolescence because they felt rejected, or they felt they were made to work too hard, or because they were ashamed of the parent's occupation or behavior.[1]

Such evidence helps interpret Dinkel's findings [2] of conflict between the generations when the older is rooted in a rural culture that believes in strict obedience, hard work, and other pioneer virtues, while the grown children rebel and establish themselves in the new ways of life that emerge in city and town in repudiation of the parents' way of life.

We would expect relationships between aging family members and their own parents, to be related to the amount and the nature of social change that has occurred in the lifetime of the individuals, and how well the various family members had been able to keep up to date as times change both in the social scene and in the shifting scene within the family life cycle. Upwardly mobile family members may be expected to have less in common with their aging parents than more conforming individuals. Persons who marry within their own group usually experience less conflict with their own parents than do those whose marriages have been less homogamous. Some family members love, revere, and welcome a chance to serve aging relatives, even in a culture that calls for individualism and independence of family members. Other families find older parents a burden assumed only reluctantly and as a last resort.

The problem is especially acute when the elderly one is blind, crippled, bedridden, or so senile that he or she needs protective supervision. If the family must provide the constant supervision that such care entails it can become a severe mental and physical strain unless a companion or nurse is employed to share the load. In cases where institutionalization is indicated, the family has not only to carefully select the most suitable resource, and prepare the senile one for it, but also must cope effectively with the feelings of guilt and implied rejection that "putting a loved one away" has meant in our culture.

Fortunately, this dark side of the picture is but a small part of the relationships between aging families and their extended family mem-

---

[1] Ruth Albrecht, "Relationships of Older People to Their Own Parents," *Marriage and Family Living*, Vol. XV, No. 4, November 1953, pp. 296–298.
[2] Dinkel, *op. cit.*, pp. 412–419.

bers. Only a small percentage of older persons are helplessly disabled, as we have already seen. Most families find that the later years are the harvest years in family warmth and closeness. As the older family members get into the latter decades, the differences between parents and children often level out in the sheer fact of all being retired together, able to relax and enjoy life, and to plan together for present and future pleasures. Success in this task is often closely related to effectiveness in the developmental task of keeping alive and interested in the world around in active participation through the years.

KEEPING A LIVELY INTEREST IN THINGS AND PEOPLE OUTSIDE THE FAMILY

Aging husbands and wives tend to become less active than they may once have been in community activities. Some are not physically able to get about as they used to do. Others lack transportation for getting places. Many have lost interest as time goes by, and spend more and more time by themselves at home.

A study of men and women over 65 years of age in rural New York found physical inability, lack of interest, and lack of transportation the three most frequently given reasons by the aging for letting up in organizational participation, as we see in Table 33.

Over one half of these rural aged belonged to no organization. It may

TABLE 33. *Reasons Given for Less Time Given to Organizations by 143 Men and Women over 65 Years of Age in Rural New York* [1]

Reasons for Less Organizational Participation	Number of Times Mentioned
Not physically able	51
Lack of interest	41
Lack of transportation	24
Not enough time	17
Can't afford it	14
Moved to a new neighborhood	7
Other	9

[1] Roland L. Warren, "Old Age in a Rural Township," *Age Is No Barrier* (Albany, New York: New York State Joint Legislative Committee on Problems of the Aging, 1952), p. 156.

be that being rural, limits the community activities of older persons in that there are fewer recreational and commercial facilities in rural than in urban communities, fewer public and private agencies, and less available transportation than is found in most towns and cities.

The Prairie City study of older persons in a community of 7,000 population describes 37 per cent of the men and women over 65 whose days are "spotted with wasted hours, during which they merely exist, with more or less feeling of the dreariness of life." [1]

Survey of the leisure time activities of older persons indicates that the most frequent are solitary, passive, and require no advance planning: radio-listening, reading, and visiting. Gardening falls in fourth place for men and in seventh place for older women, with sewing and crocheting ranking fourth for female family members; both gardening and handiwork are relatively solitary and but slightly more active than the most frequent activities. Next in rank comes taking auto rides, letter-writing, movies, and playing cards. Clubs, lodges, and community and church work fall in tenth and eleventh places respectively among men (Table 34).

TABLE 34. *Percentage of Older Men and Women Participating in Leisure-Time Activities, Prairie City Study* [2]

Activity	Men (N = 45)	Women (N = 55)
Radio-listening	82	82
Reading	73	71
Visiting	56	73
Gardening	51	40
Sewing, crocheting, etc.	0	60
Taking auto rides	42	45
Letter-writing	18	45
Movies	16	31
Playing cards, etc.	20	25
Clubs and lodges	11	33
Community and Church work	11	31
Travel	9	14
Golf, other sports	20	4
Woodworking, etc.	13	0

[1] Robert J. Havighurst and Ruth Albrecht, *op. cit.*, p. 136.
[2] Excerpted from Robert J. Havighurst and Ruth Albrecht, *op. cit.*, p. 138.

A much higher percentage of men and women at the higher social class levels are active in clubs and lodges, community and church work, and travel than is found at the lower social class levels. Women tend to be active in all of these in larger numbers than do men, at every social class level, while men tend to engage more in golf, woodworking, etc., than do women in each of the social classes.

Older people who are active socially tend to be conspicuously happier than more solitary individuals. A study of the older men in a community of retired members of a fraternal order, finds that "men with the highest happiness scores participate nine times as much in group recreational activities (cards, shuffle-board, pool, horseshoe pitching, and bingo) than do those with the lowest happiness scores." [1]

The general decrease in social activities may account for the reduction in reported happiness in the later years as seen in two studies reported in Table 35.

TABLE 35. *Percentage of Elderly People Choosing Each of the Various Periods of Life as Happiest* [2]

Age Groups	New York (Morgan) N = 370	Iowa (Landis) N = 450
Childhood (5–15 years)	14.5	11.1
Youth (15–25 years)	18.9	19.3
Young adulthood (25–45 years)	49.1	51.4
Middle age (45–60 years)	12.4	5.8
Later life (60 and up)	5.1	4.7
Undecided or no data	—	7.7
Total	100%	100%

Of Warren's rural aged, only 12 said they were happier than at age 50, while 70 reported "about as happy," and 54 said they were less happy than they were at 50.[3] The University of Minnesota study of 416 fathers and mothers of college students concludes that social participation is definitely associated with life satisfaction for both men and

[1] Ernest W. Burgess, "Social Relations, Activities, and Personal Adjustment," *American Journal of Sociology*, Vol. LIX, No. 4, January 1954, p. 360.
[2] From R. G. Kuhlen, "Age Differences in Personality during Adult Years," *Psychological Bulletin*, Vol. 42, 1945, page 343.
[3] Roland L. Warren, *op. cit.*, p. 157.

women.[1] These trends are in line with other studies at various age and class levels in which social participation and happiness are usually closely associated. Remaining actively related to life outside oneself is a developmental task necessary for the happiness of the aging person.

When men and women over 65 are asked what things in life give them the greatest satisfaction, the largest number of them report their children and grandchildren as their greatest satisfaction. Hobbies, pastimes, and housework or employment claim the next largest number, with all others (gardening, visiting, reading, etc.) mentioned much less often.[2] Since these less satisfying activities are those most frequently engaged in, the indications are that many older persons follow the line of least resistance, rather than pursuing their own real interests through the latter decades. Here again, as at other stages of the life cycle, satisfactions come from working effectively on the developmental tasks of the period, while dissatisfaction and unhappiness accrue to those who fail the tasks of the period.

The attitudes and the practices developed in childhood are related to the adjustment to aging. One study finds 11 per cent of the over-65 population of a Midwestern community, living from day to day with interests chiefly in the past. These people were hard to live with and gave little or no attention to their appearance. Another 54 per cent had little interest beyond their immediate families. While 35 per cent were altruistic, objective about their problems and tended to project their thoughts into the future. This group of men and women enjoyed social life, met people well, and took pride in their appearance. Some subjects in their eighties were so trim and alert that special questioning had to be done to establish the fact that they were over 65. These were the people who had learned social, job, and recreational skills earlier in life; they had made a good adjustment in life from childhood on; they had good relationships with other people; were able to make decisions and face problems as they came along; and had developed wholesome attitudes toward life and themselves during childhood.[3]

It is never too late to learn. Many individuals who have not pre-

[1] Arnold M. Rose, "Factors Associated with the Life Satisfaction of Middle-Class, Middle-Aged Persons," *Marriage and Family Living*, Vol. XVII, No. 1, February 1955, p. 19.

[2] Roland L. Warren, *op. cit.*, p. 157.

[3] Ruth Albrecht, "Social Roles in the Prevention of Senility," *Journal of Gerontology*, Vol. 4, No. 4, October 1951, pp. 380–386.

viously had a chance to learn special skills and to develop interests find in their later years new joys in new pursuits. A neighbor learned to drive a car at 72, preparatory to a cross-country tour. Grandma Moses learned to paint late in life. Thousands of older men and women in hundreds of towns and cities are playing in community orchestras. One Chicago manufacturer, upon retirement at 65, decided to study the violin. Over 70 now, he plays in a suburban amateur string quartet. The sixteenth-century flute-like instrument, the recorder, is enjoying a revival with many older persons actively involved in recorder groups and concerts.[1] A physician over 80 bought a boat and passed the Coast Guard course in navigation. Illustrations are numerous and as varied as older people themselves.

Golden Age Clubs, Senior Recreational Centers, and other special programs especially for older people are proving their value in helping many men and women to find life full and meaningful during the later years. Professionally trained staff, pleasant surroundings, a varied program built to challenge and meet many interests of older people, yield high dividends in such programs whose worth has been well established.

Courses like the one offered by the University of Michigan on "Living in the Later Years" explicitly deal with the challenges of aging and stimulate many an older man or woman to get involved in enough of life so that his or her final years may indeed be the fullest and best yet.

FINDING MEANINGS IN LIFE

Working out a philosophy of life is a life-long task. Through the later years its importance is heightened, as the aging person reviews his experiences and comes to terms with what life means to him. It is not surprising to find that religion means more to the aging person than it has before. One study of responses that persons over 65 make to the question, "Do God and religion hold more, the same, or less meaning for you now than formerly?," finds only four who report less meaning in religion now, in contrast to 71, who report more meaning in God and religion now, as is summarized in Table 36.

[1] American Music Conference, 332 South Michigan, Chicago 4, Illinois, mimeographed release.

TABLE 36. *Meaning of God and Religion Now as Compared with Formerly by 143 Older Persons* [1]

Aging Persons' Responses	Number of Persons
Much more	46
Somewhat more	25
About the same	59
Somewhat less	3
Much less	1
No answer	9
	143

A study of the religious attitudes and practices of men and women during the later years in a midwestern community similarly shows that favorable attitudes toward religion and certainty of an afterlife tend to increase with age for both men and women. Among the over-95 age group 100 per cent of both men and women polled were certain of an afterlife. Some decline in church attendance among the very elderly was more than matched by listening to church services regularly on the radio. Reading the Bible at least once a week increased from 50 per cent among women in the 60–64 year old group to 100 per cent among the 95–99 year olds.[2]

The aging family stage is rather like a period of fall housecleaning, of putting one's house in order. One reviews one's possessions and weeds out many an object that is no longer useful, with the realization that "You Can't Take It with You." Things that have been admired by grown children or friends are given to them while they can get pleasure from their use now while the aging ones are still alive to get the satisfaction of giving and sharing. Through the earlier decades of life, all sorts of things are accumulated with the thought that "some day they will come in handy." The aging years are the weighing years when the froth and the frills are discarded and only the really important things are held close.

Some say that the aging years are "second childhood." And in a sense they are. In the years of striving through adolescence and the first

[1] Roland L. Warren, *op. cit.*, p. 158.
[2] Ruth S. Cavan, Ernest W. Burgess, and Herbert Goldhamer, *Personal Adjustment in Old Age* (Chicago: Science Research Associates, 1949), p. 58.

decades of full adulthood, the true mystery of life may escape one. Competition and struggle overshadow love and tenderness. A man or woman loses touch with nature in the hustle to get ahead on the job or get a meal on the table. A raise in pay once seemed more important than a sunset. But as one grows older, although the sight is dimmed, one sees more—the glint of dew on the iris, the glory of a storm, the sweet peace of the woods at dusk. One's ears may not hear as well as they once did, but one now can listen to music with inner peace, unharassed by the turmoil of the mind. "A beautiful day comes like a lovely gift. One suddenly notices again, as one did as a child, the form of a leaf, the contour of a tree, the fragile loveliness of the white cosmos, the bronze blaze of the Michelmas daisies; the colored pattern of a city street; the stars." [1]

Dreary is the life of the older man or woman who fails to find life's meaning in the latter days. For the fullness of life is there to be captured and enjoyed to the point where "the cup runneth over." The gold is there in the hills for the prospector who is willing to go out and pan for it. Just so, the golden years glow for the men and women who achieve the developmental tasks life sets for them in their sunset years.

SUGGESTED ACTIVITIES

1) Insurance company statisticians have worked out a simple formula by which any person can estimate his or her life expectancy. All you do is subtract your present age from 80 and take 2/3 of the difference as the number of years still left to you. According to this scheme, plot your own life expectancy, and write a letter to yourself to be opened in the last decade of your life, outlining the program you recommend for yourself. Include items covering health, family, work, leisure, civic interests, and anything else you feel would be valuable in making your own aging years more meaningful.

2) Write a paper on the topic "More People Rust Out than Wear Out." Document your points with research findings, as well as from your readings generally. Illustrate with cases known to you as fully as you can.

3) Invite a panel of persons over 65 in your neighborhood to participate in a group interview in which you and other members of your class question them as to their activities, their work, their personal and family interests, their satisfactions with life now as compared with

[1] Dorothy Thompson, "There Is a Time," *Ladies' Home Journal*, November 1952, p. 14.

earlier in life, and their plans for the future. Ask them especially what they feel the community might do to make life better for older persons. Summarize these data, giving rough evaluations of the relative success in the developmental tasks of the various members of the panel of older persons. Tell what you feel might help more of them find their maximum success in the developmental tasks of the period.

4) Produce the play "The Room Upstairs" portraying some of the typical problems arising between older people and their grown children. Ask various members of the class to identify with specific characters during the performance: Mrs. Johnson, her daughter Fran, and her son-in-law Robert, and be prepared to discuss what the various situations portrayed meant to this particular person, as well as to the family as a whole. Order the play from Human Relations Aids, 1790 Broadway, New York 19, N. Y.

5) Refute the arguments that "You Can't Teach an Old Dog New Tricks," by quoting research findings on the ability of adults to learn, and reviewing the most frequent reasons why persons of any age tend to slow up in their learning (fear of ridicule, fear of failure, laziness, a rigid self concept, feeling "out of step," or that one doesn't belong). Summarize your findings by outlining a program of adult education for persons over 65 years of age.

6) Show the film, *The Steps of Age* (25 minutes, black and white, from International Film Bureau), looking especially for the factors that make life difficult for older persons in the family. Comment on ways in which younger persons so often thoughtlessly ignore or hurt their older relatives, and suggest some of the reasons why the generations sometimes find it difficult to live together.

7) Make a financial plan for a hypothetical married couple whose children are in college that will assure them of security in their later years, without too great sacrifice in the years that lie immediately ahead. Plot their probable income and expenditures for three decades as a middleaged and aging couple. Then compute anticipated income from investments, pensions, part-time earnings, annuities, insurance and/or other potential sources of income that will keep the aging family members free from dependence upon either their children or other assistance in their later years.

8) Review the recommendations being made in the literature for housing for the older person, summarizing your findings in an outline of suggestions for aging families.

9) Review issues of *The Journal of Gerontology* and of *Geriatrics* for the past several years, tabulating the number of articles devoted to the various aspects of aging in our society. Interpret your findings in the light of what you know about the aging family in our society.

10) Write a critical review of one or more of the following novels dealing with situations faced by older persons:

Bennett, Arnold, *Old Wives' Tale* (New York: Harper & Brothers, 1953).

Bromfield, Louis, *Mrs. Parkington* (New York: Harper & Brothers, 1943).

Chase, Mary Ellen, *Mary Peters* (New York: Macmillan Company, 1934).

Lawrence, Josephine, *Web of Time* (New York: Harcourt, Brace and Co., 1953).

11) Discuss the following situation developed as a case excerpt for classroom discussion by Dr. Hazel Ingersoll, Department of Home Life, Oklahoma A&M College, Stillwater, Oklahoma:

Jane's father is old, and she is the youngest and only unmarried child of a large family. Jane feels she must take care of her father. Now that she and Bob are ready to marry, they are concerned about what to do with her father. He has a little savings but he is infirm. He is very forgetful and often childish. They are afraid he cannot live by himself, yet they are reluctant to have him live with them. What are the various alternatives that Jane and Bob face, and what are the difficulties and advantages inherent in each?

READINGS

Albrecht, Ruth, "Relationships of Older Parents with Their Children," *Marriage and Family Living*, Vol. XVI, No. 1, February 1954, pp. 32–35.

Albrecht, Ruth, "Relationships of Older People with Their Own Parents," *Marriage and Family Living*, Vol. XV, No. 4, November 1953, pp. 296–298.

Albrecht, Ruth, "Social Roles in the Prevention of Senility," *Journal of Gerontology*, Vol. 4, No. 4, October 1951, pp. 380–386.

Albrecht, Ruth, "The Parental Responsibilities of Grandparents," *Marriage and Family Living*, Vol. XVI, No. 3, August 1954, pp. 201–204.

Arthur, Julietta K., *How to Help Older People* (Philadelphia: J. B. Lippincott Co., 1954).

Bernard, Jessie, *Remarriage: A Study of Marriage* (New York: The Dryden Press, 1956).

Blau, Zena Smith, "Changes in Status and Age Identification," *American Sociological Review*, Vol. 21, No. 2, April 1956, pp. 198–203.

Burgess, Ernest W., Issue Editor, *The American Journal of Sociology*, Vol. LIX, No. 4, "Aging and Retirement."

Cavan, Ruth Shonle, "Adjustment Problems of the Older Woman," *Marriage and Family Living*, Vol. XIV, No. 1, February 1952, pp. 16–19.

Cavan, Ruth Shonle, *The American Family* (New York: Thomas Y. Crowell Company, 1953), "Family Life of the Old," pp. 588–612.

Cavan, Ruth Shonle; Burgess, Ernest W.; and Havighurst, Robert J., "Section VII, The Family in the Later Years," for the Committee on the Dynamics of Family Interaction, Preliminary Report, Evelyn Duvall and Reuben Hill, Co-chairmen, National Conference on Family Life, Washington, D. C., February 1948, mimeographed materials.

Cavan, Ruth Shonle, "Family Life and Family Substitutes in Old Age," *American Sociological Review*, Vol. 14, No. 1, February, 1949, pp. 71–83.

Cavan, Ruth Shonle; Burgess, Ernest W.; Havighurst, Robert J.; and Goldhamer, Herbert, *Personal Adjustment in Old Age* (Chicago: Science Research Associates, 1949).

Dinkel, Robert M., "Social and Economic Adjustments of the Aged," *Public Welfare in Indiana*, January, 1942.

Dublin, Louis I., "Our Aging Population," An Address at the Annual Forum, New York Chapter of the Chartered Life Underwriters, April 7, 1949, Town Hall, New York City.

Dublin, Louis I., and Yahraes, Herbert, "Adding Life to the Added Years," *Colliers*, January 13, 1951, pp. 24, 25, 71–73.

Duvall, Evelyn Millis, *In-Laws: Pro and Con* (New York: Association Press, 1954).

Eliot, Thomas D., "The Bereaved Family," *The Annals of the American Academy of Political and Social Science*, March 1932.

Fried, E. G., and Stern, K., "The Situation of the Aged Within the Family," *American Journal of Orthopsychiatry*, Vol. 18, No. 1, January 1948, pp. 31–54.

Havemann, Ernest, "Are Funerals Barbaric?" *McCall's*, May 1956, pp. 33, 96–99.

Havighurst, Robert J., *Human Development and Education* (New York: Longmans, Green and Company, 1953), Chapter 18, "Developmental Tasks of Later Maturity," pp. 277–283.

Havighurst, Robert J., and Albrecht, Ruth, *Older People* (New York: Longmans, Green and Company, 1953).

Hill, Reuben revision of Waller, Willard, *The Family: A Dynamic Interpretation* (New York: The Dryden Press, revised edition 1951), Chapter 22, "Bereavement."

Hitt, Homer L., "The Role of Migration in Population Change Among the Aged," *American Sociological Review*, Vol. 19, No. 2, April 1954 pp. 194–200.

Kaighn, Raymond P., *How to Retire and Like It* (New York: Association Press, 1954).

Kish, Henriette, *Questions Older People Ask* (New York: E. P. Dutton & Company, 1955).

Koller, Marvin R., "Studies of Three-Generation Households," *Marriage and Family Living*, Vol. XVI, No. 3, August 1954, pp. 205–206.

Lawton, George and Stewart, Maxwell S., *When You Grow Older* (New York: Public Affairs Committee, Inc., 1947).

Loeb, Martin B., "The Social Factors in the Study of Aging," Paper presented at American Psychological Association Symposium, Kansas City Study of Adult Life, San Francisco, September 2, 1955, unpublished.

Report of the Mayor's Advisory Committee for the Aged, "New York City's Senior Citizens: Our Most Neglected Resource, Our Most Important Challenge, Our Greatest Opportunity," New York City, October 1949–October 1953, Volumes 1, 2, and 3.

New York State Joint Legislative Committee on Problems of the Aging, *Age Is No Barrier*, 1952 report.

New York State Joint Legislative Committee on Problems of the Aging, *Growing with the Years*, 1954 report.

Ogg, Elizabeth, *When Parents Grow Old* (New York: Public Affairs Committee, Inc, 1954).

Pitkin, W. B., *The Best Years: How to Enjoy Retirement* (New York: Grosset & Dunlap, 1948).

Pollak, Otto, *Social Adjustment in Old Age* (New York: Social Science Research Council, 1948).

Scott, Frances G., "Factors in the Personal Adjustment of Institutionalized and Non-Institutionalized Aged," *American Sociological Review*, Vol. 20, No. 5, October 1955, pp. 538–546.

Tibbitts, Clark, Editor, *Living Through the Older Years*, Proceedings of the Charles A. Fisher Memorial Institute on Aging (Ann Arbor: University of Michigan Press, 1949).

All the world's a stage,
And all the men and women merely
  players:
They have their exits and their
  entrances,
And one man in his time plays
  many parts, . . .
          WILLIAM SHAKESPEARE,
          As You Like It

CHAPTER FIFTEEN

The dynamics of family interaction

Alfred Nobel, creator of the well-known Nobel Peace Prize, made a fortune from the manufacture of explosives. After a series of tragic explosions of his nitroglycerin factory, he set about trying to find an explosive that would be safer to handle. The story is told that when his efforts were rewarded, he went to the University of Uppsala to consult with the Professor of Greek as to what he should call this powerful packet of energy that he had discovered. The answer was dynamite, from the Greek word *dynamis* meaning power. The word dynamics comes from the same root, and literally means forces in action. When we use the phrase "dynamics of family interaction," we refer specifically to the powerful forces in action within a given family, everchanging, evermoving, everactive throughout the life of the family.

At times these energy systems within family life are explosive and result in family blow-ups that all of us know. In recent years there have been efforts to understand the forces that operate within family life in the hope that controls may be found that will give the family stability at the same time that its latent forces are harnessed to fulfill its purposes and destiny. Only a meager beginning has been made in this search for forms of family interaction that, like dynamite, are relatively safe to handle.

Some of the findings that are usable by any person with professional interest in family living include concepts that help us see what is there, even to assist us in knowing what to look for within family life. Such concepts are tools to work with, ways of seeing, perceiving, analyzing, understanding, and channeling the forces within families that may be harnessed for constructive work rather than running wild in destructive explosions. With such conceptual tools we know what to look for, and how to understand what we see in any family situation, wherever it is.

Knock on any door, and what will you find within? No one can tell you, actually, for every family differs and in many ways is unlike any other. But in another sense, if you know a few basic things about a family, you can somewhat reliably predict what you will find within it. For instance, if you know (a) where the family is in its life cycle (stage of family development as outlined in Chapter One); (b) where the family is in time (within an era of social change described in Chapter Two), and within a given season, day, and hour; and (c) how the family rates in the community (as seen in its social class status described in Chapter Four)—if you know these three things, you can tell even before you knock what the important elements to look for are, and in general what forces you probably will find in action there.

A simple illustration is found in the ways in which the forces within a family pulsate in predictable rhythms and tempos throughout time, as is seen in the section that follows.

FAMILY TEMPOS AND RHYTHMS

Families have a developmental history that is marked by periods of dynamic action and intervals of relative calm. This is true even within a brief period of time—a day, a week, a season.

Typically, the family day begins with the bustle of arising, washing, dressing, collecting the day's equipment, and getting into the day's work. The first spurt of energy is followed in many homes with the midday pause with nobody home but Mom and the dog. In the late afternoon comes the rush of homecoming, with reports of the day to each other, fixing and mending equipment, telephoning, special clean-up activities, and preparing the evening meal. In all but some lower-class families there is a pause for eating together with the family attention focused on itself. Outside pressures are then momentarily suspended and a high degree of family interaction is possible. Between the evening meal and bedtime there are many possible activities that depend upon the social life of the family, the age of its members, and its general makeup. The young parents may go out for the evening, having a sitter stay with the baby. The family may spend a quiet evening at home with the peace broken by intervals of conflict over the choice of TV programs, privacy and group demands, the telephone, and visitors from outside the home. There may be guests in, with the entertaining done as a whole family, as adults only, as children or young people only. Retiring tends to be serially routinized, with the youngest going to bed first, and others according to age and interests.

Weekly rhythms are fairly predictable in most families. There are the Monday-through-Friday routines that are built upon work and school schedules. The working week is followed by Saturday and Sunday, which in most families are the off-beat days that are filled with shopping and food storage, cleaning, and making ready for the week ahead; individual and whole family recreation (travel, trips, picnics, hobbies, movies, entertaining, and "just being lazy"); and religious services for the various family members.

In most parts of the country there are seasonal variations characterized by Spring, with its housecleaning, gardening and storage of winter clothing and equipment; Summer with more out-of-doors living, sports, and vacation plans; Fall with the settling down to the business of organizational, educational and vocational life, and getting the home ready for the busy season of heightened autumn activities in the community. Late in the Fall comes "getting ready for the holidays" in home, school, and community, with the flurry of seasonal entertaining, and festivities in various settings. By midwinter, families settle down to activities indoors and routines established for getting things done before Spring rolls around again.

The stages of the family life cycle differ in length (Chapter One), in activity, and in the intensity of family interaction. During the establishment phase the new husband and wife are hard at work in building their marriage out of the dreams and realities that each brings to the marriage. Since no two people ever grow up in identical families, each brings to marriage his or her own ideas about what is appropriate behavior, what should and should not be done, how roles are conceived, and what a family should be like. These differences may be assimilated, they may partially co-exist, one may dominate over the other(s), or they may remain in conflict. The channeling of the forces that bring the two people together in marriage is powerfully motivated, making this stage of marriage not only important but potentially an explosive one. With the expectant phase of the beginning family comes the realization of becoming immanently a family with the creative thrusts toward making a fitting home for the expected child.

The childbearing stage of the family is a busy bustling one with things strewn about, jobs never quite done, baby's demands, and parents' fatigue. When one child follows another in quick succession this stage may continue to be strenuous for some time, with none of the lull that comes in the one-child family as soon as the youngster trots off to preschool for at least part of the day. In time all of the children are in school, the family enjoys an interval of solidarity and fulfillment, and the parents get something of a breather before the quickened tempos of adolescence are upon them.

With the coming of the teen years the family is atomized, with the teenagers forming peer-group loyalties, establishing their autonomy, and pushing away from parents in the urgent tasks that must be accomplished if they are to become full-fledged adults. All this makes for anxious relationships at home with parents concerned about the safety of their adolescents, the good name of the family, and their own peace of mind.

The day comes when even the most active teenager settles down and comes home with stars in eyes to announce that wedding bells are soon to ring. The busy expensive years of the launching stage, in which young adults leave home for marriage, for work, for military service, or for college, leave the parents financially and emotionally spent, usually quite ready to enjoy the relative peace and quiet that is theirs in the middle and later years.

The latter half of marriage is typically spent as a couple; the grown children come home only at intervals with their grandchildren, the middleaged and aging husband and wife relatively free to come and go as they wish. These are the harvest years of family living, when the big job of raising a family is done and the man and wife are free to think of themselves and what they want out of life. If they have built a variety of satisfying interests, if they have warm friendships and close contact with their grown children and grandchildren, these are indeed the "Golden Years." If they are impoverished, jobless, useless, isolated, homeless, neglected, or incapacitated, these final years can be insufferably bleak and barren, "sans everything," as Shakespeare describes them.

The success of families in finding happiness and satisfaction in any one of the stages of life is dependent primarily upon how well they achieve the developmental tasks of the period. Failure tends to predispose future frustration, while success is built upon previous success. Every individual, every family, is doing well or not so well in the tasks of the developmental period of the moment. Doing well, the person, the family-as-a-whole is happy, well adjusted, competent, and relatively self-assured. The challenge to families, and to those who care about them, is to increase the incidence of success and diminish the frequencies of failure in the developmental tasks of life.

WHAT FAMILIES MUST DO TO DEVELOP SUCCESSFULLY

All families face certain basic requirements for their survival, continuity and growth. In some way every family must deal with at least six fundamental problems: [1]

1) Allocation of authority and responsibility
2) Allocation of functional roles
3) Socialization of children
4) Allocation of economic resources
5) Allocation of lines of solidarity among family members and integration of the group as a whole
6) Articulation with other important social structures in society

These six conditions are necessary for family survival, continuity, and growth and so must be dealt with in some way by all families. The ways in which families cope with any one or all of these six fundamental problems differ enormously: by stage of the life cycle (Chapter One); by time in history (Chapter Two); by basic orientation as traditional or developmental in its childrearing practices (Chapter Three) and flexibility of roles for males and females, adults and children; by social class (Chapter Four), and by the success or failure it is finding in its various family developmental tasks (Chapter Five).

Study of corn-belt farm families in East Central Illinois, at midcentury, yields three distinctly different family types in basic ways of meeting the functional prerequisites of family life.[2]

---

[1] These are called "functional prerequisites" and defined as the fundamental conditions that must be met by any group, by Talcott Parsons, *Essays in Sociological Theory, Pure and Applied* (Glencoe, Illinois: The Free Press, 1949), pp. viii, 6–7, 42–51.

[2] Eleanor Powell Godfrey, "A Construction of Family Types and Their Initial Empirical Validation," Unpublished Ph.D. Study, Radcliffe College, Cambridge, Mass., 1951.

Type I is seen as a family that is geared to the past. Family standards are rigidly upheld, with the major sanctions being religion and the mores. The immediate family is recognized as part of the larger extended family, with each individual subordinated to the group as a whole. Family government is patriarchal. Children are trained by strict traditional methods. Women's spheres of activity are limited and subordinate to those of the men of the household. The father directs the economic affairs of the family in which economic interdependence is emphasized. Family solidarity is largely work-oriented, with farming seen as a family occupation. There are close ties with relatives and with the church, but few active connections with the school or other social and civic organizations.

Type II is seen as a family geared to the present. Individual welfare is more important than group preservation, and the immediate family is separated from the larger kinship group. Public approval is the major sanction with methods of control derived from current practice and standards that are contemporary. Family government is equalitarian. Children are trained under the careful supervision of the mother according to currently popular methods. There is a well-defined division of labor between the sexes, but both men's and women's work are considered equally important. Husband and wife jointly control the money of the family and emphasize mature children's economic independence. Family solidarity is based largely on recreational ties. Farming as such is seen as a profitable business. There is little interaction with relatives, and individual family members are encouraged to be active in numerous organizations in the community.

Type III is a family that is geared to the future. The needs of the individual and the group are equally important. The immediate family is most important, although past and future generations are considered. Standards are set by individual capacity with methods derived freely from any source. The family is governed by group consensus. Child training is permissive and in terms of the nature of the individual child. The division of labor is functional, along personal lines of feasibility. Mutual economic responsibility is emphasized, with money allocated by the whole family. Family solidarity is based upon both work and play, with farming seen as a way of life. There is a considerable amount of both family and organizational activity, with relationships with relatives along lines of personal friendship.

In Dr. Godfrey's three family types, Type I is recognized as the traditional family found as typical of the family system in the past in China, Japan, Germany, Poland, Ireland, with vestiges still found in many communities in the United States. Type II is seen as the middle-class urban family in transition, broken away from the old family ties, highly individualistic, and present-oriented. Type III appears to be the developmental family (Chapter Three).

In a country like the United States, all three of these family types, and many more, can coexist in the same community. Aspects of all three types are found even in the same family. Each family is free to work out its own way of life, its own answers to the fundamental conditions of its survival and development. This tremendous variety is to be expected not only because this is "the land of the free and the home of the brave," but also because this is a time of change in which some aspects of family living have broken off from old ways and are creating new family patterns that better satisfy the conditions of our modern, urbanized, industrialized society (Chapter Two).

What family system will work out best in the long run? No one knows, for sure. But there has been enough research to date to give some hints as to what family patterns best accomplish the developmental tasks of families today. For instance, in Godfrey's study, developmental families were found to be more likely to feel secure in their social position and to have a higher degree of family solidarity than either of the other two family types. This confirms the superiority of developmental families in rearing today's children and in encouraging the continued growth of all family members as found in research report after report quoted in Chapter Three. While traditional families may have been quite adequate at one time, they generally are too rigid, too patriarchal, and not sufficiently developmentally oriented to be effective in today's rapidly changing social scene, with its requirement for flexible, creative persons.

This volume traces the various developmental tasks for each individual and for the family as a whole at every stage of the family life cycle. In each case the developmental task is the distillate of what is known to be required for the individual or the family at that particular stage of development for healthful living. The tasks are in terms of the physical requirements at that time, to meet the demands of society at that stage, in line with personal aspirations and future growth possibilities (Chapter Five).

In many instances, the immediate society does not demand that the person perform in any particular way. For instance, a quiet child, an unobtrusive teenager, a middleaged hermit or an aging person can remain socially isolated and cut off from life, and nobody will interfere in many a modern neighborhood. Yet, all evidence points to the high correlation between social participation and life satisfaction and well-being at every stage of the life cycle. So, developmental tasks call for lively contact with others outside oneself, throughout the life cycle stages.

Many individuals resent interference from experts and rebel from recommended regimens that are known to be helpful and healthful. Millions of teenagers are known to be undernourished in this richest of countries, not because of a dearth of food nor because optimal diets are not known and taught, but rather because the pressures of the peer group call for cokes and potato chips rather than milk and other health-giving foods. So too, in the emotional area of intimate interaction within the family, there remains a wide gap between what is known to be good practice and what families actually do. These discrepancies, however, do not disprove the validity of the recommendations, nor do they mean a cessation of research and education for family living. On the contrary, they call for ever more sharply defined research and more effective education for the kind of family living that is known to be good— for the development of the individual, and for the survival and growth of the family as a whole.

In summarizing this section, we quote a simple distillate of elements important for successful family living as seen by a body of qualified specialists working together in one of the work groups of the National Conference on Family Life.

WHAT MAKES FAMILY LIVING GOOD? [1]

1. It provides a stable base for the development of its members.
2. It transmits the cultural heritage to oncoming generations.
3. It cultivates the deeper, more intimate aspects of living.
4. It interprets life's experiences to its members.
5. It assures the physical and mental health of its members.
6. It encourages the expression of human personality.
7. It serves as a "choosing agency" among many ways of life.
8. It encourages the wholesome expression of love impulses.
9. It protects the human reproductive function.

[1] Evelyn Millis Duvall, *Family Living* (New York: Macmillan Company, 1955 revision), pp. 394–395, adapted originally from *Unique Values of Family Life*, Group No. 5, National Conference on Family Life, Washington, D. C., May 5–8, 1948.

10. It is a haven—a place where "if you have to go, they have to take you in."
11. It offers a place where individuals may make mistakes within an atmosphere of protection.
12. It practices interdependence rather than competition.
13. It stands for the enjoyment and the fulfillment of life.
14. It lives for something more than the moment, and for causes beyond itself.

FAMILY MEMBERS PLAY MANY ROLES

Family interaction is a process by which a family relates to life outside itself and through which one member's action is stimulated by the action of other members.[1] Patterns of action are often referred to as role, as Davis puts it, "how an individual actually performs in a given position . . . we call his *role*."[2] Hence, family interaction is reciprocal action between family members, the interlocking roles within a family, and between a family and the world beyond itself.

Each family member helps establish the roles of the other members of the family, and is in turn influenced in the roles he plays by the others in the family. The baby makes parents of his father and mother, and in turn is cast in the part of infant in the home, at his birth. The parents influence the breadth and scope and meaning of the child's early experiences and so set the stage for the young person's present and future roles in the formative period of personality development. The children on the other hand make their impact on the lives of their parents at every stage of the family life cycle.[3]

No two children ever live in the same family, nor play identical roles as brothers and sisters. Mothers have long recognized that no two of their children are alike, no matter how big the family. Recent studies of large families suggest numerous role-types among siblings of which eight are illustrative: (1) the responsible one (dutiful, helpful, etc.), (2) the popular one (sociable, well-liked), (3) The socially ambitious one ("social butterfly," usually a girl), (4) the studious one (quiet, hardworking), (5) the family isolate (self-centered, withdrawn), (6) the

---

[1] See Robert F. Bales, *Interaction Process Analysis* (Cambridge, Mass.: Addison-Wesley Press, 1950), and George C. Homans, *The Human Group* (New York: Harcourt, Brace and Company, 1950).
[2] Kingsley Davis, *Human Society* (New York: Macmillan Company, 1949), p. 90.
[3] See "Living and Growing with Our Children: Impact on Parents of Children's Growth Phases," *Child Study*, Vol. XXXII, No. 3, Summer 1955, entire issue.

irresponsible one (the nonparticipant in the family), (7) the sickly one (physically defective or hypochondriacal), (8) the spoiled one (usually the lastborn).[1]

These eight types fall into an intriguing sequence, suggesting a theory of specialized personality roles and behavior patterns in the large family that is breath-taking in the challenging leads which it opens up. Keeping in mind always the constancy of the individual child's drive for recognition and status, let us consider the eight types in the order of their presentation, which is essentially the order of frequency of identification. The first ones to appear develop patterns of responsibility because they are first and are followed by younger and more helpless siblings. The next ones, finding this role pre-empted, seek recognition by making themselves agreeable. They do not seek to wrest control from the older children; they compete with it or supplement it with their personal charms. The next children, finding these two roles pre-empted, turn from the family to the community. They become social-minded and socially ambitious. Those that follow in turn have to turn to a new avenue of achievement. These turn to the schools. They become the scholars, the studious ones, the sophisticates, the intellectuals. Finding all of these avenues under active cultivation, the next child withdraws from competition.

This is the family isolate. Or he may not withdraw his presence, only his sense of responsibility—these are the irresponsible ones, who participate but let others hold the bag. Both the isolate and the irresponsible are patterns of withdrawal and often of failure to find a satisfactory avenue of achievement. The physically defective, the sickly, and those who pretend to be—they have their excuse for relative failure to find their roles, if they wish to use it. Finally, at the end of the line is the terminal child, either pampered into relative ineffectiveness or wearing the "magic boots" to overtake the older ones." [2]

There is nothing arbitrary in these eight role types found in contemporary large families. There is nothing in the schema that suggests that these roles are universally present in families, or that they always appear in the sequence suggested. The material is provocative not only in teasing out some of the specific ways in which siblings' roles differ, but also in suggesting the dynamics of role selection by the children of a family. Younger children arriving in a family in which certain roles have already been assumed by older, more experienced brothers and sisters, are seen to develop new roles that offer opportunity for growth without too heavy competition with the already established roles of older siblings.

[1] James H. S. Bossard and Eleanor S. Boll, "Personality Roles in the Large Family," *Child Development*, Vol. 26, No. 1, March 1955, pp. 71–78.
[2] *Ibid.*, p. 77.

An everyday illustration indicates that the same principle may operate even in a two-child family. The older child became proficient at the piano from an early age, and encouraged by the approval of the family and the applause of doting friends and relatives entertained the group with her latest "pieces" on many occasions. Along came the younger sister three years later. She became a delightful outdoor girl who could match any boy with feats on the jungle-gym, but would have nothing to do with the piano or with music. When pressed to take music lessons, she flatly said that she could never "catch up" with her sister, and so refused to try.

So it may be too with other roles within the family. The mother who is *too* competent as a housekeeper, or cook, or seamstress may so discourage her daughter in her first fumbling efforts that the child gives up and turns to other roles in which competition with her mother is not so keen. The father who is a busy executive with little time for his family may "teach" his son that the costs of working so hard are just too great to struggle for. The son then becomes an irresponsible, self-indulgent fellow whose role seems to be to take it easy rather than keep his nose to the grindstone as his father has done through the years.

The interacting roles of family members tend to balance and supplement each other. This tendency works for the stability of the family, and for the establishment and maintenance of each member's identity. As each family member finds and develops his unique roles within his family, his personality is formed around these early roles which tend to persist in his further relationships beyond the immediate family and in his further development as a person.

RESPONSIBILITIES AND BURDENS OF TODAY'S FAMILIES

The part the family plays in molding the personality of its members has long been observed and widely studied. One of the earliest pieces of research on the development of aspects of character in children found parents conspicuously more closely related to the child's moral judgments than any others of his associates, as we see in Table 37.

Similar findings since then confirm the fact of the power of family influences on the developing personality of the child. The reasons are many: the family gets the child first and has the longest and the most sustained contact with him (friends, club leaders and teachers come and

TABLE 37. *Correlation between Children's Ideas of Right and Wrong and Those of Their Associates* [1]

Child and parents............................	.545
Child and friends............................	.353
Child and club leaders.......................	1.37
Child and day-school teachers................	.028
Child and Sunday School teachers.............	.002

go, especially rapidly in these days of high mobility); family attitudes are intimate and emotionalized; the child identifies early with his family, or a member of it and tries to emulate the family ways or the individual's life style; many of the child's roles are early established in the arena of interaction of his family, long before other agencies have a chance to influence him.

The family that plays its role well in the lives of its members does not try to make each one conform to any one pattern or ideal, but encourages each member (male and female, adult and child) to develop his or her own interests, play the roles that are most comfortable, and become the person he or she is capable of becoming. Such a family encourages all its members to take part, each according to his ability, in planning, assuming responsibility and enjoying the fruits of family activities. When roles conflict, or family members see things differently, the values of each are given consideration and some solution is mutually arrived at that satisfies at least part of each person's need as well as the good of the whole. Families that foster the development of their members give each as much freedom as he can assume responsibility for, from his earliest days on through the years. Members of developmental families therefore, can usually play a variety of roles with flexibility and competence, because they have been allowed to practice a full repertoire of parts, to exchange roles, to innovate, and to explore new possibilities in role performance all along.

Freedom in the selection and the playing of roles in the family has its price in confusion and conflict. There is a certain unpredictability in having no clear-cut authority or rigid ways of doing things.[2] The de-

---

[1] Hugh Hartshorne and Mark A. May, "Testing the Knowledge of Right and Wrong," *Religious Education,* October 1926, pp. 539–554.

[2] Clifford Kirkpatrick, *The Family as Process and Institution* (New York: The Ronald Press, 1955), Chapter 4, "Family Types and Dilemmas," esp. p. 86.

velopmental family cannot be expected to be as neat, or as quiet, or as efficient as the old-fashioned home ruled over by an iron hand where each child knew his place and kept rigidly within it. But within the developmental family grow the people who are developing the inner strengths and the interpersonal competence so sorely needed today.[1]

DIFFICULTIES FAMILIES FACE IN PERFORMING THEIR TASKS [2]

Historic patterns of family living and child rearing, derived from an earlier way of life now largely passed (Chapters Two and Three) no longer are adequate or even tolerable for families today. Therefore, every family is, to a greater or lesser extent, harassed, anxious or guilty, beset with perplexities and burdened with conflicts, both within the family and with the surrounding social life. Moreover, every family is under the growing pressure of various agencies, professions, and programs to modify, change, reorganize one or more of its living habits in accordance with new knowledge of what is desirable or essential.

The breakdown in the traditional definition of the masculine and feminine roles, by which men and women were guided to the performance of their obligations and enjoyment of their privileges, has brought confusion and conflict within the family. Men and women are coming to marriage today with divergent expectations and needs, which frequently clash with those of the spouse. These conflicting beliefs and expectations hamper and often frustrate the man and woman in meeting their developmental tasks as husband and wife and as mother and father.

Moreover, children are growing up in a social situation where these changes in beliefs, expectations, and conduct are taking place so rapidly that parents are unable to understand, let alone accept, what their adolescents think and do. Thus the more or less normal cleavage between generations has been enlarged and accentuated; sometimes becoming bitter

---

[1] Nelson N. Foote and Leonard S. Cottrell, Jr., *Identity and Interpersonal Competence* (Chicago: University of Chicago Press, 1955), see especially Chapter 2, in which interpersonal competence is seen to have six components: 1) health, 2) intelligence, 3) empathy, 4) autonomy, 5) judgment, and 6) creativity, (p. 41).

[2] Adapted from Lawrence K. Frank, "Foreword of the Committee on Dynamics of Family Interaction," Evelyn Millis Duvall and Reuben Hill, co-chairmen, National Conference on Family Life, Washington, D. C., 1948, mimeographed materials, pp. 3 and 4.

conflicts and resentful rivalries at the time when both parents and children are acutely in need of reassurance and comfort.

Over and above these family-focused difficulties, there is the larger social, economic, political situations in which the needs and interests of the family are not only ignored but frequently are deliberately sacrificed to the varied objectives of organizations, agencies, professions, and individuals.

As we reflect upon the developmental tasks of family life and recognize how difficult it is sometimes under the most favorable circumstances to carry on, meeting the changing requirements of a growing family and the demands of our own ongoing maturation, we must remember that for a large number of families conditions are frequently adverse and wholly frustrating.

It is becoming evident that we cannot expect families to perform their basic functions while compelled to live in houses and neighborhoods that are subhuman and degrading. How can families, charged with responsibilities of maintaining homes, providing meals and otherwise continually meeting their daily human needs, manage to do so with fluctuating and uncertain incomes, often inadequate to provide even a minimum standard of living?

FAMILY CRISES [1]

A family crisis may be defined as anything for which the usual patterns of family living are inadequate. It is the unexpected quality of much in family living that makes it hazardous, as Koos reports a New York tenement dweller as saying, "If you always know what to expect, life would be a lot of fun. But the trouble is, you *never* know what to expect, so you're never ready for what happens, so life ain't too much fun."

Family crises have been classified as those resulting from loss of a member (dismemberment), those resulting from loss of status and of face (demoralization), those resulting from the addition of a member (accession), and those resulting from a combination of demoralization and dismemberment or accession, as follows:

[1] Based upon the report of Section VIII, "Families in Crisis" by Earl L. Koos, chairman, and David Fulcomer, for the Committee on the Dynamics of Family Interaction, Evelyn M. Duvall and Reuben Hill, co-chairmen, National Conference on Family Life, Washington, D. C., Preliminary Report, unpublished mimeographed materials, May 1948, pp. 1–16.

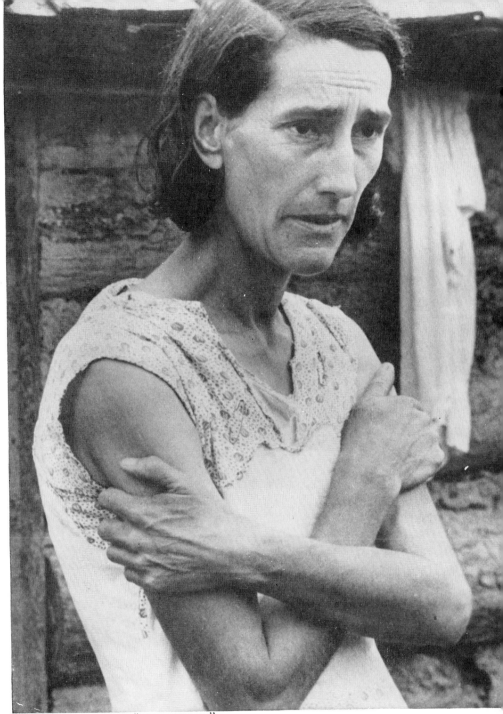

It is the unexpected quality of much in family living that makes it hazardous.

FAMILY CRISES CLASSIFIED [1]

Dismemberment only	Loss of child
	Loss of spouse
	Orphanhood
	Hospitalization
	War separation
Dismemberment only	Nonsupport
	Progressive dissension
	Infidelity
	Sense of disgrace—reputation loss
Accession only	Unwanted pregnancy
	Deserter returns
	Stepmother, stepfather additions
	Some war reunions
	Some adoptions
Demoralization plus Dismemberment or Accession	Illegitimacy
	Runaway situations
	Desertion
	Divorce
	Imprisonment
	Suicide or homicide

Despite the great attention students have given to studies of American family life in recent years, relatively little interest has been shown in the effect of crises upon the family as a family. Only a few scholars have studied intensively these disruptions, and the total number of families studied is very small. Despite this apparent neglect, the body of fact so far collected is impressive, and both the vulnerability of American families to breakdown, and the need for community supports and supplementation of family resources have been well established.[2]

[1] From Evelyn M. Duvall and Reuben Hill, *When You Marry* (Boston: D. C. Heath and Company, 1953 revised edition), p. 259, from a classification originally suggested by Thomas D. Eliot, "Handling Family Strains and Shocks," in Howard Becker and Reuben Hill (eds.), *Family, Marriage and Parenthood* (Boston: D. C. Heath and Company, 1948), p. 617, n.

[2] See especially such modern classics as: Angell, Robert C., *The Family Encounters the Depression* (New York: Scribner, 1936); Cavan, Ruth S., and Ranck, Katherine, *The Family and the Depression* (Chicago, University of Chicago Press, 1938); Goode, William, *After Divorce* (Glencoe, Illinois: The Free Press, 1956); Hill, Reuben, *Families Under Stress* (New York: Harper & Sons, 1949); Koos, Earl L., *Families in Trouble* (New York: King's Crown Press, 1946); and Komarovsky, Mirra, *The Unemployed Man and His Family* (New York: Dryden Press, 1940).

The whole problem is a complicated one, if only because crises mean different things to different people. To the low-income family, living up to and even beyond its income, there may be a quality of desperation that is lacking in the middle-class family, with reserves upon which it can draw. Conversely, the low-income family has less to lose in prestige or status, and may therefore be able to react more favorably to some crises than can the middle-class family, with much to lose in position within its group in the community. One family may have a "tight" family organization, with a firm adherence to a certain pattern of action in all family situations, while another may be groping its way toward more flexible family ways, with quite a different attitude toward what constitutes a crisis and what to do about it. Some families accept help in trouble easily and without embarrassments, others "would rather die than take help from anybody."

Crises can be precipitated by conflicting developmental tasks of family members who temporarily or permanently fail to complement each other. Parent-child differences contribute to tension and conflict, especially when the child pulls away from the family, repudiates the parent, and rebels from parental control. Conflicting conceptions of role on the part of husband and wife often lead to conflicts in the sexual, economic, home-making, childrearing, and larger relationships of the family. Cultural differences in the incomplete assimilation of two different backgrounds in a marriage can cause trouble. Differences in aspiration are common in our society where so many are upward mobile, while others remain socially conforming in their life goals. Social class conflicts precipitated by opposing class membership pressures seethe beneath the surface or are fought out in the open in many a home.

There is no *one* inadequacy. There is an initial cause which tends to create tensions in other areas of family life, which in turn become conflicts in themselves. They all may be represented in diagram fashion (see p. 494).

For example, cultural disparity may cause a lack of sexual satisfaction because of the differing ideas and standards of sex behavior, which in turn may lead to suspicion of the mate and lack of cooperation as breadwinner or homemaker, which in turn may create conflicting roles in the family and draw individual members into new positions of responsibility in the family at the expense of other members. All this may so weaken the affectional relationships and integration of the family as to render

Causes of Family Conflict

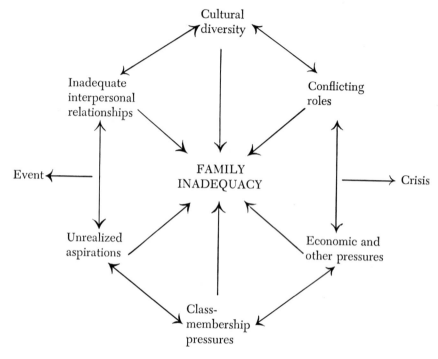

it unable to meet even a simple departure from its ordinary life patterns; the result, when an out-of-the-ordinary event occurs, is a crisis.

Studies indicate that one of the serious problems confronting the field of community organization is to develop suitable institutional aids for the family in crisis and to find ways of getting the family to use these aids where they do exist. Such unskilled individuals (in terms of human relations) as the druggist and bartender are consulted most often (except for relatives) by low-income families.[1] "Muddling through" a crisis alone appears to be the usual pattern for the middle-class family.

This relative "aloneness" of the American family presents both a serious problem and a distinct challenge. It appears that earnest steps must be taken not only to make our present institutional aids more acceptable and usable to families, but new aids must be planned and instituted if our families are to make the best possible adjustment.

[1] Earl L. Koos, *Families in Trouble* (New York: King's Crown Press, 1946).

Implications for services needed to help families meet present-day challenges and hazards are outlined below for each stage of the family life cycle. These are given with an explicit awareness of the family's urgent need to accomplish its own developmental tasks at every phase of family living. Community services in no way remove these central responsibilities from families or family members, but rather provide the resources and the opportunities for American families more effectively to achieve their tasks.

We need much more basic investigation, better research tools, and far more extensive and intensive study of all kinds of families, before we can lay down a complete list of recommendations similar to what is possible in the Basic Seven that has emerged out of many years of intensive research in human nutrition. Yet, already there appear leads that are worth following, some alternatives that definitely seem to be superior to others, some conditions for human development that are more conducive to optimal growth at every stage of life, than are others. These have been indicated for every stage of the family life cycle, chapter by chapter through the book, and are summarized in specific detail in the following outline.

SERVICES NEEDED TO HELP FAMILIES MEET PRESENT-DAY CHALLENGES AND HAZARDS

STAGE I. BEGINNING FAMILIES: ESTABLISHMENT PHASE

Challenges and Hazards	*Services Needed*
High divorce rate in first years of marriage	Extensive education for marriage in schools, colleges, churches, community and youth serving agencies Competent premarital and marital counseling
Many marriages among very young people	Courtship, marriage and family life education early in the high school years Effective parent education
Marriages of persons from different religious, racial, cultural and social class groups	Widespread intercultural education developing specific understanding of other groups, and of what is involved in mixed marriage Premarital counseling

Effective premarital and marriage counseling help a couple meet many challenges in the establishment phase of their marriage.

SERVICES NEEDED TO HELP FAMILIES MEET PRESENT-DAY CHALLENGES AND HAZARDS (*Continued*)

STAGE I. BEGINNING FAMILIES: ESTABLISHMENT PHASE

Challenges and Hazards	*Services Needed*
Marriage combined with continuing education, military service, vocational establishment, high mobility and other complicating stress situations	Education that encourages young married people to continue in school as long as feasible
	Community supports and governmental aids for young families separated by military service
	Premarital counseling and education for marriage and family living
	Apprenticeship opportunities
	Community services included in "Welcome Wagon" introductions to young couples new in the community

Challenges and Hazards	Services Needed
Low income and high costs of beginning families	Acceptable forms of family subsidy
Advertising pressures and efforts to "keep up with the Joneses"	Consumer education including explicit discussion of relative values early in high school years and continuing through early marriage
Installment buying abuses	Specific educational programs dealing with the pros and cons of various forms of financing Legislation controlling excessive buying
Inadequate housing within reach of young families	Low– and moderate-cost housing programs
Multiple roles of young working wives and hazards of homemaking still traditionally defined	Public encouragement of more flexible roles for both men and women in home and community
Taboos, misconceptions, and fictions about love and sex spread through mass media	Competent instruction and counseling in the nature of human nature from early childhood on through the years
Fallacious stereotypes about in-laws adversely influencing young marriages	Public interpretation of facts and attitudes making for success in larger family relationships
Materialism and pseudo-sophistication making more permanent values hard to establish in young families	Church and religious programs geared specifically to young married people of the community Family life education stressing relative values

STAGE I. BEGINNING FAMILIES: EXPECTANT PHASE

Challenges and Hazards	Services Needed
Sterility and infertility among couples wanting children	Infertility clinics and services freely available Continued improvement in adoption facilities and procedures
Unwanted and unplanned pregnancies	Planned parenthood programs for couples within various religious and social groups
Reproduction taboos and old wives tales	Reproduction education generally available

COURTESY OF CLARA ELIZABETH FUND FOR MATERNAL HEALTH

Courses for married couples and expectant mothers' and fathers' classes are good ways of relieving anxiety and preparing families for childbearing.

SERVICES NEEDED TO HELP FAMILIES MEET PRESENT-DAY CHALLENGES AND HAZARDS (*Continued*)

STAGE I. BEGINNING FAMILIES: EXPECTANT PHASE

Challenges and Hazards	*Services Needed*
Fears and uncertainties of pregnancy	Expectant mothers' and fathers' classes
Ignorance of child-care procedures and modern methods of childrearing	Child-care and guidance courses for young parents-to-be, grandmothers, and the public generally
High costs of obstetrical care, and hospital services	Low and moderate cost medical and hospital services
	Group health and hospitalization insurance plans covering obstetrical services
Pressures of advertising to buy more baby gear than necessary	Consumer buying guides geared to infants' real needs generally available
Sharp decline in family income as mother stops working to have baby	Specific education preparing young couples for next steps to be anticipated in family living

Challenges and Hazards	*Services Needed*
Couples often far from family supports and services	Friendly, acceptable counseling services
	Housekeeper and nursing services for families

STAGE II. CHILDBEARING FAMILIES

Challenges and Hazards	*Services Needed*
Birth and lying-in periods too often unpleasant for mother, father and baby	Wide exploration of possibilities of rooming-in plans for getting whole family off to good start the first week of child's life
	Doctors' and nurses' classes on needs of families at this period
Rigid, unwholesome child-care methods	Widespread parent education facilities
Anxious parents	Accessible counseling services for families
Inadequate, inaccessible medical aids for young families with babies	Well-baby clinics, widely available infant welfare stations, immunization services, and family focused health programs
Frequency of illness and accidents in childbearing stage	Home nursing programs in community to ready parents for competence in time of sickness
Tied-downness of young families	Community baby-sitter services
	Cooperative baby-care facilities
Housing inadequacies for families with young children	Housing planned for children within moderate price range in communities
High cost of children's clothing and equipment	Neighborhood swap-services for exchange of outgrown children's clothes, toys, and furnishings
Prejudice against grandparents' influence on young children	Public interpretation of values of interdependence with older generation
Rigid, harmful attitudes and practices in parenting in the neighborhood	Flexible wholesome climate of opinion about roles of fathers, mothers, children and families generally fostered

Nurses' classes on needs of childbearing families prepare them for making the birth and lying-in periods creative family experiences.

SERVICES NEEDED TO HELP FAMILIES MEET PRESENT-DAY CHALLENGES AND HAZARDS (*Continued*)

STAGE II. CHILDBEARING FAMILIES

Challenges and Hazards	*Services Needed*
Unwanted and neglected children	Special programs for children born out of wedlock, children with special disabilities, and children of inadequate parents
	Education and counseling help available for parents to help them enjoy their children

STAGE III. FAMILIES WITH PRESCHOOL CHILDREN

Challenges and Hazards	*Services Needed*
Relative isolation of young children in small modern families	Cooperative nurseries and preschools for small children freely accessible
Inadequate play space	Neighborhood tot-lots and block areas for young children

Challenges and Hazards	Services Needed
Insufficient dwelling units for families with young children	Housing developments designed for growing families in terms of indestructibility, play areas inside and out, within moderate and low-cost range
High frequency of illness and accidents among preschool children	Effective safety programs in the community Preventive and remedial medical services Adequate public health and nursing programs Group health and accident insurance coverage of whole family Services for exceptional children with special needs
Early evidence of mental illness in behavioral problems of preschool children	Accessible mental hygiene programs including child guidance clinics, spotter services for detecting emotional needs, and helping both parents and children Preventive and curative counseling facilities that are both acceptable and accessible
Neglected and abused children	Effective provision for children who need care beyond what their families can provide
Fragmentation of families by the various specialties serving them	Family life orientation in the training of physicians, clergymen, community workers, and all others dealing with family members Lessened demands upon the time of family members
Parents' inability to predict, understand and meet children's needs	Parent education, group and individual counseling for parents, books and discussion guides on child development

STAGE IV. FAMILIES WITH SCHOOL CHILDREN

Challenges and Hazards	Services Needed
Teacher shortage	National programs for inducement, selection and training of adequate supply of teachers

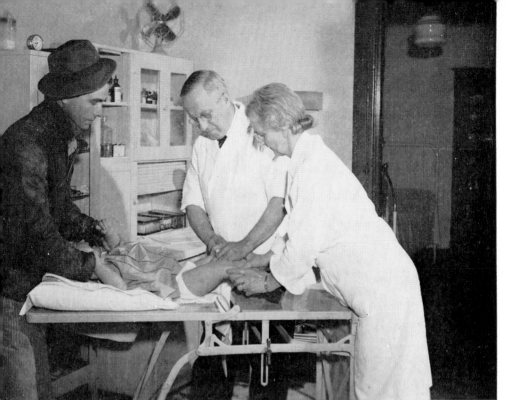

High frequency of illness and accidents among school children calls for safety-training, as well as preventive and remedial medical services.

SERVICES NEEDED TO HELP FAMILIES MEET PRESENT-DAY CHALLENGES AND HAZARDS (*Continued*)

STAGE IV. FAMILIES WITH SCHOOL CHILDREN

Challenges and Hazards	*Services Needed*
Inadequate school facilities for rapidly growing population	Rapid expansion of school building and equipment by state and local governments
Sharp increase in accidents among school children	Traffic regulation programs
	Safety indoctrination in home, school and community
	Education in first aid for parents, teachers, and among children themselves
Increased exposure to communicable disease	Effective immunization programs
	Public Health education and service
	Home nursing courses for family members

Challenges and Hazards	Services Needed
Inadequate housing for families with school children	Improvement and increase of housing suitable for families with children
Limited play space in neighborhood	Neighborhood playgrounds
Economic pressures on families with children	Financial plans to spread the costs of accidents, sickness, hospitalization, housing and education of children
Poor articulation of home and school	Parent-teacher cooperation in joint projects, and in effective PTA programs
Ethnic and racial tensions in the neighborhood	Intercultural education for all
Child behavior problems	Widespread programs in parent education and family counseling
	Readily available child guidance services
	Mental health interpretation for the public
Children with unmet needs	Community welfare programs that see that no child falls through the net of concern

STAGE V. FAMILIES WITH TEENAGERS

Challenges and Hazards	Services Needed
Youth in trouble	Delinquency prevention and treatment programs
	Guidance and counseling for all youth and their parents as needed
Truancy and drop-outs from school	Flexible programs to challenge all pupils to get as much education as they can effectively use
	Teacher education in the realities of social class and their responsibility to children of all economic and social levels
Inadequate and unwholesome recreational facilities for teenagers	Teenage centers where wholesome well-planned, adequately supervised, youth-centered programs are available for all teenagers
	Parent education which stresses need for teenagers to entertain in their homes

SERVICES NEEDED TO HELP FAMILIES MEET PRESENT-DAY CHALLENGES AND HAZARDS (*Continued*)

STAGE V. FAMILIES WITH TEENAGERS

Challenges and Hazards	Services Needed
Socially isolated and inexperienced teenagers	Opportunities for all young people to learn fundamental skills of social intercourse in wholesome settings Educational programs which help teenagers to understand and *accept* themselves Programs which help parents to *accept* teenagers—just as they are
Confusions in what is expected of teenage young people in the school, family and community	Parent-youth codes of behavior, jointly developed as neighborhood guides of what is expected at various grade levels
Worried and threatened parents	Parent education and counseling
Difficulties youth face in emancipation and development of personal autonomy	Family relationship units in junior and senior high school programs that help youth understand both their developmental tasks and their parents better Parallel programs of education for parents of teenagers
Cultural confusions about love and sex	Love and sex education in home, school, church, and community programs designed to help young people discriminate and control their feelings and impulses; sound books, and other guides for youth and their parents
Early teenage marriages	Guidance and education for marriage of early high school ages in home, school, church, and community programs Educational programs for professional people who work with teenagers
Financial pressures on families with growing youth	Part-time jobs for young people under good supervision Part-time employment for married women of older children

Challenges and Hazards	Services Needed
Health problems of adolescents	Hygiene education
	Nutrition educational programs
	Adequate programs for the detection of disease, i.e. tuberculosis examinations, etc.
	Safety education programs in the community
Rootless, "crazy, mixed-up kids"	Specific instruction on the meanings, and responsibilities, of maturing
	Youth-centered religious programs for more teenagers
	Guidance centers for youth

STAGE VI. FAMILIES AS LAUNCHING CENTERS

Challenges and Hazards	Services Needed
Inability of many able youth to continue education and training	Adequate scholarship system for young people on the basis of ability and need
Vocational complexities and confusions	Vocational guidance from early age
Problems of military service	Counseling and specific preparation for military service
Confusions in basic questions of whom to marry, when to marry, how to marry, and what is involved in being married	Effective preparation for marriage courses and premarital counseling in home, church, school, and college, including the acquisition of the knowledges, acquiring of the skills, development of the attitudes and values conducive to competence in the processes that lead to marriage
Induction of youth into responsible citizenship	New-citizen programs for induction and training young people for capable roles as citizens
	Increased acceptance of youth as capable of being participating members in the community
Troubled youth with problems	Guidance and counseling facilities
Biased emphases about youth and youth problems in mass media	Responsible press with interpretation of news stories and feature materials in line with known facts and realities

Formal and informal education for marriage clears up many of the confusions young adults have about when and how and whom to marry.

SERVICES NEEDED TO HELP FAMILIES MEET PRESENT-DAY CHALLENGES AND HAZARDS (*Continued*)

STAGE VI. FAMILIES AS LAUNCHING CENTERS

Challenges and Hazards	*Services Needed*
Economic stresses on families with young people to launch into college, marriage and the world as young adults	Public acceptance of women working Employment opportunities for married women
"Momism" tendencies in middle-class families	Encouragement of mothers to release their young people and to find other sources of satisfaction beyond their children Recruitment of middleaged women for community projects, neighborhood housekeeping, and general welfare, as well as for gainful employment Programs to help mothers of young children to develop interests and satisfactions beyond their own

Challenges and Hazards	Services Needed
	children—so they become ready to release their children
Overly elaborate wedding customs and pressures for extravagance	General interpretation of the meanings of marriage and the values to be achieved in the wedding Consumer guidance in wedding costs and choices
Confusion and contradictions over the roles of men and women in our culture	Discussions, panels, mass media treatment and general consideration given to the variety and flexibility of modern roles, with public encouragement of creative innovations Education for marriage at all levels

STAGE VII. FAMILIES IN THE MIDDLE YEARS

Challenges and Hazards	Services Needed
Plight of middleaged, middle-class women left jobless by their children's departure from home	Special education for middleaged women designed to sharpen salable skills, and fit the mature woman for several decades of useful creative satisfactions Education for husbands to see their wives' needs and how they can help meet them Employment opportunities (part-time and full-time) for middleaged women Encouragement of women in political and civic enterprises
In-law problems and stresses between the generations	Education and guidance of mothers-in-law in the acceptance and respect of married children, their spouses and families without undue intrusion and possessiveness
Confusions over independence, dependence and interdependence between the generations	Wider recognition of the values each generation has for the others and open discussion of how mutual help is best worked out
Stereotyped discouragement of grandparents' interest in grandchildren	Encouragement of grandparents to contribute their wisdom, perspec-

Hobbies, community activities, and projects help the mature man meet the challenge of social isolation in the middle and later years.

SERVICES NEEDED TO HELP FAMILIES MEET PRESENT-DAY CHALLENGES AND HAZARDS (*Continued*)

STAGE VII. FAMILIES IN THE MIDDLE YEARS

Challenges and Hazards	*Services Needed*
	tive and special gifts in helpful ways to young families
Problems of finding richnesses as a couple after years of life together as parents	Marriage education and counseling for the middleaged
	Programs preparing young adults for their middle and later years
Recreational impoverishment of the couple through the years of previous struggle to raise and launch their children	Special programs of skill- and interest-building among middleaged adults that bring variety of satisfying activities into range of their capacities now and for their aging years ahead

Challenges and Hazards	*Services Needed*
	Encouragement of joint travel, vacation plans, hobby development, service projects and other activities for middleaged couples
Social isolates among mature adults	Greater involvement of mature men and women in community organizations, projects and social life
	More recognition of and provision for the "quiet" middleager
Extremes of hoarding and extravagance in middleaged families	Education for financial well-being in the middle and aging years ahead through press, radio, literature, and community courses and study
Disillusionment and disappointment of earlier aspirations in face of the realities of maturity	Cultural climate that stresses success in many areas of life, rather than emphasizing material gains alone

---

STAGE VIII. AGING FAMILIES

Challenges and Hazards	*Services Needed*
Physical housing for the aging	Housing programs with special facilities for the aging
	Supplemental services allowing aging family members to be cared for in their homes
	Adequate programs for the senile, the incapacitated, and the institutional aged
Economic shocks and strains	Adequate retirement benefits, pension plans, public and private assistance programs
Social isolation and non-participation	Recreational programs for older persons
Health problems	Preventive and treatment medical facilities on group, clinical and individual basis
	Sickness and accident insurance to cover chronic and critical illness costs
	Food services for adequate nutrition of aging adults

SERVICES NEEDED TO HELP FAMILIES MEET PRESENT-DAY CHALLENGES AND HAZARDS (*Continued*)

STAGE VIII. AGING FAMILIES

Challenges and Hazards	*Services Needed*
	Mental health programs with special emphasis on emotional well-being during the later years
Post-retirement slump in interest and activity	Preparation for retirement programs
	Flexible retirement plans allowing man or woman to work as long as able and willing and to taper off rather than abruptly stop
	Recruitment of older people for community service
Poor recovery from loss of spouse	Death education rather than taboo, preparing men and women for realities of death, and bereavement, and loss of spouse
	Social supports for the bereaved in personal interest, and guidance in making a plan for living alone
Family frictions and misunderstandings	Education on the nature of family interaction for all family members
	Family counseling widely available
	Extension of research in the dynamics of family interaction at every phase and stage of family living

EDUCATION FOR FAMILY LIVING THROUGH THE LIFE CYCLE

There is no stage of the family life cycle when family members do not need some explicit education for what to expect, how to meet their requirements, fill their roles, and achieve their developmental tasks, both as individuals and as whole families. The need for education for family living through the life history of the family has been expressed by many people in recent years.[1] There is nothing startlingly new in

[1] See, for instance, *Education for Personal and Family Living: A Working Guide for Colleges*, "Outline of Knowledge for Personal and Family Living in Relation to Curricular and Extra-Curricular Opportunities for Its Use" (New York: American Social Hygiene Association, 1955), pp. 20–46.

these proposals. Some years ago, the American Association of School Administrators published a yearbook on *Education for Family Life,* in which "A plea is made for educators to rethink school activities with the needs and aspirations of home life in mind."[1]

Family life education has made real advances in the twentieth century, but it still faces real problems that greatly limit its present-day effectiveness in equipping families to carry their multi-fold tasks. Some of the more common difficulties family life education must meet effectively are: (1) learnings about interpersonal and intrafamily relationships are not definite, explicit, or tangible. There are no pat answers in the back of the book as in mathematics, no recipes as in cooking, nothing tangible to carry home as from a sewing class; (2) sound principles of child guidance, marriage and family relationships compete with multi-million-dollar mass media that tend to repeat outmoded superstitions, taboos, stereotypes, and old wives' tales and to exploit the love-hungry needs of persons and of families; (3) relatively few well-trained persons are as yet available to fill the rapidly growing number of posts for teachers, supervisors, counselors, and consultants in family life education; (4) curricula are already so overcrowded, it is administratively difficult to add anything as all-pervasive as family life education to existing programs; (5) highly articulate critics speak for small minorities who resist elements of family life education and overrule the vast majority of American men and women, boys and girls who favor such programs; (6) progress in the knowledges, skills, attitudes, and values acquired in family life education is difficult to appraise, to grade, and to evaluate.

No one of the challenges family life education faces in present-day United States is overwhelming. Each one is effectively being met in many programs, too numerous to list, too varied to catalogue completely. Where once school administrators hesitated to consider family life education emphases in their schools, now those who are not making some efforts in this direction are on the defensive at national, regional, and state meetings of their profession. At one time very few institutions offered courses of a functional or pre-professional nature in family life education, but now most colleges and universities offer something that

---

[1] American Association of School Administrators, *Education for Family Life* (Washington, D. C.: National Education Association, 1941), page 6.

may range from a single course or two to an entire curriculum in the field. Churches and youth serving agencies, such as the YMCA and the YWCA, have greatly expanded their offerings in recent years. Books, pamphlets, films, skits, and teaching aids of all kinds have been developed in increasing quantity and quality.

Most dramatic of all has been the increased awareness of the various professions of their interdependence with families and their need to become more family-centered. Physicians are beginning to realize they must see the family-as-a-whole if they are effectively to treat an individual family member. At the University of Pennsylvania Medical School, students are getting specific professional training in family-centered medical practice. So too, lawyers, home economists, vocational educators, social workers, counselors and guidance personnel, science educators, human development students, teachers of humanities, religious educators, health and physical educators, as well as marriage counselors and family life specialists are devoting more and more time and attention to the family aspects of their work.[1]

FAMILY DEVELOPMENT—A CONCEPTUAL TOOL

Family interaction in a dynamic world calls for good relationships between family members and effective whole-family tie-ins with other aspects of the entire culture. Throughout the entire life cycle, family members and families-as-a-whole face certain inevitable, urgent developmental tasks necessary for their survival, continuation, and development. At every stage of the life cycle, there are challenges and hazards that call for the extension of programs of proven worth and for creative innovations that will assist families to carry more effectively the burdens of twentieth-century living. Family development as a frame of reference may provide a tool that can cut into the human frontiers of interpersonal and family interrelationships with the research, education, counseling, and community services so urgently needed. Today we hack our way through the wilderness of family confusion where tomorrow our children's children may ride the smooth highways of re-established ways of family life. Road-building is strenuous work. But the dream of a nation of happy

[1] See especially, *American Social Hygiene Association, op. cit.* Part III, "Implications for the Specialties," pp. 50–110.

families producing generation after generation of strong, creative persons is a worthy one, and goal worth the struggle.

SUGGESTED ACTIVITIES

1) Plot the daily and weekly rhythms of a family you know well, indicating at what times the family interaction is most intense, and when it is least involved. Interpret and document with readings from the literature mentioned, in this chapter.

2) Review "the functional prerequisites," that Parsons discusses in his various writings, as the basic requirements for survival, continuity and development of families, for each stage of the family life cycle in terms of the family developmental tasks that have been listed through the book. Add, question, revise or delete statements of developmental tasks that are not in line with implied functional prerequisites.

3) Prepare a case history of a family crisis including the precipitating factor(s), the elements contributing to its build-up, the developmental tasks of each member involved and the family as a whole that were halted or blocked, what resources were available, and how the family weathered the trouble. Footnote your material with references to research and clinical findings in the literature cited in the readings.

4) Write a book report on Earl L. Koos' *Families in Trouble* (New York: King's Crown Press, 1946), or on Reuben Hill's *Families under Stress* (New York: Harper & Brothers, 1949), both modern classic studies of family crises.

5) Choose one stage of the family life cycle and elaborate around the outline given in this chapter its challenges, hazards, and services needed. Document.

6) Catalogue the services indicated for the various stages of the family life cycle listed in this chapter, for those that are found within your community. Make a directory of these services with annotations of who uses them, how adequate they seem to be, and what further services are indicated.

7) Invite one or more members of the Board of Education of a nearby school system to discuss with you current attitudes and practices in family life education within the public and private schools.

8) Collect a variety of catalogues of college and university curriculum and review their offerings in the field of marriage and family life for (a) functional courses related to students' personal needs and interests, and (b) professional and preprofessional courses and programs. Comment on your findings and compare with national surveys such as one recently conducted by Dr. Judson T. Landis, University of California, at Berkeley, California.

9) Review recent issues of *Marriage and Family Living* for (1) descriptions of educational programs in marriage and family living, (2) research reports on various aspects of courtship, marriage and family life, and (3) practice in premarital, marital and family counseling. Report your findings in a paper on trends in family life education, research and counseling.

10) Develop a comprehensive chart of the complementary and conflicting developmental tasks of family members at every stage of the family life cycle, as implied by their tendencies to fractionate or cement family ties.

11) Write up a case where parents who seemed to help their children achieve their developmental tasks well at one stage of the family life cycle, had difficulties at another stage with those same children. Explain and elaborate.

READINGS

Allport, Gordon W., *Becoming: Basic Considerations for a Psychology of Personality* (New Haven: Yale University Press, 1955).

American Association of School Administrators, *Education for Family Life* (Washington: National Education Association of the United States, 1941).

American Social Hygiene Association, Report of the Central Atlantic Regional Teacher Preparation Project, *Education for Personal and Family Living: A Working Guide for Colleges,* New York: 1955.

American Social Hygiene Association, Report by a Regional Project Committee, *Suggestions for Preparing Teachers in Education for Personal and Family Living,* New York: 1954.

American Social Hygiene Association, Report of the Midwest Project on In-Service Education of Teachers, *Strengthening Family Life Education in Our Schools,* New York: 1955.

Bossard, James H. S., *Parent and Child* (Philadelphia: University of Pennsylvania Press, 1953).

Bossard, James H. S., and Boll, Eleanor S., *Ritual in Family Living* (Philadelphia: University of Pennsylvania Press, 1950), Chapter 7, "Family Ritual and the Family Cycle," pp. 135–153.

Bossard, James H. S., *The Sociology of Child Development* (New York: Harper & Brothers, Revised Edition, 1954), Part II, "The Child and His Family Setting."

Cavan, Ruth Shonle, *The American Family* (New York: Thomas Y. Crowell Company, 1953), Part Three, "The Cycle of Family Life."

Child Study Association of America, *Living and Growing with Our Children: Impact on Parents of Children's Growth Phases,* 1955 Annual Conference Report, Summer, 1955.

Corson, John J., and McConnell, John W., *Economic Needs of Older People* (New York: The Twentieth Century Fund, 330 West 42nd Street, N. Y. 36, 1956).

Crow, Lester D., and Crow, Alice, *Human Development and Learning* (New York: American Book Company, 1955).

Duvall, Evelyn Millis, *Family Living* (New York: The Macmillan Company, 1955 revision), Chapter 22, "Improving Family Life."

Duvall, Evelyn Millis, and Hill, Reuben, Co-chairmen, *Report of the Committee on the Dynamics of Family Interaction*, National Conference on Family Life, Washington, D. C., 1948, mimeographed materials.

Duvall, Evelyn Millis, and Hill, Reuben, *When You Marry* (Boston: D. C. Heath and Company, 1953), Chapters 12, 13, 14, 15 and 21.

Erikson, Erik H., *Childhood and Society* (New York: W. W. Norton and Co., 1950), Chapter 7, "Eight Stages of Man."

Foote, Nelson N., and Cottrell, Leonard S., Jr., *Identity and Interpersonal Competence* (Chicago, The University of Chicago Press, 1955).

Havighurst, Robert J., *Human Development and Education* (New York: Longmans, Green and Company, 1953).

Hill, Reuben, *Families Under Stress: Adjustment to the Crises of War Separation and Reunion* (New York: Harper & Brothers, 1949).

Hill, Reuben, revision of Waller, Willard, *The Family* (New York: The Dryden Press, Inc., Revised edition 1951).

Hurlock, Elizabeth B., *Developmental Psychology* (New York: McGraw-Hill, 1953).

Kirkpatrick, Clifford, *The Family as Process and Institution* (New York: The Ronald Press Company, 1955), Chapter 4, "Family Types and Dilemmas."

Koos, Earl Lomon, *Families in Trouble* (Morningside Heights, New York: King's Crown Press, 1946).

Kuhlen, R. G., and Thompson, G. G. (Editors), *Psychological Studies of Human Development* (New York: Appleton-Century-Crofts, 1952).

Levy, John (M.D.), and Munroe, Ruth, *The Happy Family* (New York: Alfred A. Knopf, 1938).

Overstreet, H. A., *The Mature Mind* (New York: W. W. Norton and Company, Inc., 1949).

United States Department of Health, Education, and Welfare, Social Security Administration, *Memorandum on Strengthening Family Life in the United States*, mimeographed materials, 1956.

Growth of the family development concept

When a man goes into battle he needs to know how to use a weapon without necessarily knowing anything about the history of firearms, interesting as that may be at a more leisurely moment. When a woman has to feed a hungry family, she needs the immediate know-how that will help her get a palatable meal on the table, with culinary history reserved for less hungry times. When a person is faced with the challenges and problems of American family life, he or she needs tools to work with that assist in making sincere efforts effective, with the story of how the concepts were developed left until later.

This volume deals with concepts that have been in the process of formulation for many years, with hundreds of persons contributing to their development. Many of these creative workers have been acknowledged in footnotes throughout the book. For the scholar with technical interests, this fuller historic footnote may be of value. It further serves to point out that a work such as this rests upon a broad base that goes back in time, with this but the current status of the concept. Even more important is the recognition that this is in no way final or complete; for there is promise of further elaboration yet to come as others refine the concepts.

THE DEVELOPMENTAL TASK CONCEPT

When I returned to the University of Chicago in 1941–1942 to complete my residency for a Ph.D. in Human Development, I was fresh from seven years active community work with teenage youth and their parents. At that time "impulses" and "drives" were popular ways of interpreting adolescent behavior. Such concepts appeared to remove responsibility for their behavior from young people, and to make it seem to them and to those who worked with them, that adolescents were, as one writer in a book for youth put it, "human puppets on an invisible string." Such a point of view interpreting human behavior in terms mainly of biological drives was inacceptable to me.

Another concept that had gained considerable acceptance was that of "needs." This had the advantage of recognizing that people, like all other growing organisms have needs that must be met if they are to grow satisfactorily. It had the disadvantage of being ambiguous, and capable of being interpreted in many ways. Even more serious from my point of view was that so often "the needs of youth," were discussed in terms of the limitations and inadequacies of schools, families and community agencies in meeting these seemingly inexhaustible requirements. Youth was too often seen as an empty cup impatiently waiting for someone or something to fill it. Problems were seen as reflecting unmet needs. Growth of young people was likened to that of a tomato plant, which, given the proper amounts and kinds of nutrients, sunshine, moisture and other requirements would flower and bear fruit in due time. Again, the person himself had little responsibility for his behavior, development or destiny.

It was with this immediate background that I found members of the Committee on Human Development exploring the possibilities of the concept of the developmental task. Work in classes, seminars and professional workshops with Daniel Prescott, Director of the Division of Child Study of the Commission on Teacher Education of the American Council on Education, and a member of the faculty of the University of Chicago first introduced me to the developmental task concept. Study with Robert J. Havighurst, who had just come to the University of Chicago as Chairman of the Committee on Human Development, acquainted me with the history of the developmental task concept to that time. He credits Lawrence K. Frank with first using the term in his hearing about 1935, at one of the many meetings of the staff of the Progressive Education Association's "Adolescent Study" under the direction of Caroline Zachry.[1] It is probable that the original idea came from Frankwood Williams, who several years earlier had published essays stressing what youth must do to work through his developmental problems.[2]

Peter Blos of the Adolescent Study Staff referred briefly to adolescent adjustment problems as "tasks," in his book that appeared in 1941,[3] as one of several volumes published by members of the staff in which adolescence was increasingly recognized as a time of life in which certain essential tasks must be mastered if the young person is to emerge into effective adulthood.

The first published work giving a central place to the developmental task concept was a chapter written collaboratively by Robert J. Havighurst, Daniel Prescott, and Fritz Redl, for the North Central Association's *General Education in the American High School* in 1942.[4]

The developmental task concept satisfied my search for a frame of reference that dealt dynamically with the challenges of human development, keeping responsibility in the hands of the developing persons, and still allowing room for the helping and assisting roles that family members, school personnel and community workers might play. It satisfactorily met the objections raised in the use of "impulse," "drive," and "needs," and yet covered the realities implied in each of these concepts. Further, it seemed adequate to cover not only the developmental sequence of the teen years, but appeared to be quite as effective throughout the entire life cycle.

In 1943, The American Council on Education undertook, through a committee chaired by T. R. McConnell, to prepare an outline of objectives and courses in general education that would be appropriate for members of the armed forces. Ernest W. Burgess, of the University of Chicago chaired the subcommittee, of which Reuben Hill, Oliver

---

[1] Robert J. Havighurst, *Human Development and Education* (New York: Longman's Green and Company, 1953), p. 328.

[2] Frankwood Williams, *Adolescence-Studies in Mental Hygiene* (New York: Farrar and Rinehart, 1930).

[3] Peter Blos, *The Adolescent Personality* (New York: Appleton-Century, 1941), p. 275. (This reference was mainly illustrative, with developmental task still to be recognized as a key concept.)

[4] B. L. Johnson, ed., *General Education in the American High School* (Chicago: Scott, Foresman, 1942), Chapter 4.

Ohmann, and myself were members, commissioned to draw up an outline of a course in *Marriage and Family Adjustment.*[1]

As a result of this assignment Reuben Hill and I were appointed by the United States Armed Forces Institute to prepare a workbook on marriage and the family for the use of members of the armed services. This eventuated in the text, *When You Marry,*[2] the first to be written functionally to satisfy student interests and readinesses, from "first date through last baby." It was during this collaboration that the life cycle approach well-known among sociologists, and the developmental task concept emerging in human development began to be seen as a series of developmental tasks through the life cycle.

In 1947, Reuben Hill and I were asked to work together in the preparation of background papers for the forthcoming National Conference on Family Life held in Washington in May 1948. As co-chairmen of the Committee on the Dynamics of Family Interaction, Dr. Hill and I prepared a two-dimensional outline for plotting the developmental tasks of children, and of parents, for each stage of the family life cycle with implications for services arising out of the challenges, hazards, and problems involved in the achievement of each developmental task in our culture. Eight sub-committees of specialists at the various developmental levels, were appointed by the co-chairmen to prepare reports on the various life cycle stages, as noted in the original outline, p. 520.

In referring to this committee's work, Dr. Havighurst credits it with creatively contributing to the development of the concept:

This committee made a step forward in the use of the concept by showing how each member of the younger, middle, and older generations in the family has his own developmental tasks, and how the successful achievements of one person's tasks is dependent on and contributory to the successful achievement by others in the family of their appropriate tasks.[3]

The work of the Committee on the Dynamics of Family Interaction appeared in several hundred pages of mimeographed working papers used as background study for the National Conference on Family Life.[4]

[1] American Council on Education Studies, *A Design for General Education* (Washington, D. C., 1944), pp. 74–84.
[2] Evelyn Millis Duvall, and Reuben Hill, *When You Marry* (Boston: D. C. Heath and Company, and simultaneously New York: Association Press, 1945).
[3] Robert J. Havighurst, *op. cit.,* p. 331.
[4] Evelyn Millis Duvall, and Reuben Hill, co-chairmen, *Report of the Committee on the Dynamics of Family Interaction,* National Conference on Family Life, Washington, D. C., May 1948, mimeographed materials.

NATIONAL CONFERENCE ON FAMILY LIFE

Committee on Dynamics of Family Interaction
Evelyn Duvall and Reuben Hill, Co-Chairmen

Developmental Tasks of Children and of Parents Throughout the Family Life Cycle, the Challenges and Crises which Ensue and the Implications for Program. Coded for Authorship by Sections as of February, 1948.

STAGE IN FAMILY LIFE CYCLE	DEVELOP-MENTAL TASKS OF CHILDREN	DEVELOPMENTAL TASKS OF PARENTS MOTHER FATHER	CHALLENGES, HAZARDS, CRISES, PROBLEMS WHICH ARISE FOR EACH STAGE	IMPLICATIONS FOR SERVICES NEEDED, AIDS EDUCATION
Early Marriage and Expectant Family		Judson T. Landis, Michigan State University		
		John F. Cuber, Ohio State University		
		David Treat, Director, Clara Elizabeth Fund, Flint, Michigan		
Childbearing Family (Birth to 30 Months)		Loyd W. Rowland, Director, Louisiana Society for Mental Hygiene		
Preschool Family (2½ to 5 years)		Marion L. Faegre, United States Children's Bureau, Chairman		
		James L. Hymes, New Paltz Teachers College		
		Caroline Chandler, M.D., Johns Hopkins University		
		Henry Work, M.D.		
School-Age Family (5 to 12 years)		Ralph Ojemann, State University of Iowa		
		Afton Smith, Iowa Child Welfare Research Station		
		May P. Youtz, Iowa Child Welfare Research Station		
Family with Teenagers (13 to 19 years)		Leland H. Stott, Merrill-Palmer School, Detroit, Mich., Chairman		
		Robert G. Foster, Merrill-Palmer School		
		Robert J. Havighurst, University of Chicago		
		Fritz Redl, Wayne University, Detroit		
Family as Launching Center (early twenties)		Henry Bowman, Stephens College, Columbia, Missouri		
		W. Clark Ellzey, Stephens College		
		Homer Rainey, Stephens College		
The Aging Family		Ruth S. Cavan, Rockford College, Chairman		
		Ernest W. Burgess, University of Chicago, Consultant		
		Robert J. Havighurst, University of Chicago, Consultant		
Families in Crisis		Earl L. Koos, University of Rochester, Chairman		
		David Fulcomer, Drew University, Madison, New Jersey		

Nearly ten years have come and gone since the report first appeared. In that interval, many others have worked over the original materials at such centers as: Cornell University, Florida State University, Iowa State College, Merrill-Palmer School, Oklahoma A&M College, and the University of North Carolina. Faculty members of several university centers have generously shared criticisms, questions and further elaborations of the original materials that have helped bring it to the present state of development.

FAMILY DEVELOPMENTAL TASKS

The idea of developmental tasks of the family-as-a-whole emerged out of the first interdisciplinary workshop on marriage and the family, held at the University of Chicago during the Summer of 1950 which, as Executive for the National Council on Family Relations, I called and directed. One of the subgroups of that workshop set itself the task of carving out a multidisciplinary way of studying families that would have creative possibilities for research in family development. The calibre of the members of the work group; the recency of Eleanor Godfrey's graduate work with Talcott Parsons; Reuben Hill's growing interest in stimulating sound family research; Dorothy Mummery's close acquaintance with the problems of rural families; Leland Stott's planning for a a series of longitudinal studies of family life at Merrill-Palmer School; Richard Stewart's recent success in measuring husband-wife interaction and empathy with the Minnesota Multi-Phasic Inventory; Mildred Morgan's and Letitia Walsh's responsibility for graduate research in family living through their respective home economics departments; David Fulcomer's research in family crises; and my continuing interest in family development—all served to make this group an outstandingly creative one.

This 1950 Work Group in Family Development research was the first to formulate the concept of family developmental tasks as such. In its report, it defined family developmental tasks as "those which must be accomplished by a family in a way that will satisfy (a) biological requirements, (b) cultural imperatives, and (c) personal aspirations and values, if the family is to continue and grow as a unit." [1] Using the structure-function approach, this work group carved out an outline of family developmental tasks for Stage I of the family life cycle. Since then, this outline has been greatly elaborated and extended to cover the entire family life cycle and developed into the present volume.

---

[1] Quoted by Reuben Hill in his report of the workshop—Reuben Hill, "Interdisciplinary Workshop on Marriage and Family Research," *Marriage and Family Living*, Vol. XIII, No. 1, February 1951, pp. 21–22.

With such a history, it should be clear that a book like this is the work of no single author alone, but that literally scores of the most creative minds in the various professions with central concerns in family living have actively participated in the thinking that is brought together in this volume. For this reason, it does not suffice to merely acknowledge these others' contributions, but rather it is appropriate to recognize them for the collaborators they all are in the development of this work.

As author, I have had, and still have, misgivings about publication of these materials now. I am especially aware that the concepts herein, and their implications and applications are by no means "finished." Motivation for assuming the responsibility for publication at this stage stemmed from two realizations: (1) the mimeographed materials that had proven so provocative to so many, went out of print with little chance of duplication in their original form; and (2) the recognition that only as the present status of the materials became widely available would the stimuli for further work be provided. It is the desire to pass on to others what there is, so that future work and responsibility may be widely shared, that accounts for the appearance of these materials in published form at this time.

List of Charts and Tables

Index